100

No-Nonsense Things that ALL School Leaders Should STOP Doing

Compiled by
Rick Jetter, Ph.D.

Edited by
Rebecca Coda

100 No-Nonsense Things that ALL School Leaders Should STOP Doing
Copyright © 2022 by Pushing Boundaries Consulting, LLC and Rick Jetter, Ph.D.

The rights of each named author for each respective chapter within this book have been asserted by him or her in accordance with sections 77 and 78 of the Copyright, Designs and Patents Act of 1988.

All rights reserved. No part of this publication may be reproduced in any form or by any electronic or mechanical means, including information storage and retrieval systems, without permission in writing by the publisher, except by a reviewer who may quote brief passages in a review. For information regarding permission, contact the publisher at pushingboundariesllc@gmail.com.

Locations and names within the stories have been changed to protect the rights and anonymity of those mentioned. Any similarities in real life names and titles are the result of coincidence.

> This book is available at special discounts when purchased in quantity for use as premiums, promotions, fundraisers, or educational purposes. For inquiries and details, contact the publisher at pushingboundariesllc@gmail.com.

Published by Pushing Boundaries Consulting, LLC
Tonawanda, NY
www.pushboundconsulting.com

Cover Design by Rebecca Coda
Editing and Interior Design by Rebecca Coda

The interior icons were designed by Rating: Freepik, Emotional: Freepik, High Five: Freepik, Heartbeat: Freepik onFlaticon, Decision Making: Freepik on Flaticon, Stop Sign (Surang), Danger (Freepik), Trophy (Freepik), United (Freepik), Opposition (Parzival), and Winner (DinosoftLabs) from Flaticon.com.

Library of Congress Control Number: 2022921819
Paperback ISBN: 978-1-7370390-4-4

PUSHING BOUNDARIES
CONSULTING, LLC

Dedication

I am grateful for all of the wonderful mentors & school leaders that I have had the blessing of meeting, knowing, and working with throughout my career. This book is written for you and for those I have yet to meet.

Proclamation

How many times have you learned a new protocol, system, or strategy during leadership training only to add one thing to your plate while never eliminating anything? Sometimes the best new habit is to simply "STOP" the practices that don't positively impact your faculty and staff. YOU might be an incredible leader, already, but just haven't found the right words to buck up and influence your circle. Until NOW. Sugarcoating everything in K-12 education is not what we wanted to do with this book. Using the word "STOP" means that we love and value educational leaders so much that we are willing to flip the typical educational narrative to ensure award winning results that your staff and students deserve. That's why we wrote this book with firsthand insights, by leaders like yourself, so that you don't have to repeat the same mistakes.

Plus, this book is not just for NEW leaders. It is for anyone aspiring to influence another. It is a platform for leading realistic conversations that establish norms, beliefs and expectations using a common language all aligned to a common goal. It may even guide community stakeholders to better understand what should and should not be occurring in award winning districts. There are many incredible leaders out there AND there are some terrible ones too. You know it and we all know it. It is OK to encourage a colleague to "STOP" doing something if it will influence the community to better serve our students. Sometimes doing what's right requires accountability, transparency and stopping bad habits, altogether. It is our hope that by the time you are done reading this book that you will be well-equipped to confidently and professionally initiate liberating and achievement-aligned conversations among your leadership teams that will set the bar of distinction.

The RED Book

If you are familiar with *"the RED Book"*, which was the first in the *#100StopSeries* and written for teachers, you noticed that all contributing authors shared personal narratives and past mistakes within their classrooms and grade level teams. Many also shared the productive difference it made when they tried an entirely different approach or strategy or stopped something altogether. Every one of our *#100StopSeries* authors wholeheartedly love our profession and contributed practical in-the-trench relevant conversations that are sure to benefit anyone rallying for high quality K-12 education. *100 No-*

Nonsense Things that All Teachers Should STOP Doing zeroed in on the mighty power that teachers possess when they are reflective enough to *STOP* the simplest ineffective practice and/or replace it with a new habit or self-discipline within their own classrooms. The feedback passed along to our 103 teacher authors was overwhelmingly positive. Many teachers and leaders shared that having the *100 STOP* scenarios created a common language, supported the consensus of expectations, and aided in developing a school-wide process for handling interpersonal challenges related to teacher efficacy. In some cases, grade level teams and school-wide staff incorporated additional *"STOPS"* of their own. Coming to a consensus on high quality teaching and learning practices, cultivating trust among peers, and preventing ineffective practices from creeping back into their classrooms and schools during times of stress, was a huge win. Faculty-wide commitments to one another became the foundational reference for "reigning in" one another or anchoring back after long breaks to maintain high achieving and thriving schools. Synergy and success were a product of wrestling with those challenges that all teachers and their leaders face at some point throughout the year.

The BLUE Book
This is the second book in the series and was written by educational leaders for educational leaders. It is our hope that you harness your influence and power by taking a strengths-based approach in sharing this *STOP* concept with those trusted within your care. When leadership malpractice requires a *STOP* approach, consider those in your organization that are already leading effectively in that habit, skill, or disposition. We encourage you to look for talents and leverage strengths as a mentoring approach for supporting collective district and state goals. As community influencers, many of you will experience the joy and satisfaction even amidst crises or challenges because you understand that growing pains and failure are necessary ingredients if second order change is to transform your organization. Lately, the political and social unrest in society has muddied the waters. News headlines and social media have pitted adults against adults and derailed the focus of high-quality educational leaders to ideologies, political division, and fear of safety. This deters a focus from the day-to-day functions and leadership practices that frame others proactively for success. We must stay focused on high quality teaching and learning while also navigating varying lifestyles, political beliefs, religions, and values through stakeholder voice. The blue book isn't about changing THEM, it is about listening and refining your own practices and sharpening your own leadership skills to a successful point of distinction.

The stories and testimonies used within this book have been protected by both name and location pseudonyms to protect the rights and anonymity of those narrativized for this work. Any similarities in real life names and titles are the result of coincidence.

Contents

Fast Foreword AMY FAST, Ph.D.
Sharpen Your Own Responses RICK JETTER, Ph.D.
Collaboration Isn't Always the Right Answer WENDY RICHARDS, Ed.D.

STOP "Winging" Culture
This Type of Nonsense Blocks Synergy among Your Teams

1 Asking for Opinions when You've Already Made Up Your Mind ALLYSON APSEY	2
2 Thinking that You are the Smartest Person in the Room JARED SMITH, Ph.D.	7
3 Holding Back from Sharing Information that Everyone Should Have KYLE NIX, Ed.D.	10
4 Delegating Your work Unintentionally SVETLANA POPOVIC	14
5 Ignoring Staff Members' Problems HEIDI MANOGUERRA	18
6 Thinking You are Above Doing any Job or Task at School TIKA EPSTEIN	22
7 Trying to be Friends with Staff HOLLY BLAIR, Ph.D.	25
8 Showing Favoritism KRISTI SLAUGHTER LATIMER, Ed.D.	29
9 Letting Rumors Pollute the Culture PJ CAPOSEY, Ed.D.	32
10 Being a Hypocrite AJ BIANCO	35
11 Being a Martyr JUSTIN ASHLEY	39
12 Making Promises that You Cannot Keep TODD SCHMIDT, Ed.D.	42
13 Expecting Respect Just Because You are the Leader DAN KREINESS, Ed.D.	45
14 Lowering Staff Expectations SHANNON MOORE	48
15 Fearing Change MICHAEL LUBELFELD, Ed.D.	53
16 Forgetting to Celebrate MELISSA RATHMANN	57

STOP Allowing Emotions to Encroach
This Type of Nonsense Prevents Staff from Delivering their Personal Best

17 Being "Moody" Where No One Knows What to Expect BRANDON BECK, Ed.D.	62
18 Reacting Emotionally Rather & Engage Strategically PETER LOEHR, Ph.D.	65

19 Worrying What Others Will Think of You LARRY DAKE, Ed.D.	68
20 Holding Grudges about Staff Members' Mistakes DAVID GEURIN, Ed.D.	71
21 Violating Confidentiality Standards DEANNA OLIVER, Ed.D.	74
22 Ignoring Your Own Biases D. NILMINI RATWATTE-HENSTRIDGE	76
23 Believing Only One Side of the Story KRISTEN KOPPERS	80
24 Offering Unsolicited Advice PAUL O'NEILL	84
25 Wearing Rose-Colored Glasses SILAS KNOWLES & JASEY KOLARIK, Ed.D.	85

STOP Interacting Harshly or Irrationally
This Type of Nonsense Prevents a Strong Sense of Belonging

26 Talking Crap About Others LISA TOEBBEN	90
27 Publicly Humiliating Staff KRIS FELICELLO, Ed.D.	93
28 Comparing Staff Members to Each Other BREANNA BURKE	97
29 Judging Staff SANDRA DONAGHUE	100
30 Dreaming of Staff You Want & Support the Staff You Have JONATHON WENNSTROM	105
31 Interrupting Others CHAD DUMAS, Ed.D.	108
32 "Stealing" Conflict DOMINIQUE SMITH, Ed.D.	111
33 Blaming Staff for Poor Student Achievement TRISTA S. LINDEN-WARREN, Ed.D.	115
34 Evaluating Staff with a "Gotcha" Mindset HEATHER L. KEAL	119
35 Intimidating or Using Secondhand Information as a Weapon REBECCA CODA	121
36 Abusing the Phrase "Or Other Duties as Assigned" EDWARD PALMISANO	126
37 Wanting to Always Do Things Your Way JASON MCDOWELL	131

STOP Misunderstanding Yourself and Others
This Type of Nonsense Holds You Back from a Healthy Career

38 Talking About Self-Care for Staff GREG MOFFITT	136
39 Calling Staff Your "Family" WADE STANFORD	137
40 Confusing Stress-Behavior with Misbehavior BRAD HUGHES	140
41 Beating Yourself Up Over Past Mistakes ANDREW MAROTTA	143
42 Carrying Baggage from Past Positions into Your Current Position LISA BLANK	147

43 Prioritizing Your Career Over Your Family SYNDEE MALEK — 151
44 Working Long Hours at Home LENA MARIE ROCKWOOD, Ed.D. — 154
45 Staying Late at School or the Office NICK POLYAK, Ed.D. — 159
46 Underestimating the Power of an Empathetic Leader MICHELLE OSTERHOUDT — 161
47 Doubting Yourself LIVIA CHAN — 164
48 Trying to Be Perfect JESSICA REED — 168
49 Avoiding or Ignoring Mental Health Needs SHAWN BERRY CLARK, Ph.D. — 170

STOP Making Decisions Haphazardly
This Type of Nonsense Stalls Action-Oriented Achievement Outcomes

50 Obeying Orders Without Questioning When Something Isn't Right CORY RADISCH — 178
51 Carrying Out Initiatives that Only You Enjoy AGGIE SALTER — 181
52 Saying "Kids First!" When You Make a Decision JILL WORLEY — 185
53 Forgetting that All Staff Play Major Roles in Supporting Students RON O'CONNOR — 187
54 Squashing Staff-Generated Ideas or Interests MAGGIE COX — 191
55 Ignoring Feedback of Any Kind from Anyone VICKI WILSON — 194
56 Ignoring Voices of School Leaders and Staff AMANDA SHUFORD MAYEAUX, Ph.D. — 198
57 Thinking on a Small, Local Scale RAE DUNN — 202
58 Thinking that Purchasing Software will Fix Student Achievement HOLLY KING — 206
59 Hiring Staff Without Sound Practices, Procedures, or Courtesy JEFFREY EVENER — 209
60 Accepting Substandard Work from Staff HEATHER CALVERT, Ed.D. — 211
61 Letting Misbehavior go Undocumented LINDSAY TITUS — 214
62 Sitting on the Fence Rather than Deciding TERENCE TONG — 217

STOP Wasting Time
This Type of Nonsense Impedes Productivity

63 Work that Doesn't Support the Mission & Vision SEAN GAILLARD — 224
64 Introducing More Initiatives Just Because You Learned Something New MAGGIE FAY — 226
65 Assigning Tasks that Lead to Nowhere STEPHANIE ROTHSTEIN — 229
66 Being a Paper Pusher CHRISTOPHER DODGE — 234

67 Running All the PD or Faculty Meetings Yourself RACHELLE DENÉ POTH   238
68 Calling "One-and-Done" Training, Professional Development ERIK M. FRANCIS   242
69 Having Meetings that Only Provide Information MICHELE RISPO HILL   248
70 Scheduling Everything during Teachers' Planning Time JAY POSICK   251
71 Sending Pointless or Blanket Emails LAURA STEINBRINK   253
72 Failing to Communicate Changes or Decisions MARCUS BELIN, Ph.D.   256
73 Preaching or Soapboxing KRISTINA MACBURY & SHERRY MACBURY, Ed.D.   260
74 Administering Assessments that No Longer Have Meaning BRIAN MCCANN   263
75 Obsessing with High-Stakes Testing NAOMI RYFUN, Ed.D.   268
76 Rushing Through Tasks and Not Paying Attention to Details MIKE DOMAGALSKI   272

STOP Forgetting the Capacity of Community
This Type of Nonsense Prevents Maximizing all Stakeholders

77 Micromanaging Everyone EVAN ROBB   278
78 Drawing Lines-In-The-Sand with Stakeholders COURTNEY ORZEL, Ed.D.   281
79 Mocking Parents, Guardians & Families CARRIE LABARGE   284
80 Over-Complimenting Everyone without Specificity STACEY GREEN   287
81 Seeing Students as Numbers JAMI FOWLER-WHITE   289
82 Ignoring the Cultivation of Student Leaders ISAIAH STERLING   294
83 Stop Placing Sole Responsibility of ELL Students on the ELL Teacher ANDREA BITNER   299
84 Fearing or Fighting with the Teachers' Union DAVID FRANKLIN, Ed.D.   303

STOP Making Everything About You
This Nonsense Prevents Dynamic Off-the-Charts Leadership Presence

85 Forgetting Where You Started Your Career JESSE LUBINSKY   308
86 Believing that Teachers Can Afford It CATHERINE BARRETT   310
87 Taking Yourself Too Seriously BRENT COLEY   314
88 Making Excuses for Your Own Lack of Leadership ERIC NICHOLS   316
89 Inadvertently Harming Staff PAMELA HALL   320
90 Complaining About How Busy You Are RACHAEL GEORGE, Ed.D.   324

91 Being an Invisible Leader MATTHEW B. FRIEDMAN, Ph.D.   326
92 Being an Under-the-Radar Leader JILL PAVICH & RICK JETTER, Ph.D.   331
93 Waiting for an Invitation to Visit Educator Classrooms JULIE WOODARD   338
94 Trying to Be the Smartest Person in the Room LAURA MCDONELL   341
95 Gloating about Your Accomplishments, Honors & Credentials COREY CALDER   343
96 Power Tripping MARK FRENCH   346
97 Thinking You Must Climb a Mythical Superintendency Ladder RACHEL M. KENT   348
98 Stepping on Others to Get Ahead CORI ORLANDO   353
99 Using Others to Further Your Own Agenda GREGORY M. GOINS, Ed.D.   357
100 Leading in Any Role if You Don't Love the Profession ROBERT A. MARTINEZ, Ed.D.   360

What if there were more than 100 No-Nonsense STOP topics?

STOP Dismissing Reality

This Type of Nonsense Clings to the Comforts of the Past Rather than Leading Courageously in the Present

101 Pretending as Though Things Are Back to "Normal"? CHRISTOPHER MANNING, D.M.   364
102 Stop Trying to Be Somebody that You're Not SUSAN MACK-OSBORN   365

There is No Counter-Argument to Stopping Nonsense JON CORIPPO

References

What's Coming NEXT?

Fast Foreword
AMY FAST, Ph.D.

I vividly remember my final interview for my first admin role as Curriculum Assistant Principal. My Superintendent was known for being a no-nonsense kind of lady. She didn't mince words. Ever.

I sat down and looked at the blank yellow pad of paper sitting in front of her and quickly realized there were no curated nor preconceived questions. This conversation was going to be more of a dance than an interview. She began, "First question, Amy: You think you're always right." I looked over at my soon-to-be boss and high school principal with a look of "you're kidding me, right?" And she just shrugged. I spoke slowly and carefully in response. "… I'm not sure … that's a question?" But she just stared back at me waiting.

Saying "Yes I do" would not be a good look. Saying "No, I don't" would contradict her and make me sound argumentative. So, I just sat back and said, "Alright. Let me have it." And I proceeded to get an earful of all the things my Superintendent wanted me to stop doing if she were to promote me to this new role … first and foremost she wanted me to stop assuming my opinions were inherently right.

Our Profession is a Human Endeavor
If there is anything I think we've learned these past few years, it's that if we are going to lean into the real work (the work of growing humans) and not just the job (the paperwork and politics), we must STOP leaning on programs, policies, or bureaucracy. Rather, we must lean into--as my dear friend and office manager would say--"real talk." Because our profession is a human endeavor, educators are collectively an encouraging bunch. We're kind. We're loving and optimistic. And sometimes what we could use is a little more brutal honesty. I can't think of a better place to start than this book.

The thing about us leaders is---because we are "the boss," we often don't have a mirror held up to our work, our style, our efforts, and sadly even our impact unless we ask for it. *100 No-Nonsense Things That All Leaders Should STOP Doing*, reads like a comprehensive list of everything you've ever wanted to say to any lackluster, gutless, burnt out, or ineffective school leader under which you've ever worked.

As a former 5th grade teacher and instructional coach, I can't tell you how many times I wanted to scream from the rooftop to those in positions of power, "Stop seeing students as numbers!" or "Stop fearing change!" or "Stop micromanaging everyone!" But instead of approaching the boss with real talk, I'd put my head down, close the door to my classroom, and focus on the kids.

The problem with that approach is we know the impact of feedback on student achievement. But how often do we elicit it for ourselves? We, as school leaders, would do well to recognize the correlation of honest and sometimes painful feedback to our own effectiveness as well. This book is full of practical, relevant, and sometimes harsh truths. Moreover, it is written by some of the most well-respected leaders in the field. Dr. Jetter and contributing colleagues are some of the very leaders I have personally turned to over the years when I've embraced the oftentimes overwhelming task of helping humans to grow and thrive.

Often the best advice I have received in return is not about a new practice that I should embrace, a new skill set to develop, or a differing mindset to consider. Often the best advice I've received is to stop doing so much of what we have been conditioned to do and even rewarded for doing … as it prevents me from doing the work.

In fact, I underscore what Dr. Rachel George asserts as the 89th thing school leaders should stop doing immediately: saying we are too busy to read it. There has likely never been a harder, but also a more meaningful time to be an administrator, and I'm not sure there is a more all-encompassing and straightforward text that will help us through it.

Leading in a Time of Jarring Equilibrium

As a current high school principal in McMinnville, Oregon, I know I am in good company when I say that these past few years were some of the hardest of my life, professionally speaking. In a society experiencing such jarring disequilibrium, the field of education has become increasingly more complex and increasingly more important, making the job of a school leader increasingly more difficult. Usually, I love a good challenge and even pride myself in surviving on hope and creativity when faced with the absence of a solid plan. Afterall, I'm not someone who likes to follow a manual. But real talk? These past few years I really could have used one. School leaders, I present you with "the manual." Stop what you are doing and read it.

Dr. Amy Fast is a high school principal, author, and education commentator.

Sharpen Your Own Responses
RICK JETTER, Ph.D.

No matter what your leadership superpower is, adversity will strike. Addressing *No-Nonsense Things* before adversity happens will help your leadership team(s) navigate adversity with a level head, grace, dignity, and the confidence that "doing what is right" is embraced at every level of leadership within your district, county, or state. When transparency through leadership truth is established, dynamic off-the-charts educational leaders push boundaries for students. This is your opportunity to lead as a distinctive proclaimer all things effective, as you andragogically adjust your leadership style and practices to meet the unique needs of the diverse teams you lead. Consider leading these *100 Things* to foster a laser-like focus on high-yield leadership practices while nurturing a sense of belonging and balance in any educational setting.

In this book, you will experience a variety of voices and perspectives of national leading experts owning up to past mistakes and empowering you with concrete ideas that will raise the quality of your leadership teams. Rather than shining a light on classroom malpractices, Book #2 focuses on eight distinct areas for leaders to *STOP*: "winging" culture, allowing emotions to encroach, interacting harshly or irrationally, misunderstanding yourself and others, making decisions haphazardly, wasting time, forgetting the capacity of community, and making everything about you. Yes, we want to *shock* you into becoming a better school leader NOW, rather than failing miserably, LATER.

The chapters in this book are organized in such a way that they could be read in isolation as your curiosity is piqued, or you may read it cover to cover, with threads of you feeling the same way WE might be feeling. This mindset is the perfect way to launch your school year as you create school-wide norms and faculty social contracts. What a great baseline to start with! If you are a school leader or an administrator, why not head off the problems before they even begin (or become bigger)? These insights are also essential for school leaders in training within university or district level induction programs all the way up to highly aspiring five-star school-leader-of-the-year-recipients. More than anything, the ideas in this book are for the courageous, bold, and excellence-seeking boundary pushers that are willing to be intentional, disciplined, and strategic.

Over a four-year period, we started to notice a trend with teachers and school leaders as my interactions broadened within social media. We took notice of the types of questions and trends that started to emerge. We noticed that school leaders primarily focused on discussions about the differences in management and leadership, but they also wanted to express what their colleagues should STOP doing. From there, we decided to start tracking responses by simply asking the following, basic question (to all educators): What are ten things that school leaders should STOP doing? That's it. That was the question. This book reports the findings of over 1200+ educators, like yourself, who want to know the top 100 tips to help schools become highly effective schools.

The chapters are story-based and are gathered from real educators telling it like it is. Some chapters are funny. Some are serious. Some are tear jerkers. Some are wake-up calls. Every author in this book narrativizes from a perspective of we-can-do-better and you-can-learn-from-my-mistakes too. We bet you will find that you follow many of our contributing authors on social media and find them to be forerunners of excellence, uplifting, inspiring, and innovative educators doing transformative work in the field of education. They have spectacular advice--just amazing insights! A huge thank you goes out to all our authors who have made this book a reality.

Sharpening your own responses will help you navigate the societal fear that has decimated many functions within your district. You may face challenges like the ability to hire effective leaders. As a state, district, or school leader you are in many cases lucky to retain teachers or onboard new ones. The reality of fear, anxiety, and societal pressures has deterred many good teachers from returning. Every holiday break seems to produce attrition and deficits which require additional hiring, a challenge nearly impossible to get out in front of in preparing and developing high-quality teachers to have on deck. Even when districts have enough teachers hired to fill classrooms other challenges are also in play. A mix of multi-generational teachers, all with varying views of effective teaching, ideologies, backgrounds, academic foci, and social behavior require a courageous and intentional leader to follow.

Healthy state organizations, districts, and schools do not just happen. They require highly attuned leaders that offer mentoring, collaboration, systems, and resources all aligned and anchored to a belief in the mission, vision, values & beliefs. Establishing routine conversations for the sake of making commitments, agreeing to a consensus, planning for adversity, and leading effectively is undeniably necessary. The *#100StopSeries* has provided an avenue for educational leaders to connect, reflect, recalibrate and to not only know better, but to do better. The fact that you are reading through the eyes of courage and integrity means that you are up for the challenge. Well played.

This no-nonsense, cut-to-the-chase, running-out-of-time perspective is meant to stop you in your tracks so that you can achieve your most audacious goals within education. Promoting five-star classrooms, synergistic school cultures, and magnetic off-the-charts dynamic success is the aim of every author who jumped into this project. Pre-planning for how you will respond when adversity strikes is a toxicity cleanse from anything holding you back from high and masterful achievement. Although this book is written in the "negative" ("stop" or "knock-it-off") perspective, don't let that scare you away as the disclaimer warns you. This series was written in this manner to address issues powerfully and passionately for current and practicing school leaders.

Every author in this manuscript is in your court cheering you on to your greatest school or district-wide success. Our 100+ authors masterfully provide realistic advice collected from authentic been-there-done-that experiences. It is our aim that you will do incredible things and achieve with such impact that your success is not only contagious, but it will permeate throughout your entire community. It's time to make sense of past nonsense! Sure, we came up with 100 "things," but we bet you can think of even more that impact your school community.

A New Twist and a Major Spin
Dr. Wendy Richards is currently a Director of Student Services and is known as an esteemed school district leader in NY State and has been for a long time (even though she is NOT old). She has taught and led the academic transformation of numerous schools. When we came across her perspective our reaction was, "Holy smokes . . . this is the OPPOSITE of how we would tell others to lead, BUT it is SO TRUE in so many ways." Collaboration is NOT always the best leadership strategy. Wendy's preview is a relevant new twist and a perspective shifting START to STOP. We hope you enjoy this preview of what you will experience throughout this BLUE Book!

Dr. Rick Jetter is a Co-Founder of Pushing Boundaries Consulting, LLC; author of various books for educators, speaker, trainer, and the Assistant Head of Schools at Western NY Maritime Charter School in Buffalo, NY. Rick is also ranked #6 in the World's Top 30 Global Gurus in Education for 2022.

Collaboration Isn't Always the Right Answer
WENDY RICHARDS, Ed.D.

Collaboration: *The action of working with someone, to produce or create something, to achieve a goal.*

In every administrative course, I was taught that to be a successful administrator, one needs to *ALWAYS* get "teacher buy in." How many times have we heard, "If you collaborate with teachers and they own the solution, they will work harder to achieve those efforts? Guide teachers to come up with THE solutions that you, as the administrator, want and make teachers *THINK* that it was *THEIR* idea." This is a great idea, in theory, but a bad bit of advice for all situations as most teachers are smart enough to know what is happening *TO* them.

I have had the pleasure of facilitating many successful collaborations over the years with community members, educators, and administrators. Some of the most impactful plans and outcomes we have ever produced were the result of working together as a no-judgment, divergent audaciously big dreaming team. In my educator journey, I have been fortunate enough to have collaborated with some of the most grounded, innovative, and solution-oriented minds. They weren't scared of hard work and were welcoming of moving their school forward by doing what is best for kids.

Many of these brilliant minds did not even share the same position or perspective that I had at the time. It was an all cards on the table experience where all input was valued, and a common goal of student success was the desired outcome. In retrospect, I relish and appreciate those collaborative moments and alternate solution minded educational professionals because it pushed my thinking to an entirely new level. We gave ourselves permission to shift our mindsets based on growth and new information. That experience is what effective and sustainable collaboration looks and sounds like.

I challenge you to consider this question: "What happens when you are hired with a written or unwritten expectation to change the status quo environment and processes in which teachers have become accustomed to?" When educational malpractice is a daily occurrence, the organization is deeply rooted in the stagnation of the status quo. When this occurs, there is no time left to collaborate. Uncovering leadership truth is a call for ACTION even if it crushes status quo egos.

What Every School Board Member Really Needs to Know about Change

When a board of education places a leader in a position to change the status quo in the quality of hiring, the process of curriculum adoption, or developing high-impact leaders, they are setting that newly hired educational change agent up for failure unless they are ready to vocally and publicly support them. School boards must be willing to understand that realistically, change in education does not happen overnight and rarely does it happen within the first couple of years. Second order change requires three to five years at a minimum. Sure, you will see incremental growth, but second order change requires changing the systems and coaching/mentoring leaders into refined systems with succession plans through ongoing professional development and mentoring opportunities aligned to the mission and vision. School boards members are rarely familiar with the process of second order systems change because it is not typically discussed at the operator level. Many school board members believe they are voting on immediate results based on community opinion and input. There are even times when school board members have little to no knowledge of how public education functions and how the daily operations are vastly different than those of a business.

Unfortunately, there are instances where school board members serve on a school board as a stepping stone into a bigger future political arena with their eyes advancing to more powerful positions. School board members need to support the chain of command within the building and should be redirecting teachers, parents, and community members with such guidance for a healthy system to exist. There is also a need to understand that not all people will be happy with the changes and the ones who hate to change the most will be the loudest constituents trying to undermine the process. Yes, yearly board training should focus on these items, but do they? Again, collaboration and training go hand in hand, but RESCUE attempts at quickly fixing a failing system do not always have the luxury of collaborative time to get things turned around. Expectations and systems do not always go hand in hand with collaboration. Likewise, collaboration does not always go hand in hand with second order change.

Collaboration Doesn't Fix a Mediocre System

At one point in my career, I was hired at a school to change their mediocre system into an effective system that would net high student achievement. I began by holding meetings with staff members to gain their input on how to make their school a more successful environment for their students. After allowing them to flush out their ideas and share their insights, I shifted to co-developing norms. I knew that conversations would get sticky and having norms would provide a way to redirect conversations to our common goal of high student achievement. As I shifted to the development of norms, I expressed that as a group, we needed to come to a consensus (which does not mean everyone agrees; it means everyone agrees to support the decision). After the norms were co-created and agreed upon, I passed out the current and longitudinal academic data trends and achievement outcomes by grade levels and subgroups so that we could roll up our sleeves and start making connections to the changes we could make.

As soon as I said the word "data," I noticed body language shift, facial expressions change, and eye contact instantly wane. Immediately, it became evident that our staff took this work as a personal attack on their professionalism and teaching abilities--especially after presenting them with the data linked to their achievement outcomes. Even though I listened to their ideas and recommendations and had established norms as a new working group, teachers threw up invisible defensive shields ready to deflect the truth about their outcomes. Collaboration, at that point, would have only added a ten-gallon drum of fuel to an already crackling bonfire of denial.

When presenting the hard truths about student achievement, there was an excuse about *EVERYTHING* from about one third of the staff. The vocal one third were the ones with the lowest scores that were unable to reflect on their own practices and were fired up and placing the blame somewhere else. Some teachers had valid "excuses," such as excessive student absenteeism while others had invalid (and demeaning) rationales such as, "These kids can't handle Algebra." This was not the time to produce something through collaboration, but rather to convey clear expectations and processes moving forward based on the mission, vision, values, and goals of the school.

Spinning Your Wheels and Getting Nowhere Fast

So how do administrators take a group of people who don't believe students can be successful and collaborate with them about increasing student performance? Consider starting out with Admin 101: The things inside and outside the locus of our control. It is as easy as making two columns on a simple spreadsheet: things a school can control and things a school cannot control. There are some things, while very important, we cannot control. We cannot control whether a child goes to bed at 1:00 a.m. We cannot control if their parents need them to babysit instead of going to school. We cannot even control what they learn before coming to our classrooms. Our goal is to take students from where they are and lead them to where they need to be. Items we cannot control should NOT be the focus in any 1:1 or collaborative setting. That's what we call "spinning your wheels and getting nowhere fast."

As administrators, we are told that it is our job to persuade others' thinking to increase student achievement. How do effective leaders navigate such philosophical differences and beliefs about students and learning? Even when some teachers embrace change, are they willing to come up with NEW solutions and try out *NEW* methods of teaching while the ones who do not embrace change try to sabotage solutions and bully their colleagues into thinking like them?

What will happen if *YOU* get a call from your school board president who wants to meet with you about your "rough" tactics that do not embrace collaboration even if it is in the name of high expectations and student success? What if your school board president says to you, "There are teachers who are upset with what you are asking them to do; it's just too much. Just let them do what they want so that they are not upset. Oh, and by the way, we are still holding you accountable to increase student performance."

Collaboration Doesn't Eliminate the Comfort of Adult-Driven Platforms
Students are being allowed to fail all over the country for the comfort and security of adult-driven platforms. We will never move forward if teachers are handed the power to undermine school leadership, their colleagues, and the families of the school that they serve. Undermining efficacy by being outspoken to the highest leader in power, isn't collaboration, it is manipulation. Status quo busting leaders are empowered by district administrators and school board members through communication (not collaboration) to make tough decisions that are in the best interest of ALL students. That statement alone will ruffle feathers and awaken the status quo to deflect, demean, or deny anything in the name of comfort and ease. We will never move forward when school boards move away from policy management to favoritism, nepotism, or micromanagement.

School and district-level administrators, *ABSOLUTELY* want to create an inviting culture of joy, are valued for their expertise, and have a sense of fulfillment and purpose. There are times for collaboration and shared decision making, but there are also times when a leader needs to decide on behalf of the students and the school. The reason you are a leader is because you have demonstrated that you can make decisions and provide directives when. There is value in your leadership expertise and ability to exert decisions. EVERY decision is not collaborative.

Dr. Wendy Richards is an educator, speaker, trainer, professor, and educational consultant. She has worked in the field of education for over 29 years and has held positions as Special Education teacher, Coordinator, Assistant Principal, Director of Curriculum, Principal, and Head of School.

STOP "Winging" Culture

This Type of Nonsense Blocks Synergy among Your Teams

Stop Asking for Opinions when You've Already Made Up Your Mind
ALLYSON APSEY

Wisdom is the reward you get for a lifetime of listening when you'd have preferred to talk. -Doug Larson

When I ask teachers what they most want from their principals, they never say chocolate. They don't even say "jeans days". They don't talk about money. What do they say? They say they want inspiration and motivation. They want to feel valued with a sense of belonging and to feel part of a bigger cause because they are carrying out their purpose and making a difference. And they want to be heard.

A Seat at the Decision-Making Table
Leaders often talk about getting "buy-in" for new initiatives, tech tools and/or curriculum adoptions. But what exactly is "buy-in?" Jokingly, but mostly serious, many educators would define "buy-in" as an active agreement for a decision that has already been made "to" them. This is along the same lines as being "voluntold." As we saw in Dr. Richards' examples there most certainly is a time and place for communications and actions to be shared in a top-down approach. I would argue that even the smallest amount of time dedicated to collaborative conversations can have a long-lasting impact. These are conversations with a high yield investment because they seek input from teachers who are in-the-trenches. It may not change the directive or initiative, it most likely is not presented during an all-staff meeting, but insights from participants may offer insight into the manner and variables that could impact the initiative or goal.

Before long-lasting or even last-minute decisions are made "to" them, teachers deserve collaborative conversations because they understand the domino effect of change(s). They are a value-added asset for effective transition and implementation of new initiatives, goals, and expectations. Wouldn't it make sense to include those that are implementing the initiatives with real students in real classrooms to provide a voice of input during the planning stages?

Whether it is for the sake of efficiency or because leaders want to control the outcomes, oftentimes important stakeholders are not given seats at the decision-making table. Educators of all positions desire an active voice and deserve to share their input, expertise, and opinions. Conversely, educators despise being consulted or "voluntold" without having a voice in the new initiative or the manner of its implementation. Withholding a seat at the decision-making table certainly does not build a rapport of inspiration, motivation, or value among educators. This requires a leader to have discernment of the initiatives, the knowledge of the composition and strengths of their staff, and to have considered the ripple effect it may cause. Leadership discernment requires you to pause to consider, "Is this an initiative or a directive? Does this warrant whole faculty or staff collaboration? Do I need to invite varied positions to the decision-making table for their input?

As leaders you are making short-term, long-term, and on-the-spot decisions. Take moments to pause and consider how you will engage your staff to ensure the most positive outcome for the situation. Whether there is a directive or decision to be made as a leader or a long-lasting initiative of impact, what is most important is that your staff knows you are being intentional about the inclusion or exclusion of educator collaboration. There are certainly no absolutes in educational leadership and effective leaders are keenly self-aware of the way they share information.

The Healthy & Powerful Aspect of Ideation
When I first became a principal, I remember one day early in the school year when a teacher reached out to me for some advice. I offered an idea thinking we were bouncing around ideas and waited to hear her response. I was shocked when she said, "Okay," and turned to exit my office to go implement the idea. Immediately I reacted to her leaving without a response, "Wait, it was just an idea and may not be the best solution. Could you tell me what ideas you have?" Since that day I have intentionally become self-aware of how careful any administrator must be to clearly communicate that any idea offered is just that, an idea extended as a collaborative partner, not a boss. From that experience I realized that it is within human nature and professionalism to do what our boss suggests. K-12 education is different from corporate America in the sense that we all must work together arm in arm and shoulder to shoulder to create an off-the-chart positive learning experience for all students. To do this, as leaders, we must lead our staff with a mindset and school-wide belief that we will solve problems together with equal value.

Vividly I remember all the feelings I experienced when I had a "guess what I am thinking" type of boss. It was so frustrating to be asked questions knowing that my job was not to give my perspective but rather to guess what my boss was thinking. It was exhausting, taxing, annoying, divisive, and a time waster. I vowed to never be that type of leader. This experience motivated me to learn as much as I could about effectively leading educators through mutual trust, inspiration, and efficacy. One of the best training I have received as a school leader was offered through Adaptive Schools.

A profound concept that I learned through my Adaptive Schools training was to "not crawl up on the table with my ideas." Without realizing it, this is exactly what I did with the teacher that walked into my office asking for advice. I could have asked additional probing questions, I could have asked what the teacher had already considered as possible solutions, but instead I crawled on the table with my ideas. As leaders, when we throw potential solutions up on the table it is important to let the idea sit there by itself, not tied to our ego or power as leaders.

Effective leaders regularly convey the healthy and powerful aspect of ideation. Through a design or "redesign cycle" stakeholders should be encouraged to analyze, deconstruct, and even pick apart new ideas or approaches to effective teaching. When the focus shifts to the process of a "cycle of improvement" through collaboration, it removes the barrier of personally offending the risk-taker. The criticism shifts to the practice or solution rather than the person that brought the challenge. In fact, focusing on collaborative ideation proves that risk taking is an embedded attribute of a healthy school culture. When this mindset becomes part of your school culture, it enables anyone in the school community to become risk-takers within their own teams, committees, and stakeholder groups. This is a pivot toward high quality teaching and academic achievement.

There are appropriate times when decisions must be made free from collaboration. There may be a time constraint, or you may not want other opinions and, if that is the case, don't ask for input and instead focus on communicating the reason for the decision. When you only ask questions that you legitimately want answers to, teachers and staff will trust that their opinions are valued and will become your biggest champions in implementing new initiatives or processes.

Communicate the Scenario Type & Level of Input You Desire
When seeking input from staff, it is essential to be very clear about the type of information you are looking for otherwise it can go sideways and turn into a free for all gripe session. This may take some time and practice, but you can embed clear and concise expectations right into the question you ask. Below are three very different scenarios that have varying questions, purposes, pros, and cons to consider when approaching staff with challenges to overcome or changes that must be implemented.

1. No decision has been made.

Scenario	The decision has not been made and there is opportunity to influence the outcome.
Questions	Let's brainstorm solutions and flush out every possibility. What ideas do you have knowing that all ideas are good ideas?
Pros	Everyone has a voice. Listing ideas and solutions often initiate additional ideas that lead to great ideas.
Cons	It may be difficult to consolidate or narrow in on one solution when there is a wide array of ideas. Several in the group may have to settle for an idea that differs from their own.

2. Part of the decision has already been made.

Scenario	The decision is close to being made but there is opportunity to influence some part or aspect of the decision.
Questions	This is what I am thinking and why, what specific roadblocks or challenges do you foresee that could add to the success of implementation? These are the choices within the new initiative, what specific roadblocks or challenges do you foresee for our school/team/content area that we can head off to ensure an effective rollout? What might be the best timing for the rollout?
Pros	Educators have a voice and added value for leaders to consider in the process of roll-out, implementation or vital details surrounding the implementation.
Cons	The overall practice or initiative most likely has already been made, and any non-trusting educators may grumble and may still shut down.

3. The decision has already been made.

Scenario	The decision has been made and there is opportunity to learn the why behind the decision and ask clarifying questions.
Questions	Here is the decision I have made and why. I'd like your input on a successful rollout and implementation. How might we work together to ensure everyone is successful? What questions do you have?

Pros	Communication can clarify simple misunderstandings or differing opinions. This is an opportunity to understand decisions made at the district level because they typically have a domino effect that isolated grade levels or schools may not know about.
Cons	It may go against your belief system or beyond your knowledge base. Moving forward into the unknown with an expected learning curve is scary and teachers respond in passive aggressive ways or avoid implementing the initiative all together out of fear.

No matter the scenario type you must convey, teachers appreciate knowing what type of input leaders are looking for and where their own perspective will be used in the process. If you share these scenario types with your faculty at the beginning of the school year and make it your own commitment to each other and refer to them at points of decision making, it will surely save you time and emotional energy in the long run. Educators are flexible and knowing what they are walking into and what they are responsible for will save time and heartache.

Who You Ask Can be Just as Important as What You Ask

Teachers are some of the smartest people I have ever met. Every single time I turn to staff for help in solving a problem, they amaze me with their creative ideas. Not only do they come up with innovative solutions to problems, most also identify potential issues and roadblocks that might not have ever crossed my mind. When considering who to consult, I often ask myself these questions:

> Who might have strong opinions about the outcome of this decision?
> Who will have to implement this change?
> Who will be impacted by the solution to this problem?
> Who might have a read on how the staff will feel about this?

Leaders don't have time to bounce from classroom to classroom seeking input on every decision that needs to be made. And not everything is appropriate for an all staff gathering. It is unrealistic. However, there is power in taking a sampling. Asking ourselves these questions can help us carefully select individuals to ask so we can leverage our time effectively.

The Bottom Line

There are times when leaders will have to make decisions single-handedly. That is okay. It is not okay to ask for possible solutions when you have already made up your mind. It is not okay to be a "guess what I am thinking" principal. If we are clear about the type of input we are seeking, teachers will trust us with a very special commodity--their honest opinions. Honesty truly is the best policy and starts with us, as leaders, providing effective communication processes and tools that nurture a highly productive risk-taking culture of impact.

Allyson Apsey has been a school leader for nearly 20 years. She is the author of several books, including "Leading the Whole Teacher and The Path to Serendipity". Allyson is an associate with Creative Leadership Solutions, and coaches leaders and teacher teams across the country to help them achieve their goals. She is a national speaker and loves supporting educators in creating school environments where students and staff can thrive. Recognizing the significant impact trauma has had on many of our students, staff and families, Allyson is a Certified Trauma Practitioner in Education, and she is an Educator Wellness Coach with Opportunity Thrive.

Stop Thinking that You are the Smartest Person in the Room
JARED SMITH, Ph.D.

A couple years back a community member approached me at a wrestling meet. The individual wanted to better understand our upcoming bond referendum and was looking for an answer to their question. Although I had baseline knowledge, to say I had a deep comprehension of the facts and figures surrounding the bond referendum with the same level of precision of our school finance department, was a stretch to say the least.

Superintendents Don't Always Have the Answers

At that moment I immediately honed in on the fact that I did not have an answer to this community member's on the spot inquiry. Internally I was slightly embarrassed, so I proceeded to give my best response and audibly admitted that I would need to follow up with a more-definitive answer. I handed the community member my business card and assured them that I would have their questions fully and completely answered.

Disappointment consumed my emotions upon leaving the wrestling meet. I took pride in sharing accurate information, and believed it was my job to help others. Not knowing exactly what to tell this curious stakeholder left me feeling overwhelmingly inadequate. "Surely if anyone should have known the answer, it should have been the Superintendent," I silently lamented to myself.

Tap Into Your Experts & Follow Up
Leaders often experience self-doubt when they don't know something right on the spot. There is an underlying worry among leaders of being exposed as a "phony" or an "imposter" if they can't cite every detail about every department that rolls up to their position. Sometimes not having all the answers is a matter of where your mind is functioning at the time. It could be that you just left a meeting, or you were researching and deeply entrenched in another initiative. In that exact moment retrieving a finite detail to answer a question of precision, may not even pop into focus. Other times you may not have an answer because you have highly skilled and specialized people that you rely on for such esoteric information. As the chief operating officer of the school district most likely you see systems and the domino effect within the context of the big picture. Someone specializing in math curriculum may not know the details of running the cafeteria. As a leader of systems management, it is impossible to know everything about everything even though you may want to. I know I wished I could have retrieved the exact and immediate response for our community member the night of the wrestling meet. But it wasn't reasonable at the time to have that information readily available.

What I have discovered is that rather than consuming myself with the pressure to know everything, I have adapted as a leader and learned to be comfortable in NOT knowing everything about everything. Instead, I exert leadership presence by extending value to the questioning stakeholder by putting them in touch with a school or district specialized expert as follow through. Being vulnerable enough to tap into others with specialties and expertise is an essential culture building skill.

Ask Questions Until You Understand
In *"The Little Big Things"*, Tom Peters recommends that you, "Swallow your pride by asking questions until you understand". The "dumber" the question, the better! Bosses, managers, and leaders are all prone to falling into the trap of not admitting when they don't know the answer or are struggling to integrate or attach a specific concept into their schema. The fact is, we should readily admit when we do not know or haven't grasped something fully or deeply. Impactful and dynamic leaders actively seek to learn, grow, and know more about the question(s) posed in the room. It may sound counterintuitive, but as leaders we should give ourselves permission to ask as many "dumb questions" necessary in any setting, to ensure efficacy in communication. Asking questions sends a clear message to stakeholders that their work is valued. Just as in cognitive coaching, asking additional probing

questions is a model of strategic active listening that adds clarity to solving important problems. Effective leaders of impact possess a sixth sense for cognitively questioning by asking basic, underlying questions for a strategic purpose.

When high impact leaders bring "dumb questions" to the surface three things can happen:

    1. Clarity is provided to the topic being discussed,
    2. Permission is given to others in the room to be vulnerable, and/or,
    3. Stakeholder(s) share key learnings and information in their expert area which becomes high added value to the organization.

Consider the various meetings you attend. Do you believe everyone around the table has a deep understanding of every topic discussed? Often, attendees are limited on the broad range of details and organizational impact of the topic or concept(s) and therefore may not fully grasp the rationale behind system-wide decision-making. Oftentimes rather than publicly admitting confusion, colleagues may remain quiet, nod their head(s), or fly under the radar alongside peers and leaders. The fear of not knowing can be paralyzing especially in a room full of decision makers.

Effective leaders' sense when to pause discussions in progress or when things just aren't working. You may notice body language shift from several in the room as participants appear uncomfortable, disengaged or eye contact diminishes. Reading body language and knowing the strengths of the people in the room can give you the feedback needed as a facilitator to pause the discussion to re-engage or clarify. The ability to skillfully re-engage participants requires confidence and humility by the leader, and when applied properly, results in efficient outcome-based meetings based on informed decisions.

Slow Them Down and Make Sense Out of What They are Saying
Being comfortable "not knowing" also comes in handy with salespeople. When you move into a leadership role, suddenly everyone wants your business. Architects, engineers, vendors, consultants, agencies, marketers – these people appear out of thin air when you become the person in charge.

Salespeople are skilled at their job and their mode of operation is to share information so quickly that it's hard for one to process all the decision-making factors. Whether intentional or not, salespeople flourish when others are afraid to ask questions for fear of looking stupid. This is a game advantage for them because before we know it, we have signed a contract and have no clue what we signed up for.

The worst possible thought response in this scenario is, "I'm the school leader; I should know this stuff." Keeping your mouth shut and nodding your head in agreement can turn around and bite you later. Do not fall into this trap! Just because you are in a leadership position does not make you an expert in every school-related topic. And if you believe other leaders have everything figured out - you're wrong. They may be just as confused as you.

When leaders feel pressured to do something they don't understand, they must calmly declare, "I'm sorry, but you're going to need to slow down so I can make sense of what you're saying," then ask clarifying questions.

I'll be the first to admit - I still don't have school finance figured out. There are still many questions outside my area of expertise. But rather than beat myself up, I feel comfortable saying "I don't know, but I'll get back to you with an answer." Many leaders believe they earn credibility by having all the answers. Leaders earn credibility by strategically posing all types of questions.

Dr. Jared Smith is the Superintendent of the Waterloo (Iowa) Community School District. With more than 10,000 students and 1,700 employees, Waterloo is among the 10 largest school districts in Iowa. Jared has taught and coached at both the middle school and high school levels. Prior to becoming a superintendent, Jared worked as an assistant principal and principal for ten years. Jared holds a BA in Elementary and Middle Level Education from the University of Northern Iowa, an MS in Educational Leadership from National Louis University, and a PhD in Educational Leadership from Iowa State University. Jared is an award-winning blogger, professional speaker, and author of Learning Curve: Lessons Learned on Leadership, Education, and Personal Growth.

Stop Holding Back from Sharing Information that Everyone Should Have
KYLE NIX, Ed.D.

When it comes to information, leaders can be as tight-lipped as they come. Leaders keep things close to their chests for a variety of reasons. Sometimes leaders hesitate sharing information prematurely because they are still vacillating in a decision and want to mull it over further or gather more information before giving others the details or final answer. Other times leaders withhold information out of fear, fearing the inevitable outpouring of questions and criticisms that typically follows any decision that district leaders make. And then there are times when we hold back information because we think that if we share it too soon, people will forget knowing that if shared too late staff may complain that there isn't enough time to be prepared.

We have all been there. Yes, you have been there, I have been there, those before us have been there and those after us will be there. Whatever our reasons may have been, we have held back information that, quite frankly, should have been shared even though we held it back for the noblest of intentions.

Communication, or a lack thereof, can make or break you as a leader. It's time to stop holding back information that everyone should have, and start communicating in a way that makes you, your school, and your community successful!

Social Media: Friend or Foe?
In the age of social media, information can be shared in real time and become viral the moment you press "send." This one act can become your greatest friend or biggest foe. Leaders are well equipped to communicate with stakeholders on multiple social media platforms to disseminate vital information instantaneously or even virtually showcase live school events with the community. The pros of virtual communication through social media platforms is that it is typically positive community leverage for school leaders. On the flip side there are cons that can easily put your district or school in a tailspin. All it takes is that one rogue post sent by someone outside of the leadership team that can send your school community into haywire because of withholding information or inconsistent messaging.

>**Withholding Information:** This is especially true if a leader is holding back information from stakeholders and stakeholders begin sharing assumptions through social media. A lack of communication or information can lead to speculation, and speculation can become truth in the eyes of the uninformed. You can't control what people post, but many times you can get ahead of misinformation by sharing vetted and confirmed accurate information instead of holding it back. Calendaring this with your leadership team in a process can head things off.

>**Inconsistent Messaging:** Clear and consistent communication and messaging is key. Share the same information with your faculty and staff that you are sharing with your students, families, and community members. Use multiple platforms to relay pertinent information and make sure you are communicating that information clearly. Tell your faculty and staff exactly how you want things communicated and the protocol that has been established to ensure the

same message is shared minimizing confusion. One voice, one message. Be the proactive voice for your school and spread the message you want everyone to hear!

You Will Always Have Your Critics

No matter what you are communicating to your stakeholders, you will always have your supporters and you will always have your critics. Sometimes your supporters will be your critics, and sometimes your critics will be your supporters. Such is life. You cannot hold back information because of a fear of questioning and criticism. Just as in the previous chapter, Dr. Jared Smith shared that asking questions and considering possible criticism can help you gauge the clarity of your follow-up messaging. If something isn't clear enough, fix it, share it, and move forward. Our school community is very active on social media. Although it can be frustrating at times, I have learned to view it more as a blessing than a curse. When stakeholders are questioning policies and procedures, it helps our leadership team to see how we are viewed by those outside of our building and how we can potentially improve them. We may not be able to make everyone happy, but we can often use this type of perceptual feedback to make adjustments that will improve the way things are run in our school or leadership team(s). Perception is reality and listening and engaging is key.

Social media posts can also be used to open a channel of communication with stakeholders who are frustrated or confused over things happening in your school. Even when you believe you are communicating clearly, oftentimes there is room for misinterpretation. When I am notified of an upset posting on social media, I believe it is important to call the person who posted the response to determine how our leadership team can help the situation. Nine times out of ten, having a direct conversation with a frustrated stakeholder will help resolve a situation, or will at least provide new perspectives to consider for all parties involved. Communicating information with the intent to better understand the needs of the school community is a win-win.

More is More

My first year as a principal was in the 2020-2021 school year. What a year to begin! That year our school community was dealing with the rapidly changing policies and protocols of life in a pandemic as well as having to navigate the waters of having a new leader. It is safe to say that everyone was a little scared, myself included. Truthfully, there were times I was flat out terrified to share things because (1) the status quo and policies were ever changing, and (2) I had no idea how people would react. I knew as an educational leader and as a parent, especially in an unprecedented time of unknown, I would want to be as informed as I could be. I also knew that the available information was ever-changing, so, as a leader, I would need to communicate clearly and consistently to ensure my community had the correct and most up-to-date information.

With the help of my school team, I started confidently making decisions that I knew were the best for my school and community and got into a pattern of sharing information efficiently as often as possible. I haven't looked back. Sometimes the information I share changes within the hour, or the day, leading to multiple messages for clarity. Sometimes the information I share is taken in stride, while other times it is met with frustration and backlash. Sharing information is not easy, but I found very early on in my principalship that the more well-informed I equipped the stakeholders in our community, the better off we all were. I quickly discovered that the more consistent I was with communication, the more trust I gained from our school community.

Less is more for many things, but not when it comes to effective communication. If you want things done, and done correctly, it will require communicating the needs of your school and expectations often and in a timely manner. The biggest key to sharing information with your stakeholders clearly and consistently in one voice, one message. When sending a school-wide message, share that message on every media platform available to you. Some stakeholders will listen to the auto dialer but won't read emails and vice versa. Others rely on your website for information and some exclusively use social media. Share the exact same message on all platforms to attempt reaching all stakeholders. Be positive, consistent, and clear. One voice, one message.

One of my dear friends and mentors shared with me very early on that I, as the principal, would be the strongest advocate for my faculty, staff, students, and community. This is a synergy activator rather than community mayhem. To this day he still reminds me of the importance of communicating effectively to build synergy among teams rather than "winging" it. Award-winning schools consistently share information proactively and showcase all contagiously exciting things about our faculty, staff, students, and their community. We are the voice for our schools, and we possess the positional power to ensure our school voice is an amplifier of thriving and wildly successful students.

I implore you to stop holding back from sharing information that everyone should have and harness your communication superpower. Be a leader who takes control of the messaging for your school, shares information in a timely manner, faces questions and criticism head on, and advocates for their faculty, staff, students, and community. You can't just "wing" it.

Dr. Kyle Nix has 16 years of experience in education and is currently serving as a Middle School Principal. She is a board member for the Tennessee Association of Secondary School Principals and is an active advocate for educators and education leaders. Dr. Nix currently resides in Middle Tennessee with her husband and two children.

Stop Delegating Your Work Unintentionally
SVETLANA POPOVIC

"Delegating what not to do is as important as deciding what to do." -Jessica Jackley

"You're micromanaging, learn how to delegate."
"You have too much on your plate and are overwhelmed, delegate."
"The first rule of management is delegation."

As educational leaders, we have heard these mantras before, and then some. I'm not suggesting you STOP delegating, but rather to leverage the delegation of work for a mutual benefit to all. Just be intentional about it. High-capacity teams are built by being given the opportunity to lead and exposure to shared experiences. Intent is a noun and action.

Intentionality Multiplies Team Capacity

Have you ever caught yourself walking down the hall and someone approaches you with a new idea and the first words out of your mouth are, "Great idea, thanks, I'll get right on that"? You continue to your office and your admin assistant says Mr. Hines is on the phone and before another word can be said, you've already answered, "Put him through please." As you sit down to take the call, among a myriad of sticky notes, legal pads full of notes from previous meetings, and a desk with multiple computer monitors with over 20 tabs all open and running, you respond to the call and engage Mr. Hines in a conversation. Your eyes then catch an open document on one of the monitors, your hands begin to write down the new idea just pitched to you in the hallway on yet another sticky note and your mouth is saying, "Uh huh, I understand Mr. Hines." Does that sound like you? Not to worry. You aren't alone.

Can this style of leadership endure? Is this leadership behavior sustainable? Is having a competent, responsible, high work ethic leader a bad thing? What is the effect on this leader's social and emotional well-being? Are the decisions this leader is making well informed, aligned, and intentional? These are all very good questions. Although disorganization and inefficiency can be a huge breakdown in managing a leader's workload, we aren't here to share calendar management and work efficiency tips. This chapter is about building thriving, high-capacity teams within your school, district, or organization and understanding how to delegate with intention.

It's Not About the Leader, It's About Building the Team
Learning to intentionally delegate responsibility effectively can become one of the most capacity building strategies for building a cohesive team culture, not to mention efficient. Effective servant leaders understand the power of intentional delegation as a tool for growing leaders, sharpening skill sets, and uniting staff in a strengths-based approach. Imagine if you didn't intentionally delegate and develop your team. What happens to collective efficacy? How do you live your mission, vision, and values? Who's responsible for talent recognition, and bridging relationships across stakeholder groups? The answer can't be the leader if you are trying to achieve sustainable impact for your organization. Multiply your team's capacity and watch the effect on morale and organizational culture rise.

Lead Like a Clockmaker
As servant leaders, you have explored the literature of many brilliant leadership minds and read a plethora of organizational studies. It doesn't take long to discover a consistent theme of how 'great leaders behave'. Highly successful leaders make it look easy, because foundational systems are intentionally put in place through strategic planning to build high-capacity teams working together efficiently. Effective leaders lead like Bavarian clock makers, they lead with precision and coordinate all the moving parts, each part having its purpose and perfectly in sync with the blueprint and plan. It may look effortless to an outsider, but the reality is that it took planning, development, and intentionality by design of a masterful and skilled builder. Master builders of educational success invite conversations full of inquiry with the intent that their teams will be challenged to grapple and grow through productive struggle. Successful educational leaders intentionally delegate projects and tasks when they know the talent of everyone on the team and take time to invest in collective efficacy.

Intentional leadership delegation is not about taking something, (or just anything), off your leadership plate and giving it to someone else on the team. It is about thinking through and matching the project or task complexities with the strengths of individuals or teams who have the talent to best carry out the work. It is not about perfection but rather risk and failing forward. It is about engaging members in the work and driving their job satisfaction as a plan of staff retention and capacity building within your organization or school. It's a formula for sustainable impact and successful succession when the time comes.

Collaboration or Delegation?

Dr. Wendy Richards shared that collaboration is not a necessary process for every decision. After all, it isn't doable or an efficient leadership process to collaborate on everything all the time. In Chapter 1, Allyson Apsey gave examples of how collaborative conversations can positively influence school culture when stakeholders have a seat at the decision-making table rather than pretending they have a stake when the decision has already been made. Intentionally delegating is about a leader's skill of searching for opportunities and then pairing of strengths. This requires relationship building and visibility to know your team's strengths and when to provide opportunities for growth.

Delegation Requires Two Things . . . a Belief and Opportunity

Every leadership action is an opportunity to empower your team. When we invite others to lead alongside us, it shows our shared commitment to a quality informed outcome. The people you lead are watching your decision making and when they see that as the leader you are inviting and trusting in their abilities then you are establishing a culture that is risk-taking positive and creative. We've all heard that the answer to any problem is always 'in the room'. A mindset of intentional delegation is not only about the opportunity to tap into educator talents and expertise, but also an opportunity to increase work engagement and satisfaction through a shared commitment to the depth and breadth of results-driven teams. Delegating can be one of the highest yielding strategies when leaders have spent time in collaboration, have buy-in from the decision-making table, are committed to coaching and mentoring, and do so at the right time for the right reasons.

Delegating Too Soon Is a Rookie Mistake

The best advice I was ever given as a new leader was to focus on developing relationships to fully understand the climate and culture of the environment I would be leading. Conversely, the worst rookie mistake I could make would be to start delegating duties and tasks right away. I am grateful for that advice and have certainly found it to be true over the years and timing is everything. When administrative leaders delegate a task or duty to others, even if for all the right reasons, and haven't had the opportunity to do it or live it themselves, how will they ever know the mark of success, or the necessary skills needed to select someone to delegate to? By no means does every task or duty need to be felt/done by the leader first, but as a leader, be careful not to miss your own opportunity to engage and really understand the roles, skillset, and job descriptions of those you lead and the tasks that they perform before you start delegating.

Delegating too soon in any new leadership role can easily become an obstacle that can lead to serious miscommunication and expectation gaps between you and your team. If you've ever had the job-embedded learning opportunity to shadow a fellow colleague or even job-swap, then you also know the incredible appreciation you have for your colleague. Every educator, faculty member and staff have their own unique life experiences, talents, and style. Individually we possess varying schema because we are all cut from a different piece of cloth, like a square from a quilt. When we take the opportunity to wear our colleagues' 'cloth' for even just a day, we see and understand their world more clearly and see the quilt more holistically. Taking the time to learn these attributes and qualities of your staff and the relevant demands of their jobs, creates a common bond and provides valuable information that then can be used when intentionally delegating tasks and projects to others. Knowing exactly what you are asking others to do and how those experiences will stretch and grow their capacity, is key to building high-capacity teams.

"Do the best you can until you know better; then when you know better, do better."
~Maya Angelou

Svetlana Popovic is an Educator, Leader, former Assistant Principal, Regional Education Coach, and current Elementary PreK-6 Principal. She has supported Chicagoland area districts from rural to urban bringing about a whole systems approach to improving culture and climate. Her current role as Principal allows her the opportunity to implement her learning and effect change in her school community so all students achieve. Svetlana holds a BA from Elmhurst University, a double major in Psychology and Early Childhood Education, a MA in Reading, Ed.S. in Administration and DEI certification from Northwestern.

Stop Ignoring Staff Members' Problems
HEIDI MANOGUERRA

Synergistically dynamic leaders' views problems or adversity as opportunities to capitalize on solutions. They are fueled by the audacious challenge to succeed against all odds. This category of leader embraces transformative leadership and can envisage a future of opportunities and myriad outcomes for their team, students, and stakeholders. As leaders, they are patient, they recognize the need for change, facilitate that change, and support others in finding solutions to a kaleidoscope of concerns. This is the type of leader that everyone wants to work for because they foster productive outcomes, high expectations and student achievement. So why doesn't a solution mindset always transfer to staff members and their individual or personal problems?

Cultural synergy will only be present when administrators and district leaders connect, acknowledge, navigate, and support individual staff members' problems. When staff problems are ignored, dynamic leaders aren't viewed as so dynamic any longer because they become viewed as managers of operations rather than high-functioning instructional leader with a shared vision. Award winning leaders extend agency by taking the time to navigate the individual needs of educators' professional pedagogical practices, their valued relationships, and their personal needs.

Have Faith in Your Team

Although most educators hold multiple advanced degrees, they often find themselves being micromanaged by administrators. Such administrators call into question the intrinsic motivation of highly trained professionals to ensure that learning is happening in their classrooms. This is not to say that some individuals do not need support and continued growth or have totally missed the mark, but that is vastly different from being micromanaged. An effective administrator has faith in their staff's commitment, abilities, efficacy, and pedagogical practices.

Compared to other professional careers, teachers are all too often unsupported and underpaid. Now, as the administrator on site, one cannot control the payroll and funding. However, a leader can and should strive to intentionally build a climate and culture, where their entire staff feels supported, trusted, and frequently acknowledged as a valuable and successful member of the team. A healthy climate and culture will foster a community in which engagement is high, collaboration is the standard, and disciplinary issues are reduced so that the learning environments are protected.

A vital element to this dynamic is that one's staff does not interpret feedback as punitive. Teaching is not for the faint of heart and most teachers are highly reflective and critical of themselves and their performance. Most educators seek out professional development and ways by which to show continuous improvement to best meet the needs of their diverse learners. When the feedback they receive is constructive and leads to improved pedagogical practices and increased growth shown in their data, this benefits the entire community. A successful administrator teaches their staff to "catch the fish" rather than give them the fish to eat. A leader who has built a team of self-efficacious educators has built a foundation brick by brick that can withstand the cacophony that surrounds the education system in our communities, country, and around the world.

As a leader, one must have open, honest, thoughtful, two-way communication with their staff members as a group and with everyone. This is the only way to build trust, to secure group consensus for one's vision, and to create a prosperous learning environment for our students. A healthy, supported staff lends itself to a healthy, supportive environment for our students. This should also be a model for how the staff then communicates with their students, peers, and other stakeholders.

A leader's own social emotional intelligence or (EQ) is critical in connecting and responding to the professional, cultural, or personal problems that will arise. It is important to acknowledge when you are not perfect, that mistakes happen, and model how you monitor and adjust when a mistake has been made. If a leader models this behavior, their team will feel safe to do the same in their classroom and around campus. On a healthy campus with a positive culture and climate, the team's growth in intrapersonal skills will coincide with the collective growth of the entire campus. A high EQ leader provokes others to reflect, promotes productive self-talk, and mentors EQ practices that increase the capacity of those they lead.

Build Academic Trust

Chloe began her teaching career as a new hire joining our school's already high functioning kindergarten team. When she joined our school team, I had already had a strong working relationship with her new teammates as the instructional mentor on campus. She had a best-case scenario as a new hire as she was welcomed "into the fold" of trust with open arms and without question. This gave her a feeling of ease as she learned the strengths and expectations of her team, the culture and routines of our school, and the strengths and deficits of her new student community. Teaching kindergarten was a completely new experience for Chloe and there was an adjustment period for her and her students. We all rallied around her and listened, guided, and supported her efforts. Weekly during our professional learning team meetings our conversations were laser-focused on pedagogical efficacy and adjusting teaching approaches in a response to student data. During this protected time, we would construct and analyze common formative assessments, unpack the standards, and review our collective data. Through these conversations, the team developed a cohesive and constructive meeting model that resulted in their students' growth that closed multiple learning gaps as the school year progressed.

Their time together evoked casual pedagogical conversations and promoted a growth mindset that permeated across our campus. This veteran team also knew these relevant conversations supported the goals of their individual evaluations. Their trust and transparency promoted a collective school-wide failure mindset of safe risk taking because they knew with confidence that voicing struggles would never be used as a punitive measure (such as a "gotcha" moment). This trust building growth mindset created an environment of professionalism and vulnerability in voicing failures for the purpose of improving their instructional and pedagogical practices.

In November of that year Chloe approached me in the front office with work samples from her students. She was frustrated and stumped as to why her students were not making the progress she was expecting them to make. Her data did not reflect the learning she anticipated. I asked her some targeted questions about her instruction, about her students' prior knowledge, and about the quality of the assessment. Together, we unpacked the learning targets, and we determined the learning gap that was interfering with her students' advancement. She decided to provide a more targeted assessment that broke down the skills even further to determine if the students' gap in learning was truly the hurdle impeding progress. Proudly, she came to the realization on her own that such a gap existed because she had tapped into the power of academic trust. With this new information she explicitly taught the missing sub-skills needed, retaught the original standard in a different way with scaffolding and experienced academic success. She had moved her kindergarten students forward on the specific standard and improved her confidence as a teacher. This may not have happened in her first year of teaching if she hadn't experienced the power of building academic trust as a team.

Offer Empathetic Support for Personal Circumstances

Samantha was an exceptional educator. She was a warm, demanding, protector of her students and her data/student growth was outstanding. She had been married for 46 years to her husband. Unfortunately, her husband was battling cancer during the 2010-2013 school years. As the 2013 school got underway, her husband's condition worsened. As her principal, I could not in good conscience ignore her unique circumstances. As important as our student growth was, it was equally as important that she had personalized support systems in place at work so that she could be present for her husband. This required a community approach for supporting her students with their learning needs when Samantha couldn't.

She needed a system of support and deserved flexibility. When she needed to leave a little early to join him for a doctor's appointment, our team worked together to ensure that her students had a highly qualified person in her room continuing with the learning. If she needed help with substitute plans, her team helped. When she needed a shoulder or an ear, my door was open. To me, this demonstrated the simplest kindness and empathy that each person deserves based on their unique circumstances. Synergistic leaders recognize that the professional sphere of impact does not exist in solitude and will inevitably intersect with the personal lives of students and staff. Each situation that you encounter on your campus deserves special attention and compassionate understanding.

Despite her personal circumstance, Samantha continued to deliver outstanding and effective lessons, maintained meaningful connections with her students and parents, and set the bar high academically with her academic achievement data that reflected significant student growth. Samantha's grit, grace, and heart led her through a very difficult year while supporting her loving husband, her own children, and her students. One can only speculate on how the year would have gone if she had not received the support from her work family that she so deserved. If we had ignored her situation, it likely would have worsened her personal situation and negatively impacted her students, families, and team.

Building a thriving community school requires awareness through personal connections. If we ignore our staff and their problems, whether at work or home, our teams will not function at a high academic capacity nor with a healthy culture for staff and students. Your strategic, compassionate, and intentional actions will build synergistic teams that take pride in high expectations, pitch in where needed to support one another, and work together synergistically to ensure high achievement and success for all.

Heidi Manoguerra, over the last two decades, has served in a variety of settings throughout the K-12 education system that include teaching kindergarten through sixth grade, assistant principal, principal, curriculum coach, and as a professional development facilitator. She is looking forward to pursuing her doctoral degree in social justice in education. She is passionate about social justice, equity, and efficacious pedagogical practices.

Stop Thinking You are Above Doing any Job or Task at School
TIKA EPSTEIN

"If serving is beneath you, leadership is beyond you." -Anonymous

School leaders are the models of the school community. All eyes are on what we do and what we don't do *ALL* the time. We focus on student and staff safety, analyze students' academic achievement, initiate teacher collaboration, talk with families, and make hundreds of split-second decisions every day. Even though we have what seems like a never-ending list of responsibilities, we need to remember we are not above any job or task for our school. We are the support staff to our teachers, instructional assistants, office staff, and custodians.

> *"The school takes on the personality of their principal. If the principal is mean, the staff will be mean to the kids, and the kids will be mean to one another. If the principal is full of energy, excitement, and enthusiasm, the teachers will be energized to teach, and the students will be excited about learning! The principal can either extinguish a flame of positivity or ignite a flame of hope. The principal is responsible for the culture and mood of the school."*
>
> --Dr. Marcus Jackson

Take Pride in Your School
Since your school takes on the personality of the building administrator(s), the question really is, what type of personality do you want to create for your school as a leader? This question may feel like a lot of pressure to place on yourself as an administrator, and it is, but that is because you are in a position of great power within your sphere of influence. It is your job to exude energy, excitement, and enthusiasm even with the simplest of daily tasks. Take for example picking up trash around your camps. It is a monotonous task, but someone must do it, right? Why should the custodian be the only person responsible? If we pick up trash, others will notice. Then, they will pick up trash, too! Pride and integrity can be contagious when leaders model kindness and care even over something as small as

picking up trash. Isn't that the end goal, for everyone to have pride in our school environment? Remember, school is a second home for all of us. And just think when you work together to keep it clean, your custodian will be appreciative of your support just as Heidi Manoguerra shared in the previous chapter. Even your custodian will take pride in their work and work even harder when you notice and value their work too.

Work in the Lunchroom
Serving lunch to hundreds of hungry kids is not a task for the faint of heart. The lines are long, the trail of trash is sticky and bottomless, and the noise can mimic a rock concert. It is my favorite part of the day. Lunch duty is a time leaders can spend building relationships with their students on a personal level in a non-academic environment. It is incredible what a kindergartener will share with you while helping them open their milk carton. I will never forget when a first grader introduced me as her "grownup" during the first week of school. This sweet student described me as the nice lady who talks with her at lunch and passes out the ketchup. It did not matter that she did not know I was the assistant principal. Because of this lunchroom opportunity, I built a relationship with her and I'm happy to say that eventually she started calling me by my name. What was more important was that she knew she could count on me to initiate a conversation with her and assist her anytime with straws and ketchup packets. You never know what a quick check-in while opening a milk carton or sweeping a floor will mean to someone else.

Participate with the Roles Reversed
School leaders often share professional development on the importance of a growth mindset and expect teachers to model it in their lessons. Sometimes we have to ask ourselves, "How are we modeling the importance of having a productive struggle while learning something new?" I make it a point to attend all professional development shared in our building as an active participant. It is essential to be part of the learning process and to show some vulnerability, too. Your district leaders, teacher leaders and coaches are invested in their training, and your engagement sets the tone and value for transferring the practices to the classroom. If you are invested, they are invested.

Our students need to see us learning as well. Take a chance and sit in a class that might challenge you. Learn alongside students. As a novelty, many school leaders trade places with students for the day. It builds camaraderie and students love it. The students attend leadership team meetings and events and learn about the decision-making process. The role reversal gives them the chance to ask questions and reflect on what is happening. The school leader understands what the students are learning and can reflect on the routines through a different lens.

The most important part of this novel exchange is the conversation you hold afterward. This is an opportunity for the students and school leaders to reflect on the changes they can make. When the principal takes the role of the student and talks to the student asking questions as though they are the principal, new ideas, solutions, and culture enhancing conversations take place. Collaboration through role reversal empowers students with a voice in a novel and unthreatening manner and provides powerful insight to the leader on implementing new initiatives or new approaches that will improve the quality of school.

Team Teach or Even Teach on the Fly
Let's face it, filling teaching and support staff positions is never easy. There are thousands of openings all over the country and not enough quality candidates to fill them. School leaders have protocols for cover classes and want solid plans for all students to receive the best education possible even when their assigned teacher is away. Have you considered periodically teaching a class that needs to be covered? No matter your position, we are teachers first. Serving as a guest teacher for our students is not beneath an administrator, ever. Instead, it gives us time to teach the strategies we have focused on in professional development, refine our own teaching skills, model transparency and vulnerability and learn more about the needs of students in the academic setting.

There are times where we must teach on the fly because of extenuating circumstances but what about scheduling to team teach once per quarter as an instructional model for a new teacher? This will give additional time for co-planning and reflection and an opportunity to model your reflection and thinking process as a reflection afterward. Team teaching and teaching on the fly shouldn't become a part time job and it isn't ideal to serve as the administrator and the classroom teacher. When you dedicate time to stay relevant through teaching, it communicates that you are the instructional leader, first and foremost.

Generate After School Conversations
It is rare when every student is picked up on time at dismissal. What do you do while the student waits? Grab a chair and ask them the best part of their day or find out what they like to do after school. Take the time to learn something new about this student. Not only will this personal connection give the student a sense of belonging, but you will also have a "good thing" to share with the family member or caretaker that is picking them up. Conversations create community value, and the benefit is that you will all go home feeling connected and valued.

Cut It! Paint It! Fix It!
Keeping up the school grounds is a fulltime job. There is always a wall to paint, grass to mow, and a sink to fix. Sometimes, the custodian does not have the time, and the grounds crew is only at our school once or twice a month. Even though you may be wearing khakis and a polo, a suit, or a dress, a little dirt or grease never hurt anyone. The bottom line as the leader of your school is that it is up to us to keep our school in tip top shape and running efficiently no matter what. I'll never forget the time I

watched my principal grab a can of spray paint to refresh our parking lot signs or get behind the lunchroom floor cleaning machine and drive it like a mini-Zamboni. Administrators are partners in the upkeep of our buildings.

Principal Kafele said, "I am a leader. I am a provider. I am a nurturer. I am an encourager. I am the number one determinant to the success or failure of my school." We are never above any job or task at our school. We are there to serve our students, our staff, and our families and we can model synergistic teaming while having fun making the best of it too.

Tika Epstein is celebrating her twenty-seventh year in elementary education. She is a proud mom of two adult children and is thankful for her amazing husband of twenty-five years. Throughout her educational journey, Tika has taught Kindergarten through fifth grade, facilitated professional development at the district and state level, has written blog posts for Achieve the Core, served as an instructional coach at the school and District level, guest moderated several "educhats" on Twitter, was a winner of the 2018 Heart of Education Award (The Rogers Foundation), and contributed to three educational books. She currently, proudly, serves as an assistant principal at J.T. McWilliams Elementary School (Clark County School District) in Las Vegas, Nevada.

Stop Trying to be Friends with Staff
HOLLY BLAIR, Ph.D.

Humans are social beings, and it is natural for us to find others in which to connect. Being a building leader is a very rewarding, yet very lonely job as many of you already know. There are some who are fortunate enough to have another administrator in the building ~ however many are completely alone. Singletons. There is no one to talk to, vent, or share feelings when things are not going well with budget, staff evaluations, irate parents, misbehaving students, or angry secretaries, etc. They cannot go into the staff room at lunch and share "war stories" about what is going on in the office. It is natural to want someone to confide in and be a thought partner. Unfortunately, when you are the one and only administrator in the building, you cannot.

There is a natural desire to be friends with those close to you in the building. There are many instances where the building leaders go out for drinks, dinner, social hours, and connect with other staff outside of school hours. This happens especially when the building leader was once a teacher in the same building and built personal relationships with others before moving up into a supervisory position. Unfortunately, when a move such as this occurs, it changes the dynamic of the relationship with the rest of the staff and can negatively impact a positive culture. If you want to build synergy among your teams, stop being friends with your staff and deliberately become professional colleagues instead.

They Could Be Viewed as Favorites
Mr. Stone had been a principal for five years before moving to a new school in a new district. When he first moved to the building, he knew no one. Being a social person and wanting to have the staff realize that he was a caring, fun, likable person - he often invited many of the staff out for drinks after school on Friday. In his opinion, all were welcome to join, but there was only a handful of his staff who joined him every week.

Naturally because of this routine connection he became "friends" with those who joined him socially outside of school. That year on any given day, it wouldn't be out of the norm to see any or all these socialites in his office after school, joking around and laughing. More time equaled more connection and before long their social interactions extended into family gatherings at another's homes.

In February, Mr. Stone sent out his typical mid-year "let me know how you think I'm doing" anonymous survey. He was quick to realize that he was viewed as having favorites on the staff and that he treated them significantly better than others. The results showed that his "favorites" received all their budget items where others in the building had cut items. While this wasn't accurate because there was an equal cut across the board - those who perceived him as having "favorites" felt that they had their items cut to better fill in the needs of those who were his friends. Whether it was true or not didn't matter because their perceptions of him treating people inequitably was viewed as damaging to the school culture.

As Mr. Stone dug deeper into the surveys, he discovered another glaring trend among the staff who did not socialize with him on a regular basis. The "non-socialites" did not feel safe going to him with any issues that may have involved one of his "favorites." While Mr. Stone was trying to create an open and lighter atmosphere by socializing, he was in fact creating a divide among the staff - causing hard feelings that blocked synergy building trust.

Sympathy Could Be Viewed as Conflict of Interest
Ms. John was an elementary school principal who had an open-door policy. She had a rocking chair

in her office that served both her students, families, and staff well when it came to de-escalation. Everyone was welcome to come in, rock, and most of the time, share what was on their minds. There were many who used this space as a mini-therapy session.

The school was a difficult one, full of a lot of sad stories. The teachers were exceptionally supportive of their students and families, and often put the weight of those stories on their shoulders. Many of these teachers would use Ms. John's rocking chair on a regular basis to process the day or wrestle with feeling defeated. Like Mr. Stone, when other staff came into the office, they would routinely see the same staff members rocking in the rocking chair and leave with the same hard feelings and perceptions of favoritism. Although Ms. John wasn't out having drinks after work, the perception was that more time was spent with certain staff and that those relationships were more important than their own.

When it was time to write staff evaluations, Ms. John was finding it difficult to separate the classroom performance of the "rocking chair teachers" from their personal lives. It was in a leadership evaluation calibration meeting where she discovered that she was giving more grace and leeway to the "rocking chair teachers" than the quieter or less-personally involved teachers. Rather than solely relying on her observational data and script she realized she was giving them a higher score simply because she knew more about what they were facing in their personal and professional lives. She knew she struggled with keeping the evaluations fair for everyone and from that point forward she was determined to be consistent when it came time to formally observe. Ms. John still believes in the rocking chair and has an open-door policy; she just leaves the rocking chair stories in the chair when it comes time to write evaluations.

What Can You Do to be Friendly but Not Friends?
It is important to have a collegial relationship with staff and we certainly can't ignore staff members' problems either. There is an acceptable and delicate balance. Administrators shouldn't "wing" culture and must create a positive culture that builds synergy among teams. Below are three considerations that will aide in maintaining professionalism while being in tune with the needs of your staff and, without becoming personal friends:

    1. Do Not Work in the Same Building as You Once Taught: There is a train of thought that becoming an administrator in the same building where you were a teacher is a benefit because you are familiar with the building, staff, students, and community. While this is true, it is very difficult to continue having the same relationship with the people you once worked beside. You are now their supervisor and will have to make difficult decisions for the betterment of the school that may not make you popular with your once very close friends. Sometimes these decisions are made for personnel reasons that cannot be shared with your staff~ this makes it very difficult for both the administrator and staff.

2. Celebrate as a Staff: Find ways to celebrate as an entire staff. Have a Friday potluck in the staff room where there is a "No Shop Talk," rule at lunch. This is a great opportunity for the entire staff to get to know each other. As the building administrator, you have the opportunity to see how everyone, in all positions, does their job. Write them a note telling them something specific that they did that makes a positive difference in the school. Keep track of who you write the note to so that you can be sure to recognize everyone the same number of times. Whether you want to believe it or not they are keeping tally even if you aren't. So don't "wing" it, be strategic even in your celebrations.

3. Find a Cohort of Other Administrators: Connecting with people who share the same position as you is necessary - especially if you are the only one of you in the building. If you are a principal, find a cohort of other principals to meet with on a regular basis and just talk even if these are virtual connections in a different state. You will be quick to hear that although the specifics of situations are different, the challenges that you face are very similar. You are not alone. Every state has a Principals' Association who can help connect you with others in your region. By having the ground rule of "This is like Vegas - what is said here, stays here." These regional meetings are a place for you to share challenges and get feedback on your own "rocking chair" challenges. The principal who thinks they have all the answers is most likely a synergy blocker.

Administrators have a vital role to play in the professional relationships with everyone in their building. They need to be supportive, caring, and provide guidance and a listening ear to all. This is most easily done when the people they work with are not their personal friends. If the administrator does this, the entire staff will feel comfortable, welcome, and supported. THIS is what the staff deserves. THIS is what students deserve. THIS is what the administrator deserves.

Dr. Holly Blair is the Executive Director of the Maine Principals' Association Professional Division. She is in charge of providing high quality professional development for educational leaders throughout the state of Maine. She works with educators and presenters from all over the United States. She has served as a classroom teacher, a teaching principal, and a principal in several school districts. In addition to being the Executive Director, Holly is an author, presenter, speaker, and school law college professor. Follow her on Twitter and Instagram @HollyBlairMPA.

Stop Showing Favoritism
KRISTI SLAUGHTER LATIMER, Ed.D.

"Leaders who practice favoritism in the workplace have no chance to build a culture of trust"
-Robert Whipple

I can still remember just as if it were yesterday. Sitting in the school parking lot, in my car, making a phone call to a friend. I felt as if my entire life had been shattered. Thoughts were racing through my mind going back and forth between self-pity, pride, and angry ranting. "What was I going to do?" I cannot believe how they betrayed me!" "Why me, why did I deserve this?" "I worked so hard and cared so much!" "They won't get away with this!" "How dare they?!" "What are people going to think?" Two days later I was cleaning out my office, late at night, when only the custodians were around. "What are you doing Ms. Latimer?" They asked. I replied, "I am just cleaning out a few things while there is no one here to distract me." No one knew. Until I was gone…

Now for the Rest of the Story as Paul Harvey Would Famously Say…
My principal at the time, Mrs. Masterson, had always had a reputation--and not a good one. From what I had heard she was negative by nature. I was forewarned by several prior employees who shared, "Unless you are in her clique you will never fit in. She allows her 'teacher friends' that she oversees as their administrator, special privileges such as coming in late or leaving early without any consequences. She talks about staff members to other staff members behind their backs. Mrs. Masterson is not liked by the parents and that's putting it nicely, they know she is fake. Mrs. Masterson said that she cannot stand being in a school that is predominately made up of minorities." Those are some serious allegations and major red flags.

As a rule of thumb, I typically don't take in unsolicited gossip from others as fact and believe in giving others the benefit of the doubt. Innocent until I see and hear things for myself and cast my own judgment. I am wise enough to know that there truly are two sides to every story.

I wish I could say that the rumors turned out to be untrue. I witnessed Mrs. Masterson's teacher friends come and go as they pleased; allow them to wear jeans when they were not allowed; spend countless hours in her office behind closed doors gossiping about other teachers; rolling her eyes at employees because she just disliked them; continually spreading gossip about upper administration to anyone that would listen; and taking two-to-three-hour lunches while I manned the ship solo on numerous occasions. The list of atrocious behaviors goes on and on and on. And, to top it off, her best friend, Mrs. Chadwick, was also a supervisor in the building. As the assistant principal I was literally left to fend for myself manning the building for hours on end, solo.

Of course, these unethical work conditions shook me to my core, but what could I truly do? I continued to work hard, take care of business, build up staff and students, and ensured that everything worked like clockwork. Regardless of what was going on around me, I wanted my work ethic and actions to speak louder than my words. These conditions went on for four years. I always knew that if I ever said anything that I would face some type of consequence. So, out of fear and intimidation I bit my lip and kept my nose to the grindstone.

One afternoon I was called into Mrs. Masterson's office for my yearly evaluation. She gave me an "exceeds the standards" designation in all areas except community involvement (which is subjective in my opinion, but that did not bother me). Then she said these exact words, "You are the most intelligent person on this campus and a valuable asset. We are so lucky to have you. You work harder than anyone I know. Just continue to share your wealth of knowledge with us in the coming years." I was happy about the outcome, left her office and went to lunch.

While taking a break for lunch she called me on my cell phone and asked me to meet her at the central office around 2:00 p.m. I said ok and headed there. When I arrived, I was extremely surprised when I was taken into a small office with some upper administrators and my principal. I sat down and the assistant superintendent at that time told me that due to a "reduction in staff" initiative that was happening all over the district, I would not have a job for the next school year. He said, "You can either resign on your own, or we can fire you and you will not be able to get another job because we will put a hold on your certifications." I was stunned. I felt as if everything was moving in slow motion. I asked, "I do not understand. I just had an evaluation, and it was terrific." Then he replied, "Well, the other supervisor, Mrs. Chadwick, had a higher score than you did in one area (community involvement) so we determined she would remain the administrator based on evaluation scores."

Right then and there, four years later, it all became clear. Favoritism. In its most raw and horrific form. I was not chosen because I didn't have enough community involvement. I wasn't chosen because I was not her best friend. It had nothing to do with my job performance, ethics, intelligence, race, gender, or religion. Only favoritism in my estimation. Now back to where my story began. After that meeting I sat in my car, made a call, and then I went home for the day. I called in sick to work the next two days so I could decide what I needed to do. Two days later I cleaned out my office, left a letter of resignation and placed my keys on Mrs. Masterson's desk, and I left a career I had loved.

Was my decision the right thing to do? Some may say I should have stayed the rest of the month or that I should have sought legal counsel. But I just couldn't. My heart and my pride would not allow them to continue to use me, let me do most of the work, talk about me, and act as if they did nothing wrong. I had to leave. I felt I had to make a statement that people should not be allowed to be treated in such a disposable manner. I don't regret giving her the benefit of the doubt or maintaining my integrity even when she and Mrs. Chadwick took advantage of the system. And I might should have had a courageous conversation with both earlier on and or talked with human resources. But that would have been a career ending approach in a world of favoritism.

There is much more to the story after that, but I will conclude with this: I landed on my feet, completed my doctorate degree, and I have a career that ignites my very passion, and I can live my "why" free from the nonsense of favoritism and unprofessionalism.

Yes, I have forgiven all of those that were involved. Yes, it was one of the most horrific events I had happen in my life. BUT! The most invaluable experience that I gained through all that muck, was to know better, do better, be better, and to tell my story so it may help others extinguish favoritism.

Dr. Kristi Slaughter Latimer currently serves as an Associate Professor at Odessa Community College facilitating teacher preparation courses, child development, and adult ESL. She previously taught first grade, sixth, and eighth grade history, and was an Assistant Principal at both elementary and secondary levels. She has a servant leadership mentality and believes that forming authentic relationships is the foundation of all great things.

Stop Letting Rumors Pollute the Culture
PJ CAPOSEY, Ed.D.

"Gossip dies when it hits a wise person's ears." -Unattributed

Nothing is more important for a leader to manage and tend to than school culture. Many leaders struggle to understand what school culture truly and deeply is and how the behaviors exhibited within each school shapes, molds, and influences the synergy among their teams every single day. To help explain culture, I ALWAYS start by asserting the three maxims below.

Maxim #1: A great culture begets a great climate and not vice versa. Culture and climate are confused even by the most seasoned educators. Climate is volatile, easy to influence, and important within a school. Culture is difficult to move, hard to influence, and quite possibly the MOST important element within a school. Spend your time working on culture; a great culture begets a great climate and not vice versa.

Maxim #2: Culture is the way we do business around here. Culture in a school is like the character of a human. The culture of a school is what we repeatedly do. It is a synthesis and amalgamation of all the behaviors and micro-decisions made within the school over time. Said simply, "It is the way we do business around here."

Maxim #3: You are only as culturally strong as the worst behaviors that you tolerate. When it comes to establishing culture in schools, the behaviors you model and tolerate, are the same behaviors that will ricochet back and define your culture. In many instances these are positive behaviors that are modeled. When behaviors that are not aligned with your stated values are tolerated it makes things worse. These commonly tolerated negative behaviors among your teams are what really define your school culture. In other words, your organization is only as culturally strong as the worst behaviors that you tolerate.

A Series of "Rumor Mill" Impact Questions to Ask

When it comes to the "rumor mill" you cannot ignore them, or the division and synergy blocking will only get worse as time goes on. If you are reading this as a 'leader' (and to be clear, EVERY educator reading this is a leader), ask yourself the following questions to further understand the impact of rumors, gossip, and divisive and unproductive dialogue among your staff and teams.

1. Values. What values have been established within your organization? Do your own behaviors align to those values? Do you diplomatically work to ensure others' behaviors align with them as well?

2. Behaviors. How will you lead your team when the most tolerated behaviors do not align with the organization's values? How will you determine the strengths and weaknesses of your current culture based on these values? How do you (with brutal honesty) describe the culture of your team/school/district?

3. Culture. A common culture killer is blaming others, complaining about current circumstances, and defending current/past behaviors. Which culture killers have crept in and devalued your teams? What mode of operation do your teams function to further block synergy in your school's rumor mill?

4. Conversations. After thinking about the culture-killing impact of rumors, what is one conversation you need to have with someone whose behavior runs counter to the values and goals of the organization? Failing to facilitate courageous conversations is a failure to lead. Undeniably, we all have conversations that we know should be leading, which we avoid. If you were being honest with yourself, could you tell yourself WHY you are avoiding these conversations?

Three Reasons why Rumors Exist

I think as we attempt to tackle the complexity of rumors in schools and what leaders should STOP doing, it is important for leaders to process the three key reasons why rumors exist in schools.

1. People have a natural tendency to gossip. Talking things through is a feedback mechanism to make meaning out of one's surroundings. Educators talk whether in the hallway or in the car driving home to process challenges or happenings. When conversations turn into speculation based on thin air and inaccurate perceptions, the official rumor mill has been initiated. Leading with norms or social contracts address rumors before they happen in a proactive and professional way. Get ahead of the rumor mill and address the bad behavior before it even begins otherwise it will reoccur pervasively.

2. People will fill in the gaps. When there is a lack of communication or understanding, assumption fills in the void. Just like Dr. Kyle Nix shared in Chapter 3. If you are not communicating often or clearly enough, then people will start to close the gaps in communication with guesses, proclamations, assumptions, and innuendos.

3. You allow them to exist. Leaders are part of the problem when they know that the rumor mill is active and still choose to look the other way or refrain from intervening.

Leadership Actions that End "Rumor Mill" Pollution

1. STOP assuming culture does not need daily monitoring, cultivating, and intervention. There is a common perception that we can influence culture by doing nice things from time to time and having a staff potluck or jeans days. That is climate work - that is not how you establish culture. We establish culture by trying to ensure alignment between our stated values and the behaviors that *EACH* staff member exhibit *EVERY* day. We create culture by influencing behavior and aligning that behavior with stated values and primary purpose. *STOP* sitting on the sideline.

2. STOP allowing BCD (Blame, Complain, and Defend) behavior to exist. Rumors exist in many forms, a prevalent form of this is when we blame others for our problems, complain about our circumstances, and defend our own problematic behavior. BCD behavior is emblematic of a rumor-filled culture that does not have a deep understanding of the organizational values we desire to define our culture. Stop allowing people to participate in BCD behavior.

3. STOP choosing 'political capital' over values-based accountability. In many instances, leaders will choose "political capital" over having difficult conversations when they know toxic behaviors such as gossiping are taking place in their building. The simple answer is that every time we allow negative behaviors to persist, we are losing political capital. Relationships are NOT built by choosing to allow others to not behave in alignment with the stated values of the organization. That is not political capital - that simply means you are being taken advantage of. Stop fooling yourself into thinking you ever gain political capital by not holding someone accountable for toxic behaviors. Abdicating our responsibility as leaders to engage in difficult conversations to move the culture forward benefits only ourselves. And in that, it only benefits us by providing short-term relief of potential long-term discomfort.

4. STOP tolerating or participating in behaviors that run counter to the culture you are attempting to build. Synergy among teams cannot be built if we cannot manage our own behaviors as adults. Everything listed above means nothing if we take part in gossip and rumor-spreading. Many leaders will make the excuse that when they do this, it does not pertain to their building. IT DOES NOT MATTER. If people observe their leader participating in negative behaviors, it implicitly gives them permission to do the same and feeds the flame of distrust. Stop spreading rumors, allowing rumors, tolerating rumors, or gossiping with your staff. If you need to process something, take Dr. Holly Blairs's advice in Chapter 7 and reach out to the appropriate professionals.

This work is NOT easy and some days it is minute by minute survival. You are the CEO of culture building and the synergy built among your teams will become what you build it to be. Never doubt your own influence and the impact you can have on your school community. Stamping out the toxic cultural tendency of spreading rumors is real and brave work. You got this; you can do it. JUST KEEP LEADING!

Dr. PJ Caposey is a dynamic speaker and a transformational leader and educator. PJ began his career as an award-winning teacher in the inner-city of Chicago and has subsequently led significant change in every administrative post he has held. PJ became a principal at the age of 28 and within three years was able to lead a small-town/rural school historically achieving near the bottom of its county to multiple national recognitions. After four years, PJ moved to his current district, Meridian CUSD 223, as superintendent and has led a similar turnaround leading to a myriad of national recognitions for multiple different efforts. PJ is a best-selling author and has written 8 books for various publishers. His work and commentary has been featured on sites such as the Washington Post, NPR, CBS This Morning, ASCD, Edutopia, the Huffington Post, and was featured in a Global Leaders Forum thinkpiece alongside the likes of General Petraeus and General McChrystal. He works in the Education Department of two universities and in a myriad of capacities with the Illinois Principals Association including Principal Coach and author of the first complete stack of MicroCredentials offered in Illinois. PJ Caposey, was named the 2023 Illinois Superintendent of the Year by the Illinois Association of School Administrators.

10

Stop Being a Hypocrite
AJ BIANCO

"Do as I say, not as I do is not an effective way of teaching anything." -John A. Garraty

"Do as I say, not as I do," is a quote that we have heard many times in our lives. There are others of a similar variety like, "Rules are for thee and not for me." These types of standout phrases, although simple, help remind us to pursue distinction and become models of clear and high expectations. Sometimes avoiding becoming a hypocrite is as easy as fixing our eyes on someone we greatly admire and asking them to hold us accountable as mentors. As leaders, we must keep these types of quotes in mind, to ensure that we are strong models of trust, loyalty, dependability, and follow through. The goal is for our words and our actions to coincide so there is no doubt about our ethics or character. And just as PJ Caposey just shared, make sure you have no reason to become the topic of the hypocrite "rumor mill."

All Eyes are Always on You
The moment you step into any leadership role (yes teachers too), all eyes are always on you throughout the day. As the leader of people, you set the tone for appropriate behaviors, actions, and processes. When you accepted your position as a school leader you took on the responsibility of clear messaging by consistently setting a positive tone by example. This is a tough profession and anyone who takes on their position for personal glory, praise, attention, and accolades is in for a rude awakening. There are all too many school leaders out there right now who want to be the center of attention, and somewhere along the lines have forgotten that their primary responsibility is to lead their teachers and students to greatness and success. Any "leader" that is in it for the wrong reason is just a boss. Educator bosses set a bad tone for not only those in their school, and their community, but also for our profession in general. This brings a spotlight of bad news press and simply causes more problems down the road. Educator bosses are viewed as hypocritical and are not sustainable within our noble profession.

Don't Break Your Own Moral Rules
Hypocrisy, as defined, is the practice of engaging in the same behavior or activity for which one criticizes another. Or the practice of claiming to have moral standards or beliefs to which one's own behavior does not conform. In education, we continue to second guess decisions that impact our way of doing things. This happens with classroom teachers, building leaders, supervisors, and even at the district level. There are plenty of times that teachers second-guess the actions of their school leader throughout a school year. We look at the decisions that were made, and continuously believe that we can do better, or do something differently. When we look at these decisions and actions in broad terms, we think we can do better. However, it is not until we are put into these other positions that we take on too much and make mistakes that we swore we would never do. It is the failure to follow one's own expressed moral rules and principles that creates a hypocrite.

Throughout my years as an educator and leader, I am guilty of judging others and voicing my displeasure for a variety of decisions made by the "higher ups". I thought, in many situations, that I could make better decisions when it came to grading practices, school climate and culture, and of course discipline. I challenged myself to look at these situations and figure out what I would do when

I would be put in those situations. Now that I am in a leadership role, I admit that it is not easy to make these decisions. I see myself as a hypocrite as my actions do not always match my words in some situations. I have caught myself breaking my own moral rules at times. It is important that I preach the idea of "do as I say, not as I do" to my staff so that I can change negative behaviors when they become apparent and to hold me accountable as the leader of maintaining my own moral rules. As leaders we must reflect on our own behaviors to ensure we maintain educational leadership rather than becoming hypocritical educator bosses.

Synergistic leaders intentionally schedule routine checkups to evaluate their own actions and words to make sure that they are still aligned to their beliefs. We need to make sure that our staff, students, and community see us doing exactly what we say that we are going to do. Here are a few integrity building examples to keep you out of the hypocrite hot seat.

1. Get out of your office. Leaders, we are being hypocrites if we tell our staff that we want them in the hallways greeting each student, and visibly engaged, but we find ourselves stuck behind a desk. We continuously say that we want to be visible, and that we want to be part of the school day, however, there is no way this can happen if you are sitting in your office while instruction is taking place. We all have a ton of work that we need to get to throughout the day, but our priority needs to be on the teachers and students in our school. We need to make sure that we are out and about in the school, building relationships with students and teachers, and not sitting behind our desks. Block off times on your calendar weeks ahead of time and protect a certain amount of time to get out of your office. The school won't burn down, and you will find that others will support protecting this time for you. We ask teachers to be present during the passing periods and to be up on their feet moving around the room during class time so to avoid being a hypocrite, get away from your desk, and get into classrooms at least once a day.

2. Always turn the praise onto others. It's not about you. Of course, we all want positive praise, and recognition for the hard work we put into each day, but we must remember - this is not about us! Being a leader is not about self-promotion, or being part of the headlines, it's about putting the people we lead out front. It is our job to focus on our staff and students and promote the amazing things that they are doing for the school. You are being a hypocrite if you are putting your achievements ahead of those from your students and staff. Even worse, you are being a hypocrite if you are taking credit for the work your students or staff create. You are there to support and push your people to do more. Be humble, be proud, and be excited for the accomplishments that come from those in your school. You would be kidding yourself if you thought for a moment that you would succeed without all their teamwork and sweat equity. Forget promoting what you do, whether in the school or outside of school, and remember to put your students and staff on a pedestal. Always accept compliments kindly and add the list of people behind the success. Accept praise on behalf of the school, or team, or standout team member. Be a leader of praise not a boss of self-absorption.

3. Set clear, high expectations and inspect what you expect. It is important to establish clear, high expectations at the beginning of the year for staff and students. Making sure these expectations are clearly stated and posted throughout is essential for following through with fidelity. Some of the expectations for your staff may include communicating with families, whether it is through email or over the telephone. Most likely you are required to make at least one positive phone call home per quarter to establish a positive connection with families. Staff are expected to show up to school on time, stay after school for students, if necessary, have their sub folders set up in case they are absent, and take daily attendance so that attendance records are accurate. To avoid being a hypocrite, we must inspect what we expect, and be willing to have courageous conversations and documentations, when others do not follow the expectations. When leaders follow through with high expectations, they are holding their end of the bargain for integrity and trust. This includes student discipline, an angry parent who is out to get one of our teachers, providing feedback to help teachers grow, completing observations in a timely manner and answering questions or emails from staff as soon as possible. If we can't do these things for our staff, then we are not leading appropriately, we are hypocrites.

4. Be a collaborative leader. Leadership styles are changing, and we must stay relevant by changing with the times. Top-down leadership is no longer what is best for schools. We continue to look for input from all stakeholders when making some decisions, but we don't look for teacher input when it comes to classroom instruction, curriculum, grading practices, or discipline. You may want to go back and reread Allyson Apsey's Chapter 1 about making decisions for staff and asking for opinions when you've already made up your mind. You are being a hypocrite if you are leading from the top down and ignoring the ideas from your staff. She covers this idea of collaboration and teacher voice in depth. Teacher voice and creating a shared vision can drive instruction and create a school climate and culture that stands out beyond anything you've ever experienced before. It's time to embrace the ideas of building a collaborative consensus when it comes to teaching and leading initiatives. Stop being a hypocrite by making decisions for them and give teachers (and students) a voice in how things might be carried out differently in your school. Allow teachers, students, and families to have a leadership voice where they feel like they are making a difference in how the school is operating daily.

5. Never lead from your email. Technology has changed education over the last few years, and when used correctly, it has become a game changer. I am a huge proponent for the use of technology in our schools and classrooms, and I absolutely love to see new tools, apps, techniques, and methodologies used to leverage and accelerate learning. Some of the new technology being introduced to schools enhances effective communication. A variety of these apps and tools allow us to stay connected throughout the day for a myriad of reasons. But one of the most disruptive tools we utilize daily is email. Email is necessary; however, you cannot decipher the tone or disposition of the sender in an email like an in-person conversation. It is very easy for leaders to sit at their computer sending emails, waiting for replies, and maintaining an email thread behind a screen. It's time to get away from the constant sending of emails, and waiting for replies, and instead get out of the office to have conversations with our staff. We would not expect our staff to go back and forth with families through an email if there is an important situation that needs to be discussed. Stop being a hypocrite; get away from the email and build relationships through conversation with your staff and other stakeholders.

If you want to avoid being perceived as a hypocrite, continue to ask yourself; What do I want to correct? What have I corrected in my role? And What is going to happen moving forward? If you are aware of your actions and can reflect on your values, goals, and high expectations, then you will make the positive changes that will ensure award winning synergy among your teams. Take time to eliminate your own bad habits and create a system of accountability with someone to keep you in check. There will be times where we slip back into our bad habits but recognizing what we can do to stop this before it starts will be the difference between a strong leader and one who is a hypocrite.

AJ Bianco is a husband, father of three amazing children, and currently is the Assistant Principal of East Brook Middle School in New Jersey. AJ prides himself in creating a positive school climate where everyone is respected, valued, and appreciated. When it comes to the ideal classroom, AJ believes in relationships first and is an advocate for technology tools and methodologies. He is a proponent for Blended Learning practices, Personalized Learning, and the Flipped Classroom model to enhance student learning.

11

Stop Being a Martyr
JUSTIN ASHLEY

Have you ever seen the poster that reads, "Our kids are worth whatever it takes"? That was my mindset the first few years I taught...and it worked. My students performed at high levels. News outlets were doing stories on our class projects and simulations. My principal and parents gave me high marks. I had earned teacher awards for my school, district, and the state of North Carolina.

What's the problem with all the success? Somewhere along the line I became a martyr. I laid my life down on the altar of education...and it landed me in rehab. My martyrdom had literally left me with

$100 in my bank account, a wife who was ready to leave me, and a son who I wasn't connected to. And that wasn't all, being a martyr also lured me into prescription drug dependency on Adderall, Xanax, and Ambien with a diagnosis of anxiety and depression. I wasn't literally dead, but I felt like my life was quickly breaking apart, piece by piece.

The Broken Leader
As a superintendent, district leader, principal, assistant principal, or campus leader have you ever felt like every aspect of your life is breaking down because of your commitment to being an effective educator? Have you caught yourself in any of these scenarios below?

- You spend so much time answering emails, making phone calls, and attending meetings that
- It feels like you are being pulled an inch in one hundred different directions.
- Your to-do list looks more like a book than bullet points.
- Your family texts and asks, "When are you going to come home?"
- You worry about so much at night, you can't quiet your mind and fall asleep.
- You left the school for the night, but the school never left your focus.

If this is you, you may not be on the path to rehab quite yet, but you are on the road to martyrdom. It's a scary place. A helpless place. You may have avoided becoming a hypocrite so much so that you set out to do 'whatever it takes' for students. You took your mission, vision, and values to such an extreme that in retrospect you realize that 'whatever it takes' could mean your marriage, health, and happiness. AJ Bianco talked about one end of the spectrum addressing being a hypocrite, martyrdom is the other end of the spectrum, and equally dangerous. Both are nonsense and if not addressed sooner than later, will block synergy among your teams.

Something Has to Die
What if instead you made a different sacrifice? What if you sacrificed an idea? What if you shed this idyllic facade that you must be the perfect principal? Consider shedding the ambition to do 'whatever it takes'. What if you gave that up and replaced it with a new mantra- "I will give everything I can give within the context of maintaining my health, family, and finances." Something has got to give to become more balanced as an educational leader. Playing the role of a martyr is not sustainable. Continuing down the 'whatever it takes' path will only produce ultra-consuming highs followed by extreme and low emotional crashes. Self-awareness followed by strategic self-regulation is key. We are still humans with vulnerabilities who whole-heartedly want to lead at school, home, friends and in the

community. You can be that thriving synergistic leader of teams; it just requires balance and strategic boundary setting to maintain.

Rebirth

I'm blessed to say that I somehow survived as a teacher martyr. Better yet, I was reborn. After rehab, I joined a boxing gym and began working out each day. I took control of my health and am now free from the chains of those prescription drugs. My wife Samantha and I began going to marriage counseling. We recently celebrated our 14th wedding anniversary together. And some of the best moments of my day involve reading, shooting basketball, and playing Oculus video games with my son, Cole.

A few weeks after I got home from the hospital, my wife and I went to a different hospital for an altogether different type of visit. This time I found myself in the hospital to celebrate the birth of our daughter, Savannah. She was born on an intriguing month and day in 2015, July 7th (7/7). Seven is a lucky number for gamblers. There are 7 days in a week. In religious texts, 7 represents the number of completion . . . an ending. For me, it was a sign from the heavens as an ending of the old martyr version of me and the birth of the new balanced and self-regulated me. I wasn't only an effective teacher, but I was also a devoted husband, father, and genuinely content person. The new me no longer suffered from the extreme highs and lows but rather operated within a realm of consistent contentment.

The Kintsugi

This is a term the Japanese use to describe their practice of repairing broken pottery. They don't just sweep up the broken shards from a cup or dish to discard in the trash. They painstakingly retrieve each individual piece and glue them all back together with a golden lacquer. Not only does the golden inlay make the broken piece more beautiful, it also makes it even stronger and more valuable than it was before.

Maybe you feel broken as a leader. The job isn't what you thought it would be. Societal demands have pushed your role to an unsustainable level. The challenges are hitting you from every angle of accountability and transparency. Even at that pace I'm here to tell you that you don't have to be perfect. You don't have to quit the profession. You don't need to risk your health. You just need to have the courage to start setting boundaries of self-preservation, pick up the broken pieces in your life, and glue them back together with gold. Does this require strength through vulnerability? Absolutely. Does this require strategic planning? Absolutely. Does this require dropping the ball on your commitments and deadlines? Absolutely not. This is about giving yourself a break, reprioritizing, and being willing to shift your focus to balance. If you are a leader martyr, my hope is that this chapter will inspire you to make this year your year of the kintsugi.

Justin Ashley is a nationally recognized, award-winning teacher, published author of "The Balanced Teacher Path", work-life balance coach, and motivational speaker from Charlotte, North Carolina, where he began teaching in 2007. He earned his undergraduate education degree as a NC Teaching Fellows Scholar at UNC Charlotte and holds a master's degree in Educational Leadership from Wingate University. In 2011, Justin was named the Charlotte-Mecklenburg Schools East Zone Teacher of the Year and in 2013, he became the only teacher to ever win two state titles-the North Carolina History Teacher of the Year and North Carolina Social Studies Teacher of the Year-in the same year. You can find Justin on Twitter at @justinfashley or by visiting www.justinfashley.com.

12

Stop Making Promises that You Cannot Keep
TODD SCHMIDT, Ed.D.

"Don't ever promise more than you can deliver, but always deliver more than you promise." -Lou Holtz

One of the biggest challenges for any site leader is building and sustaining a positive and motivated climate of academic success. Crafting dynamic, effective and engaged teams of positive culture requires establishing and maintaining positive relationships with students, staff, and members of the school community. One of the quickest ways to damage any of those relationships is by being a hypocrite just as AJ Bianco discussed in Chapter 10. The worst thing that can happen to you as a leader is when the people you lead begin to question whether you will live up to the promises you make. It only takes the smallest incident for perceptions to shift, and your integrity is lost in an instant. Breaking promises not only blocks synergy among your teams, but it also kills their confidence in you as a leader of integrity.

You Can't Build Culture if You Can't Keep Your Promises
I remember vividly when this lesson became glaringly evident to me. I had just put the finishing touches on a holiday string of plans that have become a tradition we do at our school called "The 12 Days of Chrismukkah" (based loosely on that 90's show, "The OC"). "The 12 Days of Chrismukkah" is

a series of days during the holidays where we plan something fun each day to keep staff spirits up and keep students engaged during this high energy time right before Winter Break. We included a Holiday Movie Line Trivia Contest, a fully stocked popcorn bar, and a day where the staff must leave to go home after dismissal right after the students do (always a favorite!)

One of the biggest days I had planned was an all-day Holiday Lucky Duck raffle. I purchased rubber ducks from the internet and numbered the bottom of each one. Staff came in and picked their duck that would serve as their raffle ticket. Throughout the day, the plan was to call out different numbers for various prizes including personal delivery of favorite coffee drinks, lunch from a favorite local restaurant, and the grand prize was a Get Out Of School Early (GOOSE) card where I would cover the last hour of a staff member's class or assignment so that they could go home early. The day was so much fun, and you could hear cheers from classrooms every time I announced a different set of numbers. My plan had been to allow the staff to cash in on these raffle prizes when we came back from the holiday break. While I had the best of intentions, a myriad of responsibilities began piling on my plate at the start of the new year. I started making excuses and made tentative plans to reschedule. Weeks turned into months, I forgot about it entirely, and just moved on to the next thing.

On the last day of school, I was sitting down with my wonderful attendance clerk, wrapping up the year, talking about next year, and discussing summer plans. As we were finishing up our conversation, she paused and asked me if she could share with me something uncomfortable but necessary. It was at that point that she let me know that several staff members had come to her about the unfulfilled raffle prizes and expressed disappointment that I had not lived up to the commitment I had made all those months ago. When I inquired why no one had said anything, she told me that everyone saw how busy I was, and they didn't want to add more to my plate by adding something that on the surface seemed so trivial. But as we delved into it further, it became readily apparent that this lack of follow-through on my part had damaged my efforts to create a positive staff climate. My attendance clerk gently let me know that my tendency to take on so much meant that smaller things tended to fall through the cracks. I'm glad she had the courage to let me know how much my broken promises had disappointed so many staff members. I know now just how deeply they were crushed. My staff had lost faith in my integrity and I'm positive some may have even viewed me as a hypocrite. Not only had I caused disappointment in others, but I had created disappointment in myself. I had overcommitted with the day to day needs of the school community at the cost of under delivering to my own staff.

Lessons Learned

After this "tough-love" conversation (and I am still forever grateful that she had the courage to come forward and kindly let me know my shortcomings), I spent the summer reflecting on ways that I could avoid this in the future. I shared these strategies and my plans with my staff at our back-to-school staff meeting to kick off the New Year to give them permission to hold me accountable. Consider the preventative measures below that I put in place to ensure I keep my word even on the littlest promises.

1. Keep big goals to a minimum. In his book, "*When: The Scientific Secrets of Perfect Timing*, Daniel Pink shares that if we really want to get things accomplished, we should only have 1-3 big goals that we are pursuing. Any more than that and we run the risk of not getting ANYTHING accomplished.

2. Enlist the support of an accountability partner (or two.) When I was planning various events, I asked my wonderful attendance clerk and one of my classroom teachers to help hold me accountable and to not only make sure that what I was planning was manageable and I wasn't overextending or over promising beyond what I could reasonably carry out. I also asked my accountability partners to remind me of our 1-3 goals for the year, especially if I seemed to start getting distracted by shiny new ideas or initiatives that strayed outside those goals for the year. They kept me in check and dialed me back when I was encroaching on over-promising because my plan became too extravagant, not doable, or unreasonably grandiose.

3. Apologize, make amends, and reestablish trust. When you make a mistake, it is imperative to be willing to apologize and make amends to reestablish that trust. I sought out each staff member that I had disappointed. I let them know how sorry I was, that my first order of business was to follow-through on those promises, and I assured them that something like this would not happen again.

Keep these things in mind as you move into the next chapter with Dr. Dan Kreiness. He provides even more examples that show how keeping your promises is a key ingredient in gaining respect as a leader.

Dr. Todd Schmidt is a proud elementary principal in Los Alamitos, CA. An educator for the past 25 years, when he does have spare time he is reading, exercising, being a die-hard Chargers and Padres fan, and hanging out with his wife and two teenage daughters!

Stop Expecting Respect Just Because You are the Leader
DAN KREINESS, Ed.D.

"Nobody cares how much you know, until they know how much you care." - Theodore Roosevelt

In his book, *The Five Dysfunctions of a Team*, author Patrick Lencioni suggested, "Trust is the foundation of real teamwork." When I think of the word 'foundation', my mind conjures images of a concrete structure which supports a house at its base. Therefore, trust becomes the entire support system of teamwork which makes an organization function successfully. In my opinion, trust and respect in leadership are synonymous. You can't have trust without respect and vice versa. However, some leaders, especially leaders who are new to an organization, seemingly forget or neglect the importance of establishing a new foundation of respect as they get started. Sometimes veteran administrators expect to be respected by positional default before they have truly earned respect in the context of the new environment. According to Lencioni, "If we don't trust one another, then we aren't going to engage in open, constructive, ideological conflict. And we'll just continue to preserve a sense of artificial harmony." Expecting respect just because you are the leader only perpetuates the ever-dangerous artificial harmony that can doom any organization.

What Research Says about Trust and Respect

Leaders, regardless of how new or seasoned, must stop relying on their titles to "wing" organization-wide culture. When respect is demanded because of an entitlement type of mindset, it will always block synergy among teams. Why? To become an influential leader, fostering respect and building a strong foundation of trust is a progression of opportunities and encounters that you intentionally create. Synergy doesn't come with the title, building teams of synergy is a product of your consistent integrity and interactions distributed and proven over time. I challenged myself to better understand transformational leadership practices and began to research this topic more in depth. What I discovered was that school leaders who are most respected and trusted take a collaborative approach to establishing organizational visions, for example. An important step in the vision process unique to transformational leaders is to include and empower followers to contribute to creating the vision (Metcalf & Morelli,

2015). School leaders use transformational leadership when teachers and other non-administrative staff are recruited to participate in school leadership processes. When leadership processes are shared between leaders and followers, research indicates higher levels of organizational trust and, of course, respect. In turn, teacher perceptions of a school administrator's leadership style are likely to have a profound influence on school climate (Allen et al., 2015). This falls right in line with what Allyson Apsey and Dr. Jared Smith shared in the first two chapters of this book. Leaning on your stakeholders and giving them a voice provides input and collaborative consensus in decision making. When your teams are active participants, it builds trust and respect which build synergistic teams which build transformational organizations. Everything culture related is interconnected when it comes to effective leadership.

Regardless of which leadership style or theory a school leader chooses to portray, leadership practices influence followers either positively or negatively. In educational settings, teacher perceptions of a principal's leadership style influence the overall school climate (Allen et al., 2015). Furthermore, quantitative findings have indicated a statistically significant positive relationship between transformational leadership and the following seven dimensions of school climate: order, leadership, environment, involvement, instruction, expectation, and collaboration (Eliophotou-Menon & Ioannouz, 2016). When school leaders implement transformational leadership practices, not only do instructional practices improve over time, but the building's culture and climate among teachers improve, including rapport, motivation, trust, and respect for the leader if it isn't artificial.

Avoiding the Dreaded Artificial Harmony
It is easy for educational leaders to fall into a compliance trap, and it seems obvious as to why. Many federal, state, and local mandates and accountability measures have, over the years, led to schools, their staffs, and their students being forced into what I consider extreme conformity. Such conformity sees leaders succumbing to mandates rather than leading organizational efforts where staff can commit to agreed-upon methods that may increase organizational success. Commitment is a function of two things: clarity and buy-in (Lencioni, 2002). Without those, leaders will almost certainly find it impossible to earn or maintain respect among their staff.

Lencioni (2002) discussed the dangers of artificial harmony in any organization. Leaders who do not go about earning the trust and respect of their staff in appropriate ways can fall victim to this unfortunate phenomenon. We have probably all heard of - and perhaps worked for - leaders who talk a big game. Or, like Dr. Todd Schmidt confided in the previous chapter, made promises that he couldn't keep. Big game talking leaders are the ones who make a lot of demands, seem disconnected, do not honor their staff, and are unwilling to hold themselves accountable but are very quick to do so with everyone else. This often causes a scenario in which the leader has blinders on. When this occurs, staff cannot truly gauge the morale of their staff or their organizational culture or climate.

This approach never garners respect from the staff or organizational stakeholders. The best these "respect demanding leaders" can ever do is create artificial harmony. If the staff appears to be happy, or at least content, despite a disrespectful leader, there is almost assuredly a bogus sense of respect for the leader. Like a boomerang, artificial leadership produces artificial responses to leadership. Teams may even seem successful and are meeting goals at a literal level, but, again, that success is despite artificial harmony and not because of a belief in an influential leader.

A Little Can Go a Long Way
During my first couple of months as an administrator, I was asked by a teacher to make a very specific announcement over the PA system at a very specific time during the school day. I should add that this teacher was one who routinely pushed back hard on administrators' decisions and knew the union contract inside and out, just waiting for opportunities to use it against them. For the sake of anonymity, let's call her Dana. I knew I needed to come through on my promise to make the announcement at the right time. I came through. Dana found me at the end of the school day to tell me how much she appreciated me making the announcement and how grateful she was that I said exactly what I was supposed to say at exactly the time when I was supposed to say it. I knew I had just earned more of Dana's respect than with any of the tasks or decisions I had been a part of up to that point.

My time at that school was very short but Dana respected me very much for keeping my promise even though to me it seemed like a small thing. She was one of the few teachers who maintained contact with me as a mentor and continued to reach out over several months after I had left. Each time Dana called she would tell me how much she appreciated my leadership style and would specifically reference how much respect I showed to the rest of the staff. The moral of this PA announcement story? A leader simply cannot earn respect on title alone. Respect is earned through trust especially with the littlest of things. Respect is earned through reciprocation. Respect is earned over time. Respect is earned through actions, not titles.

Dr. Dan Kreiness is an instructional coach for digital learning and innovation with the Norwalk Public School District in Norwalk, Connecticut. Dan holds a doctorate degree in leadership and master's degrees in adolescent education and educational leadership. Dan hosts the popular Leader of Learning podcast. He is also an author who has published works as a contributor to 100 No-Nonsense Things that ALL Teachers Should STOP Doing, Edumatch Snapshot in Education (2017) Volume 2: Professional Practice and The EduMatch Teacher's Recipe Guide: Survive and Thrive in the Kitchen and Beyond. Dan is an expert presenter on topics including leadership, growth mindset, podcasting, student engagement, various instructional technologies, and using social media in education and is currently under contract to publish a solo book about how leaders can inspire growth in others.

14

Stop Lowering Staff Expectations
SHANNON MOORE

"High achievement always takes place in the framework of high expectations" -Charles Ketter

One of the best things about the education profession is that we have the opportunity for a "do over" at the beginning of every new school year and another reboot or relaunch after the long winter break. These times of the year are a gift that offers rejuvenation and reflection to fill in gaps and reset goals and expectations. Whether it is an educator's first year of teaching, or a superintendent's last year before retirement, every school year, cycles in phases that impact synergy among teams. If you use any search engine on the internet you can find a graph from the New Teacher Center, entitled, Phases of First-Year Teachers Attitude Toward Teaching. Leaders have the power to create synergistic teams when they strategically maintain high expectations through each of these phases.

Phases of Attitudes Throughout the School Year
Anticipation fills the last few weeks of summer leading up to the new school because they are filled with preparations and idyllic hope for what is to come. Educators launch the year as their best selves because the summer brings a renewal that allows us to push the pause button and reset; we get a chance to be reflective and remember why we entered the profession in the first place. Once recharged, we spend time reviewing curriculum, previewing rosters, and connecting with colleagues to gain momentum. We even meet over the summer to collaborate as a team to review resources with the hopes of finding gems that will revitalize relevancy and student motivation. We find ourselves in a

variety of stores together excited about the perfect decor to welcome our students back. We seek out effective pedagogy, new skills, and high-impact practices in the form of social media posts, blogs, vlogs, and video livestreams.

The first few days leading up to the opening weeks of school are filled with never ending mandatory professional development that always includes a motivational speech from the principal in an attempt to reinforce the mission, vision, values, and goals of the school site. New programs and procedures are introduced. Expectations, norms, and staff wide social contracts are established which encourage accountability, consistency, and a growth mindset. As the day's countdown to the first day of school, teachers vacillate between being excited and nervous for what's to come and mourning the end of vacation. In the end, educators are purpose driven and willing to do whatever it takes to ensure they are proactively prepared for welcoming their new group of students into a thriving learning environment filled with belonging and high expectations. And then the cycle begins…

> **August & September: Anticipation.** Teachers are still energized and giving their best while striving for excellence because everything is still novel and new. They are learning their students, their families, what works for their new cohort of students, and finding a rhythm within their own team. These same feelings never go away whether a principal or district leader. The beginning of the school year generates a "waking up before your alarm" level of anticipation.
>
> **October & November: Survival.** After the novelty wears off, leaders, teachers, and students find themselves tired and in such a clockwork routine that they may find themselves carving out ruts in the road. Things start to slip and sometimes even deadlines are missed. Last minute tasks, random meetings, memos, new initiatives, and interruptions start popping up. Little by little exceptions are made even if initially for good reasons or as an extension of grace. People are worn down and keep slipping into a rut of survival.
>
> **December & January: Disillusionment.** By the end of first semester, many educators (not all) find themselves burned out and resorting to the bare minimum to get through their day. In some cases, the leaders enable a "get through the day" mindset because they view burnout as a valid enough reason (or they are too busy to address it). The problem with allowing expectations to be lowered is that high performing educators that are still carrying out high

expectations find themselves becoming irritated and annoyed that some teachers are just allowed to skate by. Synergy is stopped when efficacious teachers see their colleagues as subpar. Disillusionment causes division when all students do not receive high quality teaching and learning every day of the year. To add fuel to the disillusionment fire, there is every gathering, event, class party, student concert, conference, and before and after school meetings for just about everything. Even though there is typically a two-week winter break in the middle, the tasks and events that fill these months can be an insurmountable amount of pressure. Semester report cards are due, assessments are administered, IEPs reevaluations are in play, classroom evaluations take place, and everyone is pushed beyond survival into a state of disillusionment.

February & March: Rejuvenation. By springtime the semester is in full play. Everyone can see the end in sight with spring break mixed in and summertime on the horizon. Relationships have been built, classrooms have taken on their own personalities and teams have been solidified. As teams look at their data there is much growth to celebrate, and educators typically breathe in a deep breath of satisfaction knowing that they made a difference.

April & May: Reflection. The final months of the year are typically reflective for effective and synergistic teams. Even though they plan together for the weeks ahead, they are also reflecting on areas of strengths and what might be approached or implemented differently the following year. When high expectations fall by the wayside at this time of the year ineffective teachers lose sight of bell-to-bell instruction, effective checks for understanding, timely feedback, and grading practices. When leaders lose focus on expectations, their teams do too. In many cases this is the path of least resistance for busy administrators.

There are no absolutes in these phases and their exact timing, but the cycle is a predictable pattern of behavior for many educators. As a leader, being keenly aware of the disposition, mood, and stress level of your teams is essential. This realization will give you the insight needed to motivate, encourage, inspect, hold accountable and celebrate the people you lead. Maintaining high expectations is not only respected, but it is expected of any leader, superintendent, teacher, principal or otherwise. Without it, you are just "winging" the culture within your school or organization.

Locate the Epicenter
To reverse any process, one must first determine where the slow decline initializes. In what

environments do we experience a decline in expectations throughout the year?

Staff Meetings: Engagement should be an expectation. Staff meetings become meetings for giving information (that could have been in an email) rather than moments for professional development or growth. Instead of just giving information because you are uncertain as to how the meeting should look, recruit some individuals from the site to put together meaningful staff development experiences; an administrator doesn't have to feel like they must dictate all professional growth. Administrators should empower others which leads to confidence within their staff. Instead of letting the naysayers sit by and disengage by grading papers or turning their nose up at the experience, create pragmatic experiences that staff can take and easily implement the next day in their classrooms. Setting an expectation of engagement of all staff must be at the epicenter of expectations.

PLC & Alignment: Collaboration should be an expectation. All too often educators refuse to rise and meet new expectations or implement new initiatives and choose to work in silos. Most often, these individuals have been teaching the same curriculum or course for many years and feel like what they do works. These silo teachers don't engage in the collaborative PLC process and refuse to align their grading practices and assessments because "they have been doing this forever" and "don't need to change just because a new fad comes down the pipeline". This type of attitude is an expectation lowering synergy sucker. PLC collaboration is proven to be an effective strategy to enhance student learning. When educators refuse to engage, or passively avoid collaborating in their PLC teams it impacts the entire school. This mindset was focused on in Chapter 6 where Tika Epstein shared the importance of avoiding thinking you are above doing any job or task at school. It is no different than walking past a student crying in the hall or failing to help the cafeteria staff when they are backed up. There is no "i" in the word, TEAM. If teachers are allowed to isolate themselves from offering ideas and expertise, accountability, transparency, and data driven achievement, students are the ones that suffer. Education is shifting. What worked 10-15 years ago may not be the best approach any longer. Evidence-based practices coupled with student data will always tell us what our students need. PLCs provide a systematic framework for ensuring all students are at the epicenter of high-quality teaching and learning decision-making.

Classroom Practices: Regular classroom visits should be an expectation. If the last few years have taught us anything, it has taught us that instructional practices must adapt to meet the ever-changing needs of our 21st century learners in person, hybrid, and virtually. Regardless of the learning environment type, administrators must be in classrooms formally, informally, and casually observing teachers in their practices. Frequency of visits fosters trust. A high risk-taking environment is created when leaders encourage a "failure mindset" when trying new strategies or implementing new approaches. At the same time administrators must balance holding teachers accountable for evidence-based practices that lead to high quality teaching and learning by making it a priority to be in classrooms often and providing timely constructive feedback. An administrator's role is a coach and transformative leader. At the epicenter of high expectations is a leader brave and consistent enough to model, provide redirection, or offer instructional support.

High Expectations Directly Correlate with a Pursuit of Growth. Teachers who strive to meet high expectations are more likely to learn from mistakes, fail forward, and aim to be their best self, daily. Essentially, high expectations are directly linked with a growth mindset and a positive attitude. A positive attitude and a growth mindset in teachers trickles down and directly impacts their students because it becomes a part of the culture of the classroom. When administrators set high expectations for their staff it exemplifies that the principal cares enough to encourage their staff to be their best; if teachers feel supported, they will contribute more often which leads to true collaboration and a positive school wide culture. So, why do administrators start the year by establishing high expectations only to waver in their determination to uphold them? Why do administrators feel the need to justify low standards from their staff and then wonder why school wide achievement isn't where it needs to be?

They Will Always Rise to Your Expectations
At the end of the day, building synergistic teams is a balancing act. Administrators everywhere strive to set high expectations through respect and consideration of the needs of each individual teacher. Reality is this… if leaders believe that their teams of educators can perform at high levels, they will rise to the occasion and pursue greatness for themselves, their team(s), and their students. And if they don't, and leaders are willing to have courageous conversations that focus on expectations, they will rise.

As Charles Ketter said, "High achievement happens when high expectations are present and that starts with a culture shift established by those at the helm." It will be a rocky road but stand firm knowing that when those you lead know you believe in them, they will always rise.

Shannon Moore is a district Teacher on Special Assignment that values connections, creativity, and taking risks. She is a proud educator, author, wife, and cat mom. Her joy projects keep her happy and grounded-- she is one of three authors of the book Instruction Without Boundaries newly released in August 2022. #InstructWithoutBoundaries

15

Stop Fearing Change
MICHAEL LUBELFELD, Ed.D.

We cannot imagine that anyone sits back and thinks to themselves, "I am so excited that I am able to keep my classroom, school, or district living in the past." There are many challenging societal and cultural norms and demands that sometimes make it easier to stick with the status quo. Additionally, the tyranny of the urgent serves as a constant distraction preventing schools from becoming more future-ready. As unfinished leaders, it is vitally important to identify the outside forces and the behaviors that impact leaders, both as individuals and as organizational executives that serve to preserve the status quo and to kill the momentum of progress and work to mitigate these distractions. If we don't, we are merely "winging" culture.

Change the Angle
Mathematically speaking, a small change in the slope of a line might not make a significant change over a short distance. However, that same small change makes a significant difference over a longer distance. The same is true in education. When we make small changes to the trajectory of an organization or to the success of individual students, we might not see huge impacts right away. However, over time, those small changes to the angle can take the organization or the future of a child to a completely different place.

Often when the necessity of change in a classroom or organization is broached as a topic, people tend to dig in as they view it as a condemnation of their current practice. They are immediately defensive and scared, so they put up their shields. For the sake of argument, we encourage each of you to consider these questions:

> **Would your school be appropriate for someone to attend twenty years from now?**
> **How about ten years from now?**
> **How about two years from now?**

When the question is posed in this manner almost everyone says that we need to do things differently (not necessarily more) on behalf of our students. When we project into the future, we tend to drop our instant defense mechanisms. The future for which we are preparing will soon enough be the present for our youth. This should serve as the ultimate call to action as we work to create schools that will remain relevant in an undefined and sometimes intimidating future.

So, as we continue with this chapter, that is the angle we want you to look at this from. Do not look at change from a defeatist perspective of what your current classroom, school, or district looks like versus what you believe it should look like right now in a comparative sense. Instead, project forward. This allows you to dream audaciously big and to provide yourself and those around you grace as you consider the changes that need to occur. Schools should prepare students for society and as our world continues to change exponentially, our schools must do what we can to keep up.

Process vs Outcome
Now, we are going to say something a bit controversial here. An absolute and laser-like focus on short-term outcomes will kill innovation and keep organizations living in their current iteration and serve to prohibit them from considering significant change. While managers must do short term tasks and operations for the ebb and flow of the day-to-day operations, the unfinished leader is visionary and longer viewed.

Let's say this a different way by asking it as a question. Imagine we were to offer you a one-time $500,000 bonus if your students hit a lofty, but attainable goal. Would your instruction in your classrooms, your programming and support at the school or district level look the same as if we said you have two years with zero accountability to create the school kids deserve today and will deserve ten years in the future?

The answer is that the process would look entirely different. In one scenario you are chasing a finite benchmark on some form of achievement exam. In the other, you are being innovative and attempting to reimagine a school that serves the whole child. Both strategies are (or at least can be) effective but make no mistake they are varied pathways.

Let's use a non-school example that may help this sink in. If we told you that you had to lose 10 percent of your body weight in 7 weeks for a large financial reward your behavior would look different than if we asked you to design a lifestyle that would allow you to meet your long-term health and fitness goals and we would monitor progress in two calendar years.

Thus, in schools the often over-emphasis on accountability serves to spur the growth and change necessary for our schools to keep up with the change in our society and culture. This is not to discredit the rate of change in schools currently as we are growing faster than we have at any time we can point to in history. But as we change in a linear fashion our world continues to change at an exponential rate.

As a leader it is your challenge to fall in love with the process of growing and continuing to emerge as opposed to seeking a finite title, award, or monetary reward. The reward is the work. As non-sexy as that sounds, it is the truth. The most successful people we know absolutely love the work they do and are committed to their own growth and not levels of success, fame, or wealth.

Don't Forget to Lead
Much of the necessary work to become an unfinished leader is internal. It is about making a singular commitment to yourself that you will not be satisfied with present levels of accomplishment and influence and that you will continue to press forward to create a better iteration of yourself. Organizations are living and breathing organisms composed of human beings. The most systematic way to improve the organization is to improve the humans within the organization.

This work starts with you but cannot end there. We have had the experience to lead, mentor, and coach many aspiring leaders. Some have incredible ambition; fewer have incredible ambition with the necessary work ethic to match. Those that do will stay unfinished. It is simply not enough to stay unfinished personally, however.

While this may seem like a common-sense assertion, let us assure you it is not. The purpose of improving yourself and continuing to grow is so that you can better serve the organization and the people you serve. Becoming wildly well-read and refined as a leader only matters when you lead.

Are you working hard to create a better tomorrow for your students? Our hope is to provide you with some of the skills and motivation necessary to tackle the next challenge and to help create the school/district that your staff, students, and community deserve.

Nobody Leads Alone
As we imagine the future of education it becomes more and more daunting. To imagine what the future of education should look like we must imagine what the future of our world, and particularly our world of work, must look like. The point of schools is to prepare students, both academically and socially-emotionally, for their tomorrow. Thus, without a clear sense of what their tomorrow will require of them, this process becomes hard. This is really the crux of this chapter, stop letting your organization live in the past.

This is precisely why in this instance (and in almost every possible leadership scenario) leading on your own is a bad idea. There is no single educator or educational organization out there with a monopoly on the great ideas of how we can transform our schools to better serve our kids both today and with an eye to the future. Dr. Jared Smith did an excellent job in Chapter 2 showcasing why stakeholder voice, input, and expertise of others is so vital.

Let us be clear, no one leads alone. While it is imperative that a great leader act boldly and at times, it is essential that this mindset does not turn you into an autocrat. There is a dramatic difference between playing politics and seeking collaboration and working hard to build a team and being willing to distribute leadership to others. Allyson Apsey discussed the importance of collective collaboration and inviting stakeholders to the decision-making table in Chapter 1.

Certain evidence of this is apparent in any emergency or crisis. While there may be a single person at the podium giving a statement to the press, there are many behind the scenes doing the essential work to help resolve the situation. Never was this clearer than during the COVID-19 pandemic beginning in the spring of 2020. Societally, nobody was more crucial to helping us pull through this tragic pandemic than our frontline workers and first responders. At the school level, it was the teachers, food service workers, transportation staff, nurses, and buildings and grounds workers that were the real heroes in ensuring safety, food, and continuity of education for our students.

Emergency situations may call for us to live in the present and make decisions without consensus, it's incumbent upon us to make sure we do not allow our organization to retreat to "the cocoon of the past" once the crisis is over.

How to Stop Letting Your Organization Live in the Past
Leading change is hard. In this section you will find a few straightforward strategies to deploy as a forward movement to ensure that you are not letting your organization live in the past.

Evaluate who you are bringing with you and how you have empowered them. One of our Board President's likes to use the statement, "If you go out for a walk and nobody is following you then you are not leading anything". While that may be an over-simplification, the point stands. As we push you to view yourself as "unfinished" it is so that you may lead your buildings/districts forward, it is vital that you do not attempt to do this alone. Review the leadership journey you have planned (either in your head or on paper) for your school and identify who you have recruited and empowered to help you on the journey. If the list is bare, it is an indication that you are going at it alone. Leading significant organizational change will always be a collaborative effort.

Identify three significant changes you wish to see in education in the next ten years. If you cannot quickly identify and articulate long-term changes you want to see, then it is hard to create momentum to lead meaningful change. There are no correct answers or incorrect answers on this - but you absolutely must have an opinion. If this is intimidating to you and it is a struggle to think of what the future should look like, we strongly encourage you to check out our friend Thomas Murray's organization - Future Ready Schools, as they have an abundance of resources to help support you in this journey.

Analyze your production to determine how much time you are spending doing work of responsiveness, compared to work of productivity, compared to work of significance. Most school leaders struggle to chart the path for the future because they are stuck fighting the tyranny of the urgent. A simple analysis of your time spent will help you take back control of your workday. We ask that you code your calendar ex post facto on whether you spent time:

1. Responding to other people's needs
2. Getting stuff done (doing work of production)
3. Leading (doing work of significance)

What most leaders find is that they are spending most of their day responding to other people's crises and spending whatever time they have left completing their core job responsibilities. This leaves little time for acts of true leadership, vision, and significance. This distribution of time that is typical for most school leaders is inverted for the most highly successful leaders we know. As you move forward - intentionally spend more time leading and less time responding to and solving other people's problems.

Dr. Michael Lubelfeld is an award-winning public-school superintendent, published author, national speaker, and adjunct professor with a demonstrated history of working in the education industry.

Stop Forgetting to Celebrate
MELISSA RATHMANN

"Passion drives while celebration revives!"

If You Celebrate Them, They Will Stay
If you build it they will come. And, if you celebrate them, they will stay! Just as Shannon Moore shared in the prior chapter, educators will rise, so as they do, we must celebrate! Finding and retaining the high-quality teachers of this world is critical to the success of our schools. Given the current state of the public education system in our country, it should come as no surprise that more and more teachers are walking away from classrooms and never looking back. Even under these crisis level conditions, I

think we could all agree that educators who feel celebrated are far less likely to leave the profession. Allyson Apsey opened in Chapter 1 by sharing what teachers really want is to feel valued and a sense of belonging. Celebration is a synergy booster - especially when leaders are authentic, strengths-focused, and consistent.

Foster a Celebratory Mindset
In my work, it is a privilege to collaborate with campus principals to support teachers. What has always stood out to me is the optimism and positive energy that teachers exude on campuses where the administration regularly celebrates staff. The teachers on these campuses don't spend their time talking about all the things that are going wrong. Instead, they focus on the many things that are going well and celebrate the opportunity to learn from the things that aren't. I call it a celebratory mindset. Leaders who model this celebratory mindset recognize that celebrating is not just about trying to make people feel warm and fuzzy. They know that it goes much deeper to generate positive energy which in turn leads to more passionate and engaged teachers who want to come to work each day. They find ways to celebrate teachers regularly through words of praise, personal notes, social media posts, themed days, and even food. Never underestimate the power of pushing around a wagon stocked with snacks on a Friday afternoon to show teacher appreciation by celebrating another successful week of school!

When principals celebrate teachers, they feel valued and appreciated. Teachers who feel valued and appreciated are more engaged and productive in their work. We have all witnessed teachers feed off the energy of their administration and work harder when they feel celebrated for what they bring to the table. Teachers who are celebrated also have a more positive attitude. Teachers who embrace optimism seem to enjoy their work more and channel that positive energy to their students. Finally, when teachers feel celebrated, they want to stay. If leaders want to retain staff, they must create an environment rich in celebration - and not just during Teacher Appreciation Week. Leaders, treat every day like it is an Appreciation Day! After all, educators should celebrate every day that ends in "y!"

Celebrating Student Success Has Never Been So Important
As administrators, we can learn so much from the students in our building. Out of the mouths of babes often comes the purest wisdom. I was visiting a first-grade classroom during a science lesson on weather when a student eagerly told me "I like wind because it makes everything dance." Such simple words yet such a profound statement. As administrators, we must embrace this mindset and look for reasons to celebrate. No doubt, campus leadership has a lasting impact on student learning and academic

achievement. I believe that the key to celebrating student success is acknowledging both effort and achievement. It is a catalyst to self-confidence and motivation. More than ever, students need motivation to do well in school and when administrators celebrate student achievement, it will have a lasting impact both inside and outside of school. What if the practice of celebrating student success had the power to change a student's academic trajectory?

Celebration Trounces Loss

Now, more than ever, we must take a strength-based approach to recognize and celebrate student success rather than get lost in the weeds of "learning loss." Build on what is working and set new goals to move full steam ahead. After all, celebration trounces loss. And, sometimes it is in the smallest victories, the ones that you might not even realize are impactful, that you witness the most growth. These are the victories that deserve as much celebration as the bigger ones that are to follow. Recognizing that there is always a reason to celebrate student success has never been so important. Stop forgetting to celebrate. Your words and actions are like the wind and have the ability to make everything dance.

Creating a Culture of Celebration

School administrators often feel as though they are racing around trying to get everything done with little to no time to stop and appreciate - let alone celebrate - the many successes happening throughout the school building. However, leaders who still choose to prioritize recognizing others for their efforts and achievements create a culture of celebration that makes people feel seen and valued. Celebrations are a way for administrators to provide feedback by sending a message that they recognize and applaud the accomplishments and hard work of those around them. If you want to create a positive school culture where students and teachers are excited and synergized to arrive each morning and sad to leave each afternoon, remember to routinely celebrate because… passion drives while celebration revives!

Melissa Rathmann is an educational consultant and servant leader, mentor, lifelong learner, and proud mother. She is the founder of the #CelebrateED movement / weekly chat on Twitter where she has cultivated a community of educators who support, lift, and celebrate one another!

STOP Allowing Emotions to Encroach

This Type of Nonsense Prevents Staff from Delivering their Personal Best

17

Stop Being "Moody" Where No One Knows What to Expect
BRANDON BECK, Ed.D.

"You control your mind, your thoughts, and your emotions. These lead directly to your actions. It is all connected."

Moody leaders are like "brain ninjas" and breed fear and compliance. A "moody" leader can entirely disrupt and tear apart individuals within an organization from the inside out while dismantling the culture of the group. Most of the time, leadership moodiness is unpredictable and being caught off guard is piercing. This erratic and negative emotional impulse can spread like a contagion if not addressed. Not only will "brain ninjas" prevent staff from delivering their personal best, it will also lead to a toxic environment. A "moody" leader will eventually lose trust, extinguish cooperation, and retract commitment from those that they have been hired to lead. If leaders allow their emotions to encroach upon high expectations and consistency, they prevent dynamic transformation of academic excellence within their organization to remain at the epicenter.

Regardless of your leadership title or position, your thoughts and feelings are projected as energy and attached to others like magnets. If you are having a bad day, the energy you project has tsunami level results on everything and everyone in your path, unless you are equipped with the EQ to bridle it. Negative behavior floods your teachers and staff, which pass kinetically right on to your students, decimating your school's culture.

To motivate and inspire the people you lead to do their personal best, consider reflecting on three things that will prevent your emotions from encroaching.

1. Track and monitor your own impulses and triggers. Analyze your own behavior patterns to determine the reasons behind your own moodiness and plan to mitigate them.

2. Do whatever it takes to develop compassion for those who exhibit moodiness even if you possess high EQ with consistent self-regulation.

3. Consistently choose emotions that feed positive synergy and feed success.

Identify Triggers and Patterns
Your bad day, like a lawn full of weeds. Each one of those weeds has roots that penetrate deep into the surface of who you are and who you want to be. If you have a "moody" leader, chances are that deep down underneath the surface there is a reason WHY the moodiness persists. That reason may be the key to helping you understand what's really going on behind the curtain.

Why Are You Moody? Moodiness results from a combination of negative feelings that have been suppressed or ignored and taken root. A school leader whose mood unpredictably fluctuates limits his or her ability to lead with honesty, authenticity, and integrity. More simply put, something is getting in the way of your own happiness. It could be a pest gnawing at you from something or someone outside of work altogether. Everyone has bad days and faces weeds encroaching on their pristine lawn at one time or other in their lives. Extend grace and support one another. Coming together in that manner is a product of a culture where staff give their personal best.

This chapter is focusing on the sporadic and irregular mood fluctuations that leaders develop over time due to a dysregulation of stress. Stress and adversity will always be present in education no matter your position or the time of year. The question is, are you willing to get a little dirt on your hands while reaching deep in the soil to pull the weeds that you've neglected?

Any beautiful lawn requires routine maintenance based on patterns. When you understand the forces behind the weeds growing on your lawn then you can schedule regular maintenance. You know there are times of the year when your organization is susceptible to pests, when your organization needs more sunlight, or more watering. And when the first weed rears its head in the form of your emotional disequilibrium, you have a plan to take care of your moodiness and get back on track. Effective leaders self-regulate their emotions and are keenly aware of their emotions and how they impact the culture of their organization. If you don't have a handle on this already, start tracking your own rants by writing them down in a private journal. Look for patterns of "why" and not if they are big things and infrequent, or little things that escalate, times of year, times of the day, certain types of people, planned or unplanned. Analyze your own behavior responses and plan for beautifying your own lawn first.

Combat Moodiness with Compassion
Moodiness typically produces adversity and conflict as a ripple effect throughout the organization. Is it possible to coexist as a leader of high EQ who has well-regulated responses with staff members and teams that do not? Or conversely, can high EQ teachers coexist in harmony with moody leaders? If a teacher has a student who is constantly moody, they wouldn't ignore it because it would snowball eventually turning into a bigger problem. Connecting with a moody student requires trust, grace, and empathy. Any strong educator would dig deeper into the individual's story to learn a bit more so they can understand the negative impulses and help the individual further. You wouldn't ignore a student's

moodiness, so why would you ignore a school leader's emotions?

Now, I am not saying that every single leader or staff member would be willing to share their personal story with you. That would require being vulnerable through high trust and for some leaders there may be a fear of lowering their guard which can complicate things for some. The bigger point here is that you take a moment to reflect and be a bit more understanding of any co-worker in any position. It may require you to give some additional space, time, care, concern, or perhaps even create a kind gesture. If your boss is a "brain ninja" you may need to accept that he or she is moody because it is a common theme in his or her daily life.

Practice compassion to the best of your ability by offering support and authentic care. Allow yourself to be empathetic learning the "why" behind your colleague and leaders' emotions. Your job is not to fix them, but to relate and respond with compassion and to ensure you do not become the "brain ninja".

Choose to Respond with Positive Synergy
Stand strong as a leader and colleague. Observe, reflect, and learn from the mistakes of those who have lost control of their emotions. Extend kindness, always. Learn and embrace the stories of others. If you are fortunate enough to have a synergistic leader that allows you to be your personal best, then count your blessings through gratitude and continue delivering your personal best. If you have a moody colleague and you've exhausted every approach, remain steadfast in your high EQ example because you never know when the smallest thing will become a breakthrough. Just like Dr. Todd Schmidt shared in Chapter 12 when he made a lasting connection with a teacher "brain ninja".

> Moody Leaders,
> Your emotions directly impact those whom you choose to lead. If you want others to lead alongside you then be aware of your emotional inconsistencies. Certain emotions require a filter stronger than others and have no place in your leadership setting. They prevent you from transformation, progress, and positive impact in your school and community. Whether intentionally or unintentionally every single moment of your life, you choose which emotions you will amplify. You always have a choice if you have wrestled with your own emotions and have a plan for keeping the negative ones from encroaching. The perceptions that those around you make based on your emotions can either make you or break you. Choose wisely. Unlocking unlimited potential begins with you giving your emotional personal best.
> Sincerely, Your Team

Dr. Brandon Beck is a National Board Certified Teacher, speaker, coach, and author of "Unlocking Unlimited Potential: Understanding the Infinite Power Within to Guide Anyone toward Success." He is also the host of the "Unlocking

Unlimited Potential Stories Show," a live show/podcast and podcast where he interviews inspiring people sharing their inspiring stories. He has been an elementary teacher for 18 years and a monolingual, bilingual educator for over 10 years. He is also an award-winning professional soccer coach and instructor for the United States Soccer Federation.

Stop Reacting Emotionally & Engage Strategically
PETER LOEHR, Ph.D.

We all face problems every day, week, month, season, and year. All the time. Problems. Problems. Problems. Some are easy problems, "When to fill the gas tank?", some more thoughtful, "Where to invest retirement funds?". Some problems are routine, "What roads do I use when driving to work?", some more unique, "Which house should I buy? Whom should I marry?". Some solutions have little consequences, "What color car should I rent on a vacation?", and some solutions have significant consequences, "Shall I quit my job?"

Some problems have no "right" or "wrong" solution, "What's for dinner tonight?" Some easy problems, "When to fill the gas tank?" have a wrong answer if the consequence is undesirable (running out of gas on a rainy night in an unknown location).

To further analyze how emotions can encroach on our decision-making, let's look at some common ways that leaders solve problems and make decisions. Below is a list of questions some thinking processes leaders make decisions.

Strategic Thinking Questions & Processes for Decision-Making

- Identify the various options available for decisions.
- Make a list of the pros and cons for each of the options in a decision.
- Determine how quickly a decision must/should be made.
- Determine how important it is to make the correct decision?
- Is there an actual correct decision?
- What are the possible consequences if a wrong decision is made?
- Might these consequences be financially costly to you or your employer?

- Choose the first solution that comes to mind.
- Ask for the opinions of others before making the decision.
- Flip a coin.
- Sleep on the problem and hope for an answer.
- Write each possible solution on 3x5 index cards, turn the cards face down, and select one at random.
- Google for an answer.
- Select an answer/solution that just "feels good" to you.
- Research on how a similar problem has been solved in the past.
- Consult the day's horoscope for help finding a solution.
- Decide not to decide a solution that things will change on their own, and the problem will just go away.
- Delegate this issue to someone else to solve it.
- Think about yourself: If this were a problem about you, how would you want it solved?
- Make a list of seven factors or characteristics of what a "good" solution would be so you can analyze the options according to the seven factors.
- Does this decision affect others and should they be involved in solution finding?
- If the solution will cost money, select the solution that is the least costly, the cheapest.
- When you start trying to solve this problem, first determine how much time you will spend on it and decide before your time is out.
- Spend time thinking about "Is this the right problem to solve or is this only the symptom and not the real problem?"
- If this is only a symptom of the real problem, then what is the real problem that needs to be solved?
- Analyze the legal aspects of this problem before deciding, then follow the law.
- Choose the option that is best for the personal interests of your friends, family, or yourself.
- Review this list again and decide: "What is the quickest way to get this problem off your desk?"

Each of these methods have been used in making decisions by leaders and in varying combinations, frequency, and methods. Each of these methods can produce satisfactory, workable solutions at least some of the time.

The Real Question

How might decision-makers make even better decisions even in situations where there might not be a right or wrong solution? Especially, how might administrators make better decisions even in situations where there might not be a right or wrong solution? Just as we learned in the previous chapter with Dr. Brandon Beck, when making decisions based on emotions and how you feel can be damaging to staff delivering their personal best. Knee-jerk emotions emotionally encroach upon and pollute strategic and thoughtful leadership.

Six Step Process for Making Important Leadership Decisions

You will need to find a quiet place free from distractions to thoughtfully carry out this process. Set aside some time on your calendar that is protected and undisturbed. Bring a notepad and pen, chart paper, or a device if you prefer, to meaningfully carry out the following six tasks in sequential order.

Task #1: Make a list of seven factors or characteristics of a "good" solution(s) so you can analyze the options. There is nothing magic about "seven" factors, the key is that you list several different factors and persevere in thinking.

Task #2: Write a response to the question, "What are the possible consequences if a wrong decision is made?" This will clarify the significance of making the right decision. This list will also be helpful so you can take precautions to minimize a wrong decision. For example, in employment decisions a possible wrong decision would be in hiring a pedophile and a precaution would be in conducting a thorough reference and background check.

Task #3: Document your reasons for making the decision to do something and not to do something else. This is especially the case for personnel decisions (to hire or not to hire) because of future possible complaints of discrimination or "political" considerations.

Task #4: Research by Nobel Prize winner Daniel Kahneman demonstrates that when more people are involved in decision-making, better decisions are made. Each human has his/her own biases and "noise" in making decisions. To counter this, involve more people and the biases may be canceled out, eliminated, or discovered in the process.

Task #5: Determine additional decisions that must be made before making a larger or more ultimate decision. Next to each, jot down the manner in which or "how" each additional leading decision would most effectively be carried out.

Task #6: Be prepared to be questioned and to further expand upon or explain your rationale for your decision. Even though the decision may be initially embraced, things can always go south. Keep documentation in a folder and hang on to it for the next few years, especially for employment decisions.

Dr. Peter Loehr is a professor of educational leadership at the State University of New York, College at Buffalo, since 1996. Prior to that he was a math teacher, English teacher, high school assistant principal, elementary principal, director of curriculum & instruction, director of personnel & labor relations, and superintendent of two school districts. He has also been an expert witness in federal and state courts since 1987 in areas of employment discrimination, teacher-student sex abuse, school & student safety, administration procedures, and employee discipline.

19

Stop Worrying What Others Will Think of You
LARRY DAKE, Ph.D.

If you are anything like me, you have spent a lot of time in your leadership career worrying about what others will think of you. The higher you go on the flagpole, the more public all your faults and idiocracies are. In addition, school leaders operate in a public sphere. We are public servants, and our students, staff, and stakeholders have a right to transparency in our decision-making. Early in my career, this led to a lot of anxiety about doing the wrong thing, making the wrong decision, or worrying that decisions would impact how others thought of me. Even though I made solid decisions in a strategic manner like Dr. Peter Loehr just shared in the previous chapter, I still highly regarded the perception others had of me.

What Causes This Anxiety?
Most of us come up through the system as individual contributors in the larger organization. Yes, collaboration and teamwork are highly valued and research-based ways to increase student achievement, but essentially teaching and its related services are individual endeavors. While co-teaching and other environments exist, many professionals enter school leadership having spent most of their time working in isolation. As a social studies teacher, I had broad autonomy to make decisions about how I taught, how I approached the content, and how I managed my classroom. What others thought of these decisions did not impact my practice. While we all want to be liked, I knew that if

my students were successful, all would be well in the world.

This approach and thought process changes dramatically once you move into a school leadership role. There is a shock to the system and adjustment for the leader because they are no longer an individual contributor in the system, but rather responsible for the system's overall operation and success. Just as Shannon Moore shared in Chapter 14 decisions must be made well beyond the confines of a single classroom. Working in isolation is free from teaming and does not promote staff delivering their personal best. A teaming mindset always transfers to leadership as hard decisions over classroom assignments, schedules, room assignments, and other topics will always wind-up pleasing some and displeasing others. For leaders who are used to being able to please everyone, this may be a challenge, unless like in Dr. Kyle Nix chapter, you share pertinent information and gain collective consensus for effective implementation. For me, as someone who was a well-liked teacher and had a strong rapport with students, colleagues, and stakeholders, transitioning to a decision-maker that brings out the best in others, was eye opening to say the least.

Making the Transition
Those of us who worry about what others think of them have often struggled with this transition. Often, the struggle is because we don't understand how to stop the worry. The transition goal is to not let perceptions of others eat at us. Instead, we must learn to make decisions from an ethical and values-based perspective. The first leadership hurdle to cross is the realization that all decisions, large and small, will impact people in different ways. This is inevitable. As a school leader, I have never made a decision that has pleased everyone. Displeasure is not always out in the open, and often simmers below the surface in a behind the scenes kind of way and like Dr. Brandon Beck shared in Chapter 17 can rear its head in the form of "moodiness" or other attributes that prohibit staff from contributing their personal best.

Let's look at an example. As a building principal, we had the same master schedule for many years. Several principals had come and gone, and the schedule had stayed the same throughout. Master scheduling always became "next year's headache." For me, that headache came in year two of my principalship. Even though it was also the right issue to tackle because the grade-level that had the first prep time of the day had legitimate concerns. This meant that students arrived in the building at 8:55am and went to specials at 9:10am. This eliminated the entire first hour of the day for instruction; less than ideal. Moreover, this grade-level had been in this slot for at least a decade. It was time for a change, and I knew it was right for students.

Heading into this change process, I knew some grade-levels were not best fit for first hour reporting to activities. Kindergarten, for example, often takes several weeks just to get morning routines intact. That type of immediate transition was not ideal. Moreover, Grades 4 and 5 had music lessons in the afternoon and making their special time in the morning would dramatically cut into their instructional time. The best-case scenario for students was rotating among Grades 1, 2, and 3. Since Grade 2 was in the position the longest, they needed the break. After meeting with both the Grades 1 and 3 teams, we reached consensus that Grade 1 would take it the next year, Grade 3 the year after that, and then it would rotate back to Grade 2. Because I shared the important information that everyone needed as Dr. Kyle Nix suggested in Chapter 3, and it was centered around what was best for students, this major transition was initially accepted.

Emotions Still Encroach

The decision was not popular with everyone, but it was pursued ethically with broad input. This represents the opposite of not worrying what others think of you - thoughtful, responsible, ethical decision-making. When decisions are made in this way, leaders can put their heads down at night knowing that they did their best and others' opinions can stay where they are. Leaders must make dozens of decisions each day, often each hour, and worrying what others think of them will only cause greater stress and anxiety.

There are two emotional aspects of this dynamic worth noting. First, when decisions are made in this manner and others express their anger, disagreement, or displeasure, the "moodiness" reaction is more about them than it is about you as the leader. There are people in this world who dislike any level of change or discomfort, and regardless of how ethically the decision is made, they will not be happy. Leaders should realize that is inevitable. Rather than own that reaction, leaders should realize that such a reaction is more about the person reacting than it is about the decision that was made.

Secondly, it is important to realize that not everyone is positioned to understand all sides of a decision. As leaders, we possess more information than most others do about situations, tasks, people, and problems. Often, this information is confidential and cannot be shared. In other cases, it would be distasteful to share this information. For example, if as a leader we know that one of our staff members has a sick child, and we allow that staff member to leave early to attend to their family, some may view that as unfair. Others may not know the entire situation and it's not our job to justify decisions made in this manner. Rather, put your head down at night knowing that you helped a staff member in their time of need, through empathy, understanding, and. The negative nellies can take their opinions to the local watering hole in those scenarios.

Leadership Maturity

When someone says, "I don't care what others think of me," it can often be used as a callous excuse for poor leadership. However, when decisions are made ethically, responsibly, and for the right reasons, others' opinions of those decisions and us as leaders should not cause worry. I think this is the ultimate step in leadership maturity and a journey that I've been on in my 12 years as an administrator. Once I reached this mindset out of confidence, maturity, and effective decision-making, my anxiety waned which provided an environment where my staff could give their personal best.

This is leadership maturity. Leadership maturity can be described as knowing that some decisions will cause displeasure but arriving at those decisions in an ethical and responsible manner based on what is best for students. Leaders who are trusted to make good decisions can also make decisions that cause others displeasure at times. But over time, this type of leadership maturity exercised day-in, day-out builds strong culture and community. Leaders' moods and actions are contagious and when they overcome "what others think of them", it leads to confident decision-making and safe risk-taking culture. Mature leaders make decisions in a responsible manner and let the chips fall where they may, knowing that every decision will displease someone. Becoming a mature leader often takes time, experience, and represents the ultimate step in the leadership journey.

Dr. Larry Dake has served as a school leader for 11 years as a curriculum coordinator, Principal, and Assistant Superintendent. In addition, he works as an Adjunct Professor in the Binghamton University Educational Leadership program. He lives in Endwell, NY with his wife Kelly, a literacy teacher, and three children.

20

Stop Holding Grudges about Staff Members' Mistakes
DAVID GEURIN, Ed.D.

You'll never reach your highest leadership potential if you're harboring resentment or holding grudges against anyone who is among your leadership. Effective leaders make it a goal to have zero grudges. Zero. Why? Because hard feelings and unresolved hurts always show up in unexpected, destructive "brain ninja" ways like Dr. Brandon Beck described in Chapter 17.

Your grudges harm your relationships. It's not possible to be your best self with another person when there is stuff under the surface that is unresolved. The unresolved muck is going to find its way into the life of the relationship and create distance. This toxic grime always makes it harder to be supportive, encouraging, and understanding as a leader.

Clinging to resentment only harms your ability to make the best decisions for the current situation, because you're hanging on to something from the past and no longer engaging strategically as Dr. Peter Loehr shared in Chapter 18. Your grudges are unhelpful and un-leadership-like because they distort your view of people and situations in unhelpful ways.

How to Let Go
When negative emotions have festered in the past it can be difficult to let go of bitterness. It can be tough to move past a grudge. Maybe the same issues keep happening over and over. Maybe you feel disrespected, ignored, or undermined. Maybe you feel completely unsupported. Maybe you feel betrayed. Those are tough feelings to deal with as a leader. It can feel threatening to your leadership. And yet, those feelings are still valid and understandable. You feel them strongly. After all, you're human. However, you must remember that you are ultimately responsible for your feelings. And you can't allow your feelings to cause you to act out in ways that are detrimental to your leadership. The quality of your leadership behaviors should never be dependent on the quality of the behaviors of those who are under your leadership. You must remain above the fray if you are to provide an environment where everyone can deliver their personal best.

5 Tips for Maintaining your Leadership Poise and Letting go of Grudges
1. Process your feelings. When a relationship in your school creates strong feelings in you, the first place to start is with yourself. Reflect on what's happening with your inner response. Ask yourself, how can I better understand what I'm experiencing? What legitimate needs do I have that feel threatened or damaged right now? Name what you're feeling and why. When you start by focusing on understanding your own emotional response, you'll be better able to respond to the other person calmly and productively. Just like Dr. Holly Blair shared in Chapter 7, it is a good idea to talk through this with a trusted person, mentor, or a confidant outside of your organization. It's important to have other people who understand, can validate, and offer sound advice about what you're going through.

2. Address the behaviors. Letting go of a grudge doesn't mean letting poor or unhelpful behaviors go unchallenged. Often grudges begin when we ignore things too long and resentment builds. It's better to have a direct or courageous conversation early on. One way to start that type of conversation is to say, "I value our relationship, and something doesn't feel right to me. Could we talk about that?" When sharing the problem, focus on things that are observable and avoid generalizing. For example, you might say, "When you asked others on your team to ignore what was decided for the building, it felt disrespectful and undermined our values and goals. When we come to a consensus as a staff or there is an expectation, I need you to stand by the decisions we make because they demonstrate value and commitment to our school goals. We will always try to collect input but when the decision is made, I need to know you'll support it. Can I count on you to do that?"

3. Be quick to forgive. It's much easier to forgive when we're able to resolve an issue. However, sometimes we need to forgive even when the issue is not resolved the way we would like. Maybe the person won't accept their responsibility and continues to undermine the decision or directive. Maybe they struggle with making the same mistakes over and over. Maybe they are cold or distant or moody.

It's still important to forgive them and keep on forgiving them. Most people are doing the best they can with the information they have and the mind-frame they're in. When they act out, it probably says more about them than it does about you. Don't take things personally because it isn't about you. So don't forgive them because they've earned it. Forgive them because holding a grudge is harmful to you and harmful to your leadership. You'll be a stronger leader when you are strong enough to forgive even if you need to follow through with a formal course of action later. Keep in mind forgiving isn't necessarily letting them off the hook. Instead, it's letting yourself off the hook and not being controlled by a grudge. You may still need to take corrective or disciplinary action against the individual. You might even have to let someone go. But it should be based on their performance alone, and not your inability to forgive or let go of a grudge.

4. Recognize and reinforce the good things. You will know you've forgiven someone when you find yourself cheering them on without reservation. Forgiveness allows you to commiserate when they are hurting and celebrate when they're succeeding. It's so important to continuously show everyone in your leadership that you notice the great things they're doing, and that you're invested in their growth and success. Show them you value them. Your leadership will be more effective and more enjoyable when you focus on each person's strengths and build on the positive things they're doing. It's hard to hold a grudge when you notice a person's positive qualities and contributions.

5. Ask for forgiveness when it's appropriate. Don't forget, even the best leaders make mistakes too. It is vital to respond when someone on your team feels like you've hurt them or let them down. Maybe they felt that you weren't supportive in a student discipline issue. Be sure to validate what they're feeling. Let them know, "I never want you to feel unsupported. I want you to feel like I have your back." If you feel you could've handled something better, tell them you're sorry and want to do better next time. This type of vulnerability is powerful. It sets the tone. It gives everyone permission to own their mistakes and be held accountable. It shows that you're willing to admit to your faults and that you're continuing to grow too. In this type of environment, people work through their issues together, and as a result, it's much easier to let go of grudges or never create them in the first place.

Dr. David Geurin is superintendent of Fair Play R-II School District in Missouri. Previously, he served as principal at Bolivar High School. Under his leadership, BHS was named a National Blue Ribbon School. He's the author of "Future Driven: Will Your Students Thrive in an Unpredictable World?" NASSP honored him as a National Digital Principal Award Winner. He shares his ideas on learner empowerment, leadership, and innovation via social media, blogging, speaking, and consulting. A speaking highlight was his keynote address at the National Principals Conference in Boston.

21

Stop Violating Confidentiality Standards
DEANNA OLIVER, Ed.D.

A highly experienced school district superintendent said to me once, "A secret is your burden to carry, don't pass that burden to others by divulging the information". He provided this sage advice nearly twenty years ago and it has stuck with me as a reminder every time someone shares confidential information. It is difficult for those who have "loose lips" to understand the damage they cause to their own professional reputation when they consistently reveal information that they should not have. This is one of many skills that effective school leaders must embrace to rise to their personal best. Never underestimate the importance of maintaining confidentiality.

The Dome of Secrecy
Throughout my administrative career, I have had a snow globe on my desk with a drawing of a stick figure inside of it; this is what I called the "dome of secrecy". Any time staff needed to share a personal or professional issue that they wanted to remain confidential, I would pull out the snow globe and tell them it was "in the dome" which essentially meant that it would not be shared with anyone. This ability to be a good listener without blabbing to others, helped me to build trusting relationships. There are times even when the "dome of secrecy" is out on the table that we must share, be honest, and carry out a courageous conversation. To maintain trust within the "dome of secrecy" leaders must possess a fixed set of internal standards regarding privacy that we do not violate unless necessary. Our educators deserve for us to be leaders that understand the value of keeping their mouths shut when it comes to issues that are shared with us. Unless it violates the law or causes harm to self or others, it stays in the "dome of secrecy".

Confidentiality Requires a Filter of Professionalism
It is not always easy to filter a response to a situation. In some cases, well intended staff members will request information that they are not privy to. For example, children who are abused or neglected may be a discussion topic for educators, support staff, and administrators so that they may problem solve a solution for the child while at school. The intention is to support the child; but in the process, the details of the abuse are shared with far too many individuals thus violating the confidentiality rights of the child involved. It is important to ask yourself, "If this were my child, who really needs to know the information and how much really needs to be shared"?

STOP Allowing Emotions to Encroach

Maintaining privacy is not always easy. While serving as a principal, my building needed to make staffing cuts. I was required to honorably dismiss a teacher in a reduction in force knowing full well that the next week I would be hiring him back. Why did I do this to him you may ask? I did it to protect the privacy of another teacher who would be announcing his resignation and was awaiting his official hire from another district. This devastated the teacher who went an entire week thinking he was unemployed. It was horrible! I apologized profusely when I visited to tell him the news that he would be rehired. In the end, I hope he appreciated that I placed confidentiality as a priority for all staff. I have no regrets in this situation as I had followed the expected protocols for confidentiality.

School Leaders must set aside time to reflect on their own thoughts and actions as it pertains to confidentiality. While one may think of confidentiality in terms of secrecy, it is essentially how we show the value of all content that should not be made public. The policies that exist and those that we create should comply with privacy and confidentiality. There is value in asking yourself a few questions: With all the other tasks on my plate, how do I prioritize confidentiality and infuse it in my daily work? Are there professional learning opportunities created and required for all levels of school staff to ensure understanding and implementation of these policies? Do we demonstrate that student records and data privacy are priorities? Am I explicit in making statements and creating a culture that gossip is not acceptable and how are those situations handled? Are my coaches and athletic directors well versed in limiting interview content with journalists including medical conditions of athletes to the press? Does someone in your building need to be told to "shut their pie hole"?

Picture a switch in your brain that you flip on every time a discussion arises that requires confidentiality. Imagine this switch causes lights to flash, flags to wave, horns to blast, and a computerized voice saying "warning-impending doom". This visual should alert you to a minefield that you are getting ready to walk into and you need to be prepared to shut down the fodder, correct the behavior, and redirect the conversation. Stop the leaks of information before they start.

Prioritizing a high level of confidentiality standards for yourself and others is a required professional skill for school leaders when working with members of the school community including the board of education. It is an expectation of everyone in the school community that leaders do not slack on this task. When you fail at this, it can quickly bite you and others in the behind. Always keep in mind that there is a deeply rooted connection between integrity, trust, and confidentiality.

Dr. Deanna Oliver serves as the Assistant Superintendent at the Kane County Regional Office of Education. She has served in that role for eight years. Deanna has a long history in education including serving as a high school principal, assistant principal, and teacher.

22

Stop Ignoring Your Own Biases
D. NILMINI RATWATTE-HENSTRIDGE

One thing we are guaranteed to have in common is that we are all human. As human beings we are made with imperfections. These imperfections encompass our gifts and uniqueness that intertwine us together in this world. Without nuances, strengths, and limitations we would all be the same. Many times, our differences create novelty, perspective, and excitement that make our work environment a richer place each day. When we assume a strength-based perspective, we grow stronger because we sharpen one another as human learners, giving our personal best to ensure the success of all.

The beauty is that we are all different. The challenge is that we are all different. Because we all come with varying schemas and blueprints, we must be willing to carefully examine and consider the biases that we may encounter in each situation. We shouldn't ignore our biases, instead learn to acknowledge, unlearn, learn, and hold ourselves accountable. This will ensure that we don't let emotions encroach and dismantle teams. Addressing bias begins with comparing and fully understanding implicit bias sometimes referred to as "unconscious bias" as compared with bias.

What is implicit bias?
According to the Department of Health and Human Services, the following questions are answered:

> **What is bias?**
> Bias consists of attitudes, behaviors, and actions that are prejudiced in favor of or against one person or group compared to another.
>
> **What is implicit bias?**
> Implicit bias is a form of bias that occurs automatically and unintentionally, that nevertheless affects judgments, decisions, and behaviors. Research has shown implicit bias can pose a barrier to recruiting and retaining a diverse scientific workforce.

Consider bias versus implicit bias in the context of a student's skin color. A bias or "conscious bias" is a prejudgment about a student (or individual) identified as a specific race, and as a result, the educator responds and interacts differently with this student (or individual) as a result. In the case of bias an educator may refrain from calling on a specific profile of a student assuming they won't be able to respond with the correct answer, so they avoid calling on those students. Implicit or "unconscious" bias is similar in that it may produce the same or similar outcome, but the educator is unaware and the action(s) toward a student (or individual) was unintentional or carried out unknowingly. For example, in a classroom a teacher may call on a particular race or gender more frequently than others without even realizing it. But awareness brought about by classroom observations in data may be all it takes to plan intentionally to ensure all students have an equal opportunity to respond through equity of voice. In both scenarios these biases placed a limitation on all students having access to making thinking visible or high engagement. Whether intentional or unintentional, biases impede equitable opportunities to make gains in academic progress. That's a huge deal!

Because we are all different and come from varied backgrounds, belief systems, experiences, and ethics, we must be cognizant that our unique perceptions drive our daily interactions with one another as colleagues, leaders of adults, and teachers of students. The key is that we understand our own unique implicit bias and work to mitigate them.

Crises, social movements, protests, global events, and social dynamics "in the news" have created a world of division through racism, sexism, homophobia, hetero-sexism, able-ism, ageism, religion, and many other -isms. As we work towards understanding bias and implicit bias, we must prevent them from finding their way into education, especially our classrooms. Accent or dialect, ethnicity, socio-economic status, cultural heritage, traditions, customs, gender, and religion- create unique differences that make us each original. Limiting student success even unintentionally or unconsciously, still produces limitations in achievement.

Who 'Would You Rather' Travel With?
Many of you are familiar with "would you rather" comparisons. To further explore this concept of implicit bias, let's walk through a visualization process to further drive home this point. This task is referred to as "Airplane" of which I have modified and adapted and offer credit to the "unknown creator". Imagine that you are taking a very long flight to a destination of your choice on a fully booked airplane. You can only have one person sitting beside you the whole way and you will be vacationing together once you reach your destination. Who would you rather sit by you for the long flight and join you on vacation?

Person 1: Someone who has been to prison and has served a sentence? or

Person 2: Someone who has played Basketball at the Olympics?

Think about and justify your answer. You may be thinking that you don't have enough information, so additional information is revealed to you. The findings are that the real person who you are sitting beside and continuing vacation with is:

Person 1: Is Nelson Mandela who was a civil rights activist who was sent to prison and released because he spoke up about the Black-White Division in South America. or

Person 2: Is a Female White Paralympic Champion who plays wheelchair basketball for their country.

Is this what you visualized when you first selected the person you'd be vacationing with?

What are some biases you had?
Did you react to the word Prison?
Did you react to the word Basketball or Olympics?
Did you exhibit implicit biases associated with: race, gender, ability, prominence, or influence?
Did your mind consider their positional power or success, or how much money they made?

Think about any other considerations you may have made in selecting who you'd rather travel with and join you on vacation. Reflection assists in self-identifying our implicit biases that guide our choices especially when we have limited information. If we are to unite through allyship as educational leaders we must model intentional inclusion, equity, and diversity practices to minimize bias.

Our beliefs, ideals, and schema allow us to choose who we vacation with in real life and that's okay. As leaders of public education, we are flying the plane full of students and/or staff with varying strengths, talents, backgrounds, and schemas of their own, and we must ensure all students and staff arrive at the destination of high student achievement, belonging, and success because of our unbiased guidance is a forethought. When we address our own bias, we are on an equity trajectory for all students.

Lead Practices of Equity
Equity means providing each student the resources and learning opportunities to be successful. This requires learning individual student strengths and limitations, creating connected trusting

relationships, knowing a variety of programming resources, and working together to close achievement gaps.

This may sound difficult to accomplish in a classroom, school, or district-wide organization with a wide variety of strengths and needs. Leading practices of equity demand effective planning, accommodations, modifications, expertise, resiliency, and a lot of energy. The outcomes of implementing equitable practices bring about transformations in classroom management, nurturing relationships, safe risk-taking environments, and significant academic progress. There is no doubt that leading practices of equity for students requires seeking resources such as translators, securing breakfast and snack programs, special education, medical supports, mental health resources, students of trauma resources, refugee, and migrant liaisons, and/or modifying work to give access multi-language learners, migrants, refugees, houseless students, and low socio-economic students.

As a student myself I remember hearing the words, "I do not see the color of your skin". I remember thinking to myself, "If you don't see my skin color, then how will you understand that I am learning English as a language to communicate? Or that I left a civil war behind to immigrate? And that my entire upbringing and culture focused on making a new home because literal safety came first?" Those very thoughts as a child were my own implicit bias because I assumed others would understand what I went through and who I was based on my skin color. What I learned was that we cannot assume these things of students simply based on the color of skin. What matters most in education is that we give staff and students a voice, that we make time to hear their stories, and that we learn their strengths and talents. We cannot make assumptions about the struggles our staff and students have been through based on race, religion, gender, or any other "ism". We must take the time to know our staff and students so well that we create a safe enough environment for everyone to thrive emotionally and progress academically.

As a teacher all these years later, I still hold on to the feeling I experienced as a child of inclusion and the value of interacting daily with a sense of belonging and high-quality teaching. My own schema and practices of equity have kept me grounded as a teacher. I honor my students by getting to know them, uncovering their needs, and valuing their input as we co-create successful lessons that engage, connect, and excite them as learners in my classroom.

Ask Questions, Seek Answers, & Advocate for Change
Educators, whether teachers, administrators, or district leaders, genuinely love supporting one another.

We operate in a profession where "the answer is always in the room" when there is a need to advocate for change. If we pose questions and give students, teachers, families, and leaders a voice because we are seeking answers, we will always discover innovative solutions that lead to student achievement. The more we can inspire and support our youth and young adults to pursue their passions and gain access to higher education, the more engaged they will become as citizens in our country. As you advocate for positive change within your educational organization, consider asking:

1. How can I make a difference when I am leading?
2. How will I apply my understanding of bias types to intentionally plan for those that I lead?
3. How might I monitor and adapt my interactions to ensure gains and progress for all the people that I lead?

Ignoring our biases is not an option whether intentional or unintentional. Effective leaders are self-aware and consider each person's strengths as a key component for setting the course of success and to ensure equity for all learners and staff. We owe it to humanity and the future of our communities to refrain from letting our emotions encroach so that everyone can give their personal best in a thriving, high achieving learning environment.

D. Nilmini Ratwatte-Henstridge is a teacher at heart, she loves the journey in education because it makes a difference in the lives of students, and communities one person at a time. She was born in Sri Lanka and immigrated to Canada where she now lives and calls home. She loves connecting with others and is passionate about equity, social justice, and human rights as she builds and teaches towards an inclusive world, in our generation. She completed her Master of Education in curriculum development in equity and is an active blogger for the Teach Better Team.

Stop Believing Only One Side of the Story
KRISTEN KOPPERS

We've all been there whether you're a parent, teacher, friend, leader, or just a human being. Sometimes it's hard not to believe only one side to a story when facts are not presented as they should be. In fact, many leaders would rather push the situation under the rug before seeking out the truth. It's even common that they hear what they want to hear claiming they heard both sides of the story and conclude without reason or firsthand information. As disheartening as this may be, this type of leadership malpractice leads to teacher neglect, which then leads to distrust. We want to believe that teachers are not expendable or replaceable, so why do leaders act as if they are? Why is it that leaders let their emotions encroach to find themselves only believing one side of a story?

A Culture of Trust Matters
What are the factors that lead into believing one side of a story over another? As easy as it seems to ask, it is more difficult to explain. Some leaders do not want to spend time 'investigating' the story. It's easier for them to blame one person over another to prevent a negative school response to the situation. Sometimes leaders' own biases, grudges, or moodiness gets in the way as addressed in the earlier chapters of this section. Other times there may be individuals in their inner circle that leaders trust and opinions of secondhand information carries enough weight to believe one side of the story rather than fact check based on evidence. So, what happens to the staff member that is wrongfully blamed? Leaders who choose to believe only one side of a story without verifying information create a breeding ground for negativity among the staff. One of the fastest ways to kill culture is not allowing all sides of the story to be heard or not listening through the lens of prevailing the truth. If staff are to deliver their personal best, the us versus them culture cannot exist. There are always two sides to a story. Effective leaders insist on hearing both sides, of all involved, and listen to what's being said free of judgment, past mistakes, or secondhand information.

Imagine a teacher occasionally coming in late according to the contracted start time but, in the nick of time, is there to greet the students at the door. After a few times of this pattern, another staff member got irritated enough to approach their administrator to let them know about the inconsistent arrival times. As a result, the administrator asked the teacher to stop by the office for a visit after school. Without inquiring as to 'why' this teacher had been arriving at the same time as the students, the administrator merely asked if she had been coming in late. This teacher had no reason to be untruthful and replied yes, (as it was true) but was never given the opportunity to present her side of the story. A letter was placed in the personal file for violation of the teacher contract.

The problem here is not the fact that the staff member was occasionally late but that she was not able to explain her side of the story. This may have been an opportunity to extend grace and support the teacher because of a personal problem happening in her personal life. Even if she was an inconsistent teacher that required a letter in the file, not offering to hear her side of the story doesn't create a culture of trust. Situations like this are common in schools. Teachers are brought in to see the principal for various acts of 'misconduct.' Soon enough other leaders are brought in to judge the character of the employee. What happens now is that the employee in question feels attacked without justification, backstabbed, or tattled on. In any case, it isn't healthy.

Leaders possess the experience, knowledge, and power to listen to both sides of a story. Making rash, irrational decisions based on unverified facts creates a wedge that separates any bond between leaders and staff. The result is that the people being led will no longer give their personal best and will move to an under the radar status quo type of employee.

Effective and fair leaders will take the time to listen to both sides of the story to further understand the situation and lead through the lens of compassion and empathy when needed. Leaders of sound judgment make decisions objectively based on facts and not hearsay, opinions, or exaggerations. Dynamic leaders believe those that they lead are irreplaceable and value each perspective because everyone plays an integral part of the thriving school culture.

The Paradox of Leadership
If you are familiar with logic scenarios, then you have probably heard of "the grandfather's paradox" scenario. In this scenario, the goal is to try to understand if "the grandson" can time travel into the past to kill his grandfather. If this were to be true, the grandson would not have been born, ultimately, erasing his own history. This is a simple example of a logical inconsistency that is rather easy to understand and comprehend.

Now use this same type of logic to analyze "the leadership paradox" scenario where a 'leader' may manage the staff but is unable to manage himself. In some way, this scenario is a contradiction. Examine how "the leadership paradox" embeds itself into education. Think for a moment about what leadership is, and what it entails. Leadership is not just about saying the right thing, but it is about doing the right thing by modeling desired actions and behaviors. Leaders are pillars within the community, the school system, and engage a wide variety of stakeholders to follow their lead. What happens when a leader expects one thing but does another? What happens when the administrator expects teachers to listen to all stakeholders and all sides of a story before deciding, and yet the administrator doesn't offer the same courtesy?

Here is where "the leadership paradox" is important. At the heart of "the leadership paradox," there is a conflicting message of "do as I say not as I do," which is a contradiction and logical inconsistency to leadership itself. Just as "the grandson" would not exist if he went back in time and killed his grandfather, "the leader" will not continue to exist unless they listen, offer an open mind, and elicit an unbiased point of view from all points of view. Teachers and staff can sniff out inconsistencies, contradictions, and weak leadership from a mile away. It seems to make much more sense for leaders to stop listening to one side of the story and take the time to lead by example.

Leaders Need to be Authentic
Authentic leaders have a natural disposition and desire to hear both sides of a story no matter who the person is telling the story or what the content is about. It's in their DNA to understand perspective, timing, situational environment, and behavioral responses. Authentic leaders make decisions based on two sides of a story and by looking into the situation organically with the school mission, vision, values, and beliefs in mind. When one side of the story differs from the other, a decision cannot be made without asking the right questions to all those involved in their 'investigative' truth seeking. A non-

authentic leader disregards staff by not knowing, understanding, or being willing to seek out the root cause or truth. Authenticity is an exemplary character trait of culture builders and great leaders.

In the article, "5 Tips to Become an Authentic Leader" from the Kellogg School of Management at Northwestern University, Brenda Ellington Booth and Brooke Vuckovic share this advice.

1. Know yourself. Be aware of your unique character, values, strengths, and shortcomings. Decades of research on leadership shows that there is no one right way to lead. Instead, what distinguishes leaders is their ability to understand the impact they have on other people. "Many leaders are characteristically outgoing," Booth says. "They thrive in social settings and give bold, inspirational speeches. However, more introverted types can be great leaders, too."

2. Learn to connect. Whether you are speaking to a packed auditorium or chatting with a single employee, it is important to make a sincere connection that matches the needs of the situation. In other words, your actions should align with your words, and your words with your emotional affect.

3. Be discreet. The point of being authentic is that it frees you up to be others focused. So, you should always ask yourself before personal disclosure: Is this relevant to the task at hand? Does this contribute to this individual understanding my values and decision here?" Disclosing too much information—especially if it is highly personal—can have a negative impact on a leader's reputation and can call into question their capacity to self-monitor.

4. Play to your strengths. Every leader has strengths and weaknesses. Some are good at boosting morale; others are good at ensuring productivity. Some are natural-born mentors; others prefer to keep more distance. It is important to know your limitations and figure out how to compensate for them—possibly by making sure other leaders can assist in playing those roles.

5. Keep requesting feedback. Authentic leaders' welcome feedback, both formal and informal. Be cautious against worrying too much about popularity. People may not like what you do even if you are authentic. But if you focus on what is right for the organization, make ethical choices, and treat employees with dignity in the process, then chances are you will earn the respect of the vast majority.

Leaders are supposed to be the ones we look up to, the ones we learn from, and the ones who inspire us to be better. When a leader (or leaders) takes the time to authentically listen free from judgment and through a community-building perspective, trust is built and school culture flourishes.

Kristen Koppers, NBCT, is a blogger, presenter, self-published author, high school educator, and adjunct professor at her local junior college. She has been teaching for twenty years and is currently teaching high school English in Illinois.

Stop Offering Unsolicited Advice
PAUL O'NEILL

After about sixty seconds, I knew I had said way too much. Perhaps, I should have just listened and said nothing at all? As classes were being dismissed, a teacher asked if we could meet for a few minutes. At the end of this September day, a veteran teacher eased into a chair while releasing the kind of sigh that sometimes accompanies the busy opening week of school. As this teacher began speaking, she identified concerns regarding student comprehension with the content she was attempting to teach. After all, tenth grade math can sometimes be confusing. As the teacher outlined concern after concern, I began thinking of solutions to each of the situations she described. With each point shared, I creatively devised solutions in my head and eagerly awaited my moment to share these revelations. After a few moments, there was a break in the conversation. I began to enthusiastically share my solutions until I was met with an extended index finger and an apology.

The teacher said, "I'm sorry to interrupt you but I'm not looking for solutions. All I wanted to do was vent." You could probably imagine the look of embarrassment on my face. A few thoughts immediately rushed to my mind.

1. I owe this person an apology.
2. Instead of asking questions, I just assumed.
3. I offered the worst kind of advice...unsolicited advice.
4. Why did I feel so compelled to offer solutions?
5. Will this person ever choose to confide in me again?

After apologizing, we had a great conversation. Instead of assuming that this teacher was looking for solutions or my unsolicited advice, I asked questions which ended up leading to deep moments of reflection. Our exchanges yielded more wonder, and observation as opposed to advice. Our statements started to begin with "I notice that." Our inquiries started to begin with "I wonder if."

As the conversation ended, the teacher looked at me and said, "I'm glad we spent this time together. It really gave us a chance to get to know each other better." I smiled and couldn't agree more. On this day, I learned a valuable lesson. Leadership speaks volumes even when no words are spoken.

*"Listening to learn isn't about giving advice–at least not until asked—
but about trying to understand exactly what someone means,
how it is that someone looks at and feels about her particular situation."* - Elizabeth Debold

Paul O'Neill is an educational game changer from New Jersey who uses the power of belief to create a competitive advantage for those who he proudly serves.

25

Stop Wearing Rose-Colored Glasses
SILAS KNOWLES & JASEY KOLARIK, Ed.D.

We have all encountered the idea of "rose-colored glasses" at least once in our educational careers. Looking at the world through "rose-colored glasses" helps someone see a situation with more optimism and positivity. Typically, as educators, we approach student ability with the encouragement and optimism of our rose-colored glasses. This positivity is an essential aspect of a leadership mindset as well. However, there is a fine line between positivity and reality. Unfortunately, many administrators, blinded by rose-colored glasses, have lost touch with reality.

The two of us writing bring different perspectives to this issue. One of us is a classroom teacher and the other is a department head. While reading this chapter, try and see if you can identify the "voice" in each situation. Is it the department head? Or the educator? With which viewpoint do you identify?

Overestimating Relationships

Building positive relationships with students is an important aspect of developing a classroom environment. However, placing all your eggs in the "relationship basket" does not solve everything. Sometimes administrators are blinded by their belief in relationship building. A great example of an administrator hanging their hat on relationship building happened during a meeting where teachers were preparing to start a new school year. The question was asked, "What are the discipline procedures?" Other teachers nodded that they, too, wondered about them. The administrator's body language was that of confusion as he asked for more clarification. Finally, the teacher clarified, "What if there is a fight? What do we do?" The administrator responded sharply, "That won't happen here. You just need to build relationships." As the meeting continued, building relationships became the go-to answer to nearly every question about everything: tardies, grades, and computer usage.

While it's true that relationships create a better educational culture, they are not the answer to all issues, nor does it set the standard for high expectations and school policy. This reliance on relationships as an answer is a rosy picture that can create more problems than it solves. As the school year got underway, it did not take long for students to figure out that there wasn't a tardy policy and that there wasn't a discipline procedure for a wide variety of actions just shy of physically fighting.

On one occasion, two students did something so unthinkable that I still can't wrap my head around it. The two filled a backpack with something unspeakable and took it on a bus with the intent of dumping it on another student. Luckily, when the students stood up to commit this heinous act, the bus hit a bump and the contents of the bag hit the floor instead of the targeted student. The next morning, the teachers were called together and given a lecture on how they needed to work to build better relationships with their students. What? Did that administrator really think that relationships would have prevented the two boys from getting mad at the third member of their group for having a girlfriend, a story we learned that day when the students openly shared thoughts about the event?

Relationships also couldn't fix an issue where a student became combative when asked to return to his seat for the millionth time - a challenge many of us faced with this student. He called the teacher a string of names, and she asked him to leave. Claiming he didn't want to be there anyway, the student left. Several minutes later, the student returned and proclaimed that the principal was going to have a talk with the teacher. Administrators must wear transition lenses that move from rose-colored to clear so that they can see what is really happening in situations. No amount of relationship-building will control teenage hormones. No amount of relationship-building will overcome classroom management undermining. No amount of relationship-building will fix all issues, especially when the students know the loopholes in policy to target.

Stop Being so Full of Yourself
In my educational practice, I continually preach transparency. It's not always comfortable to put yourself out there but being honest and vulnerable helps any teacher or leader grow in their

professional practice. For administrators, being honest and transparent about situations builds staff confidence in their leader. One of the schools I had the pleasure of working in used an "academy" model. Students were allowed to focus on business, medicine, or the arts. While the organization of the school was different, the issues were like any other model.

Student motivation was a challenge as many of us face at some time in some way in our careers. A brilliant idea by a previous assistant principal was to reward the students designated as "on track" while scaring straight the students who were not. The "on track" students celebrated their status with an ice cream social. To attend, these students wore green-colored bracelets to go down to the fieldhouse for ice cream, a DJ, and fun group games for the final period of the day.

The "off track" students were given pink-colored bracelets and instructed to stay in the auditorium where they would watch Dropout Nation, a film that focused on the real-life experiences of dropouts. This is where the plan fell apart. Students were offended, the behavior went completely sideways, and students were calling parents demanding to be allowed to go home.

The ice cream social was a hit. The film screening was a disaster. And it didn't end when the final bell rang. The following day, I overheard a discussion about a parent email concerning the outcome of the event. While I cannot relay the entire email due to inappropriate language and accusations, the references to Hitler and the Star of David should give you the gist. Rose-colored glasses in full glory, the assistant principal relayed his thoughts that were quite contrary to the email. "The day went well. I think the movie frustrated the 'off-track' students. We can build on this." Are you kidding me? Did we attend the same events? What kind of Kool-Aid was served with that ice cream? It was obvious that optimism, positivity, and reality were not all in the same place because of the rose-colored glasses.

Administrators, wearing transition lenses will allow you to see through to the truth, and truth helps us grow. Suppose the assistant principal was honest with himself and accepted that he made some bad decisions with regards to the activity and logistics. That the separation of groups was punitive and not a growth mindset. He could have been an excellent model for growth if students had additional opportunities to set goals, connect with their future self, or be inspired with a comeback story of hope. School leaders need to step back and be honest with the reality of things occurring in front of them.

Everything's Coming Up Roses
During a conversation with a colleague in another district, she shared that the teachers around her

were really feeling disenfranchised from teaching. She explained that a teacher in her department was looking to enroll in a corporate training program. Another department member revealed that he was thinking about retiring early. My colleague was even more concerned after a conversation with a new teacher whose response to how the year was going was that the experience would look good on applications. Her frustration came to a head in a conversation with an administrator about her perception of the general negativity toward the district. She was told that people were being too sensitive and that they would need to get over it. "She never even asked what was going on. When will they see that there is a problem?" she asked. In the end, she said that one of the tenured teachers moved to the corporate world, one retired, and several untenured teachers left the district, and that was just in her department.

Leaders, when teachers are courageous enough to discuss the inner rumblings with you, pay attention. Dismissive attitudes may unwittingly confirm perceptions. Morale is not always as high as we would like it to be, but allowing teachers to feel heard, respected, and supportive goes a long way just as Allyson Apsey shared in Chapter1. Building relationships before adversity strikes is key.

Stopping the Spin
There is an interesting term called "spin." Wearing rose-colored glasses "spins" a negative aspect of something into a more positive one. Administrators need to be careful on this ride. While it may make them feel better about themselves, their actions, and their districts, it may be making the other riders dizzy with frustration. It is a good practice to offer the benefit of the doubt, to extend grace, and to look on the bright side, but this isn't the context we are referencing with rose colored glasses. The key to "spinning" is knowing when to be optimistic and when to be truthful. Wanting the best outcomes plus focusing on reality can lead to positive change. By removing the rose-colored glasses and stopping the "spin" during problem-solving through adversity helps school leaders to see the pitfalls that must be bridged to bring positive and long-term solutions.

Silas Knowles serves as a Pirate EL History teacher in Chicago, Illinois. Looking to create that next great experience for all students, Silas is a Master Teacher in his state.

Dr. Jasey Kolarik serves as a Division Chair for Social Science and World Language at a school in northeastern Illinois.

STOP Interacting Harshly or Irrationally

This Type of Nonsense Prevents a Strong Sense of Belonging

26

Stop Talking Crap about Others
LISA TOEBBEN

"You must use your power, your voice, for good at all costs, or it will be the termination of community and relationships in your life." -Lori Harder, A Tribe Called Bliss

Words spoken are so powerful. Spoken words are the most powerful tool that we can use within an organization. Why do we, and why would we ever think about using our most powerful tool to do more harm than good? I think all of us can admit that we have "talked crap" about a colleague at some point in our careers. We are all human. I, included. However, I do know the horrible internal feeling that consumes me after I have "talked crap" even within a toxic environment that has normalized this bad behavior. It doesn't feel good on the giving end or receiving end regardless of the level of acceptance.

I agree with the various authors throughout this book that reinforce that teacher ARE leaders. This book is about leaders and if you are a teacher, you are a leader of students, colleagues, families, and community. If you hold any role in any organization, you are a leader. You lead students, you lead other teachers, parents and families look up to you. Every day they send you their best and your community relies on you to create a high-quality learning environment where students academically achieve. If you are a "crap talker", it's time to stop this misbehavior and replace your frustration with a restorative approach, courageous conversations, and processes to maintain high expectations with accountability. Moving teams forward even through crises, adversity, dissonance, or disagreement requires mental and emotional discipline. "Crap talking" only breeds toxicity, which feeds hostility. No matter your leadership role, everyone you lead wants to experience a sense of belonging because of your leadership.

The Early Onset of "Crap Talking"
Back in my early, judgmental days, I was a "crap talker" because I lacked self-confidence. I thought everyone should do things how I would do them because that was the only way to do them and would "talk crap" if they didn't adhere to my standards. It was in those years that I was focused more on what

others were doing than what I should be doing. The early stages of my "crap talking" started because I was comparing myself to others and as a defense mechanism of wanting everything to appear perfect., it was easier to deflect my inexperience. At one point my "crap talking" carried over from a social media post by a colleague that triggered my implicit bias just as D. Nilmini Ratwatte-Henstridge shared in Chapter 22. Social media is a huge catalyst for "crap talking" because many people over inflate themselves or to the other extreme even lack confidence in their God given strengths and abilities. This trash-talk creates a toxic relationship which can spread like a contagion causing toxic teams and toxic schools which unfortunately can lead to hostility. It doesn't matter how positive the person is, or how effective they are as a leader, when acute toxicity is absorbed, it will produce a negative physical and mental outcome. This is a lose-lose situation because it removes all sense of belonging and purpose from staff and students. Award winning schools cannot co-exist with toxicity. Organizations cannot function at high levels unless there is a high level of trust, professionalism, and teaming.

Recognizing Toxic Behaviors
At the time I was unaware of how toxic this behavior was and the damage it was doing to my organization and myself. If you are in this phase of life, there is hope if you are ready to create habits and self-discipline that utilize words to unify and build one another up.

Have you ever walked into a room or meeting to notice the conversation is about what someone should have done, isn't doing, or what someone else (usually the human talking) could do better than the person who is the topic of conversation? I know I have walked into these situations. Maybe it's the colleague lunch bunch or an after-hours social committee gathering, the morning coffee crew, and the convo is all about what someone wore, something new someone tried in their classroom, or what they posted on social media. For administrators it could be in the hallway before a school board meeting, a closed-door conversation in the human resources office, or at a table during a statewide training session. Recognizing these toxic behaviors in any position that you hold is imperative to building a team that fosters a sense of belonging.

Toxic conversations have nothing to do with building anyone up, its purpose is to tear someone down in pursuit of some personal vilification or justification. When toxic behaviors become the norm, nothing thrives, time is wasted, and we fail students. When trust is broken within your team organization, confident teachers will break down after a while due to the mental damage "crap talking" causes. When teachers second guess their abilities due to "crap talking", the students are the ones impacted academically. When your most passionate teachers become quiet, it's time to look within the organization/team to find out why.

We Really Don't Have Enough Time in a Day to "Crap Talk"

If you go to work at the district office or report to a school and have time to "talk crap", then you have enough time to create new habits that build self-confidence, uplift others, infuse positivity, encourage families and community, or gain more knowledge. Confident leaders don't "talk crap" instead they do these things:

1. Dust off your mission, vision, values, beliefs, & goals. Anchor to the mission, vision, values, belief statements, and goals. Anything that isn't aligned with these isn't worth their time.

2. Be strategic about positivity. Start the day with a positive quote, phrase, or goal that sets the tone of focus for their time at work. Calendar compliments, written words of encouragement, and celebrations. Of course, compliments and a positive word is welcome anytime and anyway, but if you schedule routine times throughout the month, it will ensure that positivity is infused consistently throughout your organization and among the people that you lead.

3. Infuse gratitude. Maintains a list of gratitude and when they experience vibes of toxicity, they pull out their list to anchor back to what matters. Times of toxicity are one of the most important times to add to the gratitude list. It is enough to redirect negative thoughts.

4. Use diplomacy. When they hear "crap talking", they diplomatically address it (keeping tone of voice and body language in check) rather than just ignoring it. They use phrases like, "I'm not sure we should be talking about the person, I bet they would appreciate it if you talked to them about it. I'm not comfortable participating in a conversation about another person if they aren't here to clarify. I'd prefer to keep things professional and assume positive intent, so I'd rather not continue with this conversation if we aren't building one another up. I think the person deserves to hear this conversation rather than me. We are a team and are here for students, I'd feel more comfortable if we maintain professionalism."

5. Vent appropriately. Like Dr. Holly Blair discussed in Chapter 7, they have confidants and mentors to connect with when "crap talking" or toxicity needs addressing, or they just need to vent.

6. Decompress. Decompress after work with mindfulness, journaling, exercise, hobbies, or any other activity that releases negative energy.

Magnetic and joyful leaders breathe life into their co-workers, so their organization feels a sense of belonging. If you are a leader and know this is happening among those that you lead, help your staff and teams recognize the damage "crap talking" causes. If you are a leader and are a trash talker, it's time to get real with your own personal truth to begin living your purpose. If you are the subject of "crap talking" and/or have tried to lead by example during a trash talk session, I know, it can get lonely or cause major anxiety. Find the people that build you up, plug into them, and give these seven strategies a try. Do the inner work necessary to build confidence within yourself so you can elevate and celebrate others. I'm proud of you, keep elevating.

Lisa Toebben is a Special Education Coach that firmly believes that the foundation of success is built by instilling high vibe healthy habits into a lifestyle. She brings the high vibe mindset into her coaching daily. She has been featured on Dave Burgess Consulting Facebook Live, Teach Me Teacher Podcast, Humans of Education Podcast, and has been published in School and Community, a Missouri State Teachers Association publication. Her Elevate Your Vibe Action Planner, published by Road to Awesome LLC, is available on Amazon and at lisatoebben.com

Stop Publicly Humiliating Staff

KRIS FELICELLO, Ed.D.

"Once you squeeze toothpaste out, you can't put it back into the tube. The same is true with our words. Once we say something hurtful, we can't take it back." -LeBron James

"It is so nice to see how much you have grown as a leader since you first came to the district." The colleague who recently said that to me meant it as a compliment, but I couldn't help but wonder what flaws this well-respected educator saw in me when I first came to our district some 15 years ago. I guess it is human nature to over analyze criticism. It doesn't matter how many good reviews, positive remarks, A+'s we receive, that one unfavorable comment is the one we remember and dissect. To be truthful I was thinking, "What do you mean? Wasn't I always good?"

The conversation forced me to reflect on my time as a middle school principal in the district where I currently serve as the superintendent. My thoughts brought me back to my last day as a principal, and I cringed, not an uncommon reaction when I reflect on mistakes I made in the past. It was a bittersweet day; I knew I was leaving a special place and special people, but I was excited for what the future would bring. The staff organized a celebration where we shared stories, laughs, and tears. I remember feeling so proud as staff told anecdotes and complimented my leadership, but my favorite part of the evening was the presents! Who doesn't love presents? And as an only child my love for gifts may be a bit disproportional.

Beware of the Stare
My favorite parting gift that day was a custom-made T-shirt, red to match our school colors with a large eye pictured on the front of the shirt with the phrase "Beware of the Stare" proudly written below. This was in recognition of my apparently notoriously long stares directed at any staff member who had the gall to speak out of turn or lose focus during a faculty meeting. At the time I was proud of the shirt and what it stood for. Despite being younger than most of the staff, I was respected. On a regular basis staff arrived on time. During meetings, the staff didn't talk, look at their phones, or do anything other than show me respect. I thought I had earned their respect because they knew I would embarrass anyone who dared step out of line.

Looking back at this time in my career helped me to realize that I wasn't as great of a leader as I thought. It also hit me that 15 years from now I will most likely be embarrassed by the leadership mistakes I am making now. It helped me to understand that oftentimes the less we know the louder, angrier, and more authoritative we become.

Build Them Up to Bring Out Their Best
When I began my career in education as a physical education teacher, I was hired right out of college at 21 years old to coach the Varsity Boys Basketball team. Early in my coaching career I knew so little that I felt the need to say too much. I screamed and yelled, stomped up and down the sidelines, yelled at referees, players, or whoever would listen. I was so agitated one night during my first year that I kicked the bench, broke my foot in the process, and had to ice my foot (and ego) for a month. When I finally figured out what it took to lead a team I rarely yelled, instead I looked to build up my players and pick spots with the referees. No one wants to miss an easy shot or turn the ball over. Obviously, a better approach since I doubt anyone wants to listen to a whiny 21-year-old.

I am at the point in my career as a leader that I know those same principles apply to school administration as well. Humiliating a staff member by giving a nasty look, tapping your watch as they arrive late, or calling them out publicly for professional mistakes does not solve anything. It only creates animosity and anger. The job of a principal is to place staff members in a position to be successful, to build them up, and not to knock them down. This is not the same as being soft or having low expectations, it is a different approach, one in which you try to bring out the best in teachers so they can be their best and add value to the school. I have found the following strategies to be not only more humane but also extremely more effective:

1. Set Clear Expectations. Be clear as to what your expectations are. Communicate the non-negotiables you have established for staff members. Be sure to post those expectations, repeat those expectations, and check to make sure they are heard. In today's world we are bombarded with information, it is easy to miss something. When someone is not meeting your expectations, you have the obligation to initiate a courageous conversation to remind them but do it privately and do it with empathy. Most certainly, effective leaders do not yell or embarrass others. But rather, express why it is important to the organization, how they can make it right, and how they can avoid the mistake in the future. Shannon Moore expanded on clear and high expectations in Chapter 14 and why this is vital to a healthy and thriving culture.

2. Let it Go. I noticed that when someone made a mistake or did not meet my expectations, I had a hard time letting it go. In fact, I sometimes expected them to mess up again. This flawed mindset or unconscious bias I possessed, I am confident, resulted in many staff members meeting those failed expectations I unconsciously set for them. I found it highly beneficial when I am intentional about "letting it go" once I have addressed the situation. It does no good to harbor past grievances.

3. Separate the Person from the Performance. We all have colleagues in our lives that we care deeply about that are not good at their job. Sometimes it is because they are inexperienced, lack intuition, or are simply unknowledgeable. Even though I may encounter unskilled co-workers and staff, I still see it as my job to "see" them as people before faculty or staff. Let's face it, there are ineffective and unskilled educators who may be wonderful people and successful outside the school setting. This is one of those elephants in the room that we all face as leaders but rarely talk about. Should being an ineffective employee make us love them less as a person? Should their lack of job performance prohibit us from spending time with them or sharing laughs or positive encounters?

Just because a staff member we lead may be disappointing us professionally does not make them a bad person. Be kind. Be compassionate. Growing people requires positive connections of humanity like remembering birthdays, learning about families, and discovering the interests of the people in your school regardless of their talent as a teacher. This doesn't mean that we lower expectations or that poor teaching is ok. It just means we still need to remember we are humans before administrators as many of the authors have already addressed. When you compartmentalize who your faculty member is as a person, and keep it separate from their performance as an employee you are better able to show care for the people you lead. And when they know you care about them as a person, they will want to improve their performance as an employee and will work hard not to disappoint you.

4. Uncover Special Talents and Passions. Have you uncovered the talents and passions of all those working in your school? Do you know individually what each staff member is passionate about or good at? One of the easiest ways to start digging and mining for talents is to pose the following question(s),

100 No-Nonsense Things That ALL School Leaders Should STOP Doing

"What do you like doing right now that makes you light up and consumes most of your time thinking? What are you most passionate about?" Try this out on family members and friends just to get a feel for this process. I think what you will find is that many will jump right in and talk non-stop about a hobby, talent, concept, new learning, family, recent event, or pastime that they are good at. Other times you may experience dead silence in the airwaves as some will need to ponder and get back to you. Whether you get an immediate response, or they come back and share with you weeks later, what you will discover are uniquely special talents and passions uncovered. Uncovering individual talents and passions translate into overall added value, or as the analytic folks might say, plus sum value.

Once you uncover individual talents and passions many will often become a happier teacher, staff member, or employee. This culture building mindset cultivates joy at work. I have witnessed this approach successfully transform people and entire faculty culture in every way. As a leader it is rewarding to watch the multiplying effect of a more positive faculty that is happier, treats others kinder, and has more pride in their profession. When culture shifts from focusing on faults, to focusing on strengths, skills and assets become the epicenter of focus. Success leads to more success and a desire to keep getting better. This is a goal, I'm confident we can and should all strive to achieve.

Earn Respect

I echo Dr. Dan Kreiness in Chapter 13 where he shares that we can't expect respect just because we are leaders. I know I must do my best to serve those I lead by seeking out ways to make their job easier rather than harder. I know now…

- Earning respect requires being a servant leader.
- Strong leaders never humiliate staff, instead they look for ways to put everyone in a position to be successful and to shine in their unique talents and passions.
- That growing as a leader and as a person is the greatest compliment you can receive.
- Effective leaders support, assist, and lead with a servant's approach.
- Culture building leaders lead with heart, without the desire to prove they are in charge.
- Award-winning leaders are all about the team.
- Intentional leaders create a strong sense of belonging by building on individual strengths.

Dr. Kris Felicello has been in the field of education for over 25 years as a Teacher, Coach, Athletic Director, Assistant Principal, Principal, Assistant Superintendent of Human Resources, Assistant Superintendent of Educational Services, and he is currently the Superintendent in the North Rockland Central School District in Rockland County, New York. Kris co-founded "The Teacher and Admin" education blog with his colleague and friend Gary Armida. They also co-authored the bestselling book "The Teacher and The Admin: Making Schools Better for Kids" released in October of 2019. Although Dr. Felicello is passionate about his career and improving our education system, his first priority is his family. He enjoys traveling and spending time with his wife Rebecca and 3 sons Justin (20), Andrew (18), and Scott (17).

Stop Comparing Staff Members to Each Other
BREANNA BURKE

Imagine you walk into a meeting to review your performance evaluation. As you enter the room and sit down, you hear, "Hi Mrs. Burke, your learning targets were acceptable, but not as good as Mr. Smith's down the hall. I noticed that you had great student interaction during small group work time. Miss Young in third grade does some superb protocols for small group interactions that go above and beyond the expectations. Your lesson assessment was one of the best that I've seen. We should have Ms. White look at it to use in her classroom." While the comparisons in this example are extremely overt and seem quite redundant, they are not as far off from reality as one would believe.

This chapter isn't about how to interpret an evaluation rubric or that there should be different professional teaching standards for different cohorts or styles of teachers. Nor is this chapter about lowering the expectations on a teaching and learning rubric for teaching performance. But rather this chapter is about sharing the drawbacks of allowing the harsh and irrational malpractice of comparing staff. Building a thriving culture requires capitalizing on strengths through a sense of belonging, not unhealthy and divisive comparisons.

If you were to walk into any school across the country (or the world, for that matter) you would notice the striking differences between teachers employed in the same building, grade, or subject area. There's the vivacious teacher with colorful posters, music playing, and a theatrical performance of a lesson. There's the strict teacher, with students following each routine and procedure with almost military-like precision. There's the laid-back teacher, with students strewn about the classroom, perhaps laying on the floor or sitting on a counter with flexible seating. At first glance, you may wonder, "Which teacher is more effective"? It's human nature to begin to compare (and contrast) lesson styles, classroom aesthetic, and student interactions, among others. Creating a sense of belonging in a world of comparisons requires an intentional leader that brings out the best in each staff member free from harsh or irrational comparisons.

What Exactly Are We Comparing?

When we walk through a school, looking at staff members, what is it that we are so inclined to compare? Their teaching style(s)? Student engagement? Student behavior(s)? Test score(s)? Overall productivity? A district-wide walkthrough protocol of expectations? Without an answer to that question, it is remiss to even attempt to make any sort of comparison between what we are seeing in classrooms. We often hear that you can't compare apples to oranges, yet so often we compare first year staff members to their veteran colleagues, general education teachers to special education teachers, classroom teachers to special area teachers. When working with students, we often encourage them to "celebrate their differences" and "find what makes them unique". We do this in such a positive manner and create initiatives surrounding this thought. Further, we often tell our students, "Don't compare yourself with anyone else" or "focus on yourself and your own growth". It's almost hypocritical that we preach these ideals to our students but seem to forget their existence when we consider teachers and school staff members. Each classroom has its own unique students, teachers, support staff, curriculum, and relationships among a plethora of other factors that contribute to the functioning of that classroom. Likewise, each work area has its own set of challenges and inter-workings. What we must truly ask ourselves here is, "Do we want strict uniformity in our schools?"

Impacts on Teachers

When we walk through a school, looking at staff members, what is it that we are so inclined to compare? Their teaching style(s)? Student engagement? Student behavior(s)? Test score(s)? Overall productivity? A district-wide walkthrough protocol of expectations? Without an answer to that question, it is remiss to even attempt to make any sort of comparison between what we are seeing in classrooms. We often hear that you can't compare apples to oranges, yet so often we compare first year staff members to their veteran colleagues, general education teachers to special education teachers, classroom teachers to special area teachers. When working with students, we often encourage them to "celebrate their differences" and "find what makes them unique". We do this in such a positive manner and create initiatives surrounding this thought. Further, we often tell our students, "Don't compare yourself with anyone else" or "focus on yourself and your own growth". It's almost hypocritical that we preach these ideals to our students but seem to forget their existence when we consider teachers and school staff members.

Each classroom has its own unique students, teachers, support staff, curriculum, and relationships among a plethora of other factors that contribute to the functioning of that classroom. Likewise, each work area has its own set of challenges and inter-workings. What we must truly ask ourselves here is, "Do we want strict uniformity in our schools?"

Mentoring & Instructional Coaching

There is high added value for all teachers to be observed through a non-evaluative coaching lens. Many times, new teachers are assigned a grade-level mentor on their campus, or even a district appointed mentor to support the entry level years of teaching. When efficacious leaders observe and use their anecdotal notes to cognitive coach or make recommendations, this can become one of the schools' greatest assets. There is a time and a place to offer a menu of teachers who are strong in specific areas to observe and connect with for growth. In some schools' teachers have bought into the #ObserveMe movement where they post their area of strength outside their door and welcome any teacher to stop by to observe it in action. This open door on-the-spot professional development is a healthy example of sharing expertise to support others as a team. Comparisons can be purposeful and creating an agency for productive growth in teaching and learning, moves schools forward academically.

Purposeful Comparison

Comparing teaching practices, content delivery, classroom styles, classroom management, and assessment techniques is generally an avenue through which we can determine which ideas are best suited for our students, staff, and school. It isn't necessarily about using a right or wrong strategy, but rather choosing the most effective teaching strategies and tools to meet the specific needs of that cohort of students that year. Comparing teachers within a school or district should serve a clear purpose and have a clear and concise motivation pre-determined and articulated to all parties involved. The key in this practice is to communicate the goal of any observation or interaction, and how you will foster growth afterwards. Just as mentors and instructional coaches spend time debriefing, so too should #ObserveMe experiences, any teacher-to-teacher observation, and leader visit. Instructional coaches and mentors make it a good practice to consider one aspect at a time. That is to compare routine to routine, activity to activity, quality to quality, rather than personalizing the correlation by comparing teacher to teacher or staff member to staff member. Instructional leaders clearly define healthy comparisons which utilize professional standards and make a comparison between performance and the outlined set of expectations helps to provide a purpose in the realm of comparisons and promotes goal-setting and professional growth.

Another way to examine purposeful comparisons is through the lens of pairing strengths with needs.

We have every type of student and families arrive on our doorstep each with varying needs, lifestyles, and learning types. Embracing the talents and individuality of teachers helps administrators leverage pairing student needs with teacher strengths. Some students require a stricter environment for behavioral consistency while other students thrive in a flexible seating self-driven environment. Comparisons can be healthy and create a sense of belonging as a school community when viewed as a menu of strengths to create a healthy culture.

A Menu of Strengths

Phil Jackson once said, "The strength of the team is each individual member. The strength of each member is the team." A school leader is truly a "coach" of their school team. As a coach, working with each individual staff member can only benefit the functioning of the team. Before any purposeful comparisons can be made, a school leader must first establish solid working relationships with their staff members and create clear, consistent, and concise communication. In this role, compiling a list or menu of strengths is one way which serves to ensure comparisons are coming from a place of intentional school-wide growth and not one that pits them against their colleagues. When leaders are intentional about a culture of comparison, it creates a sense of team and collaboration between school leaders and staff members.

Breanna Burke is a primary grades special education teacher for students with severe/multiple disabilities in Kenmore, New York. She holds a Master's degrees in both Students with Disabilities and Literacy Education and is currently pursuing a third Master's degree in Educational Leadership. She resides in Niagara Falls, NY and is the proud mother of two young boys, Dominic, and Alexander.

29

Stop Judging Staff
SANDRA DONAGHUE

"It is very important to carefully observe the things we see before we judge. Things aren't always as they appear." --Ellen J. Barrier

Don't "water the rocks". Leave them behind as they sit firmly in place unable to sprout life. Rocks are like "set in their ways" staff, they are unable to grow because of their density, lack of energy, heavy weight, and immovable form. Don't waste your time on "the rocks" because it would require a tsunami to get them to budge. We have all heard these types of statements from time managers, bosses, and anyone in a leadership position rushing to get their job done. Statements like these being made about staff, sends a message that we, as leaders, cannot make any gains or immobilize our resistant "set in their way" school community members forward.

Have you stopped to think about what these types of statements are based on? Do they hold any merit? Just as D. Nilmini Ratwatte-Henstridge shared in Chapter 22, external judgments and biases are often in place as we enter new school communities or when others join our schools or organizations as outsiders. We must ask ourselves, what would happen if we didn't judge our staff or carry over biases? What would happen if instead we listen, observe, seek to understand, support, and mentor for the purpose of growing each member into their personal best? We must wrestle with these questions to ensure that emotions do not encroach upon sound leadership. When we are in the business of building trusting relationships everyone has a purpose and deserves to learn free from judgment.

Cultivate a Landscape of Learning

As leaders, we must recognize strengths and promote healthy growth. Growing a highly functional and vibrant staff that bears award-winning fruit begins by knowing your students, faculty, and families. What does building relationships have to do with judging others you might ask? The answer: EVERYTHING! The people you lead cannot give their personal best when "the weeds" of judgment choke out their ability to grow and thrive. What possibilities would bloom "if" we stopped judging our staff? Ask yourself, "As a teacher would you have been willing to let a struggling reader simply give up and never learn to read?" Of course not. Giving up on a student is simply not an option to educators and giving up on staff shouldn't be acceptable either. Let's examine a powerful and positive example of an effective inclusive leader that launched the school year free from judgment.

A first-year principal arrived at a school and two statements were shared by past and present leaders. The first statement was, "Little to no professional development had been offered in prior years. Secondly, the staff was uninterested and disengaged". These statements are very concerning to any leader and certainly could have been a very troubling scenario for any first-year principal to walk into. The principal was inquisitive and possessed the mindset to survey the landscape first before deciding how to move forward with cultivation. To do this, the new administrator sent out information in an email about upcoming workshops and professional development opportunities, inviting the entire staff. The teachers simply needed to reply to the email to be considered as part of the professional development team (there was a limited number of spots available). Surprisingly, numerous requests from staff were submitted. Many more teachers had replied wanting to attend the offered training(s) than could be sent. Instead of selecting a few and sending out an email with a list of names, all staff were invited to attend an initial informational meeting. The purpose was to get to know the staff, provide an overview of the training(s), and share the commitment and expectations that came with becoming part of the team. Even though everyone that attended the informational meeting could not formally attend the training, all staff were considered in this initial process. This judgment-free approach offered value and appreciation to the staff because it cultivated transparency and inclusion. Later that day a staff member that was chosen to become part of the professional development team, sent a follow up email sharing with the principal, "In eight years as a teacher, I have never been given the opportunity to attend professional development as part of a team. I am excited and grateful that you provided a process that was not only fair but also transparent".

This teacher wasn't a sedimentary "rock" holding down the soil in a garden but rather an uncultivated seed in need of sunlight. So why had prior leaders claimed that this staff member was unchangeable and not worth watering? In prior years judgment had been cast upon the faculty by the perceptions of managers, bosses, and/or colleagues that had rushed through their job duties rather than cultivating people. Casting judgment was easier than cultivating seeds.

Recognize that Perseverance is Required for Growth
Although the faculty appeared to be apathetic about learning and growing in previous year(s), the truth was that the school culture lacked a fair and transparent process for attending professional development. In the past, the same people had been given professional learning opportunities year after year. The rest of the teachers simply gave up and felt that they had no voice or choice in the learning culture of the school. Many were judged previously as being apathetic and immovable when really their previous boss was exclusive, played favorites, or was too rushed to be intentional.

Casting judgment and ignoring signs of disgruntled and disengaged staff members does not cultivate a staff culture of high achievement. As the landscaper of your school or organization you possess the power to, ask, invite, encourage, share, and repeat, always. Do not assume that staff do not want to learn, change, grow or participate until you ask, and ask again. Many of those you lead have never been invited to participate in a leadership or visionary team. Some staff may never have participated in a true professional development learning community cycle because they were run like team meetings in prior years. Some administrators, directors, specialists, or instructional coaches have not prioritized job-embedded professional learning or clearly articulated a strategic process for continuous learning and personalized growth. As the chief gardening officer, take the time to learn the strengths and added value of everyone in your community garden and nurture their growth.

Shaping the landscape of award-winning gardens requires leaders to create individualized learning that is free from judgment and built upon strengths, voice, relationships, transparency, and trust. Leaders must get their hands dirty turning the soil, providing nutrients, scheduling watering cycles, persevering through drought and hardships, and celebrating the various functions and strengths that each add to the overall beauty of the school community landscape.

Coach a "How Might We" Mindset
To harvest a plentiful crop or to win a blue-ribbon award for beautification, it requires a leader that has an overall vision. Visionaries recognize individual strengths that already exist as a foundation. As instructional leaders of a state, district, school, or team this means attending professional development sessions alongside staff and colleagues as a model of a risk-taking that demonstrates vulnerability as a co-learner.

At times school faculty exhibit symptoms of fear, especially of being judged for having a counternarrative, different experience, lack of knowledge, or disagreement on strategy, content, or approach to teaching. A risk-taking leader also models persevering through situations or goals that may seem impossible to accomplish or too daunting to attempt. Staff may be afraid to speak up for fear that they will be judged by their colleagues or leader. This is where a, "How might we…" approach diminishes or eliminates fear, judgment, or divisiveness.

This simple phrase can entice innovative thinking, possibility, and yes sometimes stopping a bad habit that may already be in play. A visionary knows there will be disagreements, fear of judgment, and embarrassment of inexperience. Therefore, heading off these feelings before they develop is even more important. The people that you lead will relax their shoulders a bit and be even more receptive to future learning when they know that you understand that these thoughts and feelings are normal, and that together, you will find solutions.

> "I'm embarrassed to admit that I didn't know that."
>> **How might we** work together to learn and incorporate it?
>
> "I prefer a different approach in teaching that standard."
>> **How might we** work together to ensure that each student demonstrates mastery of the standard?
>
> "What you are asking us to accomplish is impossible because we already tried that approach, and it didn't work."
>> **How might we** work together to identify the reasons why it didn't work so that we might be successful at meeting this goal?

Many responses and questions like this can be heard in staff meetings and professional development sessions on any given week in schools. Sometimes there are naysayers for the sake of negative encroaching emotions. This "**How might we…**" A cognitive coaching approach works on them too.

"The kids are too far behind to do grade level math."

How might we work together and involve families, mentors, and community volunteers to support their individual progress in math?

How might we provide support of conceptual understanding to accommodate, modify, or scaffold the information?

"There is not enough time in a day to add more intervention time unless you want me to quit teaching social studies or science."

How might we integrate multi-disciplinary content to teach grammar and vocabulary in the context of authentic reading?

"The cafeteria is too loud, understaffed, and there just isn't enough time for students to eat."
How might we work together to uncover where the breakdown is in the process so we can streamline the process and ensure equity of time?

This cognitive coaching approach is inclusive, solution focused, values every individual, and maintains high expectations. How might you alter the perspective of those that you lead to become invested risk-takers that believe in their high added value?

Understand that Good Hearts, Sometimes, May Choose Poor Methods
Visionaries model risk-taking behavior in their daily interactions to create a landscape of trust for all stakeholders. To do this we must be honest, open, and vulnerable with our learning communities so that we bring out their personal best. Visionaries intentionally communicate and celebrate a "How might we…" culture. Recognition and celebration cultivate a landscape of high standards and expectations for all. Notice and name individual and team contributions, successes, and special talents. Celebrate failure and growth. Recognize their attempts, their mistakes, and their growth, no matter the result. If we honor only the final product, some may fear judgment.

Honor the process and praise the attempt to move, learn and grow. Promote and celebrate self-learning and self-growth within a school wide learning network while watering and providing a little extra sunlight to those that may have had a rocky start. Share a love of learning with students, staff, and community. Have compassion and empathy and extend grace when teachers fail. And most importantly, know your staff and create a positive and professional working relationship.

The secret to creating a blue-ribbon award-winning landscape is promoting personal continuous learning for ALL. When leaders invite all staff to invest time into learning new strategies, provide time to implement them, allow for failure and learning through resiliency, the landscape becomes even more beautiful. Everything we do must be intentional and purposeful.

It's easy to judge. It's more difficult to understand.
Understanding requires compassion, patience, and a willingness
to believe that good hearts sometimes choose poor methods.
Through judging we separate. Through understanding, we grow.
-Doe Zantamata

To sit back and judge is very easy to do, to elevate, celebrate and cultivate learning will certainly be far more rewarding and lead to a thriving learning environment. Let's make a commitment to support others more and STOP judging. It will be so worth it!

Sandra Donaghue is an elementary school principal, OCT, principal qualification course instructor, and X-Factor author. She is currently serving as President of her provincial Association. Sandra is a passionate lifelong learner with a high energy level, zest for learning, risk taking & putting students first!! As a leader with over 15 years' experience, she remains highly engaged & energetic about servant leadership, mentoring and coaching and developing aspiring leaders.

Stop Dreaming of Staff You Want & Support the Staff You Have
JONATHON WENNSTROM

My apologies to Jim Collins, but I have never cared for the term, "Get the right people on the bus". That implies that some people aren't qualified to be on the bus, aren't dedicated enough to be on the bus, or simply aren't welcome on the bus. If a teacher said to me, "I just need to get the right students in my classroom", there would be some pretty serious conversations that followed. Why then, would I say as an administrator, "I just need to get the right teachers in my school."? It's never been about getting the right people on the bus; it's about getting all the people on the bus wanting to go in the same direction.

If a teacher lacks knowledge in an area, it's my job to help train them up and provide a mentor to support and guide them. If a teacher doesn't seem dedicated to the task, it's my obligation to inspire them and help them find their purpose and perhaps reignite their love of teaching and learning again. If a teacher doesn't feel welcome in our school, then I have some serious work to do with establishing a culture that is welcoming and inclusive to all.

A Dangerous Myth

In my 26 years in education, I have had the privilege of working in several districts and in several buildings. The idea of handpicking a team of teachers that were selected, trained, and are completely in sync with one other is a myth...a dangerous myth. It perpetuates the idea that to get a winning team, they must all be individually selected with the appropriate skill sets and attitudes. That's not how schools (or the real world) operate. The reality is that team members and administrators change and so do our students. There are many variables in the schoolhouse that can shift the dynamics of a team at any given moment. An effective leader will recognize this and stop dreaming about the staff they want and support the staff they do have. This chapter focuses on four simple ways we can support our staff members.

1. Know Your Team. The best way to know your staff members is to listen to their stories. One of the first things effective leaders do upon coming to a new school is ask people what they are most proud of both personally and professionally. This gives me an insight into who they are and what they value. Ask follow-up questions inquiring about hopes and dreams for the school year. The most common responses I have received are, "I hope to feel supported, and I dream about every one of my students becoming successful." One teacher responded to me that she hoped to, "Fall back in love with teaching." That particular response has always stuck with me because it shows vulnerability, risk-taking, and an authentic longing to be passionate about teaching. Being an effective teacher is one thing but falling in love with teaching is taking a job and taking it to a whole new level of purpose. That's exactly what I want for my team!

2. Provide a Vision. Once you've gotten to know your team, they need to know what you believe and where you want them to go as a group. Consider sharing belief statements with the group. Follow up by sharing things that they can always count on you for and things that you will count on them for. The "Count on Me/Count on You" framework was shared with me by my mentors Debbie McFalone and Derek Wheaton. They include items like "assume best intentions" and "come up with solutions to problems as a team". Take some time to develop and co-create belief statements and "Count on Me/Count on You" items. This is in the same thread as a social contract where you are making promises to each other of how you can count on one another and how you will treat one another. Teachers have co-created statements like, "You can count on me to listen free of judgment" or "You can count on me to show respect". Post this in your professional development or team meeting area. When adversity strikes, this framework of promises becomes an anchor for healthy conversations because we are committed to a unified vision through co-created beliefs. At the beginning of every school year, revisit, invite feedback, revise as necessary, and make new commitments to one another. Our core beliefs may stay the same, but our vision should expand as we grow and learn.

3. Give Them What They Need. Just like our students, each team member has their own schema, talents, knowledge, strengths, and areas of need. The experiences they bring along with the skills they have acquired will dictate how a leader serves everyone on the staff. Some may be new to their role and need guidance. Some may be skilled in curriculum, but not great at developing relationships. Others may be veteran teachers who feel burned out and need to be inspired. Education is not a one size fits all profession for students or for staff. Good leaders know what their team members need and provide them with the tools they need to be successful.

4. Model the Way. As leaders, we need to model what we wish our team members to do. It's not enough to express to them what you want, we must live out what we profess to be important. If we want teachers to start fresh each day with students when they have shown challenging behaviors, then we need to show grace and forgiveness with them too. If we want staff to be risk-takers, we need to be out in front and leading from a place of courage and vulnerability. If we want our team to be collaborative, we need to include all stakeholders in the decision-making process. Staff will follow our example more than our instructions.

Going back to the bus analogy, it's not about getting the right people on the bus. We will be on many buses throughout our careers and meet lots of riders with many different personalities and different experiences. A true leader will make sure that no matter the bus they are on, that all the riders have a clear understanding of where the bus is going and how each member on the bus can contribute to the joy, passion, and success of each mile marker as they inch closer and closer to their destination. In the world of education, our destination should be student achievement through success. The climate of the bus should reflect diversity, equity, and inclusion for all. If you want to bring out the best in everyone trusted within your leadership, then support the staff that has been entrusted to you.

Jonathon Wennstrom is a former teacher and coach and currently serves as an elementary principal. Jonathan recently completed serving his term as President of the Michigan Elementary & Middle School Principals Association. Jonathan is a state and national presenter on Educational Leadership.

31

Stop Interrupting Others
CHAD DUMAS, Ed.D.

"To listen well is as powerful a means to influence as to talk well, and is as essential to all true conversations." -Chinese proverb

Twenty-five percent of people say that their pet is a better listener than their spouse (Faunalytics, 2012). Think about that: One in four people say that their dog or cat (or crayfish) listens better to them than their husband or wife. Why? Surely one-fourth of Americans don't have pets that speak back to them, do they? Of course not. The pet sits quietly. It listens. It doesn't interrupt.

Listening Enables Influence
Why is listening important? Humans are social. There's a lot of talk these days about the importance of mental health. One in five students experience a mental health problem during their school years (National Association of School Psychologists, 2021), and at any given time one in five adults are experiencing mental illness in this country (National Alliance on Mental Health, 2021).

As stated in the film, Apollo 13, "Houston, we have a problem." The average hourly cost of therapy is $90 (Shappell, 2020b). Having personally participated in therapy sessions, and while knowing there is incredible skill in being a quality therapist, my experience was that the therapist mostly listened. And listened well. In some ways, Americans are paying billions of dollars per year to have someone listen to them (Open Minds, 2020). Beyond the gift of helping each other with our mental health (Birla, 2019), listening to others without interrupting, enables influence. "(W)hat that is said loudest is not necessarily most important. What is said the most is not necessarily the most valuable? True influence comes when we listen, not when we speak" (Shappell, 2020a).

Given the importance of listening, what steps might you take to become a better listener and stop interrupting others? Before exploring some practical aspects of impactful listening, it's important to note that good listening is as much a byproduct of who you are as what you do. To demonstrate this, ask yourself the following questions: To what extent do you genuinely care for and about the other person? In what ways are you authentically curious about what they have to say? Just as Jonathon Wennstrom shared in the previous chapter on supporting the staff that you have, developing the skill of listening because you want to, not because it's a job requirement, is the key to influence. Learn to listen better. Clear your mind, focus on the other person, and try out a few of these tips:

Pause with a Breath. As miraculous as the human brain is, the thinking part isn't terribly fast--it's the slowest part of the brain, furthest from the heart and lungs (think blood and oxygen). So, give yourself (and others) time to think. Take a breath.

A breath does two things: 1) It creates a space for thinking to occur, and 2) It gets oxygen into the blood, enabling intentional thinking to happen as a result. When you feel the temptation to interrupt, take a breath. A slow deep inhale works particularly well.

Take a Breath. A breath does two things: 1) It creates a space for thinking to occur, and 2) It gets oxygen into the blood, enabling intentional thinking to happen as a result. When you feel the temptation to interrupt, take a breath. A slow deep breath works particularly well.

Interrupt Patterns. When we interrupt, we tend to interrupt with three types of patterns: 1) Autobiographical, 2) Inquisitive/curiosity, and 3) Solution (Garmston & Wellman, 2016). Unfortunately, none of these are helpful nor influential. Self-aware and intentional leaders' "set-aside" these interrupting patterns. Let's analyze them further.

> **1. Autobiographical interruptions** are when we jump in with "Me, too!" type responses. Or even worse, we try to "one-up" the other person by sharing how much worse (or better) our situation is than theirs. No doubt you've experienced this and can agree that it's not helpful. Set it aside and take a breath.
>
> **2. Inquisitive or curiosity interruptions** are when we ask detailed questions that aren't helpful. I'm reminded of a time when a friend was telling a story about a trip, and a listener kept asking questions about the length of the trip, the type of accommodations, the quality of food, etc. None of these details had anything to do with the point of the story, and simply served to knock the speaker out-of-sync and frustrate both parties. Set aside your inquiries and take a breath.
>
> **3. Solution interruptions** happen when we jump in with answers without fully understanding the entire picture. As administrators we tend to be good at that, and we think that this is what people want (because we have largely trained others into this habit). There are two problems with solution listening: 1) It likely won't solve the problem, and 2) It just gives them an excuse to blame you when things go wrong. Set aside solutions and take a breath.

"Leading is about influence. Nothing else." -John Maxwell

Try a paraphrase. Paraphrasing does two things: 1) It helps the other person feel understood, and 2) It ensures that you understand. Of course, we have all "been paraphrased," and in a manner that was not helpful. Don't manipulate the other person by paraphrasing a version of what you want to hear. Don't paraphrase so long that they forget what they were saying. Don't start with "I hear you saying…" Just paraphrase.

For example: "So a priority for you is…," or "So you're thinking about three different issues…," or "So you're frustrated that…" And then pause and listen again. If they confirm, carry on. If not, listen, pause, and paraphrase again.

Ask a good question: After a good pause, a quality paraphrase, and a confirmation that you've "got it," questions can work wonders.

As you consider the questions that you ask, remember to avoid yes/no questions. Additionally, use tentative language, plural forms, and avoid the "why…you" stem. Regarding tentative language, terms like "might" or "could" or "potentially" open thinking and create space for dialogue. Coupled with plural forms, this frees the brain to think of possibilities and not be confined to one "right" answer. Finally, the word "why" can cause defensiveness, and coupling with "you" will set yourself up for a blame game. Here are some examples of questions that meet these tips: "What might [tentative language] be some of the things [plural form] you were thinking about when…?" "What could [tentative language] be some of the ways [plural form] you see/feel/think that this connects to…?"

If all else fails, remain silent: Silence is a good first step in stopping our habit of interrupting others. A good breath will do wonders, as will the ability to set aside certain unproductive behaviors. Combine this with the practices of paraphrasing and posing questions, and we can surely become better listeners– even better than our pets!

"Leadership is not about being in charge.
Leadership is about taking care of those in your charge."-Simon Sinek

Dr. Chad Dumas is a Solution Tree associate and international educational consultant, presenter, and award-winning researcher whose primary focus is collaborating to develop capacity for continuous improvement. With over two decades of successful leadership experience, Chad has led significant improvements for both students and staff. He shares his research and knowledge in his books, Let's Put the C in PLC, and An Action Guide to Put the C in PLC, and consulting that includes research, stories, hands-on tools, useful knowledge, and practical skills. For more information, or to reach Chad, visit www.NextLearningSolutions.com.

Stop "Stealing" Conflict
DOMINIQUE SMITH, Ed.D.

The beauty of education is that every day is a new day, and every year is a new year just as Jonathon Wennstrom shared in Chapter 30. Each year we see a new group of students arrive in our schools with different needs, unique personalities, and various behavioral strengths and deficits. As educators, we reflect on what we did the previous year, which allows us to continue the practices we carried out successfully and refine the areas where we can improve.

As I reflect on my own leadership journey, there are moments that have helped redefine my "why" and allowed me to clarify who I wanted to become as a leader. Most of those moments were related to discipline situations. I realized that I did not agree with the manner and process in which discipline was being handled in schools. Now, as this is a short chapter, I won't dive into the inequities around discipline and my discomfort from dichotomous, or black and white, discipline approaches. Rather I'd like to share the succinct idea that stealing conflict from teachers removes trust, accountability, and power from teachers. Conflict minimizing approaches, for in the name of avoidance and convenience, creates a damaging ripple effect that diminishes a healthy culture within schools.

A Package Deal
As leaders, we are primarily responsible for the well-being of the adults entrusted within our care. First and foremost, we must equip the adults to nourish the well-being of students interwoven in a strong partnership of academic success. We continuously use strategies and incorporate new initiatives to support academic learning, social emotional development, and mental health of all students. We do this so that when we go home at night, we can feel at ease knowing we created a safe risk-taking learning environment that is thriving in deep connected thinking that produces high academic achievement. To accomplish this our focus must be on knowing and meeting the needs of the staff that "we do have" just as Jonathon Wennstrom shared. We are charged to lead our teachers, students, families, and the local school community as an interconnected system. It's a package deal. Yes, we make student-centered decisions based on data and observations, but we must first consider the needs of the adults

on the front lines who teach, care, and know our students best. Unfortunately, punitive discipline approaches are used to address minor infractions all too often. We leaders spring into action anytime teachers ask for help, and that must change. We think we are providing a service. But are we, or are we causing harm from our well-intended actions? Let's examine the following scenarios and their outcomes to better discern how we might respond differently in the future.

Classroom Management Scenario

Jesse is a well-meaning, full of energy, "trying to find himself" 7th grader. He tends to be very much engaged in the classroom and loves to participate. While Jesse loves to participate, he also struggles when students disagree with his responses. Recently the class was having a conversation about a current event in the news. As Jesse shared his thoughts on the current events another student shouted out, "Well I don't agree with you, and I think you are way off on what the teacher is trying to talk about." This didn't sit well with Jesse and in that moment his impulses told him to confront that situation. Jesse yelled back at his peer and chose to say some inappropriate things. At that moment, the teacher felt uncomfortable addressing this as a teachable, coachable moment, and instead sent Jesse outside to cool down as she called for support from administration.

What typically happens in similar types of situations? Administrators come to the classroom, take the student to their office, and discuss what happened to determine the consequences. This is common practice, right? We see this time and time again. Let's look more deeply at what was really happening and what was likely to happen next:

1. The student doesn't have emotional regulation skills when being confronted.

2. The teacher is worried about classroom management skills and removes the student so there isn't a bigger situation.

3. The student is now outside of learning and probably not reflecting about what they have done wrong. In fact, Jesse is likely becoming more upset with the teacher and the peer with whom they had the altercation.

4. The administrator is now going to "steal the conflict."

5. The teacher lost the opportunity to build community-wide relationships, teach emotional regulation, or maintain their social contract with Jesse and his peers and lost a perfect opportunity to reset expectations.

6. The administrators establish new expectations that might not be aligned with the teachers' expectations.

7. The cycle has been established and will occur again and again with more intensity and frequency in the future.

Emotional Outburst Scenario

Malik was a 10th grader enrolling in a new high school. He didn't have many friends and was not only missing his old school, but also struggling with new content. While in his English class, he was called on to share out what he circled as his favorite phrase in the text. He didn't respond, his teacher quickly snapped in agitation, "I'm not moving on until I hear your voice." Malik responded in a voice of outrage, "You wanna hear my voice? Well then fine, I don't care, I hate you, this class and this f'ing school." Malik was immediately written up, dismissed emotionally, and in haste sent to the office. After arriving in the office, he met with the vice principal who listened to his side of the story. The leader realized that this student was missing his old friends, struggling with school, and just had an outburst after being emotionally prodded by the teacher. The VP had compassion and dismissed the behavior with Malik because he empathized and encouraged him to have a better day and sent him back to his class. What just happened?

1. The student left the classroom angry at the teacher.

2. The administrator took the time to listen to his story and empathized with the student.

3. The administrator focused on returning the student back to the learning environment.

4. The student returned to class still angry with his teacher.

5. The teacher felt that administration is not supportive of outbursts in class.

In the scenarios above, the students didn't live up to expectations of the classroom and were removed from the classroom and had similar outcomes: administrators stealing conflict. Leaders, we must own the fact that we do this all too often, even if unintentionally. We see a teacher in need, and we rush to save the day. We take over the situation, remove the students, and then solve the problem. These situations of conflict are compounded with more conflict which fail to equip teachers and empower students with a problem-solving process. Each time we steal the conflict from our teachers we are sending multiple messages. We are sending a message that:

- Teachers can't handle the situation.

- Teachers don't have power.

- Teachers don't have time for you.

- Teacher voice doesn't matter.

Lead as a Liaison

As a leader, when you meet with a student, do you already have a clear idea of the teacher's expectations and the process established for resolution? Hopefully you do, but you may not. If you don't already know the classroom social contract, norms, rules, or behavioral expectations then you probably don't have any business mitigating them. Take this opportunity to learn the expectations of each classroom and return the conflict to teachers.

This can be as simple as requiring teachers to post their social contract, rules or norms are in every room or space of the building as a multi-tiered system of support. It may involve visiting each classroom at the beginning of the year and inviting students to share the expectations with you and allowing for you to ask follow-up questions. Reinforce that you are the liaison between teachers, students, and families and that you will always expect them to attempt a resolution first. Assure the students that you are there as a guide to healthy dialogue, self-advocacy, and liaison of leadership.

Teachers deserve to experience the process of resolving the conflict because of your liaison leadership approach. This allows teachers to model self-regulation, boundary setting, and high expectations. Teachers deserve an allotment of time to communicate how the students' choice(s) broke the promises of the social contract or class rules to impact teaching and learning. Teachers deserve the opportunity to take part in reestablishing restorative practices and to recalibrate emotions for student success. Conflict resolution must offer teachers and students a voice in the encounter that builds relationships, addresses the root cause, and is restorative in nature. Consider how this might look. A minor infraction has just occurred in a teacher's classroom. A teacher texts, calls or emails for support. An administrator shows up to the room for support and asks the teacher "Would you like me to address the conflict, or would you like to take it?" As the teacher says, "I would like to take the conflict." The leader then goes inside to support the learning in the class and uses it as an opportunity to build relationships and act as a liaison. The teacher steps outside with the students and shares:

"I don't want you to leave the learning today. I want you here. You didn't abide by our social contract/rules/norms which is why we are talking. Unfortunately, you chose to ____ which broke the promise that we all made to each other at the beginning of the year. I'd like to see you successful in class today and I can tell something is bothering you? How can I help you resolve this situation so that you can be successful in class today? What can WE do to finish our day strong?"

Certainly, you would want this to be an authentic and organic conversation and not a script, but you get the essence of the type of conversation that maintains expectations and care. Can you imagine the culture shift your school would experience if every teacher had the luxury to work through a conflict? Empowering teachers to engage in conflict resolution while also giving students a voice builds trust across the board. When administrators stop stealing conflict and instead facilitate as a liaison, student and teacher relationships remain mutually respectful, trusted, and may even be a turning point for academic growth. In this case, the leader supported both stakeholders and allowed amicable resolution for the issue that arose. So, I beg you, stop stealing conflict!!

Dr. Dominique Smith is a principal at Health Sciences High and Middle College in San Diego, CA. Dr. Smith's research and focus is around restorative practices, school equity, SEL and leadership. Dr. Smith continues to work across the world to help schools make transformations that benefit all students. He has published multiple books with Corwin and ASCD.

Stop Blaming Staff for Poor Student Achievement
TRISTA S. LINDEN-WARREN, Ed.D.

Playing the blame game will never lead to student success. Those that are on autopilot for placing blame are not investigating the origin of the problem. Nor are they analyzing the root cause for gaps in learning or low academic growth. As leaders we must stop pointing fingers solely at current year teachers for deficiencies in student achievement or overall poor performance. Instead, all stakeholders must make a joint-effort to own the responsibility and seek strength-based approaches for meeting the student where they are to ensure growth. To move from autopilot to a synchronous multi-plane airshow, we must welcome teamwork, collaboration, purpose, precision, confidence, and meaning to the pre-flight practice routine to master them in a live performance. Leaders, teachers, families, and community members are all vital contributing members that collectively assume ownership and advocate for student achievement and individual goals. The challenge is aligning everyone to head in the same direction as a team.

The Sum of the Entire Team

A high school student is a product of every staff member in every grade level experience leading up to the one that you are teaching. Teacher efficacy in teaching matters, but this doesn't mean that teachers own the quarterly benchmark scores and summative assessment results, solely. Student achievement is the sum of every member on the team. The reliance upon family, community, and friends is vital for encouragement, support in promoting self-trust, self-regulation, and self-motivation. Students are capable of learning to become the pilot of their own learning by relying on the guidance, direction, support, and mentoring of their instructor, co-pilot(s), and crew.

> *"If you are not willing to learn, no one can help you.*
> *If you are determined to learn, no one can stop you."*
> *Zig Ziglar*

Those students who have a desire to fly will learn at any cost (with or without the guidance of all stakeholders), while those who do not have a desire will always find excuses to remain grounded. Blame is one of those excuses. If school communities are working together in synchronicity, one student may lag on a tilted course while another may require additional practice or time. As co-pilots, and a learning crew of stakeholders, it is our job to retrain and offer practice sessions in tandem until students are prepared to perform effortlessly. When we stop blaming instructors, solely for student learning deficits, the possibility of high academic student achievement takes flight.

Students Require Meaningful Purpose

Whether in kindergarten or a senior in high school, students are the pilots in the learning process because they are the active participants. Taking responsibility and accountability are key components students must learn. For this to happen, students must be given the opportunity to participate in tasks that mean something to them. This work must have a meaningful purpose. If students are solving an authentic problem that impacts their lives, they will connect and learn. Rather than telling students that they have a test over the debate process, let them debate on topics of their choice. Before the debate, offer time to debrief the purpose and elements, providing an opportunity to voice their opinions about the process as it relates to the debate simulation, before sitting down to take the test.

Generation Alpha is far different from any profile of student than ever before. Students today desire meaningful purpose before they can demonstrate knowledge mastery on a standardized assessment. In elementary school, students participate in hands-on learning. They are engaged. Elementary students need to learn to read, write, and do arithmetic to live in the world. They have a purpose for what they are learning.

By the time students reach adolescence, educators must begin to help students discover their passions and direct them to those pathways. When students reach high school, they want to apply their knowledge. Let them follow the path of their passions, continuing to explore through internships and problem-based learning that lets them experience the failure that comes with ideation and the design cycle. Student-centered learning must come to the forefront if we are to create a strong sense of belonging.

Instructors Teach Failure and Resiliency
In the world of education, teachers are required to facilitate learning through the teaching of standards but the key to high academic achievement is to authentically teach what matters to the students. Education with 100% teacher-centered learning is a bygone. The focus should be on the students, allowing them to have input as to the subject matter. Student to student as well as teacher to student should be occurring regularly through activities that involve critical thinking, effective questioning, and well-planned lessons that offer depth of learning. Oftentimes, the teacher must provide necessary scaffolding and the teaching of skills in the learning. Teachers serve as coaches, mentors, and instructors who intentionally provide challenges to their students so they are prepared to respond to failures and future obstacles that they will face when they take flight. Effective flight instructors require teamwork, communication, and resiliency while providing support through scenarios. Teachers must help students identify their talents, strengths, deficits, purpose, and plan of resiliency for learning.

Communities Provide Opportunities
In the world of education, opportunities must be explored and taken. However, the opportunities must also be presented and shared with the student learners. Education is what you make of it, but if you are not aware of the multiple opportunities available, then you cannot take advantage of them. Therefore, community resources/opportunities must be shared with students, school districts, and

families. Opportunities available for students, should partner with the schools and get involved. Local businesses, chambers of commerce, financial institutions, non-profits, volunteer organizations, etc. have so much authentic learning that can be provided to students. These opportunities and partnerships will guide authentic work and collaborative design of problem-based learning in the classroom. Choice and personalization of the learning process will then develop, and the ownership of learning will occur.

Families Partner in Success
Family members serve as the first teachers of their children during the early years. As children progress academically, teachers, as experts in content knowledge and pedagogy, progressively assume most of the content teaching as instructors. Even though there is a gradual release from the nurture and human development that shifts from families to teachers, the responsibility of learning and growth development does not end when their child starts going to school. A healthy partnership between home and school offers the greatest potential for success that a child can receive.

In the world of education, families will benefit most when there is intentional and well-informed communication that provides opportunities for families and students to engage meaningfully. Families know their child best. High impact educators empower their families and engage their local community members that removes barriers of blame and instead focuses on success through partnerships. This does not mean that there is a new expectation for parents to co-teach content learning at home. Families as partners are provided opportunities to engage and have a voice in the educational process and are invited to communicate with the educators. This is a team effort that requires a genuine focus and dedication on each pilot's aeronautical precision and stability.

Some families may need to learn to trust their flight instructor's ability to facilitate the skills necessary to demonstrate proficiency in learning. Teachers are highly trained and skilled instructors trained to effectively teach to the depth of content standards as it applies to the real world. Creating relationships through family engagement is an essential component to creating a positive learning environment for all students. The more that families are on the flight line encouraging and supporting, the better the students will perform when they take flight. And when they do, everyone will be proud of the community teamwork.

Collaboration and communication are key components in creating a strong sense of belonging for all stakeholders. It is harsh and irrational to solely blame staff for the success and achievement of students.

We must all take responsibility in educating our future leaders. Merriam-Webster defines blame as to find fault with or to hold responsible. Aren't we all responsible for the achievement of students? Yes, cliché, but it truly does take a village to stop blaming the staff for poor student achievement. Whether all stakeholders accept this partnership challenge and investment, we must as leaders continue to make this our goal and do everything within our power to engage all stakeholders. When we teach students to own their own learning, we allow them to learn from failure, find purpose in authentic learning, and follow their passions. If we fill in for stakeholder gaps, we remove blame and instead create teams of students that thrive and academically achieve.

Dr. Trista S. Linden-Warren is a 26+ year public educator who supports innovation in education. She opened and was the founding Superintendent of a STEM designated public high school in 2015 and continues with forward thinking education as the Executive Director of LEAF, a non-profit that assists students and families in making pathway connections beyond high school.

Stop Evaluating Staff with a "Gotcha" Mindset
HEATHER L. KEAL

Do you remember when you were a teacher in the classroom? Do you remember being evaluated by your principal? Do you remember the emotions that accompanied the scheduled observations or the steps you had to do in order to prepare? Why is it that some of us forget these details when we become administrators?

The fact is, there is absolutely no reason for us to make teachers sweat their evaluations. We do not need to enter into it with a "gotcha" mindset or a checklist of things they're doing wrong. Evaluation should be viewed as an opportunity for teachers to reflect on their practices and get better at their craft. It's a chance for them to sit with another education professional and discuss strengths, areas they can grow in, and goals they have for themselves. Our job is to focus on their development as educators and center the conservations around growth. The components of an effective evaluation are rather simplistic.

Communicate Clearly. When scheduling your evaluations, don't let communication act as a barrier between you and the teachers. Be clear with the procedure in scheduling the pre-conference, observation, and post-conference. Share the evaluation tool/rubric with the teachers and give them the opportunity to ask questions. Be transparent with your expectations and don't leave educators wondering what they need to do to prepare for their evaluation.

Demonstrate Reliability. Once you have your pre-conference, observation, and post-conference scheduled, do everything possible to stick to the dates/times you agreed upon. This will demonstrate to any educator in the evaluation process that you care about their instruction and value their time. They have worked hard to collect their work samples and write the lesson plans. They have endured many late nights focused on meeting the evaluation expectations. If for some reason a meeting/observation needs to be rescheduled, offer the teachers choices of dates/times. There is nothing more crushing to an educator than to have planned effectively and to live the anticipation of being evaluated, only to have to plan in that level of detail again. If there is an unavoidable circumstance, offering the teacher choice shows them that you respect their time and effort, and want to provide them with the best scenario possible to succeed.

Be Authentic in Your Conversation. When meeting with educators, keep the conversation real. Ask them to share their strengths and successes as well as their focused area(s) of growth. When going over samples, scripts, or evidence, encourage them to elaborate on what they've brought to the table. Most educators are proud of their work and are more than excited to share their growth and passions in detail. Take time to ask about their professional short-term and long-term goals. Uncover what they would like to pursue as a next step in their career. Even during a post-conference, keep it conversational while providing clear feedback and posing reflective questions.

Trust Them. Trust that the teachers are doing their job to the best of their ability. If you see/hear something that seems "off" during a lesson, ask questions before jumping to conclusions. Rely on your many observations and interactions you've had with the teacher in the past. If these have been positive, then it's safe to give them the benefit of the doubt while waiting to hear the answers. Remember, if your boss walked into your school, you would want him/her to do the same for you. Trust is essential in creating a strong sense of belonging.

Be Fair. An evaluation is not usually based solely on one lesson. There are many things to consider- walkthroughs, observations, professional learning, collaboration with colleagues, communication with families. Be fair and examine all of these when determining a teacher's rating. Also, everyone can have a lesson flop. Remember that it's how the teacher reflects and learns from a botched lesson that shows their growth mindset. If adjustments are made for next time and the lesson goes smoother, then it's fair to say that the teacher is showing growth.

Ultimately, just like with so many other aspects of life, relationships play a role in evaluations. How you speak to the teachers, the feedback you provide, and your genuine interest in them and their success, all matter. Are you an administrator that offers support and wants to see your staff succeed? Or do you walk into their classrooms with a "gotcha" mindset?

Listen carefully. If you want to see your staff accomplish great things, then your own attitude needs to be positive and focused on growth. Do not make evaluations scary or confusing, and remember, having a "gotcha" mindset doesn't benefit anyone.

Heather L. Keal is a wife, mom, and proud principal of Mayfield Elementary in Middletown, Ohio. She is passionate about urban education, equity-centered leadership, and championing for the students that we serve each day.

35

Stop Intimidating or Using Secondhand Information as a Weapon
REBECCA CODA

"Experiencing the world through endless secondhand information isn't enough. If we want authenticity we have to initiate it." -Travis Rice

Every educational leader will inevitably encounter challenging situations of adversity. Whether you are in a role as a superintendent, district administrator, or school administrator you will be put to the test at some point in your career. Leaders may encounter an employee that is a direct report who is underperforming, undermining, unstable, or even blatantly gone rogue. How you respond to any of these scenarios will create seeds of culture that are planted within your organization. Your actions will determine if the people in your care can grow and be tested in how they will respond in future scenarios. If you embrace a "gotcha" mindset as Heather L. Keal shared in the previous chapter, it will come across as intimidating and lead to opposition and disengagement.

When leaders rely on tattling or believing secondhand information when making decisions, it will pit people within the organization against one another. Secondhand information should never be the fuel for making public or private decisions. A healthy organization with a strong sense of belonging requires clear and high expectations, inspection of those same expectations, and provides routine feedback and/or courageous conversations. Anything less from a leader becomes a perceived emotional weapon of intimidation and haphazard decision-making across the organization.

Stay Above the Line

Regulating emotions in a profession of tightly knit and personal relationships can be one of the toughest parts of educational leadership. This is what makes education so different from corporate America. Those in district leadership positions often landed their role because of a long history of trust, proven performance, and even garnered friendships. It's no wonder that navigating adversity becomes even more tedious when personal feelings are attached. While serving as a K-6 Director of Curriculum & Instruction in a small town where everybody knew everybody's personal business, it became clear that we needed to master navigating emotions so that we could make decisions objectively. This was necessary if we were to accomplish the district's mission, vision, and goals. One way we accomplished this was by proactively leading "above the line" leadership to create a common language when faced with adversity.

The Conscious Leadership Group (CLG) has a phenomenal video on YouTube entitled: Locating Yourself – A Key to Conscious Leadership. In the video, it describes how we are always above the line or below the line of emotional self-regulation and that as leaders, we must continuously reflect and respond based on our current emotional reality. Their website (conscious.is) offers free printable infographics that can be utilized in leadership meetings and enlarged into posters as reminders in our collaboration space(s) that we must always locate so that we respond wisely rather than harshly or irrationally. According to CLG, we are either above the line or below the line and within varying degrees of each.

ABOVE THE LINE ↑
open, curious, committed to learning, responsive, growing, accepting, trusting
OR
___
BELOW THE LINE ↓
committed to being right, defensive, closed, reactive, defensive, recycling drama, resistant, threatened

Depersonalization is a necessary practice if leaders are to effectively address, coach, or mentor situations of adversity. Consider several other chapters within this section that could be remedied by simply sharing this simple concept as a behavioral expectation of interactions WHEN there is conflict. Why wouldn't you want to be prepared when faced with the following nonsense outlined in this section of the book?

- Talking crap about others
- Publicly humiliating staff
- Interrupting others
- "Stealing" conflict
- Presiding with a "gotcha" mindset
- Always wanting to do things your way

Establish an "Intimidation Free" Zone

Establishing a culture with a strong sense of belonging requires consistent and predictable intentionality by you, the leader. Establishing norms or social contracts, revisiting goals, and referencing how educators are expected to interact are all practices that diffuse intimidation. Committing to large-scale and cyclical PD can assist with the way you do business, authentically. As Heather L Keal referenced, authenticity is a necessary ingredient when providing feedback, coaching, mentoring, or even facilitating a courageous conversation.

Dissolve the "Pressure Cooker"

Believing secondhand information is nothing more than being stuck in quicksand if you don't address it when it begins to convince others, unfortunately. Leaders rely on their trusted colleagues and those employees directly reporting to them to carry out their work with integrity that is aligned to the mission, vision, values, and goals of the district. There are appropriate times for closed door conversations of confidentiality that provide a "heads up" to prevent further adversity. There is a high level of emotional intelligence and leadership discretion needed to delineate between an authentic concern and a pressure cooker situation that if unaddressed could blow, leaving behind a hot mess. Consider the following pressure cooker situations:

Underperforming Director

A district director is not meeting deadlines and producing mediocre and status quo work. The superintendent only knows this because her next-door neighbor is friends with the director's direct report who had complained to her about the mounting frustration while loose lipped at lunch over the weekend. The superintendent's neighbor then shared the information with her while standing on the driveway after work one day.

> **Below the line response**: This secondhand information then prompted the superintendent to start asking around to see if anyone else was frustrated with the director. Then based on more

secondhand information begins leaving the director off the all-staff agenda as a silent punishment that takes the superintendent below the line.

> **Above the line response**: The superintendent schedules a meeting to meet with the district director to check in with them. She then assumes positive intent and shares the secondhand information and follows up with, "is there any truth to this?" or "is there more to the story?" "I'd like to follow up in two weeks just to check in and ensure that you have the support you need to proactively carry out your job."

Undermining Assistant Principal

An assistant principal disagrees with the new car line pick up and drop off procedures and is agreeing with parents at the car pickup line, fueling the fire of conflict. Although not overt or directly defiant, the assistant principal is publicly undermining the credibility of his principal. Later in the week a mom made an appointment to speak with the principal about the inefficiency of the car line and spouted out, "and even the assistant principal agrees with me."

> **Below the line response**: This secondhand information then prompted the principal to give the assistant principal inside duty during drop off and pick up rather than having a courageous conversation about staying above the line.

> **Above the line response**: The principal jotted down the exact words that the mother shared on a notecard along with the date and time. That night, the principal scheduled a time to meet privately with the assistant principal the next day. The principal assumed positive intent by sharing the details of the meeting including her exact words. When the assistant principal confessed that he did in fact agree with the parent, the principal went on to pose specific questions about the difficulties and confusion with the car line. After listening with curiosity and responsiveness, the principal shared that she valued his input and would like to work together with the mom to implement some changes to make the process smoother. She then went on to remind the assistant principal of the values and commitment they made to one another as staff to stay above the line as committed leaders of safety and learning. She created a learning opportunity free from harshness or irrational behavior and, instead, created a sense of belonging and high expectations of professionalism.

Unstable Curriculum Specialist: A high school STEM Specialist has become narcissistic and continuously posts selfies while airing personal and professional life on social media. Although the postings do not violate policy or the district's code of ethics, it is not aligned with the mission, vision, and values of the district. There is no distinct violation; yet it doesn't represent professionalism either.

Below the line response: The director of curriculum and instruction caught wind that her STEM Specialist was oversharing on social media. The director has her neighbor follow the STEM Specialist on TikTok, Instagram, Facebook, & Twitter and send screenshots of postings via texting. The director then texts the screen shots to her colleagues to share what is being posted and talks crap about her. This becomes an ongoing mini-series drama of text exchanges and exhibits below the line behavior throughout the year. Nothing is addressed and awkwardness and tension only create unspoken and unnecessary toxicity.

Above the line response: The curriculum director sets up a time to check in with the STEM Specialist first checking in to see how they are doing and the status of their current progress on projects. The director references their social contract or norms and shares that they had heard people in the community perceiving the social media posts as unprofessional and attention seeking. The director reminded the STEM Specialist that she would like to encourage her to consider that she is a representative of the district and that even personal posts can possibly jeopardize the standard for students, families, and community. The intent of the conversation was to look out after their best interest and to inform them of community perceptions.

Blatantly Going Rogue: A principal does not follow the curriculum guidelines and allows teachers to teach alternate content.

Below the line response: The assistant superintendent of curriculum finds out from complaints sent to the teacher's union that this is happening. The assistant superintendent informs the superintendent, and they devise a plan to request that all principals need to attend the teacher's union meeting that evening. Following the meeting, the superintendent scolds the principal group and has the assistant superintendent set up meetings at every school to meet with all staff on each campus in order to review all assigned curriculum and expectations for the state and district. During the meeting, leaders and staff are forewarned of the consequences if they are caught going rogue.

Above the line response: The assistant superintendent sets up a meeting with the principal. He shares the content and nature of the complaint submitted to the teacher's union regarding the curriculum being taught. He asks if there is any truth to it and to share any pertinent information. The principal goes on to share that his data does not show that the current scope and sequence in the curriculum is working and that his students are falling further and further behind in academic proficiency. He shared that he met with his lead team during PLC's and they offered a plan that would get students back on track. The assistant superintendent jotted down notes and acknowledged the good faith effort to do what was right for students academically, but that decisions at that level could become legal issues and must be made with the right stakeholders at the table. The assistant superintendent set up a follow-up meeting with the district math and reading specialist in order to hear the specific academic needs of the students based on their most recent benchmark data. They agreed that adjustments needed to be made and met with the original team of teachers to co-plan and adjust the pacing of the curriculum and plan for scaffolding support, together. The principal learned a valuable lesson by not overstepping his power and clarity appeased the teacher's union. A new process was also established at the district office which would allow principals to propose changes.

Below the line leaders turn the heat up on the pressure cooker through intimidation and the weaponization of secondhand information. Effective leaders pause before approaching a sticky situation of adversity and release the steam before taking off the lid. Transforming educational leaders respond with courage, high expectations, and dignity. Everyone deserves a sense of belonging in the zone above the line.

Rebecca Coda is the Co-founder of Pushing Boundaries Consulting, LLC and publishing agent for Encodable Impact Publishing, LLC in New Orleans. Her work focuses on leadership adversity, educational innovation, childhood trauma, family engagement, and spiritual resilience.

36

Stop Abusing the Phrase "Other Duties as Assigned"
EDWARD PALMISANO

"But when the deed was done, not a single golden egg did he find and his precious Goose was dead."-Aesop's Fables

Pull out your HR handbook and review your job descriptions. I'll bet almost every description has the caveat: "Other duties as assigned." The phrase is often thrown in like an afterthought, but the way it is enacted can permeate a school culture. Sometimes the phrase is bolder, directly connecting the expectation to following the supervisor's directives. Too often "other duties as assigned" is a boss' way of saying, "Because I said so." If an employee doesn't comply there could be repercussions under the heading of "insubordination", which employees know can directly influence a cause for dismissal. The phrase is anything but a throwaway comment.

Now look at your evaluation rubric. Do you have "other duties as assigned" as an area to evaluate? Unlikely. Within a Danielson Framework you might be able to work it into the final Component 4e regarding professionalism and following district directives, but that should be roughly 3% of the evaluation. When describing good teaching practice, Component 4e is listed last for good reasons, for it may have very little to do with teaching ability. Be careful: marks here may be more about compliance and punishment than what makes that employee an effective educator.

Cover Sideways
There are three kinds of "other duties". The first is the kind that asks an employee to "cover sideways". This is when you might ask your school psychologist to help with evaluations in another building or to help counsel a student in crisis when the social worker is out of the building. The US Office of Personnel Management refers to these as "interdisciplinary" because there is a similar set of qualifications required. "Other duties' are designed so that an employer does not have to anticipate every scenario. These interdisciplinary situations are perfectly acceptable if the employee isn't effectively doing the load of two positions without reducing part of the original load.

Cover Upwards
The second situation is when an employee is asked to "cover upwards". This could include when a teacher with an administrative license is asked to be in charge while a principal is called to the district office for a brief meeting or to lead a meeting in a supervisor's absence. There have been court cases where employees have sued for back pay when this is abused, but if these duties are requested only occasionally many educators who are looking to advance may jump at the opportunity to gain experience or to prove they are ready for additional responsibilities and pay. According to the OPM these opportunities are allowed but the employee may be eligible for a change of grade or classification if the duties "are a regular and continuing part of the job, are performed for at least 25% of the time, and involve a higher level of knowledge and skill that would be a factor in recruiting for the (current) position."

Cover Other Duties
There is a third kind of "other duties": when employees are asked to cover areas for which the duties do not correlate to the general job expectations or up to the level of qualifications needed. Perhaps a degreed professional is being asked to take responsibilities that could be performed by a person without a college degree. This is where we have a more unspoken problem if a pattern persists. Rather than take legal action (as in the second "upward" type of grievance), many may simply vote with their feet. Remember the memes: "People don't leave bad jobs; they leave bad bosses."

Union, Non-Union, & Contracts
A smart school leader will be very careful to read the teacher contract regarding extra duties, avoiding

a grievance. But how do you deal with those non-union employees like your related service, support staff, or even your assistant principal? Do you lump those "other duties" on them because you know they don't have the same grievance protections? Be honest. Maybe you give extra duties to your loved employees who just never say "No" or just seem good at them. Do you let them say "No"? Are you asking them because you want to help them advance or just because you are afraid of asking someone else who might resist? When you are short subs, whom do you pull away from usual duties?

Going a bit deeper - who fulfills the duties of those non-union staff members if you pull them to do something else? I have spent my career close to special education. I routinely have seen social workers and psychologists pulled to fill in various holes or paraprofessionals acting as subs, answering phones in the office, or making copies for all school mailings. Whom are you pulling to fulfill IEP minutes? My guess is "Nobody." The students most in need tend to bear the brunt of poor management.

A Crisis or an Excuse
Let me just take a moment to point out that a great cohesive staff will bend over backwards to help each other out in hard times. If there was a crisis "all hands, on deck" moment because a fellow teacher was incapacitated, I cannot imagine any caring human educator not stepping in. Teachers and other educators routinely go above and beyond because great teaching does not happen without some level of passion, caring, and duty. However, "all hands, on deck" can get overused. Educators are smart and they can tell the difference between a crisis and an excuse. You may be short a staff member, but educators will notice when the job opening has not been re-posted or you are not being more aggressive looking for a replacement. If a staff training scheduled months ago means you will need guest teachers, but you do not have them on game day, the staff sees that not as a crisis, but something avoidable and predictable. It gets old.

I do not mean to imply that educated educators should be above doing certain tasks for the school, as Tika Epstein shared in Chapter 6, but there is a line that can be crossed when it happens routinely. From a management point of view, why are you effectively routinely paying an hourly salary 3x the level you should be? Eventually, those who bend over backwards get tired and hopeless - even angry. When your staff member doesn't appear happy or even questions the amount of extra work that takes them away from their core responsibilities and students, do you accuse them of not being a team player? The one whom you accused of not being a team player will eventually start to wonder what kind of manager he or she is playing for and might go free agent.

Have you ever seen one of your "Golden Geese" walk away or die professionally? You know the story: A goose lays a golden egg once a day and the farmer makes more than enough money every day. But he gets greedy and wants more, eventually cutting open the goose to get more golden eggs. Of course, the goose dies and gives no more, leaving the farmer with nothing. Poor management or taking your staff for granted may cause your Golden Geese to burn out and leave the pond.

Educators Know their Value

The best educators have passion. They are confident. In their own training they put in significant time, effort, long nights, family sacrifices, and quite a bit of their own money earning their (often advanced) degrees. They know their value. Yes, they even have a bit of pride, but the good ones have earned it. When you continue to assign other duties that are not consistent with their job descriptions and training, those educators will feel that you either do not recognize their training or that you do not value the benefit of what they have been hired to do. If you keep pulling them from their primary job to do other things, how could they NOT feel like their work doesn't matter? The message that you seem to think something else is more important will be received loud and clear. If you really want to incense a passionate educational professional, start sending the message that their students aren't worth the time or quality that should be afforded to them, which is bound to happen over time. Even when your staff is with their students, instruction may suffer because they may be feeling resentful towards administration, angry, distant, or just burned out.

When you hired your certified staff, they realized that you chose them over so many other people because of their special skills. Your new staff members felt valued. During the interview it is unlikely you didn't ask about how well they might do their "other duties." After a pattern of different duties, your staff may start to question if you ever really valued them. Instead of opportunities for advancement, they may feel they went backwards professionally. They feel lied to. When the only way to catch up on their required work is to do the work at home, they feel that you don't care about their time or their relationships with their families. The passion starts to fade. They start to question if all the professional sacrifice and student loans were worth it. You know that trope that teachers do it for the outcome, not the income? When they are spending much of their day being both underpaid and underappreciated without a chance to affect more positive outcomes with their students, they begin to question why they stay.

As a personal example, when I was trying to get back into administration from my middle level position, I was willing to do upward tasks. These opportunities become more limited, and I was basically told to stay in my lane. I was not receiving support or training to improve myself professionally with PD opportunities turned down, once so I could assist with picture day. Meanwhile, the amount of coverage duties, substituting, directing car traffic, and student monitoring increased. I certainly was not putting my advanced degrees to work. I did a time study analysis (because that's what school psychologists do) and found that I had averaged over 40% of my work hours with student monitoring or other duties while my work at home increased. For one week, I logged 63% of my time in student monitoring or other duties. If "covering upward" over 25% of job hours was an unpaid promotion, I felt like I was in an overpaid demotion. I was losing excitement and gaining stress. Blood sugar and blood pressure increases at work that would come down when measured at the doctor's office. It was time to leave that position and that is what I did. The majority of the related service staff under similar conditions also left that same year. We did what we had to do personally and professionally. Unfortunately, this is a familiar story in many districts. Assistant principals get "other duties" dumped on them while being overlooked for promotions due to not having enough leadership experience. Teachers leave hoping for greener pastures. The Golden Geese fly to other ponds or die professionally, sometimes leaving the field altogether.

Nurture Your Golden Geese
As you ponder how to be a good manager and an even better leader, look bravely and honestly in the mirror. Remember the passion you had for getting into education and recognize that others have that same fire inside. Stop dampening the flame and give it some oxygen. Give that great educator a chance to strive higher. Nurture your Golden Geese. Let them graze and explore on their own. Treat them well, fairly, and provide a patient environment that will help them continue to contribute those golden eggs for their students. Have faith that those under your wings are ready to fly.

When a crisis day hits, jump in with the crew and lead from within. People will follow, but they will be more willing if they see you diligently working on finding more crewmates so that they don't have "all hands, on deck" for the entire journey. Your crew needs to refresh, and they need to be successful in those special areas that make them shine. As you hire new staff, be transparent and clarify what your "other duties" are. If you find that a position consistently takes on additional or different roles, you owe it to current and future staff to update your job descriptions accordingly. Forgive yourself for screwing up in the past and pledge to look forward, anticipating your potential staffing needs. Ask yourself not how you can use your staff, but how you can make it so your educational staff can do what they are trained to do, what they love to do.

Edward Palmisano has been an educator for over 25 years and has served as a school board member, special ed coordinator, and school psychologist in IL and IN. Ed loves to assist local parents as an advocate as they attempt to navigate legal issues and special education. He has also been a dedicated test prep tutor for over a decade. Ed lives with his wife, two incredible teenagers, and eight parakeets in Beecher, IL

Stop Wanting to Always Do Things Your Way
JASON MCDOWELL

School administrators make some very difficult decisions daily. Some are very basic while others have a direct effect on our students' educational experiences. Throw in multiple stakeholder groups that may have differing opinions on decisions being made and you have a strong case for why many administrators feel that they need to have every decision be made either through them or from them. It's a common phenomenon of leaders who know that "the buck stops here" with them in their building. While it's important to be in tune to what's happening in your building it's also important to empower others in your building to make decisions and lead teams and initiatives. For this to happen effectively we, as school leaders, need to stop wanting to do things our way all of the time.

Let's face it, most of the decisions that are made every school year have a direct impact on others around us. It may be students, teachers, parents, or all of the above. Bringing in some of those voices to help in the process is good for the culture and climate of your building. It builds people up. I mean, who doesn't like being asked for input on an important topic that relates directly to them. By no means am I advocating for this to be overused. Only bring others into the decision-making process when you're willing to take value in their thoughts and ideas. To save their time and yours, only seek big ideas from others if you're willing to put your own premeditated thoughts to the side and run with what is brought to you. Probably the most important aspect of the idea of being open to doing things a different way through someone else's ideas is to resist trying to put your stamp on it. A great idea is a great idea plain and simple. Don't be the leader who tears down others' thoughts and ideas just to turn around and build up a nearly identical plan of your own. It's productive to collaborate on plans and ideas but not even close to productive to crush and rebuild them.

That Idea Sounds Okay
Many years ago, I worked alongside an administrator that suffered from what can debilitate leaders the most. John suffered from the inability to take any input or advice from others. This happened even when he asked for the thoughts and ideas of his staff. The pattern was usually easy to spot. John would seek out others to see what they thought about a certain plan or idea. He would appear to listen only to be formulating in his mind because the thoughts that were being given to him were in no way going

to work. Once John gave his opinion on the thoughts and ideas he received, he would unveil his obviously "superior" plan. Many times, what he came back at you with was a mix of his own thoughts as well as the ideas from the very person he had asked advice from in the first place. The only difference was that this was now "his" idea. Other times John would pull a group of stakeholders together for brainstorming sessions and in the end, he would go in the exact opposite direction that was proposed to him with no real explanation. Over the next couple of years John carried on with this same pattern as people slowly stopped sharing much at all regarding ideas. We all knew that if it wasn't his idea then it wasn't an idea worth trying. We all had more pressing things to spend our time on than to be reminded of this. How many collaborative moments were lost due to John's inability to empower others? How could opening up to new ideas regarding processes, procedures, curriculum, and discipline have affected students' lives? We'll never know. What I do know is that as an educator, that was an uncomfortable couple of years that seemed to squash creativity in the building with many teachers feeling less valued than before he arrived in the district.

We May all Have One, but We Sure Don't Want to Be One
There's a "John" in every school, business, or organization across the world. That's why it's important that we recognize these traits and make sure that WE aren't the ones following in John's footsteps. As school administrators it's important that we take a team approach whenever we have the opportunity. If we have an issue that pertains to the maintenance of the building, then pull in the maintenance supervisor and other affected staff and brainstorm for possible remedies. Out of these remedies some may be great, and others are duds. Some may be usable and others not. If the solution of the problem comes from the group and not just from the top down, then the benefits will show themselves. You'll have more buy in from the people carrying out the tasks towards improvement. Those involved in the decision making will take more pride in the finished product.

As building administrators, we strive to bring in the top talent for each of our teaching positions. We have a wealth of knowledge behind every classroom door. By loosening up and allowing others to run with ideas that they may have, we are empowering teachers, and gaining more traction to effectively implement initiatives. Over time this style of leadership will increase the positivity in the building showing up in a boost to culture, climate, and morale. In the end this will have a positive impact on student learning and outcomes. We can do so much more together as a team than with alone in our offices.

Jason McDowell is a public-school administrator who has served in Northwest Missouri schools for nearly 20 years. He was honored as the 2019 NWMAESP Exemplary New Principal. Jason has served two terms as Mayor along with giving time to various community causes. He was recognized for this service by earning the 2020 NWMSU Alumni Association Public Service Award. Jason believes that in order to take your school to the next level you have to promote the greatness happening in your school district.

STOP Misunderstanding Yourself and Others

This Type of Nonsense Holds You Back from a Healthy Career

Stop Talking About Self-Care for Staff
GREG MOFFITT

I was doing all the things I was supposed to do. Daily exercise? Check. Mindfulness app on my phone? Check. Eating healthier? Check. Self-help books? Check. Hobbies (is watching TV a hobby)? Check. Setting boundaries (no work email after 9pm or on the weekends)? Check. More time with friends and family? Check. Seeking professional help? Check.

I was doing all the right things and yet, I was still burnt out. I was still ready to quit education. Because here's the thing: no amount of breathing, boundary setting, or bubble baths are going to change the fact that being an educator is incomprehensibly difficult at times. Are breathing, boundaries, and bubble baths important? For sure. Especially if you like bubble baths. Personally, I think it's gross to sit in your own dirty water. But maybe that's just me? Regardless, the point is that a bubble bath isn't going to make the system better for educators.

And when we continue to remind educators about the importance of self-care without changing the actual systems and structures that create the need for those reminders, we make the situation even more challenging. Worse, we reinforce the idea that if educators "just" spent more time on themselves, things will be better. And that's not necessarily true. In fact, it is a false positive that exacerbates root cause issues and holds us back from creating academically healthy schools.

Our Job is to Make the System Better

Stop telling staff about the importance of self-care and instead, show them that you care. And that begins by asking, "What does genuine care and support look like?"

Making the system better requires checking in, listening, validating, empathizing, and doing whatever we can to make things easier for staff to do their jobs well. Certainly, this will look different for every staff member because what makes one staff member feel supported may not work for someone else. And what works for each teacher may not work for each team or group. To better understand the support that is needed, administrators must build relationships with staff and seek to discover what works for them. Educators are bombarded from every angle and simply reminding them that "self-care isn't selfish" isn't enough to address all the things that come their way. Even though the message is well intended, it isn't enough to impact systemic challenges. So instead of telling staff about the importance of self-care, we need to ensure that effective structures and systems are in place to help educators manage all the "stuff" that educators need to manage and that they have the time and place to make self-care an actual priority as part of the system.

Take Care of the Cup

We all know by now that "we can't drink from an empty cup." Refilling, rest, and rejuvenation are all important. Yet no matter how often we fill and refill our metaphorical cups, toxic and stressful systems will continue to put cracks in them unless we change the system. How many times, as administrators, do we reinforce those systems while we require teachers to juggle multiple cups at once? No bubble bath in the world is going to solve the exhaustion that comes from too many initiatives! Step back and focus on a systematic approach that ensures educators are getting what they need so they can focus on making things better for kids. Actively seek out ways to make it easier for teachers to teach and learners to learn. Remove the stuff getting in the way. Provide the time and space for self-care. Genuinely show care for those we serve. It's time for us, as educational leaders, to help create better systems that truly support our staff.

Greg Moffitt was an elementary school principal in Northern California and now works as the Director of Principal Development for the District of Columbia Public Schools. He does not like bubble baths but loves working to make schools awesome for both kids and adults. He believes that students and staff, working together, can make schools better and change the world.

Stop Calling Staff Your "Family"
WADE STANFORD

FAMILY is a term that we all are familiar with and either provokes positive or negative memories from our childhood. The thought of family drives more of a feeling or emotion than physical characteristics. The unity and closeness of family is an atmosphere that all of us strive to create.

100 No-Nonsense Things That ALL School Leaders Should STOP Doing

Our notion of the family unit was developed during our childhood days. Each of us vividly remembers the structure that we grew up in, and no matter the design, most likely, we have both positive and negative memories. For some of us, our memories are heavier on the closeness and feeling of love that permeated each day. We recall entering a home that was cheerful, happy, and full of laughter. This atmosphere created a sense of safety and well-being in us. For others, we recollect arriving home to a house that was in constant conflict. We may look back on a time full of tension, emptiness, and far away from safety.

It Always Falls Short
As administrators, we have been striving to create a positive environment on our campus or in our district, and many times, we label the culture we are working towards as a "family" atmosphere. Regardless of what childhood memories dominate our recollection, we pull the positive pieces of our family memories and attempt to create a parallel feeling with our staff. And at times, we vividly remember the negative traits of our family and work diligently to design a culture precisely opposite of that memory.

Our administrative efforts have been centered on chasing an elusive feeling of closeness, unity, love, and united focus. We have poured our energy into attempting to rally our staff around mission, vision, single purpose, and agreed-upon convictions. While developing a family atmosphere is a noble cause, it typically falls short of the intended outcome.

Family Gatherings are Dysfunctional
When we genuinely pull back the layers of family, we discover that all families are dysfunctional at some level. This thought may set some of you back, and it is sure to deeply upset others. While this is understandable, think of the last family gathering you attended. Picture walking into the space the gathering was being held, and if we are honest, we will admit that we immediately tried to locate "the person" we did not want to sit next to and spend the next hour hearing their story! For some of us, this person is a sibling, and for others, it is a distant family member. No matter the relationship, we listen, and then as soon as possible, we escape and find another person with whom we can visit. Because it is family, we never address the issue these family members create when they capture us in a conversation. This lack of action is the catalyst for the family structure being dysfunctional. This lack of action is driven by a love for family and a desire not to hurt or damage a loved one. But by not addressing the behavior of the family member, we promote the continuation of the negative behavior and the dysfunctional family culture at all future gatherings.

As administrators striving to build a family culture, we are guilty of developing an atmosphere that mirrors that of the family gathering. We all have a few staff members that the rest of the staff avoid and do not want to spend time listening to them. But because we have created the family culture, and nobody wants to hurt another staff member, no one addresses the negative behavior. And then, at every future staff meeting, there is a rush to fill chairs to stay away from the "staff member" nobody wants to sit by.

Because of this dysfunctional behavior, as administrators, we must strive to develop an atmosphere that is more conducive to creating high-functioning behavior. We must grow a culture that honors transparency and authentic conversations. We must offer social contracts and norms with clear expectations on how to behave when someone falls short. Effective organizations and work teams desire a spirit of honesty, growth, forward-thinking, and accountability that focuses on all members' improvement. We all flourish in a culture where interdependence and continuous improvement are paramount. And that doesn't always occur in a family setting.

Building Highly Effective Teams
To get a glimpse into how to create a culture of this nature, we can explore the inner workings of highly effective teams. On highly effective teams, the team members discharge their egos and invest in a united purpose or goal. They do not wait for others to hold them accountable; they adopt a mindset of self-responsibility and strive for excellence every day. Highly effective team members coach and collaborate and embrace a growth mindset that builds a culture of continuous improvement for every single member.

Most importantly, highly effective teams are composed of team members who will not tolerate continual subpar performance or a noticeable lack of effort. When team members witness this behavior, they intervene with coaching, encouragement, and an empathetic heart. Their mission is to bring the wayward team members along and grow them in capacity. This coaching approach will continue until it is apparent that this process will not work, and progress will not be made. At this time, team members will have an authentic and honest conversation with the underperforming team member. Their intent is not to hurt the individual but to be straightforward about the objectionable behavior and agree that their future behaviors and actions will align with the team's united purpose. On a highly effective team, team members are not waiting on a coach to address misguided behavior but instead, they handle it immediately since they put the team above themselves!

Administrators' goals should be to duplicate the culture of highly effective teams. The people we lead deserve leaders who promote an environment that emphasizes a united purpose, a mindset of self-responsibility, authentic collaboration, and continuous improvement. Misunderstandings will be minimized when leaders foster coaching, encouragement, empathetic hearts, and authentic conversations that promote alignment to the desired student outcomes.

As administrators, I challenge us to stop singularly focusing on creating a family atmosphere and calling our staff family. That type of nonsense will hold any leader back from a healthy career. Instead, let us take the closeness and love of family and inject all the characteristics and qualities of a highly effective team into our culture to lead a staff that feels like a *FAMILY* but operates as a *TEAM*.

Wade Stanford has served in public education in various roles for the past 39 years. In the last 6 years, Wade has served as Superintendent at Westwood ISD. Prior to that he served as Athletic Director, Assistant High School Principal, High School Principal, Director of Human Resources, and Assistant Superintendent. He believes and lives by the thought that you should approach every task as though it were the moment that will define you. Wade is passionate about leadership, building the capacity in those around him, and mentoring aspiring leaders.

Stop Confusing Stress-Behavior with Misbehavior
BRAD HUGHES

"If disruptive behaviors are a signal of autonomic stress, why do our schools' resort to punishment instead of first soothing the distress through loving human engagement?" -Dr. Mona Delahooke

"Calm begets calm." -Dr. Stuart Shanker

School leaders, educators, and caregivers devote considerable time and energy--and frequently conflict, heartache, and sleepless nights--to addressing so-called 'misbehavior'.

It's time we all learned the important distinction between misbehavior and stress-behavior, and shifted from demanding compliance to engendering co-operation through compassion with children who are dysregulated, traumatized, or in crisis.

A Shift to Co-Regulating
This shift to a focus on co-regulation promotes connection and well-being for all students and community members. This leadership mindset shift recognizes that we frequently conclude that misbehavior is willful when negative student responses may be a maladaptive response to overstress-- and signals the need for the adult to co-regulate with the child.

Stress is part of life. It may be positive or negative, visible, or hidden, minor, or toxic. Self-regulation is the aptitude and action that requires recognizing self-limitations and consciously responding to stress in such a way that its balances negative energy, perception, and tension with a productive response that dissolves and diffuses negative feelings.

Learn the Stress Domains
Many students are not choosing to be inattentive, disruptive, or confrontational. Nor should they necessarily be accused of not having enough self-control. Research in neuroscience and physiology reveals that challenging behaviors may be attempts to adapt (however undesirably) to stressful situations. On his website, self-reg.ca, Dr. Stuart Shanker identifies The Five Domains of Self-Regulation in The Shanker Self-Reg® Framework as well as a Five-Step Method for enhancing self-regulation in children, youth, young adults, and adults.

THE FIVE DOMAINS OF SELF REGULATION	THE FIVE-STEP METHOD FOR ENHANCING SELF-REGULATION
1. The Biological Domain	1. Read the signs of stress and reframe the behavior
2. The Emotion Domain	2. Recognize stressors
3. The Cognitive Domain	3. Reduce the stress
4. The Social Domain	4. Reflect: enhance stress awareness
5. The Pro-Social Domain	5. Restore energy

Left unchecked, stressors in any of these domains compound and multiply into stress cycles that impact behavior. I encourage you to further explore these domains and methods to deepen an understanding of yourself and others to ensure a healthy work environment. Just as in section one of this book, you can't "wing" culture and hope for a healthy career.

Leaders must seek to learn those pervasive family and community distresses that impact their ability to self-regulate - job or housing loss, food scarcity, family illness, or death. Any one of these in the short-term or systemic and generational challenges make for dysregulated, stress-related people in our school communities. Understanding your own self-regulation triggers, dysfunctions of those that you lead, and limitations of community stakeholders are the first steps to enhancing self-regulation.

Interfering or Self-Soothing?
While children can be coached to regulate their own stress in "less interfering" ways, we must try to pinpoint and reduce the stressors upstream–rather than assuming that their primary motivation is to find ways to intentionally interfere with our teaching and learning. That child that taps, clicks, hums, interrupts, or finds other ways to disrupt may in fact be trying to regulate internal or external stress. Self-soothing behaviors are signs that stress is too high, and the student is unintentionally trying to

keep from tipping over or shutting down. The child that is yelling or explosive may have experienced trauma or otherwise adverse experiences. Their alarm systems are hair-triggered--primed for threats and self-preservation. Their stress load is already so high that unmet needs, expectations, or any additional stresses overwhelm them. We may not know why. They may not know why. These responses are occurring on an autonomic level. Sometimes the why can only be uncovered through trial and error--or after the storm has passed. After we have companioned them through the stress--to calm. Our job at that point is simply to reduce stress for them.

The Iceberg Below
In an article on her personal website, monadelahooke.com, Dr. Mona Delahooke challenges us to look deeper than the tip of the iceberg--beyond the observable behavior--to the many factors below the surface that help us understand why the behavior may be occurring. Dr. Delahooke shares:

> *"We have a preference, indeed a bias, towards "top-down" causes of behaviors. When we have a top-down perspective, we believe that children are doing things on purpose, seeking 'negative attention', or are otherwise willful. This top-down perspective is agnostic of the critical role the body plays in children's behaviors, which is a bottom-up or 'body-u' perspective. Until we understand the difference, we will be prone to mistakenly engaging with the end-product of a child's needs (behaviors) while ignoring the root causes, all those things beneath the tip of the iceberg."*

Reflecting on what is deep below the emotional surface as triggers and catalysts of pain or misbehavior for students (and adults), can become one of the greatest harbingers of restoring positive energy. You can read in depth on this topic in her book, *Beyond Behaviors: Using Brain Science and Compassion to Understand and Solve Children's Behavioral Challenges*.

Upshift and Downshift in Co-Regulation

Our own stress naturally rises with the bombardments, distractions, and disruptions around us. We can get caught in our own stress cycles and lose access to our reserves of patience, problem-solving, and our own "wells" of capacity. Our physiologies continuously upshift and downshift with those around us through tone of voice, pitch, speed, facial expressions, gaze, posture, gestures. Leaders possess the power and influence to use these limbic signals to co-regulate not just individuals, but entire groups. Use your power to soothe and reassure. Use your power to calm others' nervous systems when they cannot regulate themselves. Just showing up, listening with intention, and sharing our calm energy may make all the difference in reducing stress and restoring positive energy.

Learning to distinguish between misbehavior and stress-behavior is an essential skill I had to learn as a leader of emotional intelligence who serves all students--some with autism, a documented or suspected history of trauma, some who experienced prejudice due to a history of previous behavior challenges, or who have not benefited from typical behavior-modification plans and interventions. Learning to pinpoint and reduce upstream stress gave me a greater purpose that was grounded in curiosity, not compliance.

We can shift from judgment and reactivity to empathy and compassion. We can start to unlock solutions and competencies that stress is masking. By identifying and reducing stressors, we uncover the wells of capacity within each of us.

Brad Hughes is an elementary school principal in Ontario, Canada. He is passionate about improving kids' lives by loving and supporting the adults that serve them. Brad is a Training and Development Specialist with the Teach Better Team, and the host of The Good News, Brad News Podcast, amplifying the inspiring work of heart-led educators around the world.

41

Stop Beating Yourself Up Over Past Mistakes
ANDREW MAROTTA

Keep rolling. That's what I always say. That's what I try my best to do. #Keeprolling. Tomorrow will be a new day of school, the sun will rise, the bell will ring, both the students and staff will move on to the next activity, and Friday will come.

Why do we as school leaders feel the need to always be perfect? Why do we get embarrassed when we make mistakes and errors? It happens. It happens everywhere in every walk of life, yet we, as school leaders, feel the need to hold ourselves to the highest standards of perfection. Yes, but mistakes happen, and yes, we make them. Know that. Understand that and be prepared to deal with making mistakes. It is part of the job. It's also important to recognize that mistakes can be turned into opportunities for growth

In this chapter, I write through two lenses: one, that of a principal of 20 years, two, as a former Division 1 men's college basketball referee for 19 years. Through these two experiences, I have made my share of mistakes and keep surviving and thriving. Yet how? How can we stop beating ourselves up over past mistakes? To do this, leaders must understand why we make mistakes, reflect on how to minimize the mistakes, and explore ways to get past the mistakes.

Why We Make Mistakes

The jobs of a school leader and referee are quite similar, minus the leading and inspiring of staff and students. Think about it: both jobs are in the spotlight, both jobs require you to make quick decisions, enforce the rules, and deal with people yelling about your decisions. Outside variables affect what happens during both of your work periods, and both jobs need you to be able to withstand unbelievable, insurmountable, and unfair amounts of criticism. Throughout these pressure-cooker situations, we are going to undoubtedly make some mistakes. And here's why:

- The speed of it all. The day, the periods, the flow of the work is all very fast.
- Not all the rules apply to everyone the same way. You treat everyone fairly, not the same.
- We forget. We forget what we said, the rules, the meeting...we flat out missed it.
- We're unorganized.
- We get behind.
- We don't pack our own parachute. We let someone else prep and take care of things and we did not inspect what was packed to ensure that it meets our expectations.
- We get duped and tricked out of our own skin.
- We don't get enough rest or drink enough water.
- We misjudged, overestimated, or just were flat-out wrong.
- We didn't seek to understand first.
- We didn't listen.
- We just didn't know and didn't take the time to find out.

The list could go on and on, and I've made a mistake with each one of these categories and more. Before you read on, I challenge you now to put the book down for just a little bit. Take some time to reflect on the mistakes above through taking a walk, a short meditation, and/or a good night's sleep. Think about mistakes you've made and how some of these categories might have affected you.

Ways to Minimize Mistakes

I'm trusting that you took time to take note, reflect, and think upon past mistakes that have gnawed at you in the past and others that may still be eating at you. Moving forward from past mistakes requires minimizing them. I'm sure any regrets that you are still wrestling with as a leader have ignited a need to better position yourself to make better decisions that will lessen your mistakes in the future. Here are a few strategies:

- Be quick but not in a hurry. When things are not clear, slow down and grip the wheel.
- Set out your plan for each day and do your best to stick to your schedule. Adapt when needed.
- Say "I need some think time about that" when you need some time to digest and reflect.
- Trust your best people and make many of your decisions based on: what would the best people think? (Thank you, Todd Whitaker, for this leadership tip.)
- Take care of yourself: rest, hydrate, and exercise each day no matter what.
- Get a mentor or two who are awesome at their roles. Ask their opinions on things and bounce things off those you trust.
- Trust your gut. Your first impression is usually right.
- Read, learn, and grow in the position. Build each day to get better, smarter, and more experienced.

These are just a few of my favorites that I have learned over time and yes, through mistakes. When you start working these tips and tricks into your routines and practices, you will start to see things a little clearer, feel more confident, and overall, make better decisions that you feel good about.

Get Past the Mistakes
The magic sauce is the ability to stop beating yourself up over past mistakes. The path to success and a healthy career relies on understanding yourself and others.

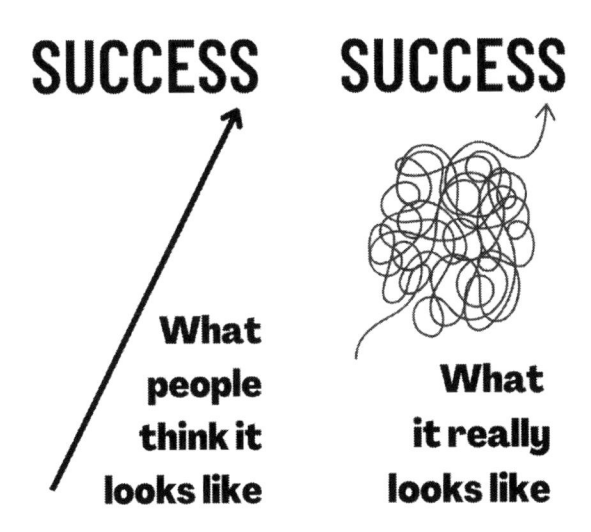

SUCCESS — What people think it looks like

SUCCESS — What it really looks like

I first saw the picture above during the great George Couros' presentation at the National Principals Conference in Boston, MA. It became crystal clear to me that getting past my mistakes wasn't going to be easy, clean, or perfect . . . helping me understand that it was ok to make some mistakes and get my hands dirty on my path to success.

100 No-Nonsense Things That ALL School Leaders Should STOP Doing

Over time I've discovered the ingredients to the "magic sauce" that have empowered me to move forward as an understanding leader in a healthy career. These ingredients have allowed me to put my head on the pillow at night to rest easy and pop out of bed in the morning ready to go. Take them, use them, make signs, make recordings, and get tattoos…whatever you must do to remember what's in the magic sauce.

Magic Sauce Recipe

1. Admit it, fix it, and move on. These are simple words that come with a lot of healthy releases. Just say it. Own your mistake. While we might feel afraid that people will think less of us when we make mistakes, people deeply respect us more when we admit that we made a mistake. We don't have to beat ourselves up nor take a public beating, yet admit it, fix it, and move on.

2. Mix in the five SW's (so magical!).

- **S**ometimes it **W**ill
- **S**ometimes it **W**on't
- **S**o **W**hat!
- **S**omeone's **W**aiting
- **S**o, **S**tick **W**ith it.

I love these magic words. They sum up the best way to *NOT* beat yourself up. Say them to yourself, say them out loud, and say them when you make a mistake. Stick with it! You got this.

3. Get the next play right. When I officiated at Duke University, I heard this yelled from the bench. Duke missed a shot or had a turnover, and the loud yell came from the bench: "Next Play!" I turned and said to myself, "Man that is awesome!" I began to implement this into my officiating mindset and then into my role as a school leader. Next play, next situation, next person, next scenario, next time, next decision, next period, next day, next year, next meeting, next teacher, and so on. There will always be a next. It doesn't mean you don't do your best with whom and what you are working with, but if it goes sideways, you get the next play right!

4. Say you are sorry. When it happens, and it will, say that you are sorry for your mistakes. After admitting it, fix it, and move on, and own your mistakes. People will respect you more and you will be able to move on from it and not beat yourself up. You owned it. Forgive yourself and let it go. Say that you are sorry when it's your fault. You are a leader. The captain of the ship takes ownership to steer the ship in a moment of truth when things go south, and mistakes are made.

5. Don't make the same mistake twice. But it will happen. You didn't want it nor meant it to happen, yet you made the mistake again. Repeat steps 1-4 above and burn number 5 into your mind, heart, and actions. Don't do it again. Learn from it, reflect on it, talk with your mentors. When the same or similar situation comes your way again (and it will), slow it down, go back to your notes, reflect, and get it right. You know you can overcome the next challenge since you lived through that mistake the first time, and the second time. You are ready to get it right!

Forgive Yourself, and Keep Moving Forward
I am giving you permission to forgive yourself when you do make a mistake(s) (not too many of course). I hope these tips will help you stop beating yourself up over past mistakes. You are a superhero helping teachers, kids, and parents on their journey. Keep rolling. This is a marathon not a sprint so keep rolling, and keep running. There's lots of work to be done and many are looking to you for inspiration. When you are filling up the hearts of others, it's ok if you spill some of the magic sauce! If I can help you in any way, don't hesitate to reach out.

Andrew Marotta, educator, author, and leader of the #SurviveThrive movement. Learn more about him at andrewmarotta.com, and on all the socials. #ELB #ELBlog #LeadershipSparks #keeprolling @andrewmarotta21 on Twitter. Reach out to him via email andrewmarottallc@gmail.com

42

Stop Carrying Baggage from Past Positions into Your Current Position
LISA BLANK

"What lies behind us and what lies before us are tiny matters compared to what lies within us."
-Ralph Waldo Emerson

At some point, it seems that every leader has "baggage" delivered to them. It wasn't asked for, but it comes our way, nonetheless. If we choose to carry over baggage from our past experiences and focus on its weight, one may opt to continue carrying it along under the guise of "flying under the radar."

100 No-Nonsense Things That ALL School Leaders Should STOP Doing

Rick Jetter expands on this in detail later in Chapter 91. Focusing on past "baggage," or past toxic trauma will only hold you back just as Brad Hughes shared in Chapter 40. Anxiety may exacerbate the situation and result in fueling failure to engage in courageous conversations. A healthy leader in a healthy career has the "magic sauce", as Andrew Marotta shared in the last chapter, down to a science. Healthy leaders strategically facilitate productive conversations and actions that spur real change and growth.

Being a leader in education is like being on a road trip. Leaders strategically map out the course of the year and are prepared to endure heavy traffic, adverse weather conditions, and crazy drivers. Sometimes you may find yourself driving on autopilot zoning from one initiative to the other. Even worse you may be so emotionally charged by past experiences that you want to pull off to the side of the road and head back. I challenge you to forgive yourself from any mistakes of your past and focus on the journey ahead. Healthy leaders don't dwell on mistakes or adverse experiences of the past but rather seek to understand the strengths, challenges, and people that they are in charge of leading.

Check the Rearview Mirror, Briefly
One of the first things a new driver learns is to check the rearview mirror. This important tool helps drivers see what is behind them, where they have been, and helps to alert them to the presence of emergency vehicles and tailgaters. The view through that rear facing mirror may cause drivers to accelerate, slow down, change direction, or pull over and stop altogether. Just as a rearview mirror impacts the actions of a driver, that same metaphorical "rearview" mindset impacts leader actions.

Looking back and reflecting upon our experiences are essential components in becoming a proficient driver. Proficient leaders drive toward building positive school culture and lead instructional efforts that transform their educational system. This cannot happen if more than a glance is applied to the "rearview." It is important to take time to briefly look in the "rearview" mirror to identify potential impacts on our actions moving forward, just not too much time. The bulk of leadership miles should focus on driving forward safely toward the destination as smoothly as possible.

Dodge Potholes, Dangerous Drivers, and Diversions
Even the most prepared, cautious, and proactive leaders will inevitably face dangerous driving conditions. You will encounter adversarial conditions including discrimination, harassment, bad politics, a back-biting school culture, revenge, or mistreatment by ego-driven coworkers to name a few. In Escaping the School Leader's Dunk Tank: How to Prevail When Others Want to See You Drown, Rebecca Coda and Dr. Rick Jetter point out that, "No school leader is immune to the adversarial conditions that can place us in (what they describe as) the 'dunk tank'." The conflict is real, fueling strong emotions and frustrations including anxiety, embarrassment, shame, a sense of loss, fear, jealousy and rage over missed opportunities, broken relationships, and perceived failures.

STOP Misunderstanding Yourself and Others

I never believed I would find myself with both hands behind the wheel of a reckless side swiping incident. Growing up in a large family, I learned from an early age to get along with everyone. I've always valued people which I why I was left dumbfounded at such an intentional attempt to take me out. I had been working on a project that served the students in my region, and not long after leading this initiative I came to find out that I was perceived as a threat. I assumed positive intent and dismissed this red flag. Being somewhat naive about such behaviors, I assumed it would just go away. I continued leading the initiative and in a short amount of time, officially became an undeniable target. One adversary turned to several and it became political. The root cause of all that happened was not personal, but it all ended up feeling very personal. For my primary adversary, the ends justified the cruel means of operation. A part of me wanted to just "duck and cover" and at the time a colleague even suggested that strategy. This was my first baggage claim as an educational leader. If I had better understood the situation at the time, I could have dodged this diversion.

Tactics used by adversaries can be ruthless, creating a whole host of emotions and impacts that are difficult to manage let alone dodge. Who do you talk to when you experience a reckless driver eager to sideswipe you? As educational leaders it seems that admitting such a challenge would be viewed as weakness in a leader. Or would it? Rebecca's and Rick's book was a game changer for me. Through their work, I learned that I was far from alone and I also discovered that I didn't have to carry this negative experience into future leadership experiences. I will always be grateful for the amazing leaders I connected with on social media who had read the book, including co-authors of the Teacher & Leader 100 Stop Series. The personalized learning exchanges in these venues provided opportunities for open, supportive, judgment-free discussion and feedback. For me, letting out what had been held in for so long was cathartic and certainly impactful in my interpretation of the view in my rearview mirror. I realized that I needed to focus on driving forward.

Many of us hang onto negative experiences of the past only to hit more potholes that require full roadside service. Consciously and subconsciously, they impact our ability to arrive at our destinations safely. Do not let negative past experiences weigh you down from moving forward. We have important work to do.

Be Careful! Objects May Appear Closer Than They Actually Are!
Observing school and district leaders in districts across many states has taught me that we can all arrive at our destinations safely and on time when we support one other. In contrast, some districts and regions have ingrained an inherent sense of competition amongst school leaders that prohibits a learning culture that fosters growth of leaders. This roadblock diminishes the power of collective work in teams and makes crossing the finish line very difficult. Catching a glance of competitive drivers in your side mirror may distort your leadership perception into believing that adverse leadership

experiences seem bigger than they truly are. If you have ever been in a previous competition driven environment, you may have been ridiculed in front of peers, been "shunned" or cut out of activities and meetings or moved laterally in a position with little or no explanation. Adversity fueled by deadlines, achievements, task completion, and one upping in the past may cause leaders to attach old feelings of embarrassment, ridicule, shame, and fear to a new situation. When this happens, we perceive the problem to be much bigger than it is. Past emotional experiences should not define us as leaders. Side mirrors are there to give you a heads up in decision making, they certainly won't get you to the destination safely. To eliminate the baggage from past positions and bolster a healthy career, leaders will need a new perspective.

4 Ways to Change Your Perspective
Shifting gears forward to a new focus can be challenging. Glancing into our rearview and side mirrors as we drive to our destinations is a necessary skill. To be productive and dodge the diversions and potholes on the path, our primary focus as drivers must be looking forward through the windshield. Consider the following four perspectives that promote forward leading:

1. Recalibrate your purpose. Keep in mind that leaders change position with great frequency. If you are experiencing a leadership related struggle, what you experience today may be very different within a year or so. In 2006, the American Association of School Superintendents found that the mean tenure of a superintendent is only 5-6 years. According to a 2019 report from the National Association of School Principals, the national average turnover rate for principals is around 4 years. When you are struggling, ask yourself, "What is my purpose? Why am I here? And, in the grand scheme of things, what is important?" Friends or close colleagues may even ask/nudge you with these questions when you really need it, getting you back on track during challenging times.

2. Break the trauma cycle. A great deal of research and related discussion has focused on resilience in our students, especially those who have experienced trauma. As educational leaders, we need to recognize the value of resiliency in ourselves. We too benefit from the practice of self-care, recognizing that trauma can exist within our environments. Consider applying SAMHSA's 4 R's of Trauma Informed Care: Realize, Recognize, Respond, and Resist. This approach was developed by the U.S. Department of Health and Human Services in 2014. Applying the 4 R's to future events is helpful in making sense of and managing adversarial actions we experience. Recognizing that our organizations may play a role in perpetuating some events that cause trauma, we should work toward corrective actions to prevent further trauma within our organizations.

3. Foster an abundance mindset. Most schools have growth mindset posters everywhere! Yet, how much of the mindset content is for educators? How about school and district leaders? An important mindset that can help us grow past the competition amongst school leaders to improve our culture, yielding productive collaboration is the abundance mindset. An abundance mindset helps us view the world as limitless, with plenty of opportunities to be shared. Benefits of holding this mindset include clarity and focus on one's purpose, gratitude regardless of circumstances, rapid growth, and feeling plentiful, creative, and inspired.

4. Lead a highly productive flow state. Flow is a highly focused mental state, which cannot be achieved under high levels of distress. Its intensity does not leave cognitive bandwidth for anything else. It is a state of profound task-absorption and intense concentration, leaving those who experience it feeling at-one with the activity in which they are engaged. In essence, that rear view is for a time closed off, leaving a rapid-fire, forward focused view that is highly productive. Flow states in the workplace are linked to high employee engagement and positive working relationships.

As educational leaders, we have important work to accomplish. Remember to glance in your various mirrors, taking time to reflect and learn, but do not live there. Lead with strategies that bring out the best in your teams allowing them to gaze at the beautiful landscape ahead. Lead with a destination in mind and a coordinated plan that focuses on arriving successfully as a team. Our students and communities are depending on you to map the course and lead the way. And always remember…

"You can't change the world from the rearview mirror."
-- Anita Roddick

Lisa Blank, a DoD STEM Ambassador, Leadership Coordinating Council Member for STEM Ecosystems, ISTE Certified Educator, and NYS Computer Science Curriculum Advisory Committee Member serves as Director of STEM Programs for Watertown City School District in Northern New York. Lisa has extensive experience in STEM Education and leadership. She has coordinated & directed multiple Department of Defense Education Activity STEM grants and has been recognized for her district level leadership in STEM education by the New York State School Boards Association and the New York State STEM Collaborative Lisa is passionate about increasing student achievement through educational opportunities that spark curiosity, wonder, and awe.

Stop Prioritizing Your Career Over Your Family
SYNDEE MALEK

Ask any educator and they will confirm that it's easy to give advice. At some point in your career, I'm confident you have caught yourself in a grocery store, restaurant, or with a next-door neighbor using your "teacher" voice to explain how to do something. I think it is a part of our teacher DNA and

Educators = Fixers

It's our job responsibility to tell others what to do . . . seriously, even if you're not a Leo, it just comes with the territory, right? Seriously, as leaders, we know best . . . until . . . it comes to ourselves!

It wasn't too long ago that I had what Oprah would call an "aha" moment...one that came with all the feelings of guilt, shame, and tears . . . that led to reflection, conversations, and changes...but the "aha" had to come first. I'd like to share a story not for shock and awe, but because it's a story I share frequently with leaders so they can learn from my mistakes. Educational leaders offer up fixes for unsolicited advice, and even faster fixes when asked.

Give Them Their Lives Back

As a beginning principal I was so fired up! My school was going to "rock it" no matter what. I had an amazing team of teachers, a phenomenal secretary, a fully staffed lunchroom with caring people, bus drivers who understood how important they were to us as a school . . . I seriously had it all! There was only one thing that I didn't realize. They could and would go on without me. I didn't miss a thing . . . first one to arrive, last one to leave. Committees? I was on them, some of which I led. Bond Elections, I had ideas to share, so I signed up! Parent Teacher Association events were my passion! Monday through Thursday I was at school from sunup until sundown and in the Midwest, at some points of the year that's 10:00 p.m. Saturdays were for me; however, Sundays were my favorite at the school, I would set up for the week, drop notes and gifts in classrooms, set up surprise breakfast for Monday morning, change the school sign, etc.

    … And then it hit me.

I had been on a leave of absence from a local Regional Education Service Agency (RESA). It was a 2-year leave of absence to serve as a principal. Nine years later, I received a call saying, "You've been on a 2-year leave of absence for almost 9 years, we either have to highlight and delete you or you can come back." Come back, really?

Fast forward, coming home and sitting down beside my husband on the couch watching the news. I said, "Hey, I got a call today . . . asking me to come back to RESA." My husband's only response without even thinking was, "Well, we would get our lives back!" Stunned, not knowing what to say "get our lives back," what do you mean? You see, I didn't realize we didn't have "our lives." I sat up straight, turned off the TV, and said in my most administrative, cognitively coached, listening voice and said, "Tell me more…"

What I heard was, "I know school is important to you, your team is your school family, you have missed weddings, funerals, reunions, and the list goes on. You tell everyone else 'family first,' however this family falls 2nd and 3rd most of the time." And the list grew longer than this book as my husband continued to talk.

The "aha's" in my brain surfaced again. I didn't realize we didn't have our lives after all we had been married for 20 plus years by then. That's when I realized I had elevated my career over my family. The truth is, I am not a control person, I believe we all lead from where we stand. My teachers led the bulk of school, I just wanted to be the supportive leader. I was one member of the crew, cheering every step of the way. My team felt supported, they understood family first and never hesitated to approach me when they needed time. I just never did that for myself. It was long overdue to give life back to my own family. As Andrew Marotta suggested, it was time to learn from my past mistakes.

As a leadership development consultant, (yes, I went back to RESA) I used the stories of my own misunderstandings to lead others to healthy careers. Since that time, I've been conscientious about leading by example. I've learned that there is nothing more important than prioritizing family over career. Below are some tips that worked for me. My hope is that they will resonate with you leading you to a healthy career.

Educational Leaders = Fixers + Planners

While we understand that Educators = Fixers, it is also true that Educators = Planners. The key to maintaining a healthy career as an educational leader is to strategically plan for all aspects of the family. Consider:

- Calendar your date nights for the school year as actual appointments on your digital calendar. Pick a color and color code anything that is family so that it contrasts your work appointments.
- Schedule your wellness visits, exercise, meditation and anything health and wellbeing related.
- Add all your special family events, your OWN kids sporting, dance, scout events. Birthdays. Anniversaries. Family traditions . . . maybe a winter weekend trip?
- What else do you need to remember? Maybe a family meeting, (for us it's in late April), to begin looking toward mapping out the next year.

You'd be surprised how many times the pinging sound of a calendar appointment notification shifted my focus from the work I was consumed in, to the importance of family as a priority. Calendaring will save you from the encroachment of time, preserving healthy family dynamics.

Involve Your Staff

Anyone on your campus who draws a check deserves to support and be supported in the preservation of family over career. Spend some time together with your faculty developing your own campus-wide

STOP list. Elicit their ideas on what needs to STOP and ideas for support. Below is a list that may help get you started.

- STOP doing things last minute! In May, hand your staff the opportunities calendared out for the next year.
- STOP doing things because it's easier if you just do it. Shared leadership/responsibility connects your team and pays greater dividends.
- STOP adding on and really look at the traditions, events, and necessary meetings your school needs. Being at the school 24/7 isn't healthy for anyone. Limit the number of outside meetings/events. Stick to what matters most and enjoy the evening/Saturday...quality over quantity!
- STOP adding to your calendar when you know you are double booked. It's okay to say no, or respond, "I'm sorry, that time doesn't work for me. Can we find another time to connect?" No explanation needed.
- STOP aiming for deadlines; plan to be ahead of the game. Calendar out your evaluations with spring break as your deadline and your springs will be more peaceful.
- STOP saying YES to others and NO to yourself.

When leaders strategically prioritize families first, healthy careers are nurtured.

Syndee Malek has been working with Leaders for over 30 years. She works with one of the largest RESA's in Michigan and has served as Associate Executive Director of the Michigan Elementary and Middle School Principals Association. Syndee is currently working as a Suicide Prevention Coordinator for Growth Works, a non-profit organization that supports struggling youth. When Syndee is not planning professional development or leading leadership retreats, she enjoys spending time with her family, reading, gardening, and dreaming!

44

Stop Working Long Hours at Home
LENA MARIE ROCKWOOD, Ed.D.

Is there such a thing as work-life balance? What resonated with me from Syndee Malek in the previous chapter is that work-life balance only happens when it is planned intentionally. Managing time wide-open on the calendar after hours also deserves some harnessing.

Harness Harmony Rather than Trying to Balance the Scale

Several years ago, I chose BALANCE as my one-word focus for the year. I engaged with many others on social media in the one-word activity that launched the new calendar year with individualized focus. I was very mindful of the time that I was spending on school related tasks at home and felt I needed to establish balance between work and life. As the year progressed, I was intentional in my awareness of how I was spending my time. There were some areas of my time management and scheduling that needed attention immediately if there was to be any progress in reclaiming balance. The year progressed and I was able to fine tune some daily habits to work more effectively during the school day. As I was preparing for the next school year to start, I revisited my one word and concluded that there was no such thing as balance for me. I decided what I was really looking for was harmony between work and life.

> *"Balance is a feeling derived from being whole and complete; it's a sense of harmony.*
> *It is essential to maintaining quality in life and work."*
> *--Joshua Osenga*

Balance suggests there is an even or equal distribution of time in work and in life. It is unrealistic to think we can have equal quantities of time for each - it does not work that way for me. Trying to find balance was adding stress to my life and I was losing sight of my intended goals. Harmony made much more sense because it suggests an arrangement that creates a pleasant effect. For me, combining work and life to co-create a pleasant overall living experience resulted in HARMONY as the better description for what I was looking to achieve.

Educators have some obligations throughout the school year that demand more time be spent at school events outside the school day. There are times when life demands we not be at work because attention is needed at home. Harmony is created when we can acknowledge that work and life each pull our attention in various directions and sometimes compete for our time simultaneously while other times they can integrate synonymously. Sometimes work time and family time blend together when there are activities or functions at school where your family joins to support your work. These can result in very rewarding experiences that do not feel like work but accomplishes the work goal while balancing life in some way. The effect is harmony. There is no perfect schedule but there is a realistic one. Intentionally finding what is realistic for you is the key to finding that work and life harmony.

Do What You Enjoy So It Doesn't Feel Like Work

My dad was an amazing man! He was one of the most content people I have ever known. As a truck driver who earned his GED when he was in the Army, he was up before dawn and enjoyed every minute of his workday. His philosophy was to do what you enjoy so it does not feel like work. This is something that we have all probably heard before. His wisest words included the advice to remember that you have a job to enable you to enjoy your life. He felt that if your focus was solely on work, you may have more money, but you would not have time to enjoy life. Those words have always stuck with me and became even clearer as I worked to find balance during that year. I'd like to offer the same question to you that my dad often asked me while growing up, "Do you work to live or live to work?"

"Either you run the day, or the day runs you."
--Jim Rohn (Motivational Speaker)

If you are spending several hours on work related tasks outside your work hours, you might want to ask yourself a few questions. Does it make you content to work long hours? Is your overworking fulfilling another need? Is your ambition to advance causing you to overwork? Are you working inefficiently? Why do you need to work long hours? These questions are a good start for better understanding the healthiness of your career. No matter your answers to these questions, attention is needed to avoid working long hours at home.

Schedule What You Prioritize
Workaholics often create work and as a result end up working inefficiently. Long hours can result in increased stress which has a negative impact on productivity. In addition, stress can lead to sleeplessness which leads to a myriad of other issues that can impact your ability to do your job. You might be more susceptible to health issues that lead to absenteeism that leads to more stress and the cycle continues. The ability to make decisions, monitor your reactions to a situation, and general communication can be impacted as a result which will hinder your ability to lead. Leaders set the tone and model the way, so we need to be mindful of how our actions are perceived. Valuing overworking is not the kind of culture school leaders should promote.

"Time is the coin of your life. It is the only coin you have, and only you can determine how it will be spent. Be careful lest you let other people spend it for you." -Carl Sandburg (poet)

Most school leaders more than likely put in lots of extra hours each week. Leaders should look at how they spend those hours. Is the added work a result of an unanticipated project or event? If you answered yes, this is the harmony piece I wrote about earlier. There are times when "unexpected work" presents itself. However, if the "unexpected work" is due to inefficient planning and you should have known in advance, you will need to look at your own routines and work habits. Is it your routine to work long hours at home? You should evaluate how you work to identify the reason for the need to work added hours at home. Perhaps there is an issue with the way you manage your time. Maybe it is the manner of your efficiency when approaching a task. Whatever the reason, you will not make changes to improve if you do not intentionally assess where improvements can and/or should be made.

Assessing your work habits and routines will allow you to look at the real work you are doing. I found that scheduling some of my tasks allowed me to have a more intentional plan to get things done. A colleague once said that if she does not put even the small things in her calendar then items are often not crossed off her list. This comment stuck with me. I have scheduled small tasks in my calendar, and I have found this to be a more effective and efficient routine than a simple to-do list. The calendar event forces my attention on the task. Time can be diverted in many ways for a school leader so a calendar event may help manage your day more efficiently.

"The key is not to prioritize what's on your schedule, but to schedule what you prioritize."-Stephen Covey

Don't Forget to Make a Life
Work hours can take control of your life with negative impacts on your quality of life and living. You need to prioritize your time and include personal time in the mix. Overworking can result in broken personal relationships and professional burnout. School leaders need to avoid this. Find the things that bring you joy. Are you able to engage in these things regularly or are you too busy working? If you are too busy working to enjoy life, you should set some goals and boundaries to ensure that you are able to enjoy life too. I am a passionate reader and have always ended my days reading a book. I know when it is time to adjust my schedule and better manage my time when several days pass and I have not been able to read. The simple act of reading each day brings me joy and I feel a sense of imbalance when I do not have that reading time. I must admit that I do get a little cranky if a few days go by without reading. Other people in my life notice the difference in my mood. That is proof that how you spend your time can impact your demeanor. I am aware that my crankiness may also impact interactions in my leadership role. Knowing this about myself makes me more aware of how I manage my daily time.

Set some priorities and goals for each day so you are efficient with your time. This needs to include taking care of yourself - find something that brings you joy, find a hobby or something you are passionate about, honor family time, focus on your health and well-being. Prioritize yourself! You are important! Realize there may not be a perfect work-life balance. Taking steps to improve your quality of life will lead to more efficiency in your work while providing added time to enjoy your life.

"Don't get so busy making a living that you forget to make a life." -Dolly Parton

I can't help but think about getting ready to take a vacation. As we prepare to be away from work, we make sure we complete certain tasks and communicate important information so our vacation will not be interrupted by loose ends left at work. What if we approached the end of each day as if we were going on vacation? Plan a set time to leave school each day. Tie up the loose ends before you leave so you can prioritize your time and focus on living your life until the next morning. That might be a way to place the importance of working to live instead of living to work. This approach can lead to improved quality of life, improved work performance, and overall increased productivity. In addition, there will be more time to focus on personal growth, professional growth or both because it will not seem like there is one more thing to do.

Your Dash Tells Your Story
In the teacher book, *100 No-Nonsense Things That ALL TEACHERS Should STOP Doing*, Jeff W. Evener wrote a similar chapter about teachers working long hours on schoolwork at home. He mentions the poem, The Dash by Linda Ellis. I heard this poem recited at a funeral several years ago and it left a lasting impression on me.

The Dash Poem
I read of a man who stood to speak at the funeral of a friend.
He referred to the dates on the tombstone from the beginning to the end.

He noted first came the date of the birth and spoke the following date with tears.
But he said what mattered most of all was the dash between the years.

For that dash represents all the time that they spent life on Earth.
And now only those who loved them know what that little line is worth.

For it matters not how much we own, the cars, the house, the cash.
What matters is how we live and love, and how we spend our dash.

So, think about this long and hard. Are there things you'd like to change?
For you never know how much time is left that can still be rearranged.

If we could just slow down enough to consider what's true and real,
and always try to understand the way other people feel.

Be less quick to anger and show appreciation more,
and love the people in our lives like we've never loved before.

If we treat each other with respect and more often wear a smile,
remembering that this special dash might only last a little while.

So, when your eulogy is being read with your life's actions to rehash,
would you be proud of the things they say about how you spent your dash?

It's all about "the dash" that appears on your headstone. How does this dash define you? What filled those years of your life? Is it defined by overworking and living to work? Or is it defined by a life well lived that was filled with shared memories of strong relationships and harmony? You have the choice to write the story of your dash. You might strive to find work-life balance or choose to use the word harmony instead. Whichever you choose, remember that self-care can help improve your quality of life when it feels as if you are living to work instead of enjoying life.

Dr. Lena Marie Rockwood spent the last 22 years as an educator in the same district. The last 14 have been as an assistant principal at the elementary, middle, and high school levels. This resulted in her working with some students in the Class of 2021 since they were in kindergarten and many others for several years overall. She believes in unique and amazing experiences for all!

45

Stop Staying Late at School or the Office
NICK POLYAK, Ed.D.

As a young teacher and administrator, I worked in a school district that felt very competitive like the scenario that Lisa Blank shared in Chapter 42. My supervisors got to work very early in the morning and stayed very late at night. Whether intentional or not, the lesson to all of us was that part of our value was our willingness to put in long hours at school and this didn't even account for the long working hours at home that Dr. Lena Marie Rockwood shared in Chapter 44. This competitive climate was set by the leadership and ingrained in the organization over the years. Harmony was nonexistent as I missed many family events, either because I was working late or because I needed to get to sleep to wake up early. Fortunately, our four children were very young, and they didn't know the hours I was keeping at work. Unfortunately, my wife was very aware, and that wasn't fair to her, or to us, or to our family. As Syndee Malek shared in Chapter 43, I had fallen prey to prioritizing my career over my family. From there, I had the opportunity to move my family from suburban Chicago to central Illinois to become a superintendent.

Shift Expectations

I was following the retirement of a wonderful, long-time superintendent. He and his wife had grown children and they regularly attended many evening events throughout the school district. They were regular fixtures at sporting events, fine arts performances, and many other school and community events. During my transition, I was able to see his level of involvement and I assumed that there would be an expectation of the same from me. Aside from those perceived outside pressures, I was also putting pressure on myself. As the new superintendent, I was the only new administrator in the district, and I was also the youngest administrator in the district at that time. I wasn't going to let people think I was slacking in my new role.

I vividly remember that first day on the job - I was the first one in the parking lot that day. My prior experiences had taught me that if people saw my car in the lot first, it meant I was working hard. As it got later in the day, my wife called me and asked what time I would be coming home. I said I wasn't sure. A couple hours later, she called again and asked me the same question. She wanted to make dinner but didn't know when to expect me. Very honestly, I told her, "I don't know when people go home. I'm not sure if I'm waiting for them to leave or if they are waiting for me to leave. But I'm surely not going to ask anyone what my hours are!"

Over those next four years as the superintendent there, I tried to be who I thought I should be or who I thought people expected me to be. I tried to be at every school event possible and I tried to be the husband and the father that my family needed at home. Spoiler alert - that is a recipe for frustration and disappointment. At the end of those four years, I don't know that I felt like I had filled any of those roles as effectively as I had wanted to. With my kids growing up and getting more and more involved in sports and activities - I knew my expectations and priorities needed to shift.

Establish Priorities that Nurture a Healthy Career
For the past nine years, I have been honored to serve as the superintendent in my current school district. I was very upfront and honest with the School Board that was interviewing me. I explained that I was committed to being a superintendent who makes a difference in the lives of students, but equally committed to be the man that my family needs me to be. We had open conversations about our district placing a high value on family, both within the school community and individually.
I'm happy to report that because of this courageous leadership conversation I was able to take a markedly different approach the second time around. I still arrive to work early most mornings, but that is so that I can exercise in the school's fitness center. That is a time of day where I can take care of my own health without impacting the requirements of my job or time with my family. There are still plenty of nights where I need to work late or attend evening events. That is a reality for school administrators and that doesn't go away. However, most nights I head home right away to have dinner with my family or to attend my kids' sporting events and other school activities. Like Syndee Malek recommended I schedule regular date nights with my wife.

Set the Example

When I reflect on those early years of my career, much of my time was spent following suit of how my leader modeled the expectations. Now that I am in a leadership position, I have had to remind myself that my actions are setting the tone for the people around me. If I model the importance of family and working to find harmony, hopefully others will pick up on that and follow the lead. Certainly, it gives them permission to try to strike a balance in their lives.

At the end of our careers, nobody gives out awards for whose car is in the parking lot the longest every day. Even if there isn't a spouse, a partner, or a child at home waiting, we all need to prioritize self-care and life balance the best we can. Make time for a hobby, walk your dog, go out with friends, do whatever makes you happy and gives you purpose outside of the professional part of your life.

Working in the field of education is an honor and a blessing. The work we do is incredibly important. Every single day, we have the chance to make positive impacts on the lives of kids and help them achieve outcomes that are even better than they thought possible. Never forget that. And while that is all true, we will all retire someday and pass the reins to someone else. When that day comes, we will want our loved ones there to celebrate and enjoy those retirement years with us. If you want those people to be there then, make time for them now. Stop staying late at school.

Dr. Nick Polyak serves as the Superintendent for Leyden Community High School District #212 in suburban Chicago. Nick is a co-moderator of #suptchat, the monthly international Twitter Chat for Superintendents. He has co-authored The Unlearning Leader: Leading for Tomorrow's Schools Today, Student Voice: From Invisible to Invaluable, and The Unfinished Leader: A School Leadership Framework for Growth and Development.

46

Stop Underestimating the Power of an Empathetic Leader
MICHELLE OSTERHOUDT

"Leadership is about empathy. It's about having the ability to relate to and connect with people for the purpose of inspiring and empowering their lives." -Oprah Winfrey

The Oxford English Dictionary defines empathy as the ability to understand and share the feelings of others. Unlike sympathy, empathy doesn't involve feeling sorry for others. It is also not about how we would feel or deal with a situation. It is about putting ourselves in other people's shoes. It truly is about care, not pity. What does this have to do with leadership? This: great leaders value people. Great leaders are empathetic leaders. Scenario: I was having a conversation with a colleague. I mentioned that one of my staff members was struggling. Their immediate response was, "That's hard for me Michelle, everyone has "stuff." While I agree, not all of us have the level of resiliency that this colleague has. Isn't it a kinder approach in these times to be caring? In a world focused on the needs of our students—which I vehemently agree with—let's not forget that our educational staff have social emotional needs and struggles too. And while some of us are more resilient than others, we cannot ignore those who are struggling. Especially if we are to be successful leaders.

Empathy Guides Awareness of Employee Needs
As a leader, being in tune to your employees' social and emotional needs is paramount to the success of the organization. The last year and a half—teaching through difficult times— has proven that those of us who are deemed essential have a burden to care for others in ways that we had never anticipated, or to the level that we were expected to. When schools were shuttered due to the pandemic–parents became even more aware of the importance of school. Children across the country were feeling the loss of school and social connection. Rising numbers of depressed children returning to school has caused alarm to educators. Teachers carry the weight of their students' struggles with them beyond the school day. They need support and follow through from their leader's listening ear, the granting of grace when needed, and thoughtful appreciation for those who go above and beyond. When you listen and show empathy, your staff will be more likely to open up to you. This will foster faith and trust in our leadership.

Empathy Builds Trust
As leaders, when we are willing to lead with empathy, we build trust with our staff. They are able to articulate their needs more clearly. More importantly when they trust us, we can move in the direction we need to go in. Whether it be buy-in with new educational initiatives or building collective efficacy among staff, trust will help you! As a leader when you have trust from your colleagues and staff, you have the ability to create a culture that can drive behavior, which in turn can produce results. The power of culture lies in our ability to engage the hearts and minds of our staff members.

Just recently I experienced a bittersweet moment with one of my teachers. We were outside with a student who was dysregulated. He is in our classroom for autistic children. This teacher does a remarkable job with him. Due to the pandemic, we started this classroom with less-than-ideal support. But it's gotten better throughout the year. This particular day was a difficult day. And it was probably the third difficult day of the week. This student was outside of the building refusing to come in. He was very heightened, and several staff members had already tapped in and out to assist this classroom teacher. I came to keep her company while we kept an eye on the student. At one point, we were discussing our frustration and I offered her a hug. During that hug we both started to cry. I had never done that before–not in front of a teacher. And I maintain that it was not a moment of weakness. It was me being authentic in the moment because I was feeling as though I was a failure. I didn't have the answer for this teacher with regard to how to deal with his child. And in that moment, she realized that I was feeling the way that she had been feeling for so long. While I know this teacher has struggled and even thought about quitting, she hasn't. She said, "I know you hear me Michelle, I know you're listening, and I know you support me. I will do my best." I'm not going to assume that she didn't quit her job because of me. But I do know that I built trust with her because I showed her empathy. I also showed her that I struggle too.

Rapport and Relationships
Through some of the most difficult times in my leadership career, I have connected with staff as we struggle through complicated situations like the one above. These are the things that help build relationships with the people who work for us and with us. We can be empathetic leaders and still be "the boss.' I'm reminded of a quote from the book *Crisis Management: Effective School Leadership to Avoid Early Burnout*, by Larry Dake, "trusting relationships are centered around respect and mutual need. School leaders need strong staff, and staff need strong school leaders.".

At that moment the teacher knew that she could trust me, and I knew I could trust her. It's a mutual respect and symbiosis that Larry Dake talks about in the first chapter of his book. This didn't happen overnight. I had to grow as a leader and my staff had to grow to trust me. It took well into my fourth year as a building principal to finally feel like I had this type of relationship with most of my staff. Without a doubt I know it's because I led with empathy and listened with an open heart in mind. As I continue to improve and reflect on my practice, I believe that empathetic leadership fosters the trust and relationships needed to move staff in the right direction of doing what is best for students.

Michelle Osterhoudt is a wife, mother, and 23-year educator and community leader. Active in civil rights work within her community, Michelle also serves as the Vice President of the Oneonta Area NAACP. She currently serves as the proud Superintendent of the Margaretville Central School District. Michelle hopes to impact the ability to reach all children with equitable and diverse educational experiences that provide opportunities for lifelong learning and success.

47

Stop Doubting Yourself
LIVIA CHAN

Think back to the last time you encountered a "never experienced before" type of situation. The type where your heart was racing. Your mind was rapidly firing inaudible questions. What if this? What if that? What should I say? What should I do? And quite possibly the onset of panic set in like someone skydiving for the first time, getting pulled over by law enforcement, or presenting in front of a large and influential audience. Every leader at some point in their career has experienced anxious adrenaline pumping thoughts and feelings in response to a stressful situation. Leaders are routinely cast into high emotion-driven leadership scenarios that require pulling the parachute handle, explaining with precision to a police officer that a car that just cut you off, or facing the fear of public speaking to your colleagues and leaders.

Self-doubt can range anywhere from a waning thought to perseverating all-consuming regret. Take for example when a student discloses information that is time sensitive requiring an immediate response. Or a teacher may share their uncomfortable conflict with a colleague. A parent may show up unannounced and upset about a decision you made regarding their child. Senior Administration may tap you on the shoulder for a big district project you didn't feel equipped for. Every day, leaders are bombarded and expected to navigate a myriad of challenges on the spot and other times resolution is distributed over time. Sometimes in the moment, time seems to bend until a decision is made. Many decisions are urgent while others have the luxury of time and collaboration. In any type of decision-making scenario, self-doubt can permeate and consume our thoughts and even linger long after the resolution has taken place.

What is Self-Doubt?
Ah, enter self-doubt. Doubt is a feeling of uncertainty and insecurity and more often felt when faced with a challenge or a new situation when a person is just not 99% certain of the outcome. This is a typical feeling when those in a new role do not have the experience or enough information or confidence to determine the best course of action.

Self-doubt seems to rear its head more readily as leaders progress through new situations. New experiences, opportunities, and facing the unknown are par for the course in leadership. Some level of self-doubt is necessary as a check and balance confirmation that we are making the best decision. Assuming the perspective of the other person(s) at stake is essential in solid decision-making. But don't let self-doubt immobilize you from deciding. Timing is crucial in many situations and there's only so much time you can buy. Regulating negative feelings of indecisiveness and unsureness require forethought, a plan, and intentionality or it will complicate things.

Self-Doubt Complicates Any Situation
As if it's not difficult enough to assess a challenging situation and make a solid decision given the facts at that time, self-doubt can complicate matters, taking up additional emotional energy and unnecessary time. This happens when leaders misunderstand themselves (or others) and waver or fall prey to indecision. Yes, second-guessing is a complication. Of course, leadership choices or decisions come in varying sizes and sometimes the bigger the decision, the more self-doubt leaders' experience.

Everyone's journey into leadership looks different. Leadership style looks different because of who you encountered along the way, experiences early in your career, the opportunities you have been afforded to lead, why you became a leader, and how you've grown since. There are numerous factors that impact solid decision-making:

- Influence of family and close friends
- Cultural influences and perspective
- Past experiences and opportunities
- Personal strengths and limitations
- Values and beliefs
- Leadership knowledge and experience
- Content knowledge and references
- Level of self-confidence

These and many more factors orchestrate how every leader uniquely makes decisions or resolves situations. Likewise, these same factors can influence second guessing in any situation. Variations in leadership style does not mean one leaders' response or resolve is better than another, it just means that every leader responds uniquely differently given their schema, the timing, and information at hand. One thing is for certain, when caught off guard every leader is susceptible to self-doubt especially if they are experiencing imposter syndrome.

Imposter Syndrome
According to Psychology Today (PT), "Similar to perfectionists, people with imposterism often put a lot of pressure on themselves to complete every task flawlessly; they fear that any mistake will reveal to others that they aren't good or smart enough for the job." PT also goes on to share that, "Around 25 to 30 percent of high achievers may suffer from imposter syndrome. And around 70 percent of adults may experience imposterism at least once in their lifetime, research suggests."

100 No-Nonsense Things That ALL School Leaders Should STOP Doing

Until I learned the term "imposter syndrome" I thought I was just experiencing self-doubt. For many leaders the pandemic ushered in continuous new opportunities and like me, many were afraid to make a mistake in this new frontier of education. Self-doubt can be viewed as weak, but truth be told, testing, and stretching our capacity to respond may not be such a negative thing. It forces us out of comfortability and aids us in leveling up in our careers. I have come to see that perhaps self-doubt can serve as that meek whisper that reminds us to be humble. I am appreciative of the unprecedented situations I was able to embrace during the pandemic, because I was willing to overcome imposterism and be vulnerable enough to fail trying.

I used to say to myself often, "Who am I to...?" especially in the presence of others with more experience and/or credentials. Pushing aside self-doubt took time and practice. Believing in myself also required time and practice. And becoming my own biggest cheerleader took time and practice. I had to learn how to talk to myself positively when the imposter in me came out to stifle my progress. I'd have to tell myself that I am on my own journey and not to compare myself to others. We each have our individual strengths to share and stories to tell and they are all worthy of telling.

Get to Know Yourself
Overcoming imposter syndrome and shedding leadership doubt requires self-confidence. Your strengths, talents, and stories are all prerequisites to self-confidence. You must seek to know yourself and define what you value and believe as part of your self-confidence journey. Try combating self-doubt and imposterism through self-confidence! When you are feeling an overwhelming sense of self-doubt, stop and breath. Listen deeply to what you are telling yourself. Use the acronym T.H.I.N.K.

> Is it TRUE?
> Is it HELPFUL (or HURTFUL)?
> Is it INSPIRING?
> Is it NECESSARY?
> Is it KIND?

This type of inner dialogue will anchor your purpose as a leader in a role for a reason. You have experience behind you. You were chosen to be in this role because others believed in you. Believe in yourself. If you're finding it difficult, then draw on the knowledge of colleagues and mentors that you trust. Whether you are new to your role or not, you have many leadership qualities to draw upon. Lean into your strengths and intuition. That's why it's important to truly know who you are, your purpose, your strengths, values, and beliefs.

Opportunities Are Gifts
Leading is a gift. As leaders we are "gifted" many opportunities to lead, have conversations, build

relationships, and make decisions. Every situation is unique. If we choose to embrace even the most challenging situations, as a gift it becomes an opportunity to learn and grow. Below are some steps that may help you navigate future opportunities.

Notice and name feelings: "I notice that I feel uncertain and insecure. This is self-doubt."

Acknowledge and appreciate feelings: "I acknowledge I have feelings of self-doubt. I appreciate this opportunity to ground myself in my strengths, recognize I have experiences I can draw upon, and move forward with a decision that will be aligned with my strengths, purpose, values, and beliefs."

Embrace & elevate feelings: "I can embrace the situation and affirm that my leadership is needed. I will recognize where I put my energy. I can elevate my feelings by learning as much as I can about the situation and not feed into the problem but instead focus on the solution. I can be my own biggest cheerleader and believe that I will make the best decision as I anchor into who I am, my purpose, and our shared vision given the facts before me. I will seek help and consult with trusted individuals, if needed, to check that what I am thinking is right. We are better and stronger together.

Whether we have self-doubt or not, decisions still need to be made. Most likely you will make mistakes in your leadership role but when leading with strengths, positive intentions, and a clear understanding of information, effective decisions can be made. Instead of thinking, "What if I am wrong?" think, "What if it turns out right?" Leadership is an opportunity to effect positive change and lead others to a healthy career.

Listen to your heart. Lead with your heart. Believe in yourself and have self-confidence!

Livia Chan is a Head Teacher, Author, and a member of the Teach Better Team. She is passionate about building relationships, teaching, learning, and leading with her heart. Livia lives by the belief that it is through every interaction that we can intentionally uplift others through our kindness and gratitude to brighten their day, make an impact on their lives, and an imprint on their hearts. She would love to connect with you on Twitter and other popular social media platforms at @LiviaChanL or at livchan.com.

48

Stop Trying to Be Perfect
JESSICA REED

Along the same lines as self-doubt and imposterism that Livia Chan shared in the prior chapter, perfectionism is equally challenging to manage as a leader. Many leaders determine their worth based on an invisible standard created fictitiously in their minds based on their perceptions and expectations of others. The truth of the matter is that a perfection bullseye is inordinately unrealistic. Perfectionism is a bunch of nonsense that kills healthy careers because nobody can measure up to an invisible standard that lacks clarity and communication.

Culture is built on one's mission, vision, values, and beliefs. Academic achievement and healthy careers are built on clear and high expectations, not fictitiously created invisible lines of perfection as the expectation. Often, teachers feel as though they are held to this unspoken standard of perfection by leaders. This chapter could easily fit in the previous section that addressed interacting harshly or irrationally as perfectionism is just that. Drawing invisible lines of perfection also aligns with this section that addresses misunderstanding yourself and others. Placing healthy careers in the bullseye is always a win for building culture.

Never Let Go of Your Idyllic Dream
Teaching is not just a job but a roller coaster of passion-fueled purpose. The emotional highs and lows that come hand in hand with teaching are not taught in teacher preparatory programs. Educators, new to the profession, do not leave their undergraduate experience prepared for the demand required to survive that first year.

The biggest lesson I learned my first year was that teaching is arduous work rather than the idyllic vision I once held throughout college and student teaching. My student teaching experience was so much fun because I had the opportunity to work with a classroom filled with gifted students. Students ignited learning connections that inspired a variety of extension activities for my lessons and idyllically showcased how to have fun in the classroom. It was a dream come true. I am grateful for this fulfilling experience; however, this idyllic experience contrasted my first year of teaching which turned out to be a cold hard dose of reality. While I enjoyed teaching and bringing out the best in my students, I did not experience a sense of belonging, support, or community. I always had this perfect vision of what type of teacher I was going to be and the perfect school that I was going to become a part of. I thought that I would be a teacher that would never raise her voice, receive students that listened to all my words with excitement in their eyes, and have an administrative team that supported me in all that I did. My idyllic dream of education was crushed by administrators of perfectionism rather than people.

I have been teaching for fourteen years and have served in several positions from instructional aide, general education teacher, behavior teacher, to my current role of middle school special education teacher. My yearning for fulfillment led me to try another school. It took some time to find a school that embraced me as a vital part of the school community. My idyllic sense of belonging was crushed because I knew this was not the norm for most in our profession. When I reflect on those first years of teaching, I cringe thinking about how I was committed to behaving in accordance with meeting invisible expectations of perfectionism over people. This false perception drove my life decisions in and out of my classroom. It was not until about four years ago that I finally found a school where I knew I was meant to be. I knew my imperfect idyllic sense of belonging would be possible because my administrative team supported my crazy dreams, by openly building upon my strengths. They saw my creativity, strengths, and talents, first.

When I talk about my dream of becoming a Google Innovator and presenting at various conferences, they nurtured this goal and sought ways to support my personal need for learning. Not only did they capitalize on my strengths, but they also expected failure as part of the growth process. They nurtured failure as the pathway of success. It was liberating to teach in a perfectionist free zone. I still consider these previous administrators my friends even though they have since moved on and leadership has changed. I'm happy to report that my new principal is just as big of a cheerleader for my idyllic dreams and to this day supports, nurtures, accepts, and leads me in growing forward as a better teacher and leader. If I had given up early in my career, I wouldn't be here today in a healthy career.

Offer Perfect Strength for People Not Fear of Perfection

Just as offering perfect strength as administrators goes to leading teachers, so too does it apply for teachers offering perfect strength to their students. What type of teacher am I now? I am not perfect by any means (nor do I want to be) but I have been perfected because leaders enhanced my strengths that allowed me to be a perfect strength for my students. Offering individualization through high standards, pushing students to learn and master standards, and meeting their IEP goals is grounded in understanding of strengths.

Just as Syndee Malek shared in Chapter 43, I am learning how important it is to set boundaries between work and home because of my family. And yes, past fear of perfectionism made this a tough lesson learned. Offering perfect strength includes life outside of school. This means spending time with my 4-year-old who talks non-stop about Paw Patrol; that's what I must offer at 8:00pm at night.

Detach From a Perfectionist Persona on Social Media

Educators around the world have experienced the unprecedented pressures as we head into our third year of the global pandemic of teaching. Perfectionism is rampant as social media places compounding pressure on teachers to maintain a visibly perfect classroom, perfect relationships with families, students, and perfect collaboration with fellow teachers. It is unrealistic to maintain a persona of perfectionism that was thrust on us upon us by the upheaval and dissonance of society.

Sometimes I think that social media is going to be the downfall of so many people because things on the internet do not go away, even if you think that you have deleted a picture, it still can be found. Social media has made it very easy for people to think that "so and so" has a perfect classroom, but the reality is that it is a snapshot that is often staged for an Instagram post or the creation of a Tik-Tok video. A persona. Life is not perfect by any means and social media can ruin it for any teacher. Just as Livia Chan shared in the prior chapter, we tend to experience imposter syndrome in the classroom. If we are to be perfected as teachers and offer perfect strength for our students, we must be strong enough to detach from the illusion of perfection.

You don't have to be perfect to be in the classroom. You don't have to be perfect to be a leader. You don't have to be perfect to be the perfect teacher for a child or leader of people.

Jessica Reed is a special education teacher in Georgia and is in her twelfth year in education. She received her ED.S. in Instructional Technology from Kennesaw State University and is a certified Google for Education Trainer and a Google Innovator (#NYC19). Jessica is married to Robby and they have one daughter, Elizabeth who is four.

49

Stop Avoiding or Ignoring Mental Health Needs
SHAWN BERRY CLARK, Ph.D.

*"Your mental health is more important than your education.
Better to have a degree of sanity than just a degree."-Unknown*

Stop putting everyone and everything ahead of you. How can you possibly lead others if you ignore your own mental health? Mental health is just as important as physical health. I would be lying to you if I said I go to therapy regularly or if I manage to prioritize my mental health on "the daily."

STOP Misunderstanding Yourself and Others

Your Mental Balance is Paramount for Leading Others

Fake it 'til you make it is an overused saying and not always advisable by some (seen as power posing or lacking authentic encounters) but I use an offshoot of this concept to provide a guide for my brain to change my behavior because behavior can influence biology. I recognized how important it was to work on feeling healthy on the inside so that I could more productively build capacity and lead people.

When leaders are mentally stable, productive leadership engagement and interactions are contagious to those around them because the brain(s) of those around them either catch up or catch on. For example, some therapists advise doing pushups when you feel anxious because it is difficult to combat the endorphins that arrive while exerting yourself. Although I don't drop down and do pushups in my office, I have experienced success in minimizing anxiety, fear, or negativity. When leaders are feeling down and/or not their personal best, productive leaders strive to shake it off. You may be tasked with walking into a coaching session, a heated meeting, or delivering a post-evaluation. When these emotions surface, consider the following strategies:

> **Begin the day with habits of self-care.** There are many digital apps that are immersive in meditation and calming techniques. I like to begin most days using the "Daily Calm" or the "Daily Trip" portion of the Calm app on my phone. Using a meditation app gets me mentally set to be a better coach and leader each day. On the app there was a session called "Circuit Breaker" which dealt with grounding yourself before you attempt to console or ground others that you interact with. It's literally giving a dose of oxytocin (the "cuddle hormone") to yourself by breaking a circuit when feeling fear, self-doubt, or anxiety.
>
> **Consider your strengths and past successes.** I think of my strengths and how I have so much to offer people because I believe people can change and that it should start with me. I even have a "happy" folder in the side drawer of my desk where I tucked away nice notes people have written in the past and even complimentary emails I have received. Focusing on the feelings of past successes will feed future success.
>
> **Use positive affirmations aloud in private.** I'm sure many of us are visualizing Stewart Smally from the Saturday Night Live clips saying, "I feel good, I feel great, I feel wonderful, and darn it, people like me." And although it is a parody in jest, there is psychological truth to the positive vibes you send out to the universe. Positive self-talk goes a long way in helping you feel balanced and allows you to be grateful for yourself before you attempt to assist others. Speaking these affirmations out loud sets forth a mental perception of adding value and resolution through cooperation.
>
> **Physically pose and visualize an outcome of success:** In the book, Presence: Bringing your

BOLDEST SELF to your *BIGGEST CHALLENGES*, Dr. Amy Cuddy shares ten principles to assist leaders with posing for success. She mastered Ted Talks, faced fears, mitigated adversity, and faced some of the world's biggest challenges.

> *"Before we even show up at the doorstep of an opportunity, we are teeming with dread and anxiety, borrowing trouble from a future that hasn't yet unfolded. When we walk into a high-pressure situation in that frame of mind, we're condemned to leave it feeling bad. If only I'd remembered to say this. . . . If only I'd done it that way. . . .If only I'd shown them who I really am. We can't be fully engaged in an interaction when we're busy second-guessing ourselves and attending to the hamster wheel in our heads – the jumbled, frenetic, self-doubting analysis of what we think is happening in the room. The excruciating self-awareness that we are, most definitely, in a high-pressure situation. And we're screwing it up. Exactly when we most need to be present, we are least likely to be." (p.17)*

She talks in depth about body language, gesturing, and yes, posing physically in your office for the outcome you want. Standing tall with fists on your waist, deep breath in and eyes to the sky, a simple posture of confidence may be all that your body needs to equip you to face a challenging situation with empathy, fairness, professionalism, and productive outcomes.

End the day with self-care. While I admit that I don't always put my physical health first (as evidenced by the addition of the COVID-19 pounds gained and my proclivity for Doritos dipped in anything and everything) my mental health is super important for keeping myself in balance. I do manage to walk most days of the week and let my face and body soak up sunlight, but I engage in these tasks because it clears my head, energizes me, and forces me to breathe differently. We can't safeguard the mental health of our colleagues or students if we haven't protected ourselves first.

Your Family's Mental Stability Must Be a Priority

To piggyback off Syndee Malek in Chapter 43, leaders must prioritize their family members over their careers. Up to this point in our careers most leaders regret and have feelings of guilt associated with missing milestones and memories with family members because of work. What I am about to share is emotionally extreme because a life ended most tragically.

When my sister, Renee, needed me the most I was not there for her. She would call at least weekly to chat and check in, but I would often ignore her calls. I was working in a school with very high needs and my attention was devoted to my new job and my newfound friends. I avoided talking to her because she was very depressed and had recently exited rehab. It was draining to listen to her episodes of mania and depression, and I admit that sometimes I just didn't know how to respond when the conversation got too deep and too dark. Being responsible for her happiness and health was not a role I was willing to take on. I certainly could have taken a more active role in listening to her or providing her resources to assist with her journey towards wellness. I was one of the very few family members that had the knowledge of what she was going through, who she was in touch with, and had a good relationship with, yet I was too busy living my own life to waste time helping her navigate hers.

In February 2018 my sister and I talked on the phone for over 30 minutes, and she sounded cheerful and was reminiscing about the insane times we had as sisters. Renee texted a picture to my brother and I a few days later - it was something only we would know and laugh about from our childhood. My brother did not respond, and I simply replied with a laughing emoji. Renee went missing a few days later. It took three days to find her, only to discover that I would not have to help her through life anymore. Renee was discovered locked in her Mercedes and had killed herself using a method known as Japanese detergent suicide. I will spare you the horrid details (plus you can Google it) but I will say that the only way I could identify her body was by describing a tattoo beneath the metal belt buckle of her jeans. Her death was so well planned that she didn't want anyone harmed in responding to the scene. She considered the first responders by leaving a giant written warning for EMS workers and law enforcement so they would not be harmed upon her discovery.

There is an audio message on my phone from my sister that I keep so I can remember her voice. She called me on my birthday two years before she died, and I had the forethought to keep it because I'd always known that she might not survive much longer. Instead of worrying about keeping that voicemail, I should have made a point to reach out to my sister and find ways to get her more help. I don't blame myself for her death, but I will blame myself if her death doesn't serve as a greater purpose in my action(s) or inaction(s), forever. Your family situation(s) may be as extreme as the one I encountered or more selfish like Syndee Malek described in her chapter. Regardless of the severity or simplicity of your family, they deserve you to be balanced enough to put them first. Ignoring emotions of family members fuels rejection and resentment that will be with you for a lifetime. Productive leaders are intentionally balanced and take action to ensure their mental stability is a top priority.

Your Colleagues' Mental Health Matters Much More Than You Think

It takes 1.54 seconds (I literally timed it) to ask a colleague "How are you doing?" When the look on their face says they are struggling but their response is "fine" it takes another 3.52 seconds to reach out and touch the person, pause, and ask "No, how are you really doing?" Time and words I should have spent on countless occasions.

As a former principal I can recall many occasions when I walked down the halls, passing hundreds of students, always attending to their body language, facial expressions, and tone. I seldom missed an opportunity to communicate with a student to make sure their voice was heard and that someone cared. So why then was it so difficult for me to do the same with the adults that I worked with? With shame I admit passing by teachers or assistant principals who looked sad (some, even with obvious signs of tears or recent crying) and did not say one word. I smiled at them for sure and made eye contact but failed to acknowledge pain and emotions.

Did I consider attending to the feelings and emotions of adults as weak? Did I assume since they were adults, they could take care of themselves? Would it have made me uncomfortable or sad to hear the pain of my colleagues? Was I too busy to care or spend time chatting with co-workers about their feelings? The answer is yes to all these questions.

I was only able to truly change my ways after one interesting experience. It was an experiment on my part that opened my eyes to how much the mental health of colleagues matters for the entire organization (and anyone they encounter). Let's call my co-worker, Summer. This is the gift she gave me: Summer showed up to work often looking red-faced and not pulled together, arrived late, and missed many deadlines. Being the leader in the building I, of course, provided her specific feedback with radical candor (see Kim Scott's work) which resulted in zero change to any of her behaviors even with the comparison. I was confused because Summer was an intelligent educator with very valuable experience. I continued to hold conversations with her, pointing out the specific areas in which she was underperforming. Exhausting all my expertise on feedback, I was forced to take a different route…I simply sat down across from her and asked, "Is something wrong? Are you alright?" What Summer taught me was invaluable. She said no one had really asked her how she was doing or feeling, and we had a long talk about ways she could get help and how I could support her through the situation (Side note: Summer was struggling with overconsumption of alcohol and would come to work hungover and admitted drinking due to her isolation, depression, and anxiety).

Our colleagues' mental health matters. Summer matters. Helping each other through mental health struggles had a tremendous impact on everyone around us. Summer eventually flourished on the job, provided mentorship for her peers, and created invaluable programs for students. We all gained a sense of community and care from Summer's journey towards well-being. Much like you can't give to others unless your mindset is healthy, our co-workers cannot give their best to others or the organization until they know how much they (and their mental health) matter. Addressing mental health through a lens of belonging and support shouldn't be taboo. You will save a lot of time and heartache if you will start asking your colleagues questions . . .

Stop being silent; start asking questions.
Stop being too busy to care.
Stop pretending it will go away.
Stop thinking people will get better on their own.

Dr. Shawn Berry Clark went from GED to PhD, has over a decade of experience as an administrator and district director, and currently serves as a Lead Transformation Coach for the SC Department of Education. She is the author of Using Quality Feedback to Guide Professional Learning: A Framework for Instructional Leaders and contributing author for 100 No-Nonsense Things That All Teachers Should Stop Doing.

STOP Making Decisions Haphazardly

This Type of Nonsense Stalls Action-Oriented Achievement Outcomes

Stop Obeying Orders Without Questioning When Something Isn't Right
CORY RADISCH

"If it ain't broke, then break it" -Marc Natanagara

"If it ain't broke, then break it!" Wait, that's not how the saying goes. There are many who believe things are not broken. There is an overabundance of achievement data that points to inconsistencies in learning opportunities across demographics and a national widening of the achievement gaps in schools. That isn't even convincing enough. Worse, there are many school leaders who know it's broken, but will continue to just obey orders despite the findings. It doesn't matter that the data tells a different story. In many places, if the adults are satisfied and comfortable, many leaders choose to participate in the "ain't broke" system. My longtime mentor, Marc Natanagara, used the opening quote of this chapter with staff. He intentionally challenged the status quo while also liberating leaders from a broken system. His aim was to inspire but also to let them know it's perfectly acceptable to break the system when it needs breaking. It was appropriate long ago and it's even more appropriate today. If we are going to truly transform education, then it may require leaders to stop obeying orders when they know something isn't right. We must stop obeying orders that:

- Marginalize students
- Perpetuate learning and opportunity gaps
- Disproportionately discipline students of color
- Disproportionately have fewer students of color in AP and advanced classes
- Allow your zip code to determine what level of education you receive
- Fail to recruit and retain teachers of color
- Teach a unilateral perspective of history

"We can choose courage, or we can choose comfort, but we can't have both." -Brené Brown

Break the System Don't Blow It Up
Keep in mind, breaking the system is not blowing up the system. Breaking the system is about addressing and interrupting implicit and explicit bias in our policies, curricula, and procedures. It is about identifying the systemic root causes that inhibit student (and staff) growth. Disobeying orders will undoubtedly cause discomfort. However, we need to stop obeying orders that continue to put the comfort of adults before the needs of our students. Adult comfort should never supersede the

discomfort of the students we serve. C'mon, when has breaking something not created discomfort? As Brené Brown says, "We can either choose courage or we can or we can choose comfort, but we can't have both!"

Do What's Best for Students, Not What's Easiest

Leaders have an obligation to do what's best, not what's easiest. Heck, every day we ask kids to face and overcome challenges. We ask kids to sit in their discomfort, learn from it, and be better. Leaders need to model this same behavior. There is only one reward for taking the easy path: IT'S EASY, THAT'S IT! Leaders must stop accepting the status quo. Veteran leaders need to stop hanging on to pad a pension instead of padding our students with hope and opportunity! New leaders need to stop being afraid to make tough decisions.

Please understand that disobeying orders doesn't mean you defiantly wave an admonishing finger in the face of authority, but it does mean questioning those orders (or the system) when you believe it's not in the best interests of your students. I am not naive to the cost associated with disobeying orders. I know firsthand that sometimes doing what's right comes with a price but there's no value in compromising your integrity.

I wrote a blogpost a few years ago titled, *"Road Rage in Schools."* The post shares how I had thought about the idea that when someone's behavior on the road can be detrimental to our own children, we find the courage to speak up and lash out. I pondered about the need for "road rage" in our schools. I decided we needed an addendum to the definition of road rage as it pertains to education. So, I decided to provide my personal definition of educational road rage.

> **Educational Road Rage:** the courage to speak up when we know that a student's best interests are not being met or with those colleagues whose actions earnestly don't align with the culture.

Overcome Your Status Quo Fears

Not accepting orders can be done with grace and tact. It first requires dispelling the myth that if you confront orders or challenge the status quo, that it will automatically end in bitter confrontation. Sometimes changing the trajectory of something, starts with asking this simple question: Does doing this equitably serve ALL our students? If the answer is yes, keep doing it. If the answer is no, it needs to stop. Here are three more no-nonsense things leaders need to stop being afraid of:

- Rattling the cage of status quo
- Addressing the elephant in the room when necessary
- To do what's right, even when it's unpopular

As an example, a principal I knew led the change in their building where they eliminated a level below college prep course when they uncovered a major disproportionality of students of color enrolled in this "lower" level course versus enrollment in honors and advanced placement courses. This was an unpopular decision. The principal designed and shared with staff an extensive professional development plan to meet the needs of the teachers and to quell their concerns. This unpopular decision was met with status quo roadblocks and pessimism because the principal didn't obey the order of keeping things "as is." Remember, orders aren't always overt directives from your supervisor or central office. This principal questioned how the system had operated because it clearly wasn't working. The system "as is" produced disproportionate data that revealed status quo results, at best. Despite anticipated backlash from the staff and community, the principal maintained their moral compass that focused on what is best for students, not what is easiest. The decision was made because all demographics of students deserved equitable access and opportunity to that school's best curriculum.

Have the Courage to Conquer the "What if"
Transformation of practice in any organization will have its peaks and valleys. We must stop viewing the valleys as a problem but rather as opportunities to equip those around us with action-oriented achievement outcomes. Solutions are often found amidst conflict and chaos of facing the status quo. Things will only go wrong if you are making decisions haphazardly. Educator, author, and presenter David Culberhouse say's it best. "If you aren't willing to ask what if, you will always be left with what is!"

"I would rather have questions that can't be answered than answers that can't be questioned."
--Richard Feynman

We, as educational leaders and regardless of title, need to stop being afraid to pose questions when given orders. Be courageous, make decisions intentionally, and continually ask, "What if..."

What orders are you ready to question?

Cory Radisch is an equity advocate currently serves as a Continuous Improvement Specialist for the NJDOE working to support schools identified for support under ESSA. As a former building principal he has made equity a priority working to narrow achievement and discipline gaps. He is a dynamic presenter who has worked with schools across the country in facilitating the implementation of PBSIS and PLCs. He is currently the Co-Host of The StatusGROW Podcast @_statusGROW.

Stop Carrying Out Initiatives that Only You Enjoy
AGGIE SALTER

Since I was a young girl growing up in Poland, my dream was to be a music teacher. I always believed music can make us feel better, heal our hearts, and inspire others. That was the message that I wanted to share with the world. It didn't take me long to realize that there is much more complexity to teaching elementary music than just my idyllic childhood dream.

Electives are Always the First to Go
I did the math and realized I had seven principals and seven superintendents in the eighteen years of teaching in the same school. On average, I had the same administrative team for a maximum of three years. There are so many issues with this alone, but I am not going to go there. I quickly learned every time I had a new administrator joining our school district, there was always a chance my position or funds within this position could be eliminated. Each of these transitions would bring anxiety and the feeling of once again having to sell and advocate for my elective subject as the new administrative team was looking at budget cuts. Of course, it took me years to connect the dots and realize that the upset stomach and fatigue I was having every other August or so were brought on by the fear of meeting and trying to impress the new administrator.

The Innovation Adoption Life Cycle
As in business, there are several ways that teachers will respond when leaders adopt new initiatives, technology, curriculum, or programs. The Innovation Adoption Life Cycle is also known as the Technology Adoption Curve and originally referenced as the theory of Diffusion of Innovation by Dr. Wayne LaMorte back in 1962 and according to the article, *Technology Adoption*, on hellowiota.com:

> "The theory rests upon the fact that different people have different propensities to accept a new product or idea, and that this results in acceptance of new things taking time as they slowly build into a crescendo. The two 'adopter categories' that precede 'the chasm' are called innovators and early adopters. It stands to reason that the innovators are most scarce since only a few people have the time

and enthusiasm to constantly search for the newest project. It's hard to live on the cutting edge! Early Adopters are the group that fills out 'early market' composition before the new technology can advance into mainstream adoption."

According to Business-to-you (B2U) in their article, *Crossing the Chasm in the Technology Adoption Life Cycle*, they share a cycle of acceptance that leaders experience when onboarding a new technological product or innovation based on Everett M. Rogers book, *Diffusion of Innovations*. I would propose that the adapted graphic below can easily be applied to the various types of teachers and their willingness to change, adopt, or embrace a new way of teaching.

Change in Education Life Cycle

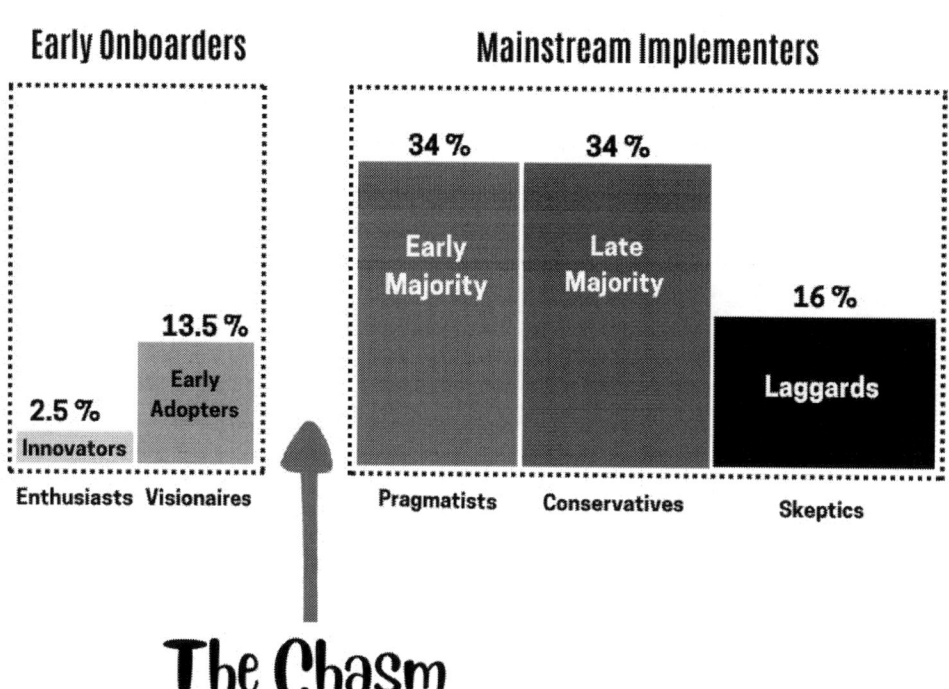

Early Onboarders
- 2.5% Innovators (Enthusiasts)
- 13.5% Early Adopters (Visionaires)

Mainstream Implementers
- 34% Early Majority (Pragmatists)
- 34% Late Majority (Conservatives)
- 16% Laggards (Skeptics)

The Chasm

Consider the following teacher scenario as it pertains to the education life cycle of change. Throughout my years as a music teacher, I witnessed all fourteen of my principals show up with their own passion projects, agendas, and must-do first-year initiatives because it is what they enjoy or comfortable doing. Luckily, by nature I am an innovator and an early adopter of a change. I learned early on to embrace change and jump right into the "chasm" of the brave. Change was going to happen "to me" so embracing change always minimized leadership conflict. As a result, I was always the first teacher that would buy into new initiatives, goals, and educational practices that would change our school. I was so good at being the early adopter, I was called "admin's pet" because I was encouraged by my principal to share my enthusiasm with the skeptical laggards.

This Too Shall Pass
Change seems to be the only constant in education especially when it comes to initiatives. In my twenty-three years in education, I have never visited a school that did not have its mission, vision, values, and goals visibly posted at their school and available on their district website. However, the educators that I meet tend to agree that each time a new administrator is hired for the building, the leader arrives with a personal agenda and educational initiative that seem to rank higher than the district strategic plan. When initiatives are administratively selected, two things happen: none of the long-term district goals are attained, and none of them have the dedicated time allotment to be successfully implemented with fidelity. Neither of which have the success of students as the focus.

Administratively adding school goals and changing initiatives tend to create a culture of, "Here we go again with the new stuff." Slowly, this type of a passive attitude solidifies the status quo just as Cory Radisch shared in the prior chapter. One of the worst phrases in education is, "This is how we have always done it." This mindset sneaks into the school climate when decisions serve the enjoyment or interests of the leaders rather than an action-oriented student achievement focus. When the status quo is accepted, the late majority and laggards wholeheartedly embrace a "this too shall pass" mindset that stalls action-oriented achievement outcomes.

Focus on What is Best for Students
In any line of business, the most critical action a leader can take to establish a solid foundation is taking the time to strategically observe. Note the strengths of individuals, strengths of systems, strengths in culture, and make a list of what is working. Even in the most challenging school, you can identify people and processes that are student focused. As you come across challenges and deficits within the system of a school or organization, consider the following questions before adding more to the plate:

- Does this require a new initiative altogether or just a new understanding?
- Are my decisions haphazard or do they drive student achievement outcomes?
- What data do I have to support making changes to, or adding additional initiative?
- Is there time allotted to carry it out with fidelity?

100 No-Nonsense Things That ALL School Leaders Should STOP Doing

- Do I have enough time and/or resources to inspect what I expect?
- Will this allow other initiatives to be removed, replaced, or eliminated?
- Do I have the relationships and culture to come to a collective consensus?
- How will I give stakeholders a voice in the adoption process?
- How does this relate to other initiatives?
- Does your new initiative come from your feelings and emotions?
- Am I passionate about the new goal?
- Do I have a strategic plan for rolling this out?
- Does this new initiative align with my purpose?
- Am I willing to visibly demonstrate through my actions my dedication to the new goal?
- Do I have a process or plan for addressing adversity when things start to fall apart?

"When leaders want to implement change, the new initiative needs to be driven by emotions (passion for the new goal), objective thinking (data that supports the need for change), and behavior (everyday actions which align with the initiative and your purpose)."–Brené Brown & Simon Sinek

When leaders implement a new initiative based solely on emotions, rather than using excitement or the fear factor to get staff on board, it will fall apart as soon as you leave or look the other way. If you move forward based on the numbers and data which documents the change needed, people may not put their heart into it because they have no emotions or personal connection toward your goal. Systemic change is successful when our initiatives sit on the three-legged stool of emotions, thinking, and behavior. In my early years teaching music, if I only focused on music and the things I enjoyed, I wouldn't have impacted my school as an early adopter. I wouldn't have been seen as a team player, and I wouldn't have impacted our school achievement goals. Likewise, leaders must not carry out initiatives that only they enjoy.

Aggie Salter is the Instructional and Professional Development Specialist/Coach and Innovation Teacher in Madison, WI, who provides training for various Midwest school districts. At 16 years old, she immigrated to the United States from Poland, received BA from Ripon College, MA from Stevens Point, and later became Apple Teacher, Apple Learning Coach, Google for Education, and NEARPOD Trainer. She shares her passion for learning and coaching by presenting at ISTE, DelCe, Google Summits, SLATE and is one of the EdCampMadWI organizers as well as the Digital Promise Global Couch Community Manager. Aggie also worked on piano instructions with Quincy Jones and Playground music. She was the Quarter-Finalist for the GRAMMY Music Educator Award in 2016.

52

Stop Saying "Kids First" When You Make a Decision
JILL WORLEY

The Real Debate
Stop taking a literal approach to the topic. All school leaders, teachers, parents, and other stakeholders want to put kids first in the sense that, as a collective whole, we want students to have a successful and enjoyable school experience. No one is debating this concept. Instead of diving into the definition and syntax of the "kids first" phrase, let's skip to why this is an issue and acknowledge how this message can generate a negative interpretation and hinder the school culture. When hearing a school leader is making a choice to put kids first, this has the potential to make a teacher or staff member feel like their own opinions are not being taken into consideration, even if this is not the reality of the situation. Asking yourself "Is this what is best for our students?" is an important step during the decision-making process but cannot be the justification for all decisions made.

Pulling the "Kids First" Card
As a school leader, the easiest way to justify any decision is to assure your audience that you are basing your decision on the positive benefits students will yield socially, emotionally, and/or academically. You can pull the "Kids First" card for almost any decision. The following questions demonstrate how this works.

Should we enforce a schoolwide homework policy?
Yes, because we want to prepare students for a rigorous next step in their educational careers.
No, if we want students to give their all every day at school, they need ample time for afterschool activities, sports, church, family, etc.

Should we host an after-school student dance next month?
Yes, our students work so hard that they deserve the opportunity.
No, we do not want to interrupt the academic focus of our students with an event that may cause unnecessary stress and drama between peers.

Despite the polarizing answers to the same question, one cannot argue that the outcome is what is in the best interest of students, however, these answers lack any input from other stakeholder groups. The answers also omit consideration of equally important factors such as current data and logistical restraints like the school budget, preparation time, available personnel, and additional resources. Decisions should be data-driven, factor social-emotional wellbeing, and be made with a holistic mentality that aligns with the mission of the school.

School leaders must look at decisions from every angle and understand there will always be opposing views. Some decisions are not what is best for every student but for the greater good. Some are even made knowing the reality of the system we must operate in (like preparing students for state testing as opposed to making every assessment project-based). At times, decisions are made to ease the burden of the teacher to avoid burnout which would have even greater consequences. Occasionally, we have to appease an angry parent and go along with what they want for their child even when we know it is not in the best interest of the student. Also, saying "kids first" doesn't work if the teacher is out of touch with reality or not progressive or innovative. How many times have you heard a teacher say, "But they should know how to..." when talking about non-standardized and/or relevant skills like teaching cursive handwriting or putting more time into spelling vs. vocabulary? When making decisions as a school leader, along with the logistics and realistic expectations, consider the interpretation of your rationale from the vantage point of all stakeholders.

In an Ideal World

Have you noticed it is the same staff members sponsoring unpaid after-school activities, setting up for after-school events, and volunteering to help when needed? Take a minute and name the people who pulled out of the parking lot at the same time as you after the last school event. Is it the same group of teachers and staff members who helped the previous time volunteers were needed? If not, consider yourself blessed with an amazing school staff. Most school leaders must spend time strategizing on how to gain collective consensus from the staff whenever volunteers are needed, or changes are coming. Let's go back to the people you named. These school success-oriented team members are the ones who naturally put kids first. You can see the passion in their eyes. They don't hesitate to put in the extra work or time if it means a better school experience or opportunity for students. They are the ones smiling when they overhear you slip up and try to encourage a difficult teacher to do something just because it is in the best interest of their students.

Let's look at the rest of your staff. We are all on the same page that it is a challenge to be a superstar every single day of the school year, but between trying to balance mental health and personal issues, some staff members struggle just to get through the day without anyone noticing they are hanging on by a thread. Due to their current circumstances, they might not currently have a student-centered mindset and are more interested in their own needs. If you try to get them to do something by drilling down the "kids first" mantra, they might start thinking about when they are going to tell the rest of their team about this awkward conversation and how they will update their resume and possibly write a resignation letter this evening. A teacher might be trying to put kids first—their own kids, which they should not have to feel guilty about.

As a rule of thumb, never ask an employee to do something you would never do yourself, but if the request involves putting the employee in a position where they must give up personal time or put forth extra energy, think about how you would like to be approached with the request. As a school leader, we have all been faced with a situation where you are trying to convince someone or a group of people to just agree to do something and the predominant and logical reasoning is because it is in the students' best interest, and we all want what is best for our students. Unless your school culture is better than most, this tactic is not ideal. Next time you have the urge to take the easy way out and use the "kids first" rationale for a decision, stop and think about how the message will be interpreted by your audience.

Jill Worley served as a school administrator and teacher for sixteen years. She is now the Operations Manager at the International Board of Credentialing and Continuing Education Standards (IBCCES) in Jacksonville, FL.

Stop Forgetting that All Staff Play Major Roles in Supporting Students
RON O'CONNOR

Education has many moving pieces. The problem is that certain groups of employees both certified and non-certified provide services that aren't necessarily seen or appreciated. For instance, the business office worries about balancing books, payroll, and purchases. Custodians prepare the physical building, but typically hear complaints on how something is not clean enough. Also, some staff don't appreciate colleagues and view them as competition. Aides, secretaries, teachers, district office staff, custodians etc. become their own cliques within districts. On a social level it is organic to spend more time with those most like you and that understand you from a day in and day out perspective. But if not tended to, haphazard leadership can divide certified staff against non-certified, disconnecting teams, and inadvertently creating a multitude of silos. Unless district leaders are intentionally driving the district's mission, vision, values, and goals with a laser focus on action-oriented achievement outcomes, they will be left putting out fires, one silo at a time.

There is no "I" in Team
Everyone is part of *THE* team. As the district team, we should be focused on the bridges and interconnections to one another that lead to achievement outcomes for students. Consider every employee in the district from bus driver, nurse, cafeteria worker, crossing guard aid, master teacher, administrator, to school board member as a group of "Super Friends" - a collective and synergistic team of people focused on providing every student a world class learning experience. No one individual can accomplish this type of outcome. Fragmented or isolated teams do exist in our profession. This may not occur in every district, but many of the examples I'm about to share do exist in our arenas.

> **Secretaries** are the ambassadors of everyone in the building. They are at the front line of our campuses and are the first ones to connect resources and people when our students are in need. Secretaries are the face of the school and set the tone for others who visit our schools. Secretaries are positionally powerful when it comes to creating community perceptions and facilitating culture.

> **Instructional aides** connect with students due to their individualized assistance. They are there to assist the teacher in a curricular/instructional role. Teacher aides bond with students, advocate for students, interact with families, and contribute to the school climate and culture. They are high value and positionally pivotal for student learning. How many times have you experienced an instructional aide picking up copies for the class rather than assisting in 1:1 instruction? Preserving their value is a "Super Friends" move. Anything less stalls achievement outcomes.

> **Custodians** are the eyes and ears of the hallways. They should be seen as a high-added value for the well-being of children, yet they are underutilized. When a challenge arises at school during lunch, transition times, or even school culture. How often do leaders pause to ask

custodian "Super Friends" how they view it from their perspective? They hear conversations that may impact a school's environment. Custodians contribute to the culture of the building. A clean, safe place is essential for a healthy environment both mentally and physically. Humming a tune, wearing an encouraging shirt, giving a kind word of encouragement, or taking a moment to model integrity all contribute to a thriving school. At times, custodians are looked to just for cleaning messes rather than contributing more as emotional support of kids and/or for being a human with emotions too. Under valuing custodians, undersells their importance as part of the educational community.

our faculty or way up yonder at the central office procure) items. Because they don't interface with students directly, nd" so easily can fall by the wayside. When part of the team g that occurs, their work can be taken for granted. The . Payroll must be accurate. Moments of thinking about ween when working in this silo. Yet, they are a vital part of iented leaders recognize every employee as a vital member ct for the 'reason' of impacting students.

urturing caretaker role because they are feeding students rally). Although this may feel routine, this is an emotional f poverty who may only eat while in your building. There ted through smells, tastes, tone, and feelings of safety and throughout their adulthood. These "Super Friends" are the curity for students.

et and the last ones to say goodbye to many students. They ne for our children's well-being. Bus drivers are the "Super k, and year of a student's school experience. This is a lot of t can comfort and set a student up for a turnaround great week all around. How bus drivers act and interact can stall a. .evement or work together as beautiful culturized team.

Every employee is part of the "Super Friends" team and should never be ignored or dismissed by staff with a hierarchy mentality. Everyone deserves a voice, a sense of belonging, and appreciation as a team.

100 No-Nonsense Things That ALL School Leaders Should STOP Doing

Examples above can be found at any school district. However, it is up to leadership to set the tone and remind everyone that they are members of a team. Remember, we are in a people profession. Every single staff member must hear it, see it, and believe it. It is up to you as a leader to remind all staff that they support students.

Everyone Serves a Purpose for a Reason

If nobody is following you as a leader, then your "leadership" is haphazard. It isn't too late to turn things around. Get out there and get to know everyone and know them by name. Show everyone they are important and that their individual work matters to the collective success. When leaders model a "Super Friend" mindset the staff can follow your lead. From there share positive experiences during a faculty meeting or in a staff email. Showcase the positive experiences happening on your campus that are student achievement focused. Invite "Super Friends" to go along with you to classes, so they can see your students in their element, and see other school staff in action. Every stakeholder deserves a personal invitation to see the fruits of their labor and how their individual contribution adds value to the team. Invite staff to interact with each other, even as simple as team building or an appreciation initiative across all staff and departments. Build it into the process of your planning.

Celebrate and feature student learning in all spaces. This can be as simple as photos of children in action, getting on or off the bus, working 1:1 with a para, at lunch, or displaying a student's project. Showcase inclusively how every staff member has a purpose and why their work matters. Share an email with pictures, a text, or short video what is being learned by students - you would be surprised how appreciative some staff can be for hearing about the classroom.

Every single person in a school deserves to know that they're there for the same reason: to promote successful thriving and high achieving students. It's up to us as leaders to remember that all our staff are part of a team that play a vital role in the achievement outcomes of our student body. Once you project positivity, it will be followed by others. The key is cohesiveness. You never know, the least likely staff member might just help a child's life and make all the difference for that one.

Ron O'Connor, SFO is the Assistant Superintendent of Business Services at CCSD59 in Elk Grove Village, Illinois. He has presented at the state and national levels on innovation, school finance, and leadership. Ron's favorite activities are spending time with his wife Karen, three kids, and two mini schnauzers. Ron O'Connor started his career in the classroom, working his way up to Assistant Superintendent. He prides himself in being a conduit between curriculum and finance. He is finishing up his doctorate to learn more on how to be an effective leader.

Stop Squashing Staff-Generated Ideas or Interests
MAGGIE COX

I think I fall into the category of "teacher-leader", an innovative idea generator who sometimes gets eye rolls in staff meetings when I ask questions or make suggestions. Of course, it was not that way when I started my career after college, because I did not initially go into education.

At the age of twenty, as the athletic trainer for the school, I was asked to assist a team create their school emergency plan. In all the schools I have worked at since as an educator, I have never been asked to assist with this task. I have volunteered to be on emergency response teams, and even then have not been included on those despite my medical background.

At age twenty I was also asked by an Orthopedic Surgeon I worked with, to present to a group of about 250 doctors on sideline injury evaluation because he thought I had something to offer them. Many years later, and about 6 years into my teaching career, I excitedly told my administrator that I had been selected to present at a national education conference, but I needed a signed permission form to be eligible to attend. My travel and registration were being paid for through a grant. However, even a full funding source did not stop the disheartening comments that followed. This principal, with a Ph.D., asked me, "Well why are they sending you? Are they paying you, typically when I am asked to an event, they pay me"? I was speechless. I didn't even know how to reply.

Coming From an Industry that is Respected
My entrance into teaching came later in my career. I recognized a need for students to be exposed to medical careers and training, so I entered an alternative program that allowed me to teach in California under a "vocational credential". Later I went on to teach in Nevada and am in my eleventh year of teaching under a "business and industry credential". Many states offer alternative programs that recruit people transitioning to a second career. This helps bring in educators to a profession that is in dire need for more participants. I have witnessed and experienced how it can become a frustration for these new teachers.

As a Career and Technical Education Teacher, I entered teaching with a completely different skill set and an outstanding reputation in my field. Still, I needed clarification on terms like Blooms Taxonomy and PBL. Truthfully, with my background in medical assessment as a Certified Athletic Trainer, with a bachelor's degree from Cal Poly San Luis Obispo (known for its motto "learn by doing"), I did not think there was any better way to teach than through scenarios requiring critical thinking and projects that required in depth knowledge and understanding to complete. I just did not realize this was called Project Based Learning until a few years into teaching. I was trying to explain my lesson to an administrator, who said "Oh, you are doing PBL". I googled it that night.

Entering an Industry that is Dismissed
I have mentored many CTE Teachers over the past years and have seen the frustration as they come from an industry where they are respected, then enter education where they are often dismissed. I have helped teachers adapt to education language, teaching them how to explain the depth of knowledge being used when they perform certain lab activities or aligned to standards. I explain how they can advocate for what they need. These skills I have learned over time, only came with much research on my own as I sought to understand the pedagogy. I also maintained learning the content knowledge of my industry which allows me to speak from a point of real-world application.

Many of your teachers enter education with a rich set of skills and knowledge that are not being tapped into, used, or even recognized. It can be very hard to keep teachers in the profession when they face disrespect or low support from administration. These are potentially some of your best teachers, but they do not know how to write a lesson plan or document it the way you would like. Go watch their lessons and you will not be disappointed. These teachers entering a second career need more support, but in a completely different way than a new teacher straight out of a traditional college education preparation program. They need assistance from a veteran teacher, who potentially entered the same way that can help them adapt what they know already into best teaching practices. They need to learn to document their instructional practice to meet school requirements. They may be exceptional with technology, and be a resource for your teachers, but they may also need support to learn the required gradebook program.

Be a Mentee at All Stages of Life
You cannot make assumptions about a first-year teacher. Ask them what they need, ask them how they learn best, and what would help them feel most supported in their new position. A new teacher, starting as a second career, may have more work experience and leadership experience than the administrator that is overseeing them. This is not a bad thing, but the administrator can recognize this as an opportunity to grow rather than showing concern that this new teacher will not step "out of place" or surpass and outshine them in some way.

I have always felt it is important to have mentors as well as be a mentee at all stages of life. If more administrators viewed it as an opportunity to work with an educator that has varied experience and less like it is an imposition to work with a teacher that does not understand all the education abbreviations used, I think it would allow both to grow.

Your teachers entering as a second career are going to view the classroom and the school through a unique and beautiful lens. This could potentially be a great opportunity for an administrator to open a discussion surrounding innovation. This new teacher may be able to help with workflow, schedules, and school culture in ways that traditionally educated teachers simply cannot, because they have not been exposed to working in a field outside of education. I am always shocked that more administrators do not sit down and strike up a conversation with their CTE or ROTC Instructors. If you are looking at some type of redesign or re-imagining of your school space, these would be the first teachers to speak to. Ask to be the mentee and learn from others that are different from you. Seek to learn corporate, military, or other professional perspective ways of doing things. Afterall, aren't we preparing students for the real world? They have lived in the real world and have this perspective to offer us.

Be Open to Receive Help or Suggestions
Just as Ron O'Connor shared that all staff play a role in supporting students. The same is true of solving problems and collaborating at a new level. The best way to begin is to get to know every educator and network to tether people together. During the pandemic I did see more educators at all levels collaborating to solve problems. Out of necessity people were more open to new ideas, and more willing to listen to suggestions by anyone, regardless of title. Whether it was planning a non-traditional graduation, that required live streaming, teaching virtually (requiring extra equipment and training), or boosting the school's social media activity. I hope that is something that we can continue to do as we move education forward.

At the point of writing this, I am still several credits shy of completing my master's degree in educational leadership. I have participated in professional development for years and bettered myself as a healthcare provider, educator, speaker, and leader. My eagerness to learn and field expertise have opened a door for consultant work, writing curriculum, presenting at state and national conferences, and yes, sometimes I even get paid to do that now, despite my lack of title.

Before You Say No
Questions to ask yourself as you engage with staff who have offered to help, or have a new idea:

1. Do I know this colleague's education, skills, talents, and background? Would they be considered a subject matter expert in the area in which they are making a recommendation, outside of the school building?

2. Do I fully understand what they are asking, and why they want to make the change? Can I set aside time to meet with this person so that I can understand their perspective and goal?

3. Why am I saying No? Has this been tried before, can I explain to the teacher, or show them why I do not think it will work, or will the teacher be able to show me examples of this being successful in other industries?

Remember that Leadership is relational and to be heard you must be willing to listen and bravely go where education may not have ever gone before.

Maggie Cox is in her fourteenth-year teaching Medical Career and Technical Education. She is Past President of the Nevada Association of Career & Technical Education and remains active in her state, region and national ACTE. She loves to present at events. Topics of interest include personal branding, social media, career and technical education, design thinking, project-based learning, iPad apps, augmented reality, virtual reality, emerging technology and educating students today to be creative, adaptive & resilient as we prepare them for jobs that may not exist yet. She can be found sharing what she teaches & learns on social media @maggiejcox

55

Stop Ignoring Feedback of Any Kind from Anyone
VICKI WILSON

Interviewer: "If you are chosen to lead this school/district, describe the leader your stakeholders (staff, students, and families) will see."

Candidate: "They will see a gracious leader - one who values trust and builds relationships. My staff, students, and families will feel listened to, valued, and see me as someone very approachable."

I whole-heartedly believe that all leaders step into their role with the intention of being approachable, establishing mutual trust, being gracious, offering authenticity, and being a thoughtful listener. But what if the feedback coming at you is tough to hear, seems inauthentic, or doesn't match your perspective? Or perhaps ….

> you disagree with the feedback,
> the person delivering it has a negative attitude,
> you are under pressure they cannot understand,

> you don't believe they see the big picture,
>
> you have considerable knowledge on the topic,
>
> you see their reasons as self-serving,
>
> their approach is rude,
>
> you don't have time,
>
> they are wrong,
>
> or you really don't care.

The Communication Gap

Regardless of any of those reasons, or others that may have come to your mind, ignoring feedback of any kind from anyone, destroys trust, harms relationships, and will obliterate your school culture. People know when they are not being listened to. Each time they feel ignored - trust, relationships, and culture take a hit. If you think they will walk away quietly and accept that you are the wise leader and simply move on, you will be blindsided later. They will find a way to be heard by someone else. They will express their frustrations to anyone that will listen and seek to find others that feel the same way. When people perceive their opinions are not heard or valued by the leader, they are less inclined to hear the opinion and values of the leader. This creates a communication gap which impacts trust.

If you truly want to be realized as a gracious leader – one who values trust and builds relationships, where stakeholders feel listened to, valued, and see you as approachable, then you must STOP ignoring feedback of any kind from anyone because it stalls action-oriented achievement outcomes.

All Feedback is Perception

Great leaders are always gathering perceptions from stakeholders. Those perceptions may be contradictory, may be supportive, or may be in total left field. Accurate or not, perception is an assessment made by a person and to them, it is the 'absolute truth'. By gathering and understanding perceptions, leaders learn how to frame their conversations, front load misunderstood information, develop leadership skills, strengthen communication skills, and improve relationships.

Part of the job as a leader is to understand first, and then flip through the various lenses people look through and assume their perspective(s). This helps a leader not only make wise decisions, but it also gives insight on how to effectively communicate those decisions, the purpose for the decision, and the benefits and/or challenges each group in the organization will experience. It is the feedback you have gathered from others that gives you an understanding of the lens they are looking through.

100 No-Nonsense Things That ALL School Leaders Should STOP Doing

For example, if you decide to adjust the start and end times of the school day, you want to understand the impact it has through the lens of families, students, teachers, maintenance, and anyone else impacted by that decision. Ignoring feedback impacts your ability to see through these various lenses. I am not implying all lenses carry the same weight - because they usually don't. Looking through all of them, however, allows you to weigh them appropriately and then communicate effectively.

Receiving Feedback

You build relationships with people by thoughtfully listening to them without judgment. Their perspective may be different than yours. Avoid every temptation to react with defensiveness and anger. Remind yourself this is an opportunity to understand someone's perspective so that you can lead more effectively and maintain trust.

First, listen without interrupting. Absorb what they are saying. Check your body language and tone of voice so you appear curious, not defensive. Look them in the eye, pay attention, and focus on the words being said. Evaluate what is being said.

Once they have shared their feedback, ask clarifying questions, and paraphrase or repeat back what they say. Be open and inquisitive to their views or new ideas. These are all cognitive coaching skills that we learned early on in our leadership journey. Thank them for taking the time to talk to you.

After receiving feedback, reflect on it and decide what to do with it. Assess the reliability of the feedback and the implications of using it or not using it. If you disagree with the feedback you were given, consider asking someone else for their opinion. Your response is your choice. Listening is always more important than nonsense stalling actions that you could take. Once you decide what to do with the feedback, circle back to the giver and let them know what you did or didn't do because of the conversation. We all know there is more than one way of doing something and when we embrace the feedback may even learn things that yield achievement outcomes.

It's Tough for the Giver Too

You are a leader, a decision-maker, and a person of authority in the school. When you are approached by a staff member, a student, or a family member of a student, wanting to give you advice, criticism, their opinion, or an alternate view, consider the brave space they are stepping into. It is uncomfortable for most people to give unsolicited (and difficult and courageous) feedback to a person of authority. When leaders truly value people and relationships, they recognize how difficult it is for the giver.

STOP Making Decisions Haphazardly

Emily is a well-respected fourth-grade teacher with strong student and family relationships. After a harmful social media post spread rampant among parents with rumors about the school, Emily's principal announced to faculty that there would be no school-sponsored social media pages. Emily was crushed. She has a social media page for her parents that had been very successful and contributed to the positive relationships with her families. Emily respected her principal and didn't want to challenge her decision, but she felt there was a great value in using social media to engage families in the classroom. A few days later, Emily still felt troubled about the decision to eliminate social media and decided to talk to her principal. Although Emily considered her principal as approachable and a good listener, she was incredibly nervous about having a conversation that would challenge her decision. Emily understood the reason for the decision, but she didn't think her principal realized the implication it would have on her role to communicate with families effectively and positively. As she sat down to share her concern, her stomach tightened with nerves. Emily took a deep breath and shared that while she understood the harm the recent social media bashing brought to the reputation of the school, she felt that the opposite could happen if we could leverage social media to positively promote the school. Specifically, school or classroom social media pages push out messages and pictures of the positive things that happen inside the walls of our schools every day.

Emily's principal listened carefully to what Emily was saying and seemed genuinely interested in her perspective. Emily's nerves subsided in response to her principal's attentiveness and thoughtful questions. Emily shared how she uses a social media page to share out quick updates and show pictures of learning and their class community. She even opened the page on her phone and showed the positive comments and gratitude posted by the parents of her students. At the end of their conversation, Emily's principal thanked her for talking to her. She also told Emily that she imagined it may have been hard to share how my decision has a negative impact on your role as a teacher, but she is glad she did. Even though Emily's principal didn't commit to changing her decision during their conversation, Emily felt heard and understood. Later that night, Emily realized that even if the decision remained, she felt much better knowing that her perspective was heard.

The next day, Emily's principal stopped her in the hallway and asked if she could follow up on their conversation. She was impressed with the way Emily used social media to positively promote the learning and joy of her classroom. It gave her a completely different perspective and she admitted that the recent social media incident tainted her view which resulted in a rash decision. She asked Emily to continue using her classroom social media page and planned to communicate with faculty that her previous decision was reactionary, and she no longer stood by it. She asked Emily if she would be willing to share with other faculty how she used social media to engage parents with the great work we do at our school. Leaders, in the story above the school principal made a change because of feedback she received. It will not always happen that way. You may reflect on feedback and take no action. The action(s) you take or don't take is not what is important. How you receive and listen to feedback and follow up, is everything.

If leaders are to avoid haphazard decisions, they must embrace feedback and alternative perspectives that may show a better way of doing things. When you realize a better way, do it. This not only validates the giver of the feedback, but it also validates you as a gracious leader – one who values trust and builds relationships, where stakeholders feel listened to, valued, and see you as approachable.

Vicki Wilson is an elementary principal in Michigan, a Solution Tree associate, and an educational consultant. She is the author of Lead with Instructional Rounds - a Lead Like a Pirate guide book and a contributing author to 100 No-Nonsense Things that ALL Teachers Should STOP Doing. Vicki is passionate about education and the potential for reimagining current practices, change leadership, and collaborative professional learning.

56

Stop Ignoring Voices of School Leaders and Staff
AMANDA SHUFORD MAYEAUX, Ph.D.

On my parents' property is a large pond filled with beautiful aquatic life, including fish waiting for grandchildren to catch. To sit on the little bench that my father built years ago, is a moment to engage in tranquility. The pond is never overgrown with algae or ever reeks from the terrible odor of stagnant water. The secret to this small oasis of beauty is a centuries old spring that feeds the pond every day. The freshwater flows in and the older water trickles out the levee on the opposite side. The water is clear and alive with small fish growing, ready to be transferred to other ponds. The constant source of fresh water means life is constantly multiplying and supplying life beyond its banks.

The pond-ecosystem analogy applies well to schools. Schools are small ecosystems of various relationships and interdependent systems. Strong school leaders manage all the elements and consistently analyze which pieces need refreshing. Some schools are unwilling to embrace fresh ideas and the people who have such ideas just as Maggie Cox, and Vicki Wilson shared in the last two chapters. Such schools are stagnant with the dying odor of unfavorable cultures. Often these schools are more bound in "how we have always done things" rather than focusing on what students and teachers need to grow and evolve. Schools need fresh voices like ponds need fresh water.

Sources of fresh ideas abound in our schools when leaders seek to listen and engage. The voices of three groups are often overlooked as potential change-makers: assistant school leaders, aspiring school leaders, and new teachers.

Build Trust

Often when new people join our school communities, we expect them to fit into the existing community. Rather, we should embrace new people as they join our teams, recognizing that they are different and require a reassessment of core values to include the new voices. Years ago, I was part of an instructional team with a core group of teachers who remained together for several years. However, each year we would lose and add a new member. We started our summer team meetings the same way. We followed a process to set new core values with all voices heard. We did not simply ask the new person to approve our prior values or just add something for them. We started fresh. This established trust that this person was equally valued. After setting core values, we did share some of the strategies and processes that had been working, but we were also willingly open to new ways of doing things. One year we even had a student-teacher who added some brilliant solutions to some issues we had been experiencing. We found embracing new people through honesty and being open to resetting our team anew, was critical to building trust.

Honor Transparency

Building and cementing trust is dependent on transparency. Assistant school leaders are a valuable voice for school leaders. In the optimum situation, assistant school leaders compliment the school leader's strengths and weaknesses. When transparency in communication exists, assistant school leaders can reveal potential stagnant elements in the school. Assistant school leaders are also a powerful source of confidentiality and accountability for school leaders and for teachers. Assistant school leaders are often a bridge between the school leader and the faculty. Such a bridge allows the school leader access to conversations and beliefs that may otherwise be hidden. If the assistant school leader feels the need to carefully guard their words and actions, transparency is lost.

Aspiring school leaders often learn more from observations of leaders' actions than words. Working with aspiring school leaders in graduate school, the frustrations I hear the most from these students is lack of transparency from leadership. This leaves them confused and unsure, which leads to a lack of trust. While leaders are not able to always agree with someone, explaining the points behind the reasoning leads to greater transparency and validates that the person has been heard.

Additionally, new teachers are often hesitant to share their thoughts when processes and structures are not transparent. School leaders reveal who they trust by the voices they seek. Transparency is revealed when leaders see all voices and have open dialogue with all members, even the new teachers on campus. One of my favorite principals ever was Glenn Delafield. My first quarter at his school he asked me what I aspired to be. I told him I wanted to be a professor of education one day. He began pulling articles and would invite me to research discussions after school. He not only read the articles but encouraged me to try out things we discussed and share my conclusions about how it worked in my classroom. This had such an incredible impact on my career.

Build Relationships
We often think about building relationships between ourselves as leaders and the faculty and staff, but powerful leaders work to build relationships between all people in the building just as Ron O'Connor shared with detailed examples in Chapter 52. For new assistant school leaders, building relationships with the school leader is critical, but building relationships with faculty is equally critical. Strong school leaders will strategically create opportunities for the assistant school leader to lead and to engage with faculty. Often leaders will give the assistant school leader tasks like managing buses or discipline. Such tasks are important, but assistant school leaders also need consistent opportunities to engage with faculty and staff in a variety of activities to build relationships, demonstrate transparency, and develop trust. Assistant school leaders also need opportunities to build relationships with students. When assistant school leaders have relationships across the school, they have knowledge and understanding to share and to use in problem solving.

Aspiring school leaders need opportunities to build relationships outside of their grade level and/or departments as Vicki Wilson showcased in the previous chapter. One weakness I often see with aspiring school leaders is they have limited experiences across grade levels and departments. One strategy would be to invite them to join the school leadership team to begin to understand the various elements of the school and how these systematically work together. Echoing Vicki Wilson in the previous chapter, engage them in peer observations across content and grade levels. Expand their understanding of the inner workings and provide the 40,000-foot view necessary to lead all aspects of a school. Intentional mentoring is critical to developing the succession of your future leadership team(s).

Aspiring school leaders are also great resources for the new teachers in the building just as Maggie Cox open heartedly shared in Chapter 53. A teacher new to the profession may need several mentors who focus on different elements from management to lesson study. A seasoned teacher new to the building may only need a mentor to help with the dynamics of the school. Mentoring is a great first step for aspiring leaders, but also a way to allow new teachers to share their voices too.

Consider reverse mentoring as a wonderful strategy to engage new teachers in leadership roles in the school. Reverse mentoring allows new teachers to share strategies and activities with veteran teachers. For example, maybe a young teacher is an expert in a great tech app. Allow this teacher to host a quick professional learning session and invite other teachers to come to the new teacher's classroom to watch the students engage with the application. Then afterwards, allow teachers to engage in a discussion and share their ideas. Build trust. Engage in transparency. Grow those relationships!

Seek to Disrupt Stagnation Before it Leads to Decay
Strong leaders value positive and powerful school culture, but also understand without fresh ideas, stagnation will eventually lead to decay. New assistant school leaders, aspiring school leaders, and new teachers are excellent voices for clues to where stagnation may be occurring. They are also sources for fresh ideas to overcome it.

School leaders that make intentional decisions focused on action-oriented achievement outcomes prevent others from becoming stagnant. The dreadful truth is that hiring solid educators and retaining them is a challenge in and of itself. Because of this, leaders may respond haphazardly by preventing strong teachers from evolving into school leaders because they do not want to lose these teachers from their building. However, preventing someone within our little ecosystems from growing will force them to seek new environments or wither.

The most critical stagnation to avoid is the stagnation of professional growth in the people in your building, including yourself. Embrace new ideas! Embrace critical feedback from assistant leaders, aspiring leaders, and new teachers. Create a culture where all voices trust you enough to share with transparency and faith in the relationships that exist in the school. Be an ecosystem of life where abundant growth occurs daily for all stakeholders.

Dr. Amanda Shuford Mayeaux is an associate professor at the University of Louisiana at Lafayette where she works with a wonderful group of peers to develop educational leaders at all levels. For the past three decades, she has been seeking the impact on the lives of children by creating high quality educational opportunities as a teacher, assistant principal. Amanda is a Milken Educator and Disney Teacher Award recipient. She is author of "Expertise in Every Classroom" and "Teamwork: Setting the Standard for Collaborative Teaching, Grades 5-9". Dr. Mayeux's research passion is focused on expertise in education whether from the classroom or at the international impact level.

57

Stop Thinking on a Small, Local Scale
RAE DUNN

Having pride in your own work is deserved . . .
Generating school spirit is a positive force . . .
Friendly competition can be motivating . . .

BUT . . . if you are doing the work as a school leader *JUST* as a professional steppingstone, JUST for the short term, or *JUST* for a small local community impact that will end if you leave. Just stop.

Get Out of Your Bubble
Early in my career as a high school English teacher in the 90's, I was consumed with the success of my students. I fretted over them, planned for their success, replanned, assessed, reassessed, cajoled, threatened, inspired, and sometimes even literally tap danced to get students to succeed. BUT I did it in a bubble; my own little world that didn't take into consideration other teachers or even the other courses my students might be taking. And since *MY* students were successful in *MY* class, I wasn't too concerned with what was happening around me.

Just after my seventh year of teaching, I was "voluntold" by my principal that I would be our site's first ever Literacy Coach. Imagine my surprise when I stepped outside my small little four-walled world and started looking around at the entire school site. Sometimes, I was amazed at what other teachers were doing. There were many teachers doing extraordinary lessons that made learning contagious in their classrooms. Students were engaged, productive, and on fire edifying one another.

Other times, I was shocked at what was *NOT* happening in classrooms and sadness consumed me as I witnessed what students were enduring. Mostly, I noticed that teachers were in isolation. Like what Ron O'Connor shared in Chapter 52, my priority focused on eliminating working in silos. To accomplish this, I knew I needed to encourage collaboration just as Dr. Amanda Shuford Mayeaux and Vicki Wilson shared in their chapters. Once we began focusing on working together towards the betterment of all the students in every classroom, the success of every teacher was multiplied by a factor of a kajillion (let's remember I am a recovering ELA teacher, so my math may be a bit off…) and the entire school benefited.

Furthermore, when I became our school's Literacy Coach this was my first big scale teacher leadership role that would interact at a district level. There was one other high school in that district that likewise appointed a Literacy Coach. I was so excited to get together with her to begin our big audacious work, because I was convinced that together we were going to change the district! However, while I wanted to talk about how to make reading relevant in all content areas, she wanted to talk about how we were going to make a name for ourselves, so we could move up into administration. I think my shocked face revealed to her that I had a different perspective on the WHY for taking this position. Now, there really isn't anything wrong with having a career goal and striving for it. Personal goals are great and I commend her on knowing what she wanted and going for it. To be honest, I personally am still trying to decide what I want to be when I grow up, but what I do know is my WHY! I happily remained in that position until I left that district to move to one closer to my home a few years later. She stuck to her plan and didn't even stay through that entire school year, leaving to take a position as an admin somewhere else. Last I heard, she has been in 3-4 other districts in various administrative positions.

Create A New Vantage Point
I went from the classroom to literacy coach, then later from literacy coach to instructional coach. With each move the scope of my lens widened from classroom to literacy blocks, then later to a view of the entire perimeter of the school. Initially in my career I had a narrow focus on *MY* students, suddenly I was paying attention to the success and needs of *ALL* students. I listened, asked questions, learned, and quickly came to the realization that Ron O'Connor shared that everyone plays a major role because everyone has a voice. Leaving the classroom made me realize I had been making decisions based on a very small frame of reference.

While I didn't set out to become an administrator or anything other than a lifelong high school English teacher and coach, circumstances transpired that nudged me out of the nest. I had been frustrated with decisions being made by district leaders. While sharing this with a mentor and confidant, they challenged me with applying for the position and do something about it or stop complaining. I experienced a big dose of step up or shut up. I took the advice literally and began serving as a coordinator of secondary education in a midsize district. Moving from a school site to the district office allowed me to once again gain another vantage point that deepened my understanding of how the entire educational system functions together, beyond one school. I began to see how everything was interconnected. I could see how things I thought were being done to the site were sometimes done for a very good reason, but the reason might not have been explained to the site. I could see how necessary vertical and horizontal articulation produced a ripple effect of decisions.

Build Collaboration Capital
Leading in a district-level role has taught me to adhere to the action-oriented focus question, "Is every decision I make one that I would make for the benefit of my very own child?" I am also very fortunate to be in a district where our Superintendent Michael McCormick models the belief that leaders must "Motivate not Mandate" and charges every leader to build "Collaboration Capital."

One of the projects I am most proud of building "collaboration capital" with is the Riverside County Education Collaborative (RCEC). This collaborative consists of 5 school districts: Val Verde USD, Moreno Valley USD, Perris USD, Murrieta Valley USD, and Temecula Valley USD; 2 community colleges: Mt. San Jacinto College and Moreno Valley College; the University of California Riverside; and the Riverside County Office of Education. The beauty of this group is that traditionally these 5 districts would be rivals in all things- athletics, state assessments, college stats etc. Because of this project we have put those things aside (mostly…) and decided that together we are fierce and powerful.

Set Audacious Goals
Working far beyond our local communities, we are even better problem solvers. Every student in each district matters to all of us equally. We have worked together with our college partners for more than seven years with very lofty goals. These goals boil down to this - we want ALL our students to have postsecondary success. Furthermore, their success should never depend on their zip code or their families' bank account. It also doesn't matter which school district they attend. All that matters is that we come up with ways to help all students walk through open doors of opportunity and access. Some may argue that not all students are going to college and there may be some truth to that. Regardless, every student deserves the opportunity to make that choice. Thinking on a large scale helped remove barriers that may have prevented post-secondary experiences to further learning. This large-scale vision allowed the RCEC team to set the following goals that would increase:

   1. Graduation rates: Increase the number of high school students graduating high school.

   2. Percentage of students that are college ready: Regardless of desire, students are prepared and eligible to make the choice.

3. College going rates: College ready students enroll in a community college, or four-year university.

4. Number of students who finish college: Students enrolled in two- or four-year college level programs complete their initial commitment.

5. College readiness: The hashtag RCEC uses the most on social media is #bettermakeroom. This hashtag focuses on seeking out students to communicate the college readiness initiative inspired by Mrs. Obama. This initiative has been so successful that colleges better start making room for the students who are coming their way, because they are coming in droves.

6. FAFSA as a Graduation requirement: As a result of the work of this collaborative, Val Verde under the guidance of Mr. McCormick and the Assistant Superintendent Mark LeNoir became the first district in California to institute FAFSA as a graduation requirement in 2018. Soon after other districts in the collaborative also made it a graduation requirement and now as of July 2021 California has made it a statewide graduation requirement in Assembly Bill 132. We do not want students to think that they can't afford to go to college when we know there's money to help them! Our work has had an outcome that goes far beyond any one district.

You can learn more about the work this amazing team has accomplished at rcec.us. The most exciting part of the dynamic work of RCEC is that it all is meant to be replicated. Everything we have done, do, and will continue to do is based on the idea that ALL means ALL, and that includes your students too.

The Heart of the Matter
One of my favorite memories in working with this inspiring team of educators was when we were presenting to a crowd in Chicago and someone in the audience asked if we would share some of the resources we had created. Our County lead, Catalina Cifuentas who spearheads RCEC stated, "Seriously? You think I don't want you to use these things? Like I might be worried that you would turn around and help more kids or something?" The room burst out laughing, but it goes to the heart of the matter. Do you know your *WHY*? What is your Collaborative Capital worth? Is your *WHY* to help the students in your schools, classrooms, and communities? Maybe you want to help the students at your school. Maybe you even want to help the students in your districts. Don't stop there. Stop thinking and making decisions on a small, localized scale. Make your *WHY* big, bodacious, and maybe even a little scary. All students deserve a team of leaders that are intentionally focused and united by action-oriented achievement outcomes. . . . ALL Means ALL.

Rae Dunn (N0- not that Rae Dunn) is a recovering high school English teacher currently serving as the Coordinator of Secondary Education in Val Verde USD in Southern California. In this role she supports all secondary teachers, professional development, AVID, New teacher Induction, Instructional Coaches, Counselors, and College/Career Readiness. Her passion is student success and is always pushing the boundaries for access, equity, and academic excellence. She believes ALL means ALL and that there can never be enough glitter.

Stop Thinking that Purchasing Software will Fix Student Achievement
HOLLY KING

Recently, I sat in a collaborative brainstorming meeting with an ensemble of building leaders, lead teachers, and interventionists where we discussed how to better support classroom teachers. The team was tasked with meeting the needs of students who were presenting a more diverse skill set than ever before. Although necessary, the task felt monumentally daunting because teachers were so overwhelmed. In the meeting, teachers were asked to brainstorm all the various needs of their students. As teachers fired off their experiences, I crafted a bulleted list on my tablet just to keep track of the wide range of needs. When prompted to contribute, I shared my thoughts as a consolidated summary that included the need for a diagnostic assessment tool, differentiated autonomous lessons to groups of students based on need, progress monitoring, learning strands that span K-12, and the list continued. Given my leadership role in instructional technology, the first action item prompted a direct statement from a leader in the room, fired off haphazardly, "We need you to find a software that will do everything on that list."

You might have read it thinking that as a statement was made in jest, but it was said in complete seriousness. Think deeply about the long-term ramifications of this suggestion.

Software is No Magic Bullet
These magic bullet suggestions would require students to sit in front of a device as a replacement for instruction. Although the gamified concept is enticing, and it holds students' attention for a short period of time, it is not a replacement for high quality teaching and learning. Completing digital tasks provide students with digital adaptive learning, but the question remains, "How much of this mastery is transferable outside of the software platform? What percentage of content mastered in the software platform is retained long term? To what depth of knowledge have students mastered the content standards? And what evidence ensures that students can apply content knowledge to multilayered, complex problems?"

Software alone is not the answer to closing achievement gaps. When funding is available to address gaps in learning and the need for individualization, instructional technology vendors are primed and ready with software that promises to reduce the learning gap. They tout results in reading and mathematics because students are engaged in responsive, adaptive, and personalized learning pathways. Vendors boast a one-stop shop for learning needs. In fact, some go so far as to suggest that the teacher can simply facilitate the use of the program for 30-40 minutes per day per subject...and guarantee student mastery of content.

While digital platforms can provide powerful insight into student mastery of concepts and skills, this data point is only one variable in a huge set of quantitative data. Software is necessary for making many practitioner-level decisions for instructional planning. However, software programs do not provide deep teaching of standards, application of content, cross-content transfer, or real-world social interactions. There are limitations when solely depending on digital learning.

Teaching Requires Anecdotal & Qualitative Feedback
Digital platforms fail to consider demeanor, social limitations, emotional needs, and student interest in engaging with the content. Anecdotal observations and personal interactions with students provide the qualitative data needed to inspire, motivate, make connections, scaffold, reteach, praise, question, or celebrate. Human interactions are essential in leveraging the social presence necessary for learning. A software program cannot answer the following questions:

- Is the student distracted or tired?
- Does the student lack the resiliency to try again, so they click through the content to finish?
- Is the student logging in for a prescribed amount of time but not engaging in the content?
- Does the student really know the content, or did they simply get lucky and select the correct response?
- Can they connect this concept to more complex situations where this content or skill is a prerequisite?
- Once students are faced with more complex problems, will this platform identify the unpolished skill and offer support?

Software Does not Replace Teachers
Communication, collaboration, critical thinking, and creativity are valuable ingredients in learning. Instructional platforms allow students to progress while bypassing these advanced skills. We have complex global issues, and we desperately need complex thinkers who can develop innovative, sustainable solutions. In short, platforms without the facilitation and guidance of a highly effective teacher fail to ensure that today's learners are tomorrow's leaders.

Is there a place for instructional software in the future of education? Yes, of course.

Educational software - like any other academic resource - can serve as a valuable resource for educators, especially those struggling to meet the needs of all learners. Software is a supplement to leverage the learning environment, not to replace it. Digital platforms inform. Adaptive technology has the power to support content spanning multiple grade levels. Digital instructional programs can provide data that informs teachers about content mastery on specific topics and standards which leverage the planning and implementation of differentiation. When faced with a wide span of learning needs, digital platforms assist teachers in quickly grouping and differentiating content for learners for additional practice that will enrich thinking. With seemingly unlimited content, digital platforms can provide teachers with enrichment opportunities for learners ready for advanced content. It can also offer additional content for students who need practice on concepts from previous instruction. With that said, any software program in existence will fail if implemented without a knowledgeable, skilled educational professional.

Teachers Make the Connections
Teachers recognize the value of human interactions in the learning process. Teachers leverage student discourse as they grapple with the integration of new concepts into their current knowledge base. Teachers create learning experiences that incorporate critical thinking and collaboration to creatively solve complex, relevant problems and present their ideas to an authentic audience. Teachers understand the delicate balance between encouraging resilience and failure fatigue, and they recognize the exact moment to offer personalized encouragement or academic support. Teachers know the ceiling and depth of knowledge required to meet the thinking and application necessary to master the standards.

Teachers Know Their Students
Digital software is one tool in the arsenal of tactics and strategies of the professional educator. However, to be an effective tool, it must perfectly match the task at hand. One software package will not solve all of the needs of all learners, nor will it support the needs of all teachers. Every program, online or offline, will fail to reach a subset of the population. There is no one-size-fits-all, especially when it comes to digital learning. Leaders and teachers must carefully match the needs of the teacher and the needs of the individual student with the specifications of the platform.

Put a Pause on Haphazard Digital Purchases
Leaders should pause purchases of instructional software that claim to be a one-stop shop for all the educational needs of the learners in the building. Provide the time and space for teachers to develop deep relationships with students so their observations and academic data can support the identification of the needs of their students. Then, and only then, make decisions on the implementation of

instructional resources - digital, text, and humans - that will support the specific needs of the students that are in classrooms right now.

Lean on the expertise of teachers. Invite them to conversations about potential solutions. Welcome them to pilot new ideas and give feedback. Focus on action-oriented achievement outcomes.

Holly King, a champion of digital tools and instructional technologies, holds an impressive record of creating and implementing innovative classroom practices in her classroom while leading others to do the same. Her leadership experience in instructional coaching transforms classrooms through collaboration, personalized professional development, and individualized goal setting. After serving as a secondary science educator for 20+ years, Holly now serves as a Director of Instructional Technology and Gifted Specialist in North Carolina where she inspires educators to transform their learning spaces, ensuring that all students are challenged to communicate, critically think, problem solve, and create every day.

Stop Hiring Staff Without Sound Practices, Procedures, or Courtesy
JEFFREY EVENER

Two scenarios typically play out near the end of the summer in school districts when human resources and/or school leaders practice haphazard hiring processes.

> **First:** We do not do our due diligence with reference checks because we are in a hurry to fill vacancies.

> **Second:** We filled a vacancy that had many applicants. We selected a few to come into our district for a first-round interview. The candidates we did not bring in for an interview are not communicated with at all, which makes the district look bad.

Mistakes in the hiring process can and do happen. From my experience, there are a handful of things we can do to ensure we hire the best candidates. Hiring new faculty and staff members can be a daunting process for any school leader. Beginning with the advertisement, to the committee invites, to initial screening procedures, to the first and second round interviews, to the final round interviews, to the formal and informal reference checks, to the final recommendation, there are many moving parts to any new hire. It is often said that the two most important things that school leaders can do to ensure a great school is to hire great teachers and recommend tenure. Getting those two things wrong can be a costly endeavor and more importantly, hurt students along the way. School leaders can do one thing

100 No-Nonsense Things That ALL School Leaders Should STOP Doing

to ensure that they get the right candidates. We need to stop hiring staff without sound practices, procedures, or courtesy. What follows is a guide based upon my experiences as a principal and an assistant superintendent for human resources school leaders can follow to ensure great faculty and staff are hired.

Four Areas of Focus Leaders Must Get Right

1. Advertising: The first area that leaders need to get right is advertising for the position. If you think simply posting on your school website is good enough, you need to think again. This might be the least effective way to draw candidates to your district. I encourage school leaders to leverage social media (Twitter, Facebook, Tik-Tok, Instagram, LinkedIn, utilize hiring websites like Indeed or Monster), contact and make connections with local colleges and universities, advertise in local news outlets, and maximize your own professional network to recruit potential candidates. Stop thinking the best candidates will come to you simply because you have a vacancy. It is wise to go to where the candidates are.

2. Strong Interview Teams: The second area leaders need to get right is putting together strong interview teams that have representation from the whole school and then making sure they are aware of their role as an interview committee. As a leader, think about the position and what members of the school community will interact with the new hire the most. Pick these staff members for the committee. Do not forget to include parents and students for your interview teams. These two voices are vital to the process. They are the consumers of our product and their opinion matters. Also, including parents and students goes a long way to ensure the conversations and debriefs stays professional and on point. Lastly, the interview team should know their role up front. This is an important part of the interview structure. You do not want the committee thinking they are there to hire the new person. Leaders are ultimately responsible for the hire, so your recommendation should trump the committee. I recommend the committee simply help you look for positives and areas of growth for each candidate. You will have to answer for the new hire at some point along the way. Leaders need to stop abdicating the hiring decision to the committee.

3. Comprehensive Reference Checks: Thirdly, leaders need to stop short changing the reference checks for the candidates. All candidates list references that will provide a glowing recommendation. Go outside the references listed. Use your professional network to your advantage. For example, place a call to a supervisor of a teaching candidate that does not list one on their resume or application (this is a red flag in my opinion). The better picture that you can get of the potential candidate the better and the more confident you can be in your recommendation. In some cases, school leaders skip this step altogether because the next board meeting is a day away. Do not let arbitrary deadlines cloud your hiring decision. Hiring poor candidates is costly not only in dollars and cents, but in work hours, and can ultimately hurt students.

4. Follow-Through with Courtesy: The last area is extending courtesy to all candidates that applied for the position. Do you want to be known as the district that does not communicate with applicants or do you want to be known as the district that treated all candidates so well that they apply again for other vacancies? All candidates deserve our attention to a degree. If you have many applicants and you only bring in a handful for a first-round interview, then at least send an automated email or letter to the other applicants letting them know that they will not be getting an interview. This will allow those candidates to move on in their search and it shows your district cares enough to let them know. Once candidates interview, phone calls need to be made regardless of outcome. A rule of thumb to live by is that if you physically see them, physically call them.

School leaders face an even bigger challenge in recruiting, hiring, and retaining the best candidates possible to serve students, and it has become even more challenging post-pandemic. Although the process is more daunting than ever, do not shortchange the process. Stop falling victim to false deadlines and the lack of time. If you do not make the time to hire the best talent possible with sound practices, procedures, or courtesy, then action-oriented achievement outcomes will be stalled.

Jeffrey Evener currently serves as the Assistant Superintendent for Instruction for Homer Central School District in Homer, New York. He has served as a teacher, athletic director, principal, and assistant superintendent during his 20-year career. His passions include spending time with his wife and children and learning about leadership.

Stop Accepting Substandard Work from Staff
HEATHER CALVERT, Ph.D.

Being an educational leader is hard work. There are a lot of proverbial plates spinning in the air at the same time, and at the end of the day everything that does or does not happen in a building is the responsibility of the building leader. Because of this, leaders are taught and expected to delegate to other staff members. In a perfect world, seeing as we are adults, all delegated work would be completed on time and of high quality. The reality, however, is that sometimes adults cut corners just like students do, and it is the building leader's responsibility to hold and enforce high expectations for all staff. When staff are allowed to perform at substandard levels, students suffer, and the spinning plates start to wobble until they eventually shatter on the ground. Accepting substandard work is haphazard and stalls action-oriented achievement outcomes.

A Breakdown in Communication

My first year as a principal, I found myself sending countless emails to staff delegating tasks. Some were to the whole staff, others were to specific groups, and a few were to individual staff members. The problem with communicating via email is that there is no way to judge nonverbal communication. I assumed that because I sent an email and the directives made sense to me, everyone was on the same page with the expectations and the documented request couldn't be denied. The problem I ran into was that others thought they knew what I wanted, and they tried their best to follow the directives as I had sent them, but many times my directions weren't as clear as I initially thought they were, important pieces were missing, or they took every detail in an extreme or literal sense.

Miscommunication can lead to substandard work. As leaders we are tasked to provide feedback on lesson plans. Because I was an instructional coach prior to becoming an administrator I assumed that all educators had been coached on components that should be included in developing a well-planned holistic yet detailed lesson plan. My first year as an administrator at a new school, I began checking lesson plans and my initial thought was that teachers were intentionally being lazy or insubordinate. I quickly began scheduling meetings with teachers to address the problem. The first teacher arrived at my office. I started the conversation by stating how disappointed I was with the quality that was submitted. Ready to 'lay down the law', I noticed that this teacher had tears in her eyes and a look of total shock on her face. I asked her to share her thoughts with me regarding the issue, and she responded that she had never had an administrator review her lesson plans before.

It was in that minute I realized I had failed to communicate clear expectations surrounding the completion of lesson plans. Did I state the components that should be included? No. Did I state the deadline for completing weekly lesson plans? No. How could teachers possibly meet these expectations and submit quality work when the expectations had never been set in the first place nor modeled with an exemplar or process that included collaboration and teaming?

It wouldn't be fair to assume that staff who submit substandard work do so intentionally. Leaders must adopt the mindset that staff are doing the best they can with what they know and understand at the time. Sometimes, rarely, staff are truly just trying to cut corners or not do the work. However, in my experience that is not the case for most staff.

Regardless of the reason why the work is substandard, leaders must take action to address the issue. Inspect what you expect. I share my experience above to bring awareness that not all substandard work deserves written reprimands. Leaders should first address substandard work through seeking more information and coaching to ensure they are not making decisions haphazardly.

Uncomfortable Conversations Protect Student Learning
I have been blessed throughout my educational journey with many amazing mentors. When I first became an assistant principal, I was in awe at how easy my mentors found it to address things with staff, even when it created an uncomfortable conversation. After witnessing a few of these conversations take place, I asked my mentor (the principal of the school) how she always seemed to know what to say. She shared that the most important part of having an uncomfortable conversation is sticking to the facts and to set clear expectations moving forward. Easy enough, right? Hardly!

As a young, novice, principal I found myself leading staff who had more educational experience than I did. This created an odd balance as a leader, in that I needed staff to respect and trust my decisions as an educator and as a leader. One instance occurred with a veteran teacher. I had been in this seasoned teacher's classroom for a walk through a few times, and had noticed that every day during vocabulary instruction, something always seemed to get in the way of this instruction. The previous week, I had made it a point to stop by her room every day during this time frame, and not one day had vocabulary instruction occurred. Every time I entered the classroom, she quickly came over to me to explain the reason for the change in schedule. One day the students were practicing their class poem for Grandparents Day, another day they were all taking sensory breaks, etc. Not once were the students engaged in direct teacher instruction or small group activities where students had the opportunity to process vocabulary development.

Unlike the first scenario in this chapter, the expectations for students to participate in vocabulary instruction daily were very clearly stated and on the non-negotiable list. As the building leader, I could have chosen to ignore this teacher's blatant disregard for the expectations surrounding student learning. However, that would mean that her students were missing thirty minutes of targeted direct instruction every single day. This was unacceptable and warranted a courageous conversation. I had to facilitate the uncomfortable conversation in order to protect student learning.

Focus on Action-Oriented Student Outcomes

I sincerely do not believe that any leader in education took the administrative position because they enjoy having uncomfortable conversations with other adults about substandard performance. Suck it up buttercup. The buck stops with you. It doesn't matter how long you have been in the field of education, or how long you have been a leader in the field. YOU are the leader in the building. YOU set the tone. YOU are responsible for ensuring everything that occurs in your building is of high quality. Other than the challenges that Heidi Manoguerra shared in Chapter 5, there really is no excuse to accept substandard work from staff. Clearly communicate, model, set and maintain high expectations. Students deserve nothing less than your commitment to ensuring high quality education from every member of the staff. Anything less is haphazard.

Dr. Heather Calvert is currently an Elementary School Principal. Previously, Dr. Calvert has served as a classroom teacher, instructional literacy coach, building leader intern, and assistant principal. She is a National presenter and has also published articles in The Reading Teacher journal.

Stop Letting Misbehavior go Undocumented
LINDSAY TITUS

It's no surprise to any school leader that thousands of decisions are made every single day. In fact, on average, we make 35,000 decisions every single day. I've heard it said that educators answer more questions per minute than air traffic controllers and doctors. The amount of information going in and out of our minds any given hour of any day is remarkable.

Following up on Dr. Heather Calvert's prior chapter, inspecting what we expect and follow up courageous conversations will require documentation. Leaders simply can't remember all the information flowing in and out of every aspect of a school each day. This signifies the importance of documenting situations, especially those involving behavior. Without documentation, we rely on our memory, which we've already determined, even on the best of days, is overloaded with information.

Documentation becomes a data point, a third point to reference especially when looking for bias, patterns, and ways to mitigate past and future situations.

Behavior Bias
We often hear about bias when it comes to racial, ethnicity or gender bias. But did you know, we also have behavior bias. Behavior bias occurs when we make assumptions about why behavior is occurring through only our point of view. The mindset we hold about all things, including behavior, will impact our ability to effectively be a change agent to those around us.

Simply put, without documentation, we rest on our memories. Without detailed documentation, the past is an illusion of perception that can change over time. We process information consciously and subconsciously. Subconsciously, we process 11 million bits of information per second. Per second! Think about that. At any point in time all this information is coming to us through our senses which impacts our understanding based on our current perception of previous experiences. Of all the information coming in, we consciously process about 45 bits of information per second. Many of the decisions we make are based on our subconscious mind rather than what we are seeing and hearing at a conscious level. Which means, we turn an objective measure, such as a code of conduct situation, into a subjective measure. We allow emotions, limiting beliefs, and bias to determine our future actions, when we aren't actively documenting the information, succinctly, as is.

Behavior Patterns
Human beings are complex and determining unmet needs takes time. Behavior situations are not typically isolated situations. Situations of negative behavior most likely began at an early point in time and multiple situations build one upon another. Uncovering the root cause or "Why" behind behavior requires analysis of behavior patterns of triggers, supports that work, and aptitude for de-escalation. Without objective documentation as data to reflect upon, we are stuck in reactive mode instead of proactive mode.

The person acting out with negative behavior is unconsciously responding to a problem. To help the person understand their misbehavior, anecdotal notes, data points, and patterns of observations captured in documentation is a necessity. Without documentation we lose the ability to identify patterns. Documentation of patterns aids leaders in depersonalizing uncomfortable conversations that must follow misbehavior by students or adults. Thorough and objective documentation moves the conversation to a third point (the misbehavior documentation) and removes the "Me vs. You" mentality. Mitigating negative behavior patterns through courageous conversations shouldn't be delivered, received, or felt as personal. It should always be about clearly communicated high expectations as Dr. Heather Calvert shared and then looking together at the data or documentation to co-develop a resolution as a team. Anything less is haphazard and will only divide relationships and fuel adversity. When leaders use data and detailed documentation to navigate people with patterns of misbehavior it helps to understand the "why" behind behavior, use the behavior to create meaning, and to find ways to serve any unmet need.

As human beings, we can overgeneralize situations, which is generally due to the biases we hold and the evolution of perceptions of past situations. To truly understand what each behavior is telling us, documentation is essential. As leaders it's important that we honor the fact that we aren't supposed to get it perfect each time. Instead of trying to get it right, 100% of the time, what if we invested in a system of reflection and refinement that would help us to better connect, strengthen our relationships, and ignite our ability to teach simpler and more effective solutions to the students we interact with daily.

Documentation: The Simple and Easy Way
Documentation does not require endless reports nor pages of information. Documentation doesn't have to be complex or complicated. In fact, I'd like to argue quite the opposite. Documentation becomes simple and easy when you have identified a system that works for you.

As a leader, are you someone who likes paper/pencil, or maybe you prefer to digitize your information? If you go digital, do you prefer to use a Google Doc or maybe a spreadsheet better aligns to you. How you document, and what you document, will automatically come easier when you know why you are documenting. Documentation is a form of data collection. And when it comes to creating a preferred data collection system, consider the following analogy of "data as a play".

> **Set the Stage:** What type of data will you collect? What information is important to remember? Do you have ways to collect data from all sources, including the student?
>
> **Main Act:** Use the system you create. Gather data and report it consistently.
>
> **Intermission:** Check in with your documentation. Is it working the way you intended? Is it giving you the information you were looking for? Use this check to refine your process and ensure that you are collecting objective data rather than subjective thoughts.
>
> **Take a Bow:** Celebrate your successes big and small. Connect with the audience and send them off relishing in the experience.
>
> **After Party:** Share the experience with others. Use this information in conversations with families, students, and teachers. Ask questions about the data and what went well, what was improvised, and how you would do it next time.

Misbehavior is going to occur within our school buildings, as behavior is a part of human development. How we react and respond to the behavior(s) has potential to strengthen and grow our students, teachers, and staff. Thorough documentation followed by courageous conversations backed by compassion, empathy, and care carries the potential to help our students, staff, and school community grow and strengthen. Understanding misbehavior(s) through an objective lens led by growth, expansion, and purpose promotes action-oriented achievement outcomes.

Lindsay Titus is a passionate and energetic educator! She uses her expertise as a board-certified behavior analyst and a former classroom teacher, to ignite the passion of every educator. Lindsay is an educational coach, speaker, podcaster, and author. She is eager to transform the mindset educators hold about behavior and use this dynamic shift to increase connections with all students!

62

Stop Sitting on the Fence Rather than Deciding
TERENCE TONG

Leadership is fearless, it requires the best of us, and it demands the entirety of us. Whether you are the CEO of a Fortune 500 conglomerate, the shift manager at Taco Bell or the principal of a small, rural K-8 school, leadership roller coasters between exhilarating highs and bottomless lows. Imposters are easily singled out and punted to the curb. The ability to make decisions is part and parcel of the role. Leaders cannot be indecisive, hide, or shirk decision making responsibilities. For the wellbeing of the learning community and stakeholders involved, it simply cannot happen.

> Shush!
> Hear that?
> The nervous pacing outside your office...
> The frantic tapping of fingers on desks...
> The anxious chit-chat by the water cooler...

Those are the sounds of your community waiting on you to make a decision. They need answers from you to quell their restlessness, to guide their next steps, or simply to know what is going on. While your community is anxiously waiting, you might even be hiding in your office, sitting there dilly-dallying, "umming and ah-ing", secretly hoping the moment will simply pass by.

Get Off the Fence

Your fence sitting, your unwillingness (for whatever reasons) to decide, will only make a situation worse. Guess what? Situations requiring you "making the call" will not pass by nor disappear into thin air, and it certainly will not resolve itself. Situations requiring your input will linger and add to the cacophony outside your office waiting for you to *MAKE A DECISION*. This is quite a different scenario than that of Allyson Apsey in Chapter 1. She focused on leaders that all too quickly make decisions "to" people without considering repercussions or how an initiative might be carried out. This chapter focuses on the opposite end of the spectrum where a leaders' fear of making quality and timely decisions can be equally blocking of synergy and recklessly haphazard.

Failure of any leader to make timely and quality decisions, erodes faith and trust of the learning community. Let that sink in for a moment, all that community building, all the positive interactions, and all the hard work you banked to earn the trust of your stakeholders – gone. Disappeared into thin air – poof. All because you sat on the fence and would not make a decision. Seems like an awful waste, and a mighty big leadership consequence. The burden and responsibility of decision making is core to anyone in a leadership position. Decisions require discernment, consideration, information, and perceptions but that doesn't mean that you prolong the inevitable. The responsibility can be overwhelming, but it cannot render leaders inactive sitting on the fence, fingers and toes crossed, merely hoping for the best.

> *"Indecision may come from an instinctive hunch that there's more you need to know - which means it is time to learn everything you can about the pros and cons of each option. You can continue on this track, however, only as long as you're unearthing genuinely new information."* - Martha Beck

What if This? What if That?

In an ideal world, leaders are equipped with all the time and information necessary to make a rational, informed decision. However, life is often far from ideal. Leadership is akin to sailing. Mere amateurs can race in the America's Cup when the seas are mirror calm. The true challenge lies when you are racing a multi-million state of the art craft in typhoon strength gusts with a shredded spinnaker in 25-foot swells. You will not have all the information you need, and you would not be afforded the gift of time and perfect clarity. It's the split-second decisions made that will determine the fate of the crew and boat. Leaders make the best decision they can based on the information they have on hand. You are in a leadership position for a reason, you have demonstrated that you can, and have made difficult decisions in the past. Instead of focusing on "what if this...?" or "what if that...?" and the incalculable permutations that exist, focus on the possible consequences of "what if you don't make a decision...?" What consequences will befall the community then? How are you serving and leading your learning community then? Indecisiveness is a poor choice that kills morale. You are surrounded by capable and rational colleagues. Seek input, weigh the pros and cons, and then decide.

Don't Know? Let Them Know!
Whether you like it or not, your community will look to you for answers. It is also unrealistic for them to expect you to have all the answers as well. There will be times where you simply do not have the answers and you don't know what to do. Not having enough information to decide is par for the course, there is no shame in that. It is not a character flaw, nor a personal attack or a reflection of you as a leader. The simple act of acknowledging that you don't have the answer is testament to your leadership capacity. If you do not know, or if you do not have an answer right away, communicate that to your community. Let them know, share with them that you do not have the answers they need, but do reassure them that you are indeed working on it, and that you will share what you can when you can. Not knowing the answer immediately is still no excuse to sit on the fence! Be vulnerable, admit you do not have the answer, consider offering an opportunity for others and for the community to problem solve together. Your community would rather you be up front and honest, they will respect your willingness to be vulnerable. Engage in dialogue and seek input just as Dr. Jared Smith shared in Chapter 2. Any momentum generated is better than passive avoidance.

"The risk of a wrong decision is preferable to the terror of indecision." - Maimonides

The Answer is in the Room
Empowering leaders distribute leadership, when possible, to raise their learning community's efficacy, because they cherish community voice in important matters. Most likely that was your message and perspective when you interviewed for the position. Mostly it is also the message you impart to your learning community and stakeholders every August. Admittedly, there will be situations throughout the school year where you "empower" your faculty and let them "hash it out" as shared by many authors in the first section of this book.

Sure, you distribute leadership and empower your faculty to make decisions to best serve the learning community. However, that cannot be your "go-to" move every time a decision needs to be made.

Asking staff to sort it out amongst themselves and then telling them this was your plan all along may work once, maybe twice? Automatically defaulting to this time and time again inevitably erodes any confidence your community may have in your ability to make difficult decisions and lead.

Just because you are empowering others, it would be foolish of you to entertain the notion that it will be easier to achieve consensus. Empowering others is equally messy. Twenty-six different people will likely give you twenty-six different opinions. You cannot come to a consensus every time for everything. Rare are the occasions where all stakeholders will agree on a path forward so stop looking around. Your wish to involve stakeholders cannot be the reason why you fence sit and delay the inevitable. The "answer is in the room" – many times it's you. You are the bus driver, you are the captain, you are the drum major - the onus and responsibility to decide falls squarely on you.

The Fear of Not Being Liked is Paralyzing
Your stakeholders will not agree with every single decision you make. Not everyone in your learning community will like you. The sooner you recognize and appreciate this, the easier your task is as a leader. Leadership will never be a popularity contest. Do not for one second think you can make decisions that will please everyone. Otherwise, you are not the person for the job! Leaders need to be credible; leaders need to be trusted, and leaders need to possess high emotional intelligence, but you (and the learning community) you serve will never get anywhere if your goal is to please everyone. Utilizing avoidance tactics to distance yourself from critique and second guessing will surely backfire on you too. The fear of not being liked cannot paralyze you on the fence, delaying the inevitable, or simply hoping someone else will make the decision for you. Be decisive, do not shy from what is expected of and from you.

> *"In any moment of decision, the best thing you can do is the right thing.*
> *The worst thing you can do is nothing." -Theodore Roosevelt*

Silence the Cacophony
Have confidence in your leadership, have confidence in your learning community. Confidence does not mean you will always be right, not at all. Confidence means you are not afraid to be wrong. Steadfastly adhere to your values as an educator and leader, be faithful to the values of your learning community, trust your "why" and let it serve as a compass for you to make the best decision possible with the information you have at hand.

"If you don't believe in yourself, respect your own decisions, or stand by your own values, no one else will and that's the quickest way to lose respect even if you are a likable character," –Shivani Bhagi

Silence the cacophony, get off the fence and lead to action-oriented achievement outcomes.

Terence Tong, an experienced international school educator has taught in Canada, Kuwait, and South Korea. He is an aspiring leader with an abundance of teacher leadership experience in leading through change. An ardent believer and advocate of "Life in the Middle", Terence is seeking the next learning community to serve.

STOP Wasting Time

This Type of Nonsense Impedes Productivity

Stop Work that Doesn't Support the Mission & Vision
SEAN GAILLARD

It was a bad day. I am not sure what the source of the bad day was. I just remember it being a day plagued with worries and negativity. Principals have their share of those days. We are in the trenches putting out the fires and taking the heat. I refer to these types of days as, "This is part of the gig." School leaders may identify with a day of this nature when the phone rings off the hook filled with complaints, problems, toxic people, and worst-case scenarios. These are the days when we move at top speed and leap over buildings in a single-bound. I was having one of those days at one of the schools I was serving as a principal.

An Unexpected Epiphany
My goal was to help our schoolhouse exit low-performing school status as designated by our state. The needs of our students and teachers were high and the sense of urgency was intensively high. I was flying at a high speed, but I was drowning in a sea of deadlines, paperwork, and administrative minutiae. This principal was a classic stress case heading straight into a dead end of wasted time and unproductivity.

It wasn't quite yet 9:00 in the morning and I remember that this bad day was becoming a candidate for the proverbial "Hall of Fame of Bad Principal Days". I had just lowered the phone in conclusion of a conversation with a very dissatisfied parent. As I placed the phone down, the chirpy ping of my inbox revealed an email signifying a past due deadline of a task for the district office. Down for the count, I rose from my desk and headed over to my lead secretary's office. I was hoping for some solace in a kind word from her and help in completing the overdue district office task. Instead, I received an unexpected epiphany.

As soon as I walked into the secretary's office, she simply said, "Fix your face and remember your purpose. Go visit classrooms." That lightning bolt of remark struck right to my leadership core. Every leader has a core--that motivating life force that compels our "Why" into dynamic action. The leadership core is the essence of our purpose. Our lead secretary had taken my words and thrown them back at me. She had heard me many times in faculty meetings extol the "Why" of our School. The echoes of conversations I had with teachers about our shared vision for our schoolhouse. We wanted to inspire our students to create a masterpiece. We believed that our work was rooted into collectively creating a masterpiece in our schoolhouse. She had heard me many times share my purpose as a school leader. She witnessed me coaching teachers through the process of forming and living out their purpose as educators.

This reminder from our lead secretary was humbling. I needed that jolt to remember my core. I had even jotted it down on a sticky note on my desk. One of my school administration professors encouraged me to do so during my days in "principal school." Yet, that purpose was literally buried memos and paperwork. I had lost sight of my purpose and gave permission to the administrative grind to dominate my focus.

Your Mission & Vision is the DNA
Often, we forget that our purpose as educators and leaders must be tied to the mission and vision of the schoolhouse. The mission and vision of any organization is the compass and guiding light for action, results, and growth. For a schoolhouse it is the DNA in service and support of students.
As school leaders, we are called to uphold the balance of dreams of the building. We are called to model and exemplify our core in alignment with an inclusive, shared school vision. Education is life changing. All of us hopefully had at least one teacher who changed our world. The mission and vision of a schoolhouse must be embedded in the school culture through the actions of our values and beliefs. It is felt, believed, and evident in every aspect of the schoolhouse. There are important tasks that we must accomplish as school leaders. There is that part of the "gig" where we do have to meet the demands of required tasks.

We do have a responsibility to shift and push the conversation to the principal work that is aligned with mission and vision. As productive leaders we must do our best to keep in concert with that move. As leaders of best practices, we are bombarded with the essential question, "How is this best for kids?" I am not downplaying that question at all. We do serve and support students. What if we shifted the paradigm to one that was more intentional with the vision of the school? What if we ensured that every decision and action we made was in support of the vision and mission of the school? Too many times we sacrifice aspiration for compliance. It is vital that we relentlessly share our core as leaders and connect it to the vision and mission of the school. In many ways, we as school leaders are emblematic of the words that form a vision and mission statement. Using the spirit of those words is an essential pivot for school leaders to commit to doing. Leaders must find relevance and meaning in the daily grind. What better way to do that than to move with the very thing that drives our passions, joys, and dreams as educators and leaders?

Protect Leadership Core
I did heed the words of our school secretary. The rest of my day was spent engaged in the energetic marrow of classrooms. I connected with students, teachers, and district thought partners. My purpose

was renewed. I felt a sense of well-being in reviving my core and connecting to the shared vision of our schoolhouse. At the end of the day, I thanked our secretary for giving me the crash course I needed in renewing my sense of purpose. She smiled as I thanked her for reigniting my purpose to the schoolhouse in which we both believed.

For the remainder of the school year, I taped the word "Purpose" to a prominent place on my desk and set an alarm on my iPhone with that word. I encourage you to do whatever it takes to protect your leadership core and uphold the vision of your schoolhouse. Do not let paperwork and deadlines corrode the momentum you have forged to make a positive impact as a leader. You are the foundation for the vision in your schoolhouse and the world is better for it.

Sean Gaillard is an elementary school principal currently residing in North Carolina. He is the founder of #CelebrateMonday, author of "The Pepper Effect" and host of the "Principal Liner Notes Podcast."

Stop Introducing More Initiatives Just Because You Learned Something New
MAGGIE FAY

The scenario below is not a climate anyone wants to create in their school. It is one that does not promote collaboration, excitement and brings forth passion. Rather it defeats the educators before the initiative can commence. Introducing more initiatives just because you learned something new is a complete knee jerk reaction that wastes time and impedes the productivity of everyone.

Scenario: School leader attends a professional development workshop, committee meeting, or visits with a colleague who shares where they learn of a shiny new initiative that worked for them. Because it was packaged persuasively and even presented as evidence-based, the leader wants to jump in with both feet and give it a try. No consensus, no collaboration, just an expectation to try the shiny new initiative that worked for someone else. The next day, week or month during the next staff meeting the leader excitedly interjects, "I have a GREAT new initiative that I want us all to implement."

Educators in the room: Eye rolling, sighing, exchanging glances with their colleague, anxious, overwhelmed, and some wondering why they are never consulted on these new ideas. The same responses that Allyson Apsey shared in Chapter 1 where the leader was "winging" culture and blocking synergy of teams.

As leaders, we want to maintain a standard of excellence in our schools. We want to try new ideas and see if they can add value to student success. However, often educators' input is not sought out. We add layers of work onto already very busy and overwhelmed educators, especially during a time where everyone is asked to pivot continuously as induced by this new era of the pandemic. Jumping into new initiatives just for the sake of a new idea is an overreaction of emotions rather than a strategic plan just as Dr. Peter Loehr shared in Chapter 18.

Please Do So with Input
What would happen to a school climate if educators were asked to form a committee where they unpack how a new initiative would impact their students? Their community? New initiatives should be tailored to your communities' needs. Ask parents to be part of the discussion and genuinely listen to what they have to say.

Being excited about new initiatives is fantastic as it means you are trying to make changes, have passion to enlist new ideas, however, please do so with input. If you haven't already done so, step into a classroom and observe what your students are doing and saying. Give them the opportunity to also have input and have a wholesome approach when you're announcing a new initiative just because you learned something new.

In our current circumstances we also need to think about how your new learning impacts digital learning. Is it a pedagogical shift in thinking practices that can be transferable to in person and online? We ask our learners, our educators, and all our staff to be reflective. So, I ask that as leaders we also continue to be reflective. Keep your passion for new ideas to be implemented but shift your own thinking in terms of how it will be approached, announced, and delivered. I honestly believe that involving our educators, students and parents in our decision making for new ideas will shift the culture of a school to being more dynamic, passionate, and dedicated.

Flip the Scenario
Flip the scenario around and ask yourself how you'd feel if your superintendent didn't provide you

with a choice about how you are to implement new policies, procedures, initiatives? Of course, sometimes we do not have a choice in how things are implemented or addressed, especially when educators are "voluntold" because of policies or state initiatives put in place. When approached by a leader for your input, most likely you feel appreciated and respected for your level of expertise. Every educator wants to feel appreciated and respected. Likewise, if overlooked or dismissed, you'd probably feel deflated. Place yourself in your educators and students point of view when introducing new ideas.

Seek the Missing Voice

Examine whose voice may be missing from the new initiative. Ask the following questions to seek out the missing voice(s):

- Who is missing that would ensure equity of voice?
- Who might need to be included to ensure that culturally responsive pedagogy that can lead the new initiative?
- Who will be carrying out the work?
- Who is the end user?
- Who is accountable for the results?
- Who are the supporters that will require close communication?

When voices and opinions are sought out and heard people will trust their leader because they trust the process that led to the implementation of the new initiative. Productivity is enhanced when a leader considers and includes students, parents, and those impacted in the school community.

Shift Your Thinking Based on Input

There is intentionality in using the words "shift your thinking" rather than "change your thinking." Many people revert to their defense mechanisms because they don't want to "change"; therefore, "shifting" thinking is more palatable and less definitive. You may not completely change your decision about a new decision, but you may tweak the plan, better define the process of the plan, or delay the plan based on the input you have gathered. You may even decide to scale things out and start with a classroom or grade level pilot of the new initiative rather than going all in. When leaders actively listen with the intention of shifting their thinking, it saves time and promotes healthy collaboration and productivity.

Maggie Fay is a public-school vice-principal in Ontario, Canada with a passion for inclusionary practices.

Stop Assigning Tasks that Lead to Nowhere
STEPHANIE ROTHSTEIN

Educational Leaders do not enter leadership roles thinking, "I'm so excited to assign tasks that lead to nowhere." Often, we leaders are asked to fulfill initiatives, solicit feedback, and analyze data. As tasks and initiatives pile up, leaders often delegate them to faculty and staff. Due dates, compliance, programs, data collection, and documented collaboration are all compounding components necessary for the function of public education.

The question leaders should consider before delegating a task is, "Does this task, email, or meeting warrant the amount of time I am requiring of the person, will it offer a mentoring and growth opportunity because of our interactions, or will it simply lead to nowhere?" Productive leaders value the time and input of everyone that they lead. Delegation cannot be a surface level value; we must value people by considering the amount of time attached to the communication and task(s). When the work of those that you lead is not meaningful, delegating tasks promote a culture of disgruntled, discouraged, and demotivated staff members. Leaders must ensure that tasks are not time fillers caught in the spin cycle of delegating work unintentionally or micromanaging as Svetlana Popovic shared in Chapter 4. Stop wasting time requiring staff to read unclear emails, attend staff meetings with no outcome, collect data that lay dormant, serve on committee meetings that simply check a box, and/or turn in documentation that leads to nowhere. Strategic and productive leaders value the time required of the people they lead.

The Staff Meeting Discussion
Consider the following staff meeting scenario:

> You greet your staff at the door with upbeat music creating a positive atmosphere. Educators are seated with a variety of grade levels, subject matters, position, and titles. An ice cream sandwich bar is even catered in the back of the room to help boost morale. You feel productive and ready to guide your staff in understanding that they are a vital part of the processes of your

school. To do this you give each table a discussion question, data overview from the previous school year, and you even ask that people at the table take on the roles of facilitator, timekeeper, and note taker. You made sure you have checked in with the facilitators ahead of time. The questions for each group focus on some of the larger problems of practice of your school: meeting the academic needs of all students, SEL, and Equity. These are initiatives of the district and you have ensured your staff that while they may not be new topics, you are now setting this conversation up differently and this will be impactful. Somehow, in this 1-hour staff meeting, you thought everything was going to change.

While there may be good intention in eliciting feedback and thoughts from your staff just as Allyson Apsey recommended in Chapter 1 of this book, the scenario above is not that. What is the end goal of these staff meeting conversations? Having staff talk without ever leading to application leads staff members to feel like their time is wasted and that they really aren't valued. As a result, what they share during these conversations will not be as honest and reflective and they will veer the conversation away from the task assigned. Ultimately, staff members want to know what you will do with these reflections. Will they be gathered for a report to document the thoughts of staff? And, if you gather them and analyze this data, what changes will be implemented based on it? None of the "actions" from this staff meeting scenario can be implemented immediately and staff are left unclear why the administrator is gathering information.

Ensure that Tasks Lead to Added Value
Instead of asking staff to "discuss" topics, provide opportunities for faculty to provide feedback with a result in mind. Are the actions you are requiring aligned to your mission, vision, values, and beliefs? As in Chapter 1, disclose why staff are gathered and how the information will be used to add value to your mission, vision, values, and beliefs. Below are three ways leaders can ensure that the tasks lead to somewhere.

> **1. Analyze student work samples to guide instructional decisions.** We do have alternatives to handing out packets of data from the previous year. It is not easy to begin a meeting hearing staff say, "None of these students are in my class anymore, why am I analyzing this old data?" And while there may be times as a leader to analyze this data to look at trends, for the educators, this task leads them nowhere. Instead of bringing data to your staff, have your staff bring their data. Use planning time to have teachers bring in student work samples to analyze current data.

This is often used in Professional Learning Circles/Communities, but this is a process that does not need to be limited to those spaces. When teachers are expected to arrive in a PLC space with relevant data for the purpose of analyzing, collaboration has value. When teams analyze growth based on the needs of their students and seek expertise from their colleagues based on the analysis of student work, educators experience high-value productivity. Strong PLC protocols must be in place to ensure a high-trust solution-oriented environment where educators experience celebrations and support. It is important that leaders invite educators to participate in this process, model the process, provide adequate planning time, and provide high quality training before diving in.

2. Provide asynchronous interactions. Not all meetings need to take place with everyone in the same room at the same time. Not all communications can be solved with a blanket email either. A post-pandemic solution that emerged that supported initiatives and committees, was asynchronous interactions. Instead of assigning staff group reflection tasks during all staff meetings provide a space and window of time to provide input. Asynchronous interactions provide individuals time to reflect on questions, gather thoughts, and thoughtfully share. Ask staff members to come ready to deliver a 1-minute pitch, artifacts, digital samples, or a picture representation for an actionable step to impact change or reach a school goal. Consider assigning a table/room/space where each staff member is invited to join you or another school leader at their convenience. Asynchronous interactions focus on sharing ideas, providing perspective, or voting on next steps. Asynchronous spaces can also be used for mentoring and guiding colleagues in setting classroom or grade level goals. These interactions or pitches provide an opportunity to make quality decisions about which group, task force, and/or committee educators may want to spearhead.

"The big idea of the sprint is to take a small team, clear the schedule for a week, and rapidly progress from problem to tested solution."—Jake Knapp, creator of the Google Ventures Design Sprint

3. Offer collaborative design thinking sprints. Voltage Control (a real-world corporation that specializes in change and innovation for businesses on voltagecontrol.com) shares in their Blog: Design Sprints vs. design thinking, What's the Difference? that a design cycle is a longer process that involves empathizing, defining, ideating, prototyping, and testing. In STEM classrooms the design cycle is highly collaborative and may span over a longer amount of time.

In contrast, design thinking "sprints" are condensed into five-day compressions. These design thinking sprints are applicable faculty-wide, in grade level teams, and even alongside students in a problem-solving setting. These short productive sprints aim to collaboratively develop actionable and tested solutions. My favorite way is using a Design Thinking Sprint - a quick burst of time when you propose a wide variety of solutions without censoring yourself. This option allows staff members to develop solutions collaboratively.

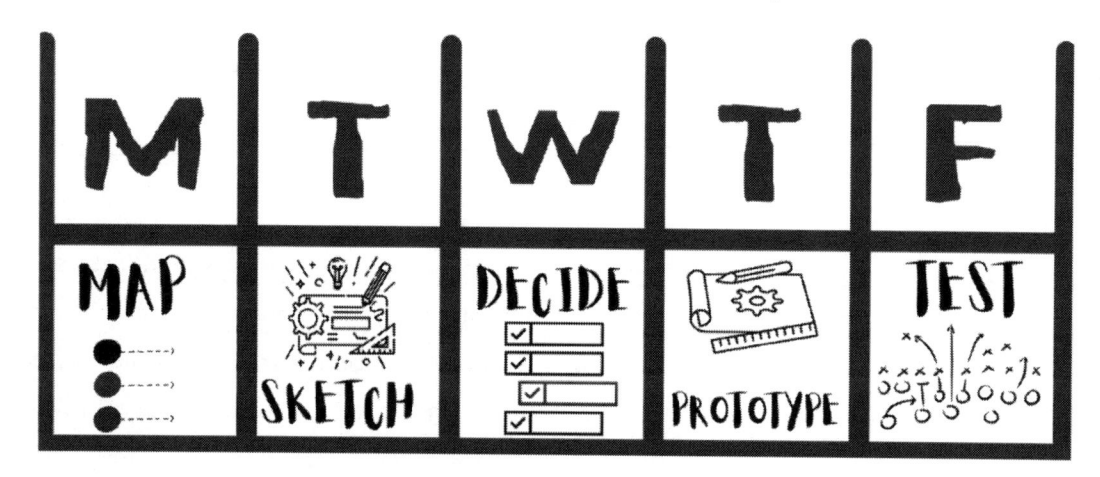

Sprints offer creative solutions that pack a powerful punch because they focus on:

- How to break down a complex problem into a focused target.
- The benefits of a diverse, cross-functional group when tackling a project.
- The power of learning through quick-and-dirty prototyping versus months of development.
- The importance of showing your work to stakeholders early to get actionable feedback.
- Plus, the need for collaboration, open-mindedness, divergent thinking, and empathy for the end-user.

Step 1: Map
To accomplish this, school faculty must understand the problem(s) and what is needed of those impacted. In this step of the cycle educators are asking critical questions, focusing on the mission, vision, goals, and beliefs.

Leaders provide an atmosphere where evidence-based practices, expert ideas, processes, protocols, activities, or strategies are explored.

Step 2: Sketch
This is a time to get creative and to divergently ideate solutions while prioritizing what is most important. Ask, "How might we" questions for the top three problems of practice.

- How might we meet the academic needs of all students?
- How might we support our students' Social Emotional needs?
- How might we evaluate and ensure processes in our school are equitable for all students?

This is a time for teachers to individualize for their classrooms, or teams for their grade levels, or content areas and start sketching and brainstorming potential solutions that can be carried out within the week.

Step 3: Decide
This process is individualized because faculty members then decide which problem of practice they want to focus upon. You can have them gather corners of the room, at tables, or sign up on a digital form. Next, pair educators up with another in the group and interview one another about their experiences with this topic and what issues impact them and their students most. Based on the responses of their partner each person develops solution ideas during the "Sprint" for the needs of their partner. This is key- they are not developing solutions for themselves. They draw out or write out solutions in 5 minutes and then present them to their partner and get feedback. Based on feedback, each person picks one solution or combination they would move forward with. These solutions can be process, content, or practice based. You can decide if you want to keep this task to remaining in pairs or if you want to have each pair present to other pairs or have volunteers share more widely. The importance is that these ideas do not end during the staff meeting. Like a "give one, get one" the objective in this stage of the process is to collect as much feedback and added value to decide what teachers will try in the classroom or on campus that week.

Step 4: Prototype
This should lead to groups or teams that focus on prototyping, or implementing solutions that are replicable, can be analyzed for their impact, and that can be reported out as successful or unsuccessful.

Step 5: Test
Teachers and teams implement their strategy, process, protocol, or activity and document the process to determine if it was successful or unsuccessful. Adequate data in the form of anecdotal observation, scores, feedback, or student work provide the evidence needed to adjust the

practice, repeat the practice, or to abort the mission.

Start Small to go Somewhere Big

Don't get hung up on a Monday through Friday calendar or a need to set aside five professional development days. Quite the contrary. This is a process that can be taught and replicated during grade level team planning, part of the PLC process, or even during weekly faculty meetings. Once educators learn the process of design cycle springs, they will feel valued because of the way leaders prioritize time together by asking them to participate in specific and actionable tasks. A key element to successful implementation is to make sure staff do not focus on tasks that already have solutions. Allowing faculty to use and analyze their own data, create solution initiatives that inform committee work they lead, and participate in collaborative design thinking sprints focused on action is key to going somewhere BIG. Let's redesign tasks that lead to nowhere to tasks that are worthy of having educators give of their expertise, voice, and time.

Stephanie Rothstein, a 20-year educator, is an Academic Innovation Leader in Northern California. Her continuous love of learning led her to become a Google Innovator, Trainer, and Coach, co-founder of GlobalGEG, creator of CanWeTalkEDU, and writer of numerous articles published on Edutopia and her own blog. She is a contributor to Because of A Teacher by George Couros, Evolving with Gratitude by Lainie Rowell, and Be GREAT by Dwight Carter. She speaks at educational conferences around the world about Design Thinking, Leadership, and Growing a Culture of Innovation and was named CUE's Teacher of the Year for 2021.

Stop Being a Paper Pusher
CHRISTOPHER DODGE

Imagine this scenario: you are at an athletic event to watch your favorite team play. The game begins and it dawns on you that something is not right. The players are on the field or court, but they are not playing well; they are not communicating well and clearly their actions are not coordinated in any way. Suddenly there is an important decision to be made that will predict the outcome of the game, and it dawns on you: the coach is not present. Chaos ensues, as the players begin to argue and fight over this decision. "Where is the coach?" you are thinking to yourself, as clearly there is no one to make this all-important call for the team. The game ends, your team loses, and you leave the game perplexed by what you just witnessed. You quickly get home to watch the post-game press conference, at which point the coach explains their absence. You watch in confusion as the coach explains that he/she was in their office during the game, completing a checklist and filing paperwork that was long overdue. The coach explains, "The league has mandated that all coaches, in addition to coaching, submit player discipline reports, practice schedules and plans, as well as player updates and game plans to the league office every week. This is hours of work that must be done in lieu of being on the court."

Leaders Are Paid to Be at the Game
The scenario above is utterly ridiculous and I am sure you laughed at the absurdity of it. A coach is paid to be AT THE GAME, coordinating the events and actions of the players involved. There is literally no scenario where you could imagine a coach not being at the game- it is why they do what they do. Even when a coach cannot be present, there is an assistant coach who fills the void. Coaches have a perspective and view that players simply cannot and should not have. Even with the most talented players, every team needs someone who is watching from the sidelines, observing, and providing feedback to the players, while creating a game plan that highlights the team's strengths and puts their team in the best position for victory. Paperwork is either done by someone else or is saved for a different time, outside of practice and the game. Time with the team is sacred. I am left with questions for leaders, "When the 'game' is happening, where are you? Are you on the sidelines watching your team and giving them feedback to improve? Or are you in your office completing the mandated paperwork that has very little impact on the team(s) in which you lead?"

Leading cannot be done through email and you certainly cannot do it from your office. In my ten years of being a school leader, I can say this with a great deal of certainty- there is not anything you will do from your office that will make a lasting impact on your school community, and I haven't read any research on high performing schools lead by a principal who stays in their office all day cranking out reports and staff mandates. As you are reading this you are likely thinking about your colleagues who spend way too much time behind their computers. I would also better that you don't consider them leaders. You consider them managers, and there are huge differences. We are paid to be a leader so let's act like it by leading the game.

The Secret is Showing Up
Make a point to be present in the school or team of people that you lead. Interact with students, families, and staff. The things you learn through dialogic conversations will make you a better leader,

it certainly did for me. I would like to think that over the years my intentional leadership presence has helped me gain trust with the staff because it is based on a culture of feedback and interaction. When people know they are important and that their voice(s) are heard, belonging, hard work, and high standards becomes the norm. When leaders are attuned to individual needs and challenges and respond authentically, educators feel understood. Be approachable at the drop off and pick up line even though you may be observing traffic patterns. Be present in the cafeteria and seek to understand the culture of the student body and the routines that are working (and not working). Be focused on instructional quality and practices in the classrooms while watching how a new program is being. Most importantly, enjoy being with those that you have been entrusted to lead. That is why we entered this profession. No educator ever signed up so they could type up reports and file paperwork. Someone once said that the secret to most things in life is simply showing up, and as a leader, showing up intentionally is one of the most important and hardest things to do.

Do the Right Thing Even if You Need to Ask for Forgiveness Later
When I first heard the coaching analogy my first thought was, "Yeah, that makes sense, but I don't have an assistant to help with paperwork." This is true, and for me I had to make a mindset shift. Intentionally I set out to make my presence and visibility my first priority and the paperwork/emails second. If it were the other way around, it would be a big waste of time to every stakeholder involved. I will never apologize for missing a deadline because I was in classrooms; it is simply that important. If my superintendent or the state is upset because I didn't get something to them on time, I would much prefer to ask forgiveness than consistently miss time in my classrooms with students and teachers. And hey there are tricks of the trade like working from the back of the room, power walkthroughs, and rotating with the assistant principal or coaches to ensure balance for all. But at the end of the day, if I am going to be penalized for delayed clerical work, then that is most likely a place I don't want to work.

Plan for Less Interruptions
For some reason, many novice leaders get stuck in a trap of never-ending email chains and paperwork that gets in the way of doing transformative work. In the past when I made a commitment, I had to be intentional with my time. I had to figure out the "how", and I am sure you are thinking the same. Most of us who are serious about the work we do and would love nothing more than to be out and about, without the dreaded paperwork hanging over our heads. My recommendation is to start small. Book one entire day a week to be out of your office or book a two-hour block of time for each day. Let your

staff and secretary know that you will not be available for meetings, and that you will be checking email at the end of the day. This time is protected, pending a life-threatening emergency. You will be shocked at how much you learn, the depth of conversations you have, and spoiler alert: the buildings do not, in fact, cave in because you didn't respond within 10 minutes to an angry parent. Leaders who block off a day a week typically expand to two days per week very quickly because of the transformation they see it making on the productivity of the school.

During the times when you are not out and about interacting and providing coaching feedback, be more intentional with your clerical work. Plan out your days with timelines and timeframes. Put as many nominal tasks as possible on your calendar and be rigid about sticking to these smaller daily accomplishments. Be approachable regarding school matters during the day, but don't leave your door open so wide that staff interrupt you over and over for casual conversations that are not focused on a culture of high-quality teaching and learning. Your time is too important. Modeling efficiency, productivity, and balance is key to self-regulation and effective time management. Plan your days, post them on your office door for transparency so that individuals and teams can be mindful and minimize interruptions. Start color coding that calendar and be amazed at how much more efficient you become. I hardly ever miss a deadline, and I spend two days a week in classrooms solely because I am now better with my time.

Work on the System Not in the System

The next question you may be thinking is: "Once I am out there, what do I do?" This is a very real question to ask yourself because I am sure it is foreign to just be present and talk to people. Leaders are doers, fixers, type A's who want to get stuff done. My first instinct was to mediate the issue between two students in the hallway, teach a model lesson for a teacher, or even run dismissal duty. My advice: don't. All the things I mentioned are well-intentioned but have unintended consequences. The first and most important is that once you interject yourself into a situation, you become the saver and that can lead to staff not feeling empowered to do it on their own. You never see Bill Belichick on the field throwing 65-yard touchdown passes, or Phil Jackson making it rain from beyond the arch. Watch your kids and staff and talk to them afterwards. Coach them. Empower them. My advice for when you are out and about come from the words of the great George Costanza: "do nothing". Go to classrooms and watch. Leave a word of encouragement on the desk. Smile and give a compliment. Work with kids. Join a P.E. class. Do some reading or writing. Observe. Reflect. Coach. Repeat. All in a strength-based approach. Your job as the leader is to work on the system not in the system. And P.S- when you are "helping" most of the staff are upset because you are just getting in the way, so on behalf of your staff, stop. Please and thank you.

Being visibly present in your school is vitally important. Unfortunately, too many leaders have the desire to be actively engaged but are caught between many competing forces and priorities. If there is something you gain from this chapter is the permission to let go of what you know is not making a difference for your students and staff, and to start spending your time where it matters most. My fear is that many leaders have left and will leave administrator roles because of the evolution of complexity- we aren't doing the work we entered the profession to do and we don't have a way out. The work of the leader is too important to waste on budget sheets, evaluation forms, and all staff emails. I am here to tell you that you can accomplish leadership balance when you stop wasting time and become strategically productive.

Christopher Dodge is an educational troublemaker, principal, and lead learner of the Thorndyke Road School in Worcester, Massachusetts. With over 10 years as a school leader, Christopher is a connected leader (@PrincipalDodge1) who is passionate about educator and student wellbeing. He is a consultant with Seaside Educational Consultants, and also works as an adjunct instructor at Assumption University in Worcester, MA.

67

Stop Running All the PD or Faculty Meetings Yourself
RACHELLE DENÉ POTH

A few years ago, teachers in my school had the option to present different sessions during one of our professional development days. A choice board was created which gave teachers the chance to learn from one another, to share experiences, challenges, concerns, new ideas, and to feel valued. Because of that opportunity, I walked away with many new strategies, interesting tips, and tidbits that otherwise I would not have become involved in. I learned about mindfulness, restorative practices, challenge-based learning, and trauma-informed teaching. I had time to share some of my ideas for what worked with my students and learn from others too. It was refreshing to learn from colleagues and offered the administrators the opportunity to interact, make interconnections, and interject in a high energy setting. It was a win for all. Providing flexibility in learning where teachers were able to decide where to go and how to spend their time learning, made a big difference. Teachers felt valued and inspired by their colleagues. Time is valued and learning is productive when teachers can showcase their talents not only within their school but in the larger school community.

When I think about learning whether it is the learning of my students in my classroom or professional development, I truly believe that regardless of which of these we are focused on, we need to have the same mindset about how to best co-create learning experiences. Productive professional learning focuses on the pedagogy of high-quality instruction, the ability to collaboratively design activities that build skills, how people exchange information most relevantly, promoting learner driven outcomes.

Provide Choice

All educators have different comfort levels with learning and engage in a variety of professional development whether in school, conferences, social media, educator networks, personal reading, or the multitude of other options available. We don't all learn the same way, we don't all make the same choices, and so it makes sense to have educators to share their unique experiences and perspectives to enhance learning for their peers and bring new innovative ideas into more classrooms for more students. Teachers deserve to be involved in the decision-making process when it comes to professional development just as students should be involved when it comes to their own learning in our classrooms.

When it comes to learning, whether for students or for educational leaders, all participants deserve access to voice and choice as part of the process for meeting our goals. We know that not all students learn at the same pace or benefit from the same activities yet there are many educators that continue to provide the exact same instruction and activities for all students, leaving little room for choice. I was that educator. Until I learned something different.

We know the importance of providing choice for our students. We know that we need to empower them to take the lead in learning in our classrooms. So why are professional development sessions still happening where one or only a few people make decisions for all educators? Only a few decide on the PD agenda and types of learning activities that are going to take place, in many cases without input from those who will be directly affected: the teachers.

Professional development is essential and having it scheduled throughout the school year creates guaranteed times to spend with our colleagues. PD topics, processes, grouping, and interactions can be maximized when teachers are offered choices that promote more meaningful, personalized interactions, and learning experiences.

Customize PD

During the pandemic many schools could not meet in person, nor provide traditional professional development days for their staff. Even leaders had to figure out how to facilitate learning remotely when schools closed. Learning the technology was a feat in and of itself for many educators. Additionally, educators were tasked with locating curriculum resources and training programs that would help them pivot their teaching to meet the needs of students and their families. This experience also uncovered individual professional needs and gaps in learning that were needed to make it through the year. Teaching students virtually required a reevaluation of the pedagogical approach to facilitating learning. Likewise, facilitating professional development virtually required leaders to reevaluate the andragogical approach to PD which involves more complex schema, effective self-regulation, intuition, time, higher ability to reason, and a faster processing time to acquire new knowledge. Although both educators and students deserved to have a say in their learning experience, the approaches, activities, and needs of students versus adults look different.

Adult learners deserve professional development choices that focus on pedagogy, achievement outcomes, content area(s), interdisciplinary connections, technology integration, and self-driven. Providing teachers with the opportunity to voice their needs and areas of focus can be as simple as setting up an asynchronous time in person or digitally for educators just as Stephanie Rothstein shared in Chapter 63. Based on this type of input educators deserve a choice on how they will drive their learning and engage in meaningful opportunities for professional growth aligned to a targeted outcome.

If we are to create rich learning experiences for our students, leaders must also experience adaptive, self-driven, individualized, and relevant learning experiences. It is our job as leaders to seek the voices of educators, to understand the needs of the adult learner, and actively plan for high engagement in andragogy-based learning. Create spaces for educators to choose from a menu of PD topics or learnings, lead asynchronous interactions in learning cycles, or provide observation and feedback support to one another. Educators deserve customized PD in this post-pandemic era of the unknown in education.

Offer Flexibility

For years and perhaps even still, professional development was a passive learning experience. Educators would receive the agenda for the day and show up as directed. It was a day of sit and get, with little time to apply or build skills together. All too often there was little room for flexibility because everyone was required to be in the same room at the same time regardless of schema, skill, content, or topic. There may have been one speaker droning information with a PowerPoint presentation with no interaction. Other times the content may not have been relevant for all teachers because of tight schedules, multiple or new district initiatives. When PD is rigid or stand alone, it can disengage educators in actualizing new learning, leading to the feeling of wasted time and talent rather than impacting their efficacy of teaching. In terms of flexibility consider the following questions:

- What practices can be applied that meet district or state requirements and offer flexibility in learning?
- How can leaders create the most authentic and relevant learning experience for all participants online, offline, or hybrid?
- How should learning flexibility be applied to adult learning (andragogy) versus student learning (pedagogy)?

Many teachers are considered experts in specific content, strategies, or skills and willing to lead a component of professional development. Leaders that network with other leaders may want to consider sharing teacher experts and providing release time to travel to other local schools to share the work that they are doing. Interconnections of "expert" teachers willing to teach, model, or share develops teachers into leaders and learners into experts. Leaders may gather local teacher "experts" to create a special learning event that is open to teachers from neighboring schools. Consider these flexible learning venues.

> **Taste of Technology:** A good friend of mine, Zee Poerio, in Pittsburgh, runs a "Taste of Technology" event open to local educators and for teachers in her own school.
>
> **Unconference:** Another example is hosting an "Unconference" that provides participants the opportunity to list challenges that they are seeking solutions for as well as strengths or areas of expertise they can offer. Informally people are grouped by strengths and need to breakout, collaborate, and share tips, and expert ideas.
>
> **Pop-up PD:** A teacher, instructional coach, specialist, administrator, or guest offers a short 15–20-minute showcase before or after school to collaborate on a featured strategy. Educators

power up together and rapidly discuss implementation, misconceptions of skill, standard alignment, and a down and dirty "how to". Teachers leave ready to implement the following day.

PLCs: Leverage the power of a PLC, a professional learning community, to give teachers the chance to self-direct and work on something truly meaningful for their practice. Provide choices when it comes to a PLC, by empowering teachers to focus on an area of interest, a book study or even a self-directed initiative that teachers want to pursue.

Transferability and classroom implementation is more likely whenever educators connect with colleagues, share challenges, explore successes, and use talents. When educators seize the opportunity to try new things and continue to grow and become their personal best. Opportunities that offer flexibility and ownership foster authentic learning experience that have a higher likelihood of transferring into classroom practice. Provide teachers with the chance to decide what type of PD they need. We all experienced different things in our classrooms and have a variety of interests and skill sets that are unique to us. Let's embrace the power of social learning and the importance of voice and choice for all learners, including us in our schools.

Rachelle Dené Poth is an edtech consultant, presenter, attorney, author, and teacher. She is an ISTE Certified Educator and serves as the past president of the ISTE Teacher Education Network. Rachelle is the author of seven books and a columnist for several blog publications.

Stop Calling "One-and-Done" Training Professional Development
ERIK M. FRANCIS

*"Too many professional development initiatives are done to teachers
– not for, with or by them."* -Andy Hargreaves

Do You Want the Rock Show or the Relationship?

That's the question I ask school leaders who contact me about the professional development that I facilitate based on the deep learning topics, depth of knowledge (DOK) and good questioning. After I describe the intricacies, depth of learning that the training will entail, and what the teachers will experience, the school leaders generally want to know two things:

1. How much time will professional development take?
2. How much will professional development cost?

This is the uncomfortable part of the conversation I have with schools. I understand time and money are the two things that most schools lack. They lack the time needed to implement professional development effectively with fidelity. They also lack the money needed to pay for someone like me to provide professional development, guidance, and support to the depth and extent it demands. I am very empathetic and sensitive to that. That's why I ask them whether they want the rock show or the relationship.

The "rock show" is just what is inferred. It's a one-and-done presentation that feels more like a performance than professional development. The key difference, however, is the performer putting on the "rock show" gets invited to the venue for one night only to perform their music to an audience who is familiar with their work and wanting to hear the songs. After the show, the performer is gone to put on the same show at the next venue for a new audience who wants to hear their music and are fans of their work. The stipulations for the professional development provider are similar. However, unlike the performer, the audience to whom the PD provider presents may not be familiar with their work or the message and methods they present. Also, there may be some in the audience who are neither interested nor wanting to hear what they are "singing". They are a captured audience who are forced to attend the training. Hopefully, they will be captivated by the performer's message and method and become "fans". It doesn't matter how much time a PD provider has to present a one-and-done training. It's still a "rock show". Like Eminem raps, "You only get one shot, do not miss your chance to blow. This opportunity comes once in a lifetime." That opportunity is not only to share the message and method but also leave the audience wanting more so you'll be invited back to work further with the educators or come back later or return the following year.

Now I'm not saying the "rock show" is bad. I'm also not dissuading schools from providing "rock shows" to their staff. There are times when school staff may need the "rock show" where they can relax, reflect, and take a respite from the demands of teaching. There are also some schools who can only afford the one-and-done "rock show" because it costs so much to bring that presenter to their school.

That time and money for the one-and-done training may be the only time and money schools have to provide their teacher such an experience.

A One-and-Done Training is *NOT* Professional Development

Professional development is a relationship. Timebound training is part of the relationship. However, the relationship between the teachers and the PD provider develops not only through continuous training but also coaching, guidance and support. The teacher knows the PD provider will be back to provide additional support on the practices and methods they presented previously. They will conduct walkthroughs to observe how the kids are responding to the message and methods the teacher has learned. They schedule time to work with the teacher to gauge how they are doing and guide them in increasing or improving their skills. They assure the teacher they are there not to make their lives more difficult or to add to their workload. They assure the teacher they are there not only to help the teacher but also decrease the pressure they have placed on themselves. Relationships through professional development require time and money. More specifically, they require schools to make an investment in the relationship. What determines whether that investment of time and money is worth making?

The Rock Show

You see, "the rock show" is when professional development providers can establish and build the relationship. It's when they can introduce a new message or methods and also themselves. The rock show performance is a time that the presenter can gain the trust of the teachers. A rock show performance acknowledges the complexity and change that must take place among the students and staff. It's also when the presenter can assure their audience, they will not be expected to make this change immediately or single-handedly. The presenter can do an Arnold Schwarzenegger imitation and let the teachers know, "I'll be back," to coach, guide, and support them in this process. Hopefully, the staff will want the present to come back – and if they don't initially, perhaps they will once they recognize and realize how the presenter shifts their role from sage on the stage to the supporter of the staff's success.

Pick One or The Other

To maximize time and productivity through professional development experiences, leaders must be intentional about their purpose, and communicate that purpose. Teachers want to know that when they come together and give up instructional time that they could be working with students or planning effective lessons, that their time is worth it. There are times when culture and community building or facing adversity should be at the center of the stage. Other times a focus on mission, vision, values, and goals should drive multi-session professional development that allows for distributive practice, failure, trying it again, and receiving feedback until the new skill is implemented effectively. So how could leaders decide whether they want the "rock show" or the relationship? Consider the following components and guiding questions that may assist you in strategically picking one, and only one, for the right reason(s).

Pricing and affordability: What can you afford? Do you have the time and funding to implement the message and methods with the help of the presenter or can you only afford a one-time only presentation? Do you have the resources and manpower support in the form of district specialists, instructional coaches, or teacher mentors that can carry out the ongoing support if you cannot afford to pay an outside facilitator for this service?

Teacher receptiveness: How do your teachers feel? How did your teachers respond to the message and method presented? Do they agree or disagree with the message and methods? Did they like or dislike the personality of the presenter? Are they committed to implementing the ideas and instruction or have they decided what was presented won't work with your school's specific student population or for them professionally? Is it worth the time and money to invest in making the change required or should it be abandoned?

Teacher wants and/or needs: What do your teachers need and want? Do they just need and want that one time to hear someone with expertise come in and provide them that message or method that will increase their effectiveness or do they need continuous coaching, guidance, and support in making the message or method work for them?

Expected outcomes: What do you want from the experience? Do you want to inspire your staff with an encouraging message, or do you want to introduce them to an educational method they can apply in their instructional delivery?

Follow-up and follow-through: What do you want the next steps to be? Are you confident you and your teachers can implement the message and methods after listening to the presenter once or do you need them to come back to help with the implementation, monitoring, and adjustment?

Capacity and longevity of the facilitator: What can the PD provider offer? Is the provider interested in returning or do they feel they only need one time with the teachers? Is the follow-up coaching, guidance, support, and training not only affordable but also adaptable to the unique needs of your school or is it a program or product you must purchase and implement on your own or with an associate from the presenter's organization?

That's why I didn't title this chapter "Stop 'One-and-Done' Professional Development, Altogether". You are instructional leaders guiding long-term life-changing metacognitive teaching and learning experiences that are individualized and rooted in purpose that will impact generations to come. The one-and-done has its place and purpose. It does. It's an excellent way to take a break or take a moment to recharge, reflect, and relax. Invite those presenters who can motivate your staff to be the best they can be. However, don't call those "one-and-done" sessions professional development because it isn't. Call the experience by what it really is – a "rock show". The "rock show" can be used to start that solid and supportive relationship where both the teachers and presenters can learn from each other. Professional development is the ongoing relationship of trial and error, perseverance, feedback, learning, failing, modeling, mentoring, and coaching based on the strengths of the people. None of which are present in a lecture, keynote presentation, or presenter. Professional development requires the active development of people through relational interactions distributed over time with a goal of proficiency.

Enduring Understanding and Growth Requires a Personal Relationship

The relationship, however, is professional development. The relationship between the teachers and the PD provider develops not only through continuous training but also coaching, guidance and support. The teacher knows the PD provider will be back to expand on the implementation of the message and methods they present. They will conduct walkthroughs to observe how the kids are responding to the message and methods the teacher has learned. They schedule time to work with the teacher to gauge how they are doing and guide them in increasing or improving their skills. They assure the teacher they are there not to make their lives more difficult or to add to their workload. They assure the teacher they are there not only to help the teacher but also decrease the pressure they have placed on themselves.

Let me reiterate a key point, this does not mean you should stop providing "rock shows" for your staff. Sometimes teachers need the "rock show" that will allow them to relax, reignite, be inspired, be encouraged, feel valued, connect emotionally, and experience a respite from the demands of teaching. They need a "rock show" that features a presenter who is skilled at presenting their message and methods in an "edutaining" manner. Skilled "rock show" presenters can be more personal than pedagogical in their presentation(s), focusing on the social and emotional aspects of teaching and learning for both the students and the staff. Or they can be so specialized in their content area that they provide a myriad of examples, resources as givers of knowledge. They are there to touch our hearts or to stimulate our minds. They are motivational, informational, or pedagogically instructional, but most certainly not relational. One-and-done presenters will not be by your side when their recommended strategy completely falls apart when you try it. There is nobody to bounce ideas off of or co-plan with for support. If the facilitator is not providing ongoing development, they are simply a presenter.

Professional development is a relationship that grows and evolves. That's why it's called professional development. It's a matter of teachers developing their professional knowledge and skills continuously. It's not "one-and-done" training. It requires follow up coaching and support to ensure the teachers are comfortable, confident, and efficient in implementing the message or methods presented by a trainer. It needs to be monitored to ensure the strategies or skills are working. If not, they may need to be modified to ensure they are meeting the specific needs of both the students and staff. It also requires schools to devote extensive time and money – two things that schools do not have. So how can we provide effective professional development in a continuous yet cost-effective manner? When trying to decide between a "rock show" or strengthening the ongoing instructional capacity of your staff based on a relationship, consider the following:

> **Purpose:** What is the purpose? Why are you wanting teachers to listen to the message or learn the methods? Are you wanting clarity on a concept or are

> **Impact:** What is the impact? What kind of impact do you want the training to have on your teachers and the school community?

Erik M. Francis is the owner of Maverik Education and an international author and presenter with over 25 years of experience working in education as a classroom teacher, site administrator, education program specialist with a state education agency and a trainer who provides professional development for teachers and school leaders. He is the author of ASCD's top selling book, Now That's a Good Question and Knowing is Half the Battle & Solution Tree Press, Deconstructing Depth of Knowledge: A Method and Model for Deeper Teaching and Learning. Eric is also ranked #12 in the World's Top 30 Global Gurus in Education for 2021.

69

Stop Having Meetings that Only Provide Information
MICHELE RISPO HILL

On a recent trip with my sisters, we visited the quaint town of Jim Thorpe in the Poconos Mountains of Pennsylvania. There were hip eateries and small shops with items such as candles, bumper stickers, and mugs. I stumbled upon a brand that was created by a woman who decided that the name of items would be based upon the politically incorrect things that people say when in the presence of trustworthy company. It was there that I found the perfect mug for a Christmas Pollyanna gift with colleagues. The mug read "Stop Having a Meeting That Could Have Been an Email"! Although it was certainly designed to be comical and get a hearty laugh, it was absolutely true.

Think about how much time is wasted in meetings that could have been covered through a simple email. Don't get me wrong, there is value in holding face-to face meetings that do more than share information, but most often, meetings are a one-way system of delivering information to others. The participants (if you can call them that) are usually on the receiving end of information.

Is it Justifiably Meeting Worthy?
Some information that is shared is critical, and it is essential that you witness that people have received the information. Procedures for standardized testing and critical operations are a few examples. In cases such as these, the meeting may be justifiable and necessary. There is no other way to ensure that they received the information and/or training than to host a meeting with sign-in sheets. These meetings are warranted and should continue to be scheduled. But so many other faculty meetings lack such purpose and accountability. Most times leaders schedule faculty meetings because they are expected to, sometimes even demanded to. (Yes, demanded or contracted) Because there are a finite number of minutes in the school day and almost every one of them is accounted for before a meeting is scheduled, leaders need to decide what is "meeting worthy" and what is not. So, leaders, PLEASE do not schedule meetings to have a meeting. This wastes time and impedes productivity.

Meetings That Are Unproductive
Leaders should set a goal for every meeting that they schedule that the staff leaves the meeting fired up

or re-energized or that there was a great take-away in terms of professional development or information. Please do not schedule meetings that:

- **Chastise staff as a whole group.** You know which staff members are not towing the proverbial line. Address them personally. When you use the blanket approach to call out unprofessional behavior, you lose the staff that are doing the right thing--and in turn, they lose faith in your leadership.
- **Read from a slide show.** If you are going to read verbatim from a slide show or document, just share the document with the staff. They are professionals. Treat them as such.
- **Are dictated by leadership.** Just as our students want to have a voice in their learning, so do our staff members.
- **Announce changes without staff input.** Change can be hard. Make sure that the staff has had some input in the decision-making process before a sharp change is announced at a meeting. You don't like being blind-sided and neither does your staff.
- **Do not honor the time of staff members.** Some meetings are necessary but set firm time limits and create an agenda and stick to it so that the meeting is not an endless event.
- **Could have been covered in an email.** If the information that you are delivering can be stated in a concise email with clear directions on what to do, please just do it. The staff can go back and reread the email for clarification at a time convenient for them. Now sometimes you have so many things that can be covered in an email, but a meeting might be the most expedient way to relay the information. If you find yourself scheduling 15 emails about the changes in the schedule for the week, you may just want to hold a meeting that can give a visual of the anticipated changes and expectations. (This is generally a rare occasion so staff shouldn't mind when it happens)

Meetings That Build Rapport

Faculty meetings are the perfect opportunity to build rapport with staff and amongst colleagues. They can also be a great opportunity for inspiring and recognizing staff members. Here are some reasons that meetings should be held:

- **Sharing of best practices facilitated by staff.** Members of your staff are experts in their field and pedagogy, so why not have them share their best practices with the entire staff? You can conduct the meeting much like the speed dating format. (We call it Speed PD) You may opt to highlight one or two teachers' best practices and show a video of the lesson and ask staff members to guide their peers through the process. Whatever design you choose, sharing of best practices is a great use of meeting time.

- **Celebrating milestones together.** (Years of service, life events, school wide accomplishments etc.) Who doesn't love a celebration? Well, truthfully, I am sure that you could name a few people, but most people love to celebrate others, and secretly, love when they are celebrated by others. Host meeting with no other purpose except to celebrate and honor the important milestones and achievements of the staff.
- **Team building activities.** Building positive relationships is paramount to any great organizations. (that's leadership 101) We often don't have time in the daily schedule to pause and get-to-know one another on a personal level. Use faculty/staff meetings to build a solid foundation of trust and rapport.
- **Take away something new, as in information or ideas.** Much like the sharing of best practices, you can utilize meetings to share important information or generate some buzz about new ideas.
- **Sharing sensitive information that impacts the school community.** (Deaths, illnesses etc.). Every organization has been affected by devastating events or news. Those things need to be shared with staff in-person with a sensitive touch. Emails do not convey the emotions attached to the sensitive news being shared.
- **Strategic plans or brainstorming sessions.** The staff wants a voice of collective collaboration when change is looming. Host all important stakeholders for brainstorming and strategic planning sessions so everyone can be heard.
- **Event planning sessions.** The African proverb says that when you want to go fast, go alone, when you want to go farther, go together. Planning the many events of your school requires people coming together and looking at all logistics. More can be accomplished if people are all in the same room, with an agenda of course!
- **Student-led staff meetings.** Staff may be grading papers and checking their phones in a normal faculty meeting, but if the students are leading the meeting, they will be more attentive.
- **Practice run-through of important events.** They say practice makes perfect. Utilize your meetings as run-through practices of the big events at your school. People often remember better by doing.

As a leader, you want to embrace transparency and good communication, but that doesn't mean that there must be a meeting to accomplish your goal. Your staff will appreciate your ability to discern what is meeting-worthy and what is not. Be that productive time-protecting leader!

Michele Rispo Hill is a speaker, trainer, blogger, and passionate educator who is currently serving as the Coordinator of Admissions and Strategic Marketing for Burlington County Institute of Technology. Michele is on a mission to support educators in their professional journeys.

Stop Scheduling Everything During Teachers' Planning Time
JAY POSICK

Teacher planning time is a vital part of every teacher's day. Planning time is used for a variety of purposes: planning for an upcoming lesson or unit, assessing student work, developing interventions and extensions, calling families, and reading IEPs. Teachers count on this time to best prepare for the individualized needs of every student. How much time is provided for a teacher is different for every district and maybe within every school within a district. If meetings are scheduled during planning time, pre-scheduled and protected time takes a back seat, deadlines might not be met, and meetings during planning time becomes practice instead of the exception. Essentially, encroaching on planning time (especially last minute) reduces the time teachers have to use to meet the needs of their students.

Planning Time is a Time of Productivity

In a We Are Teachers article from October of 2019 entitled, "Dear School Administrators, Please Stop Taking Away Teacher Planning Periods", the author mentions the following benefits for teacher planning periods:

- Planning periods have a big impact on the quality of our daily and long-term teaching practice (Common planning times allow teachers to meet with one another).
- Student assessment suffers when planning periods are limited (Planning periods allow teachers to compare assessment results and determine possible interventions or extensions).
- Planning periods are our self-driven PD sessions.
- We use planning periods to build relationships (Planning periods allow for phone calls and emails to families).
- Extracurricular activities and field trips require planning periods.
- Most importantly, planning periods contribute to our personal health (Planning periods allow teachers the chance to take care of personal needs).

As we know, teachers have both individual planning time and group planning time. Each has its own purpose, whether to have conversations about students or curriculum, or both, to plan for the coming days or to assess student work. Taking this time away from our staff is not something that should become an everyday experience. This time is so valuable for our teachers and once it has been taken away it becomes an expectation that it can always be taken away.

Planning Time Includes Before & After School
I think that it's also important to recognize that planning time isn't only the time that says "planning" or "preparation" on a teacher's schedule. Planning time also includes the time before and after school as well. Some teachers use their time best before school while others use their time best after school. This time should not be taken for granted nor should it be something we take advantage of throughout the year. Planning and preparation time are paramount to campus-wide productivity and for the success of staff and our students. Consider creative ways of scheduling meetings with teachers.

- Summer Academy dates to kick off the school year.
- Monthly Wednesday morning meetings.
- Professional development days throughout the school year.
- Release days where guest teachers cover classrooms so classroom teachers can meet regarding students or curriculum.
- Cover a class so that teachers can either meet with one another or watch each other teach.

Don't get me wrong, situations will arise that require a last-minute meeting during planning time. But last-minute meetings shouldn't be a daily occurrence. One meeting per week should be more than enough, especially when the agenda has been shared in advance of the meeting and staff have the opportunity to add to the agenda. And, if a pre-scheduled meeting isn't needed, then give the teachers back their planning time. I encourage you to stop monopolizing teachers' planning time!

Jay Posick is a recently retired 35-year educator, 32 of which have been in middle school, and co-author of Principals In Action: Redefining the Role. Twenty of those years were as an assistant principal or principal. Jay is a husband to his wife Jen and a father to their amazing daughter Lauren, an educator in training.

Stop Sending Pointless or Blanket Emails
LAURA STEINBRINK

If you were a teacher first, think back to those times when you were doing your job well, and then you receive that blanket email about what teachers were doing or not doing something. Consider how you felt as you read that email. Did it inspire you to continue doing what you were supposed to be doing? Or did you make a beeline to the nearest teacher to see if they had also read the email? Did you and a group of teachers get together to talk about the email? These are common reactions to pointless emails. Every educator has experienced pointless or blanket emails at some point in their career. Many of the emails may sound like this:

> *Teachers, please make sure you...*
> *"teach the whole hour" (pre-COVID cleaning at the end of each class).*
> *"stay off your cell phone while teaching."*
> *"aren't showing pointless movies."*
> *"close your room door when students are present."*
> *"supervise students at all times."*
> *"always wear dress shoes."*
> *"fill out the form that was sent out last week."*
> *"contact parents."*
>
> *Sincerely,*
> *Your Admin Team*

Teachers Shouldn't be Painted with the Same "Out of Compliance" Brush

Your first thought when you see emails of this nature may be, "I already do that, or I never do that." Your next thought might be, "Why are they sending this email to everyone instead of talking to the person or people who are doing or not doing whatever the email is about?"

More than likely the all-important blanket emails will go unread by those committing the offense and taken to heart by those already in compliance. Yes, there is a thought process behind those blanket emails which may be written documentation or proof of the edict. More times than not administrators see a behavior going on by more than one staff member, and a blanket email seems like a fast and efficient way to communicate or re-communicate expectations before the problem becomes even more widespread. Isn't this an electronic form of group punishment?

Some administrators may privately address the behavior with the actual individuals who failed to comply or accomplish a task. That may not seem important, but for us who follow the rules, dot our I's, and cross our T's, we need to know that the actual offenders are being held accountable and that we aren't all painted with the same "out-of-compliance" brush. Understandably, administrators are swamped with other duties or problems that need to be solved immediately, so the blanket email seems like the most efficient way to deal with the current staff situation. Whatever the reason, blanket and pointless emails are not productive, nor do they save time in the end.

Pointless vs. Blanket Emails
Some of you who are reading this right now may be wondering what the difference is between blanket and pointless emails. In many ways, they are similar. Both clog up the email inbox for everyone, open the door to those "reply all" responses that nobody enjoys, and frequently go unread by those who caused the email to be sent in the first place. There is one key difference. A pointless email doesn't need to be read by anyone, and a blanket email doesn't need to be read by everyone.

Pointless and blanket emails require exponential time and reduce productivity for both the sender and the recipients. Teachers, by and large, have one prep period a day. Emails sent out during the day might get read by teachers whose prep time comes after the email is sent, but the chances decrease for teachers who have already had their prep time. Many teachers spend the first few minutes of their prep time scanning emails in their inboxes, then shift to the things that directly affect students and deadlines. Just as Jay Posick shared in the previous chapter, teacher planning time is fragmented beyond email to lesson creation, LMS (Learning Management System) updates, grading student work or grade book updates, parent contacts, and more. Time is such a commodity that often teachers forget to go to the restroom, refresh and refill their water bottles, or find caffeine. There are even teachers who don't check email after hours, so those critical 8 p.m. emails about something that MUST be done the next day are often absorbed into their email inboxes, along with emails about unplugging for self-care.

High-functioning educators pay close attention to the rules and regulations of their building and district and respond with high integrity. Not everyone will slack off when others do, in fact, it is typically just a handful. When leaders send pointless or blanket emails, know that it comes with the great price of responsibility which will always impact the productivity and synergy of teams.

Streamline a Solution

What is the solution then? There is no escaping sending blanket emails to staff about important issues, last-minute changes, or handling emergencies. Leaders can streamline processes that will save time and increase productivity. Some of the simplest ways to minimize continuous blanket emails are to manage a Google Sites, Smore or Wakelet Newsletter, or internal website or page that deals with all the important reminders, due dates, expectations, and more. Having a digital launching pad or communication tool checks the boxes of communication, expectations, and documentation. If you decide to update the information then announce that in a meeting, over the intercom, or just set it up a routine so that the staff knows to check the website/page weekly on a specific day for the updated information or to read the newsletter with the updates each week. Does this solve the solution of one or a few staff members not meeting the expectation or doing something they are or are not supposed to do? Not necessarily, but you can remind staff that ignorance of the law does not get them out of the consequences of breaking the law. This is true in legal terms as well as for compliance with school and district expectations and requirements and falls within the evaluative box of professionalism.

Blanket Emails are Typically Negative

A final thought to consider when it comes to sending blanket emails is that they are generally negative, require documentation to turn in, complete a task, or address behaviors of staff or students. Negative emails can emotionally trigger the recipient and as a result, immediately shoot off an unfiltered and dysregulated "reply all" response, just to prove a point. Unfortunately, an email war is likely to ensue, running school culture right into the ground. This amount of time spent cleaning up a mess can be avoided altogether. Whenever possible, include in your message that, while you have addressed the issue with the few who were out of compliance, you wanted to make sure everyone was on the same page regarding whatever the issue is. Consider these two factors when sending a blanket email. Instead of typing a long email, find other ways to disseminate that information so that your tone is not misinterpreted, yet your message is nonetheless conveyed.

> **Tone.** one is important, and when you leave it up to an email recipient to determine your tone, it is the same as a batter leaving the third strike call up to the umpire instead of swinging the bat if the pitch is anywhere close to the strike zone.

Voice. Methods of communication should include voice options if face-to-face isn't an option. Apps like Voxer for asynchronous voice delivery, or Discord for synchronous group calls that are quick virtual meetings when you don't need a formal video call. Simply recording a quick video of your message and emailing it or a link to the video is still better than a blanket email. Hearing the voice of the leader can ensure a positive delivery of the message. It is so much easier to convey the tone of your message if your staff can hear (and see) you speak. Likewise, it is also very important for you to hear the tone of your staff members when they respond.

Communicating expectations will save time all throughout the year. One of the best ways to establish a protocol of communication is to co-create a plan alongside your staff and come to an agreed-upon consensus together. If they have some agency in the process, then the communication method will be more productive in the long run because you productively established multiple ways of communicating, in-person, virtual, synchronous, or asynchronous, that will benefit your school culture by saving not only time but heartache.

Laura Steinbrink has over 27 years in education and presents technology and instructional practices nationally. Laura is the author of www.rockntheboat.com, a Feedspot Top 200 blog in Education, an educational consultant, and a contributing author in 4 educational books. Laura has published articles for ISTE, Buncee, Kahoot, Getting Smart, and other educational-related companies. Laura is also a contributing author in several educational books, has co-authored a Microsoft Education course: Creative Expression and Social-Emotional Learning with Francesca Arturi of Buncee, and is a content creator for the app, Zigazoo.

72

Stop Failing to Communicate Changes or Decisions
MARCUS BELIN, Ed.D.

We have all been in situations where communication failed because someone on the team missed one pertinent detail, something did not go the way it was expected, or there was a breakdown in sharing information. Imagine a situation where you have an entire building of students and staff relying on this communication to do their job(s) effectively. This is the weight we carry as school leaders because communicating changes and making hundreds of decisions per day is the nature of the job. We are expected to communicate in a timely manner, with precision, clarity, sound decision making, and thoughtfulness. This gets even trickier with last minute changes or decisions that must reach all stakeholders with clear messaging. Miscommunication is missed productivity. All it takes is one miscommunication and it may take days or weeks' worth of time and energy to try and undo.

Nobody Really Likes Change
Most people are against change no matter how positive or strategic the messaging of communication is delivered. Change is challenging for any organization because it rattles cages for some educators and school leaders. If you layer on ineffective (or lack of) communication to the equation, tensions escalate to create adversity, resistance, and barriers. An uncomfortable situation can quickly become a heated situation if communication isn't effective. Everything that leaders do to implement change directly affects others.

It is easy to fall into this unfortunate trap where you may "mean well" and your intentions are in the right place. You may also feel that because students are the center of decision-making that you are making the best decision because of them. Yes, all leaders make mistakes that are inadvertent and unavoidable. Leaders have within their control the choice effectively, intentionally, and strategically communicate changes or decisions which directly affect others. Consider two areas that leaders can focus on to gain consensus and support to ensure the successful implementation of change:

>**Set the table of support.** Change is hard. Change is stressful. Change is inevitable. The best way to get people to buy into the change is to allow them a seat at the table. The saying, "Build it and they will come" is a popular quote from the movie, *A Field of Dreams* directed by Phil Alden Robinson in 1989. The key to understanding this is by allowing stakeholders to sit at the table and be a part of the decision-making. When you are building a culture and need to make the necessary changes that align with the vision you have as a school leader or educator, you must have the opportunity for the voices to be at the table. You may think it sounds good, looks good, feels good, and more but that is how you feel and what you believe. Refer to Allyson Epsey's Chapter 1 for examples on sharing decisions that have been made that will result in change.
>
>Any stakeholder wants to feel reassured that they understand the reasoning behind decisions. They also want to feel confident that they are equipped to support or carry out what is expected. Adding reasoning and clarity will reduce the chance that any stakeholder makes unnecessary assumptions and develop their own understanding thus controlling the narrative. Think of a time where you had a vision or a thought that required change to happen. The first thing a school leader should think of is the vision and purpose. Change events are often uncertain, risky, and stressful. School leaders should build their support for a better understanding of the change to occur.

Empower stakeholders to make meaning. When someone is empowered, they can accomplish something because they are equipped with the confidence, direction, and necessary tools to succeed. Student voice matters. Teacher voice matters. Parent voice matters. In school environments when we are making decisions that affect others, we need to make sure those voices are at the table. Empower those voices to make sense of the positives and the pitfalls of decisions. When you empower stakeholders to grow through autonomy and you regularly solicit and act on feedback, you begin to develop a sense of trust and by-in to the decision-making process.

Three Benefits of Stakeholder Empowerment
1. **Greater trust in the leadership of the school leader:** Leaders who empower other to help in the decision-making process tend to help support, challenge, and push their thinking
2. **Creativity is unleashed:** When leaders allow others to think outside of the box, they create the opportunity for others to be committed to the change and are more likely to understand the reasons why the change needed to be made. When changes are made in isolation, you may miss a better way or a more creative way of doing something to get a greater result.
3. **Belief-in vs Buy in:** Leaders always look for buy-in to a decision that is made. When a school leader empowers the voices to help understand the decision and develop a solution to the change that is needing to be made, there is a stronger commitment to believing in the change. Belief-in is stronger than buy-in. Belief in does not require proof. When a leader has people who believe in change, there is never a need to solicit buy-in, instead they come to a consensus through collective collaboration.

So How Do You Do This?
It's easy to say that some decisions just "have to" be made and there is no time to bring all the voices to the table. This is true. There are times as a school leader that you must make the tough decision because time is of essence, and it will ultimately affect others. Here are some takeaways on how to not fail at communicating.

Be clear and consistent in your vision of why you made the decision. When you create a narrative to explain how your decision is aligned to the vision and stick to it. When people understand the WHY, and can connect the decision to the way, it shows consistency in thinking and keeps the understanding clear.

Communicate the "how." People will always want to know what's in for them and HOW will this affect them. If those who are affected by the decision do know how it will affect them, they will tend to not connect or choose to not understand the change. Everyone always wants to know "What's in it for me" or "What will this change mean for me." I mean think about it.

There are people who are in a routine and a regiment of doing things and when the disruption comes to their work and they don't understand the disruption, you hear about it. Communicate often!

Understand that change takes time. If you had all the answers that worked, you wouldn't need to bring voices to the table. You could do it alone. Reality check… you can't. So take time to be vulnerable in your decision making and let those who are affected know that you don't have all the answers but you will work to find them. Save yourself some time by seeking answers from the voices around the table. Allow yourself some time to connect with those that the decision will affect and come up with the best answers and not try to have all the answers.

Use solid judgment and think strategically. Be intentional and specific about what you do for kids and the stakeholders in which you make decisions. Consider pro's and con's. Elicit support from a mentor. Reflect on similar situations in the past. Consider stakeholder perspectives. Think about short-term and long-term impacts.

Be vulnerable in your leadership and decision making. I am not saying put yourself all the way out there. I am encouraging you to continue to let people know that you are human and not perfect.

Trust your gut. Making decisions is hard work and much of our job as school leaders relies on this. If leaders do their due diligence connecting with stakeholder(s) impacted by decision(s), and consider fueled emotions and outcomes, then they should rest in the assurance of their decisions. You must weigh listening to your gut, your inner voice, and follow your instincts knowing that you made the best decision with the greatest amount of input and information available at the time.

When you think about decision making, it seems like a daunting process. As school leaders, we make an infinite number of decisions that affect many people in various ways. We won't always get it right and we are not perfect. That is the challenge of going through the decision-making process. What we can do is listen, engage, empower, and communicate with the people that are directly affected by the decisions we make.

Dr. Marcus Belin serves as the Principal of Huntley High School, National Association of Secondary School Principals Board Member, and Immediate Past President of the Illinois Principals Association. Recently Dr. Belin was awarded the 2021 National Association of Secondary School Principals Digital Principal of the Year and was named to the Class of 2021 ASCD International Emerging Leader. Dr. Belin is a motivational speaker who has reached over 5,000 school leaders and educators in the past 3 years and the host of Unapologetic Leadership, a podcast designed to tell and share the stories of leadership and the passion behind the work of being an educator. He is passionate about creating learning environments that foster social-emotional support for kids, leveraging the integration of technology to expose kids to the world around them, motivating educators, and challenging the status quo of education. He is an alum of Bradley University, where he received his bachelor's and master's degrees and National Louis University for his doctorate. Dr. Belin is the husband of an amazing wife, Monique, and a father to 3 beautiful children, who keep life exciting and active.

Stop Preaching or Soapboxing
KRISTINA MACBURY & SHERRY MACBURY, Ed.D.

There is a long history of preaching within leadership, likely drawing its origin from spiritual leaders in a pulpit, leading its members in a sermon filled with positive intentions. According to William Horton, in his book, *Leading with the Sermon: Preaching as Leadership*, he shares that preaching can help those in a congregation face its problems, coordinate resources while also making clear the mission and vision of the pastor or church organization.

Like preaching, leadership soapboxing comes from a well-intentioned place. Districts and schools face problems, they require coordinated services, and the superintendent and district administrators work to make clear the mission, vision, values, and beliefs of the district. Educators, like those sitting in the congregational pews of a church are seeking to be led to a greater purpose. Many leaders step on their professional soapbox instinctively when they believe they have a captive audience. Through cadence, rhythm, passion, motivation, and personal belief the soapbox rant can easily turn into a persuasive sermon about:

- The importance of getting certifications and training early in one's career
- Practicing self-help to prevent burn out
- Taking advantage of professional development opportunities
- Work and life balance
- Not wanting others to make the same mistakes as us
- Through our experiences we believe we know better

Many leaders can inspire and motivate others with their words, particularly if they are authentic, consistent, and aligned with your mission and vision. But, if preaching is not complemented by action, not only will your efforts be fruitless, but you will also lose credibility, momentum, and followership.

One of the top strategies a leader can implement in building culture is to lead mission, vision, values, and beliefs through active modeling. Leadership is not a one and done sermon. Gone is the adage, "Do as I say and not as I do," and quite frankly, this mentality agitates any follower of any organization. There has never been a more pressing time in educational leadership for us to understand the implications of our actions and those we lead. Our responsibility extends far beyond preaching an eloquent sermon one hour a week or soapboxing intermittently a personal belief. We have been charged to lead by example, serve through individualization, provide equity of voice, coach up, lead up, and inspire up.

The Leadership Dangers of Preaching from the Pulpit

Below are three common missteps leaders make when they choose to step on their soapbox to begin preaching (as opposed to leading by modeling). When educational leaders preach from the pulpit or get on their soapbox rather than leading evidence-based educational practices in the trenches, essentially, they are:

> **1. Weaponizing the Message:** Leaders who preach self-care end up weaponizing it for their staff while celebrating and rewarding martyrdom. Preaching and not giving the space, time or resources do not create the intentional opportunities for true self care and are dangerous and counterproductive. Without modeling a culture of self-care, as we saw in Greg Moffit's Chapter 38 and Dr. Shawn Berry Clarks Chapter 49, we ultimately reward the opposite actions like publicly thanking staff who worked all weekend, went above and beyond during their break, or being the only car hours after and before everyone else, every day. Therefore, let's consider implementing and leading the actual self-practice of self-care for your staff just as Greg & Shawn shared with us in their chapters. Leaders are well-intentioned, want staff (and themselves) to exercise self-care. However, many drop the ball when it comes to carrying it out as a way of productive well-balanced living. Consequently, the support may not be there for the people that you lead, and the soapbox message of self-care ends up as another thing a leader preaches but does not do. In any church, this would be viewed as hypocritical and ultimately the pastor becomes viewed as a fraud. Any initiative that leaders preach, soapbox, or promote that isn't part of the system of school is an unproductive weapon aimed at school culture.

> **2. Producing Toxic Positivity:** The worst and most damaging type of preaching is toxic positivity. Preaching a sermon or standing on a soapbox in the meeting room proclaiming that everything will be okay, does not make everything ok and certainly doesn't build trust. This is not the same as having a positive mindset. This is the lack of acknowledgement, when there is an issue, by being dismissive of the perception or feelings of others. Sometimes, it is prudent and necessary to step back, and reflect and address the current reality and perceptions of those

you lead instead of continuing forward. Acknowledge those you serve and be as transparent of what is to come. You are kidding yourself if you believe that during a crisis or amid an educational dilemma that educators want a rose colored, unrealistic outlook riddled with toxic positivity.

With the trends in mental health awareness and trauma of the ongoing pandemic, we often feel the obligation to empathize without the understanding or training to recognize the depth behind our "preaching." Messages like, "It's ok, you are ok, this is a blip or hurdle that we will overcome." No, please stop - it's ok to NOT be ok and leaders need to recognize their staff and their struggles. While those toxic positive messages are well-intentioned and valid to awareness, without the next steps of connecting to resources as Dr. Shawn Berry Clark shared of her tragic experience, without an appreciation that although it may ultimately end up being ok, expressing empathy and using language to acknowledge their trauma, mental health, or feelings, all you are doing is unintentionally minimizing their experiences and feelings. Be realistic, acknowledge what is, and for heaven's sake, don't give false hope through toxic positivity. Time to stop with the toxic positivity - it's time to acknowledge, respond and take actions that are authentic, heart-felt, and even look at ways you can help with relief internally (i.e., cover a class, provide time off without guilt, frequent check-ins, thoughtful notes). This is the leadership our staff and colleagues need and deserve.

3. Minimizing Equity: From the lens of equity - we are our strongest when we are comfortable enough to vulnerably share and given opportunities in a trusted environment to value diverse viewpoints and honor experiences. These productive spaces of ideation and solutions transpire when leaders intentionally create that space through social contracts, norms, and actions that value the voices of all on their team. When preaching becomes the main leadership practice, there is no room for other voices to be heard, and the potential for communities to evolve is stunted. As leaders, we often feel our staff need to hear from us, and they do want to please and measure up to the expectation set forth. Equity of voice means that we *MUST* hear from each person soft spoken and wildly loud, alike. In the book, *Educational REHAB: An Unprecedented Opportunity to Restore K-12 Public Education*, Rebecca Coda shares the following about leading practices of equity.

"When we seek to understand perspectives, we distill our reality down to community truth and when we embrace our differences for the sake of finding solutions, we create a foundation for high-impact community-wide solutions that have the power to fully restore K-12 education, because of equity."
-Rebecca Coda

Equity not only provides "things" others may need but is inclusive of understanding "why". When staff feel placated it is often the result of preaching or soapboxing rather than leading. No one likes to feel invisibly boxed, labeled, or grouped. Leaders of equity form groups, committees, advisory boards, steering committees that focus on one culture, aligned to the mission, vision, values, and beliefs of the whole. Let go of the notion that you must preach the educational gospel or soapbox as the messenger of everything. Providing each individual the opportunity to have their voices heard and share in the collective responsibility of your mission is vision will go a long way.

Keep on learning and leading forward. Don't live in the past. Know and live your mission and vision. Leave the preaching for the spiritual pulpit!

Kristina MacBury is a co-mom of 11, an award-winning principal in the tristate Philadelphia Area, NASSP Digital Principal, author of Principal Pro: An Authentic Leadership Playbook for Managing Crisis, Building Teams and Maximizing Resources and co-founder of Educate4Hope. She is a fierce mental health advocate for education and a die-hard Phillies fan.

Dr. Sherry L. MacBury, is the Dean of the Secondary Campus at Sussex Academy. Sherry has been working in the educational sphere for over twenty-five years, providing leadership, professional development and coaching services for schools and school systems, as well as serving as a strategic partner to help build capacity and improve practice. A former teacher, high-school counselor, school principal and district-level administrator, she focuses on 1-1 coaching and holds a master's degree in Community Counseling and a Doctorate Degree in Educational Leadership & Policy. Navigating the challenges of being a co-mom to 10 children, Sherry appreciates and empathizes with parents' experiences with children with mental health challenges and realizes the need to end the stigma surrounding these difficulties and build a community of support.

74

Stop Administering Assessments that No Longer Have Meaning
BRIAN MCCANN

Five years ago, I canceled final exams. Simply, I was tired of the school year ending in a whimper rather than a celebration. As a school body we strived to be a student-centered community. We created a school atmosphere that prioritized relationships from the first moment of freshman year, continuing through our four-year advisory, and culminating in a senior year individualized capstone project. Yet, this philosophy was juxtaposed against students completing intense exams in an alternate school schedule, with teachers then rushing to correct and tabulate end of the year grades. The high-stress, low impact mayhem of these last days seemed to undermine what we were doing the other 178 days of the school year. I had identified the culprit that was culture-thwarting our school as these traditional, "the way we've always done it" end-of-the-year exams. I was finally done with finals.

A History of 'Meh'

Like most high schools, we were spending the final days of school in high stakes, locally designed tests that were administered in a schedule that did not necessarily reflect the past school year. Sometimes exams were often administered by an unfamiliar teacher proctoring a summative assessment worth 10, 15 or even 20 percent of students' final grades for the year. To add to the culture-thwarting mayhem, the highest standard deviation of performing students were exempt from finals because of high academic performance during the year. And get this, sometimes their academic performance was combined with their standing in the schools, including the completion of a national summative exam that the local teacher may not receive its score for months down the road.

The exams stressed out students and families and fueled anxiety across the community. The exams stressed out teachers. And the scheduling and proctoring of the exams stressed out administrators, paraprofessionals, and even the cafeteria workers running an alternate schedule. The cold hard truth was that their scheduling took away learning opportunities from students. The tests took place over multiple half-days so they could be corrected before the year was officially over. Not to mention the final half-day of school that was scheduled for make-ups. Since almost no student ever missed a final at our school, the last day of school was like a free day for both students and teachers.

Final exams created an alternate universe at school. Every closing to the school year is in a perpetual cycle of students arriving to class, taking a multi-hour assessment, and then either reporting to their next test, or leave school early for the duration of the instructional day. In most cases, teachers distributed exams, proctored others, and began to score the assessments with little to no interaction with students or their peers at the conclusion of the testing block. Every year our community of awesome always lost its luster and digressed during testing week to become a community of 'meh' year after year in mid-June. For years, the final exam grades would be posted without any opportunity for students to see their corrected tests, clarify misunderstandings, relearn the information, or even ask questions. Summative meant, "It is finished."

In the past, we tried to set aside the final day of school for reviewing students' summative exams to provide students with feedback on errors so they could master the knowledge. But the initiative never gained any traction. This wasn't an equitable practice because it didn't even apply to the group of students that were exempt from the exam altogether. That brings me to an even greater point, how important were these exams if students could be routinely exempt from them? Do final summative exams even reflect a year's worth of deep and connected learning?

Final exams seemed like the traditional end goal of each course. Maybe we had lost our WHY somewhere along the line. Had they devolved to high-stake creations of habit that were designed merely to be corrected quickly -- almost like an unnecessary rite of passage that did not value the tenets of assessment? I felt that in my heart, I could do better as a school leader. Much better. For all stakeholders.

Returning to Our "WHY"
I returned to school blazing with questions and a mission for my school's leadership team, representing each department across the school. Just as Rae Dunn shared in Chapter 57, maybe our "Why" was focused on too small of a scale. Maybe we needed to think more audaciously or more courageously or more consistently. So, I bravely stuck my neck out and posed the following question, "Why do we still have final exams in our 21st century school?" We already had in place quarterly summative assessments that were common among courses taught in the same department that were scheduled organically and strategically in the final week of each term. Why would we even need to administer final exams in school? They had already shown mastery or minimal proficiency of the standards. The teachers initially responded with, "being serious about academics," "teaching students responsibility," and "getting our kids college-ready" which seemed to pale when followed up with, *IN WHAT WAY*? I shared with these teachers that I would gladly reconsider my viewpoint on the ridiculousness of final exam week if they could find one college program -- just one -- that met every day from September to June and had one cumulative test that might be worth anywhere from 10 to 20 percent of their course grade *AND* had built-in provisions to be exempt in certain privileged cases.

Crickets. Problem solved? Not quite so fast, we had one more hurdle: the mid-year exam.

Mid-year Waste of Time
It was easier to first eliminate the mid-year exams at my school because we already had an established

system of quarterly assessments. We had moved beyond having a rogue alternate schedule that usually landed sometime in January. By eliminating mid-year exams and finals, we were consistent across academic departments that all courses would have an end-of-term assessment four times a year.

We eliminated the anxiety and rigid formality that came with a glut of exams on any one day. Our leadership team collaborated and developed a schedule that would ensure that no student took more than two quarterly assessments on any given day. Our goal was to provide every student with a best-case scenario to showcase their proficiency in learning not to stress students into a status quo demonstration of knowledge.

By eliminating mid-year exams, we all gained more time and productivity in teaching and learning. The quarterly assessments became formative in nature rather than merely summative and served an even greater purpose. These "formative" assessments provided teachers and students with relevant data on the level of understanding and mastering content standards, gaps in learning, and classroom-wide trends. This allowed teachers to reteach or scaffold content that surfaced as a trend deficiency, provided students the opportunity to relearn or practice a skill, and presented an opportunity for new short-term goals to be co-created among stakeholders.

Risk-Taking is Rewarding
As the end of the year approached, teachers became curious about what we were going to do with the two district half days that were designated for administering finals. So, I set out to challenge my staff once again, so during a May faculty gathering, I posed another audacious mind-shifting challenge to our teachers that centered on our "Why." I cleared my throat, loosened my tie while consciously relaxing my face to a smile and asked, "Would you be willing to share a passion of yours -- whether related to your discipline or not -- with a small group of students at the end of the year?"

I looked out to see some blank stares. Necks moved. Seats shifted.

"I know I am asking you to take a risk," I posed to these teachers, "but how can we expect our students to be risk-takers if we do not model the same?" I sensed my body language shift as smiles, ideas, and passion flooded the staff (well the early on boarders anyway). I followed up immediately by sending a Google Form to capture their personal interests. In my mind I figured I could pull this off if 40 percent of the staff would get onboard. By the time I got home that late afternoon, I had heard from about seven people, including some I thought were going to be my toughest-sells.

Within a day, I had 100 percent of the staff committed to this pilot. We rolled this out to freshmen, sophomores, and juniors in class assemblies (the seniors had just graduated) and designed some old-school paper sign-ups to be done at lunch. We published a digital menu of activities over the two half-days. Our faculty offered 35 micro-experiences that included Italian cooking, geocaching, meditation, a beach cleanup, knitting for troops, wiffle ball, putting on a full musical in two days, weight room restoration, and -- my favorite -- fishing. We had old school video games, a chemistry camp, and making bow ties from wood. Some students chose to begin the Common App; others looked to bring their academic year to positive closure with some opportunities for credit recovery. Most students not only attended the final days of school but engaged in culture building transformations and experiences that would matter later in life.

Yes, sign-ups were a little crazy. Yes, I wish I had figured out a digital platform to register in advance. Yes, it seemed like there was a lot of organization, coordination, and management to occur. Rosters had to be created, revised, and redistributed. Permission forms had to be collected and vetted. But, for the first time in a long time, the year's end had a tremendous energy to it. Teachers, families, and students were happy to close out the year with tangible opportunities to build relationships, engage in talents and hobbies, in the final days of the school year.

As a high school principal who welcomes students off the buses each morning, there is nothing more unique than to see kids disembark with fishing poles! The day that our "Why" as a high school team of relationship building embraced the modeling of high risk-taking, our new legacy of "Passion Days" was born. The year ended on a higher note than I ever knew was possible. Teachers gathered data that showed how their students not only completed their course, but confirmed they were ready for the next challenge in the department's scope and sequence. The term "Passion Days" became part of our end of the year vernacular and now viewed as one of the most anticipated times of the year.

Passion Days Celebrate Community

For the past five years, school has ended on a positive, celebratory note. Our attendance, engagement and morale continue to be high until the final bell. We have transitioned to digital sign-ups using Google Forms, had 50 different choices this year, and offer teachers the option to sponsor a student-run project. We celebrate these two half-days annually with multi-day digital shout-outs on Facebook and Twitter. We have been captured on the front page of the local daily paper more than once for our risk-taking.

Removing these antiquated final assessments had no negative impact on next year's learning or what college a senior received acceptance to. Their riddance only helped build our community, nurture talent, and support balance and well-being. Stop administering assessments that no longer have meaning. Instead, use that time to return to passionately building your community - even at the end of the school year.

Brian McCann finished his 18th year as principal of Joseph Case High School in Swansea, MA. from which he graduated in 1980. He is passionate about disruptive leadership, #PositiveSignThursdays, and snow day videos. Brian is a 2011 Massachusetts High School Principal of the Year and one of NASSP 2018 national Digital Principals of the Year.

Stop Obsessing with High-Stakes Testing
NAOMI RYFUN, Ed.D.

In the prior chapter Brian McCann showcased the power of leading Passion Days in lieu of ending the year with class finals. He harnessed the power that was within the locus of his power and influence to create an alternative that positively impacted all stakeholders. Unfortunately, there are mandates that are far from our control. High-stakes testing is inevitable, but how we approach and facilitate the process, is within the realm of our control.

Don't Lose Sight of the True Purpose

A few years ago, I was invited by family friends to attend their daughter Christine's middle school open house. Upon entering the building, we were given an agenda for the evening. The principal's welcome address was just about to start, so we followed the other families and made our way to the gymnasium. After an initial, "Welcome, families! Thank you for coming tonight," he went on to say, "Your children are in middle school now. These are important, formative years.

Our job as middle school educators is to ensure our students are prepared for high school. As a district, we've analyzed the state test data and have found that students who score higher are more successful in high school. With that in mind, our focus this year in each class, every day will be to prepare our students for these very important tests." With a puzzled look on my face, I stood there trying to process what we had just heard. Question after question scrolled through my mind:

- Really? Of all the ways to welcome families and students, that was the message you chose for your opening address.
- If you believe these are such formative years in the life of a child, why would the school's focus be on test prep?
- If you were a student, would you want to focus on test prep in each class, every day? Wouldn't that get incredibly boring?
- How is "successful in high school" defined? What does that look like?
- Are all students valued here, or do you just take pride in the students who score proficient or above?
- Why is there such a seemingly unhealthy obsession with high-stakes test scores?

I imagine similar words have been spoken at other open houses, professional learning days, parent conferences, and faculty meetings by well-intentioned administrators who have perhaps lost sight of their true purpose, which is to ensure that students have every opportunity to engage in meaningful, relevant learning experiences that ignite curiosity and result in continuous growth.

Use Summative Assessments for Their Intended Purpose
Too often, policy makers assume that administrators and teachers are implementing effective assessment strategies in their schools and classrooms. Yet, research has clearly established that many receive little training in this area. As a result, there is an ongoing need for assessment literacy and an understanding that assessments are designed for different purposes.

I can almost guarantee that if you are an administrator reading this chapter, you've either participated in or facilitated data meetings where you've reviewed item-analysis reports for each student based on the results of state tests. You may have even used the tests for diagnostic purposes and tried to devise interventions for students to close perceived learning gaps. The problem with this is that many of these high-stakes accountability tests are not designed for this purpose and using assessment data in the wrong way leads to educational malpractices that are potentially damaging to students.

Summative data, however, does play a crucial role in both program evaluation and informing future instruction. If after examining trend data reported by standard, data teams discover that there are gaps in instruction at the program level, deliberate corrective action should be taken by evaluating the curriculum, aligning assessments to standards, and teaching lessons that specifically focus on essential student-friendly learning targets. Summative assessments drive programming decisions based on overall trends; they do not correspond to individualized learning goals.

Shift Your Focus
In schools where the focus is on high-stakes test results, there seems to be a wider gap in learning between groups of students. On the other hand, when the weight of accountability-imposed consequences has been lifted, the focus shifts to addressing the needs of each student. Addressing individualized learning needs requires adaptive formative assessments that provide information about the next learning target on a continuum for that student. Standards-based common formative assessments, anecdotal observations, and skills-based assessments require timely feedback for effective instructional planning to occur. I can attest with confidence that educators must shift focus.

Instead of focusing on making sure that teachers equip students for various types of assessments, why wouldn't we teach our students the difference between summative and formative assessments and how to use that information as co-partners in individual goal setting? When students have a voice and are empowered to set goals, define next key learnings, and take ownership they will be more invested and engaged in their own learning. To maximize productivity, educators must spend time upfront with students, discovering their strengths, talents, and preferences if they are to engage students in deep and purposeful learning.

Engage Students in Every Class, Every Day
In every school there are teachers who couldn't care less about their end of the year, high-stakes assessments, yet the students in their classrooms year after year their students out-perform colleagues who obsess over the tests. Why is that? It's because engaging educators build a culture within the classroom based on individual strengths, an established social contract that drives high quality interactions, a culture that values every student, and an environment that understands that failure is the pathway to success.

- **Teach Level of Thinking Required:** Provide questioning techniques that elevate deep thinking, that teach students to recognize and adapt to the various question types and the cognitive demand that each requires.

- **Co-Create Assessment Items:** Invite students to co-create assessment items based on DOK levels and cognitive demand required. Use a variety of student submitted assessment questions as a pathway to assess. Know exactly what you are assessing, as well as when, how, and why.
- **Determine the DOK Ceiling:** Analyze content standards to determine the DOK ceiling and cognitive demand required of students to reach minimal proficiency and mastery.
- **Communicate Learning Targets:** Deconstruct the standards to create clear, student-friendly learning targets that are implemented in a meaningful way all throughout teaching with all students in each class, every day. Regularly check to make sure students can explain what they are learning.
- **Provide Standards-Based Feedback:** Provide feedback and understand that for it to be effective, it must address both the processes necessary to accomplish a task and a student's effort toward achieving the desired goal.
- **Set Aside Time for Students to Reflect on Short Term Goals & Key Learning:** Give students opportunities to reflect on their learning, and celebrate their growth.

Don't be like the principal at the open house who was obsessed over high-stakes tests. It doesn't help teachers, and it's not good for students. Rather, build systems that will help your teachers provide meaningful assessment opportunities that build ownership, rapport, and high-quality learning. As high-quality engagement increases, you'll see a parallel outcome in test results. Even more important, you'll witness your teachers and students excited and engaged in the process of continuous learning.

Dr. Naomi Ryfun has served as Data Coordinator, Coordinator for Teaching and Learning, Assistant Superintendent for Curriculum and Instruction, and currently serves as the Superintendent of Schools for the Altmar-Parish-Williamstown Central School District in rural, upstate New York. Passionate about student-centered learning and assessment practices, Naomi has presented at conferences, delivered statewide professional development, and provided data analysis and facilitation services to over fifty school districts

76

Stop Rushing Through Tasks and Not Paying Attention to Details
MIKE DOMAGALSKI

If you think about it, completion can be a form of gratification. When we complete a project or task, it gives us a sense of happiness, fulfillment, and can possibly even improve our self-esteem. In the world we live in today, it is easy to get caught up quickly checking off a box and completing a task that we sometimes miss the bigger picture, the details. There is an issue that arises when leaders hurriedly complete a task and move right onto the next just as fast. Many leaders seek the fulfillment of checking a box to keep their heads above water, to stay ahead of the game, or for an immediate sense of accomplishment. The issue that results from this fast-paced box checking mindset is that it diverts focus away from details. And missing key details won't save you time or productivity in the long run. Missing details may equate to a misunderstanding or mishap with a future project, initiative, or program implementation. Attending to detail is a key quality that productive leaders possess.

An Inch Wide & Mile Deep
The phrase, "A mile wide and an inch deep" dates to 1889 when an American journalist and humorist, Edgar Nye, described the Platte River in the Midwestern part of the United States as mostly shallow and meandering throughout. Over time, this phrase became a common phrase and analogy that meant too much is happening without enough substance. Most likely you have heard this phrase used in education and leadership as it pertains to taking on so many programs, projects, tasks, or curriculum, that it becomes unattainable to carry out any successfully.

At times, leaders tend to take on too many initiatives and implement a project or program too quickly without focusing on the details that could lead to a domino effect. The scope of programming should not focus on multiple projects or tasks simultaneously because carrying out a new initiative with fidelity requires attention to detail. When any task lacks substance, or details to carry out the protocol(s) to make them successful, one can only ever land in the shallow end, missing the mark of success. Acting too quickly in decision-making allows for the program or project to simply become "one more thing" that may or may not be supported by the stakeholders, especially teachers or staff.

When looking for substance, instead of focusing on the number of different projects that are going on and trying to tailor to all of them, leaders must streamline initiatives, limit the number of projects, be attentive to details, and ensure there is fidelity through expected process and protocols. Rushed projects allow for less time focusing on the details that lead to successful implementation.

As leaders we often get inundated in the management of the job and rush through tasks and meetings so fast that relevant details may be glossed over. When key details are lost, collective collaboration and motivation of those carrying out the initiatives, may be in jeopardy. Mission, vision, values, and big idea foci are essential to going a mile deep. And all meetings, professional development, or school improvement, should embrace the intentional details that align with the overarching desired outcome. Consider anchoring your leadership focus on an inch wide and a mile deep. An inch wide pertaining to the number of changes or projects you will consider acceptable. And a mile deep pertaining to the amount of time you will protect for breaking down the details within an initiative, change, or project.

The Vacation Project
Think about a vacation you recently took. Reflect on the planning, the sites you visited, and what you took from that vacation. I was blessed to have the opportunity to visit two islands of Hawaii back in 2017, and it was an unforgettable experience. It wasn't breathtaking just because it was Hawaii. It was spectacular because we decided that we would concentrate our time experiencing the details of the trip rather than jet setting, just to cover more territory. Our vacation planning focused on the details because we were focused on a high-quality experience.

Sure, there were certain sites that we had on our list to visit. We loved everything about the Hawaii Volcanoes National Park, Diamond Head, Pearl Harbor, the North Shore, and many others. The experience of planning where we wanted to go and what we wanted to see was fun, but we all decided that we didn't want to plan more than one or two things per day. Our goal was to *NOT* over plan. We didn't want our trip to become two weeks of hopping from one place to another. We wanted time to experience the details and surroundings of what each of the places had to offer. By focusing on the details of each attraction, and not the number of attractions, it made the trip one of the most vividly memorable of any trip I have ever taken. When planning your next vacation, I suggest that you try this. Consider the major attractions you want to visit but be more intentional about planning enough time to experience the smaller details that add richness, sensory, quality, and even longer-lasting memories.

The analogy of the "vacation project" is transferable to what we do as leaders in our building. Consider the following example. It may look good to the community that you, (or the school site, or district), have several projects implemented that address the social-emotional learning (SEL) needs of your students and staff. Like planning for a quality vacation, SEL programs must focus on the details that will add richness and a quality experience to its implementation. SEL programs most certainly should not be a long shallow checklist to simply check off. Planning for covering the programs will only lead to an unforgettable or shallow experience. If the "vacation project" has taught us anything as leaders it is that planning for a quality experience focused on the richness of detail is essential for going a "mile deep." Productive leaders continuously place importance on the details of the project as part of the quality of the experience. Without an intentional focus on details (like a poorly planned vacation), the project will not be as richly memorable, nor a success

A Shopping List
Think about having to go to the grocery store. There are foods, drinks, and other amenities that you may need (or want). Productive leaders always show up to the store with a shopping list, follow that list, and get in and out in a timely fashion. However, have you ever been rushed while making the list? Or hurried through the store because you were in a time crunch? Going too quickly in making a grocery list or hurrying through a store can be very problematic. Items may get missed, there may not be enough thought put into the purchases, and the details of how all the products are going to be used may get overlooked. Even navigating through the store could become a waste of time and effort.

Anytime leaders are too rushed to intentionally list their tasks or are double booked on appointments, the result will always be time wasted. Like a shopping list it will produce additional trips to the store, wasted money, unhealthy eating habits, and/or poor time management. When leaders focus on the details of the list, or "why" you are making the purchase it will make the trip that much more successful. As leaders in education, rushing through the tasks on our checklist without focusing on the details and the outcomes, tasks simply become a box to check and ultimately impede productivity. Checklists aren't going away, but we can ensure that our decisions are thoughtful, intentional, and detailed before crossing them off the list.

Success is in the Details
The last thing we want is for a program or project to be acknowledged as "one more thing." To avoid "a mile wide" leadership we must allow others to have a voice, share the details of "Why," and facilitate a collaborative discussion about any future initiative, project, or task. When considering any new project or deconstructing any conversation that leads to how fast it can get started or how fast it can be accomplished. Share your "inch wide and mile deep" vision, motivate your team with a vacation project mentality, and model how to create a high-quality shopping list. There is no prize for being the first one to complete your evaluations. There is no prize for getting a School Improvement Plan submitted first. The gratification should be in the conversation, the planning, the collaboration, the work, and the details. Success isn't measured by checking the project off the list, success is measured by the richness of details, quality experiences, and new connections that will lead to productivity and even more success in the future.

Mike Domagalski is a recognized educational leader in Michigan and has been a middle school principal, elementary principal, a district curriculum coordinator, teacher, and coach. He has been active within the Michigan Elementary & Middle School Principals Association (MEMSPA), acting as MEMSPA President in 2021-22, named the MEMPSA Region 6 Principal Honoree and known as the founder of #MEMSPAchat, a weekly ed leadership chat on twitter. In addition, Mike is also a partner with Design Education Group, a collection of education leaders who focus on developing others within the entities of Culture, Innovation, Instruction & Leadership.

STOP Forgetting the Capacity of Community

This Type of Nonsense Prevents Maximizing ALL Stakeholders

Stop Micromanaging Everyone
EVAN ROBB

"If you're the kind of boss who lasers in on details, prefers to be cc'd on emails, and is rarely satisfied with your team's work, then—there's no kind way to say this—you're a micromanager."
-Muriel Maignan Wilkins

In the previous chapter Mike Domagalski encouraged leaders to pay more attention to the details of quality program implementation. This chapter may initially seem contradictory because he shared that leaders must attend to details to carry out high quality tasks. And that is absolutely true. Likewise, the need to stop micromanaging every detail of running a school day-to-day is also true. In Mike Domagalski's scenario, and the ones I am about to share, reflection and change require the investment of time. It isn't about not enough details or too many details, it is about productive and sound leadership based on intentional choices.

Micromanaging is Demoralizing

I often reflect on my brief time as a micromanager and how far I have moved from directing and managing every school detail. I didn't purposely engage in this management style to demean staff, show a lack of trust, or create a less than optimal culture for my school. I acted and attempted to manage every element of my school with conviction because I genuinely believed that overly micromanaging staff would increase efficiency and allow me to know everything happening in the school. Quickly, I realized I couldn't know everything that occurred all the time, and my actions, born out of good intent, were demoralizing my team. Yes, I needed to change. I needed to change to find a better work balance, and I needed to change how my influence was hurting the school I was expected to lead. Yes, I was a micromanager. I have a simple message, stop this unproductive and time-wasting approach. Micromanaging inhibits effective leadership. Instead elevate your leadership; build a foundation of trust and relationships. A commitment to building trust and relationships allows leaders to empower others and shift away from micromanaging.

They Don't Care How Much You Know

No formula exists for creating positive relationships. Effective education leaders have the skills needed to establish positive relationships. However, there are some common elements that effective relationship builders have: they care, communicate, build trust, empower, develop empathy, and have a sincere interest in others. There is much truth in this old saying, "Students don't care how much you know until they know how much you care." The same is true for adults. Productive leadership doesn't transpire without establishing relationships by showing those that you lead that you care. Remember it's the principal who sets the tone in their school, the superintendent that sets the tone for the district office, and the school board that sets the tone for the entire community. Regardless of your leadership role, positive relationships contribute to a positive tone, and that's why they must be worked on with diligence all the time. How are you cultivating positive relationships to empower staff and the culture of your community?

Intentional Risks Require Trust

Just like relationships, building and extending trust must become a daily practice for educational leaders. Trust can take a long time to be established because it is the cornerstone upon which to build positive relationships. Effective superintendents, district administrators, principals and teacher leaders foster trusting relationships by making collaborative decisions that embrace creative thinking, innovation, and empowerment of others.

Staff and students need to know and have ownership of the direction and vision of their school. Ownership allows staff members to experience relationships that build trust, empower, and value their ideas. Since trust and safety walk hand in hand, the result can be that staff are more willing to take intentional risks to improve and grow or to let go of what's holding them back, laying the foundation to build a school full of leaders instead of a school micromanaged by a "leader." What are you doing to cultivate trust and model a culture of empowerment?

Eight Tips to Stop Micromanaging and Start Leading:
1. **Communicate Expectations:** Trust and relationships develop when we communicate our expectations with clarity and consistency. This may be as big as your mission, vision, values, beliefs, and goals or as precise as the dismissal process after school. Communication should be made available to reference digitally, hanging on posters in the hallways, discussed in team

meetings, and acknowledged by all. This also requires that you inspect what you expect through positive interactions and being present to observe expectations in action.

2. **Practice Removing Yourself from The Group:** Learn to trust groups on your team. You don't need to be at every meeting if expectations and processes for follow-up documentation and communication is clear.

3. **Ask How You Can Help:** A simple gesture of asking how you can help sends a positive message to your team, a message that you care.

4. **Prioritize Your Time:** Where you put your time and where staff sees you spending your time communicates to staff what you value.

5. **Ask Staff How to Work with Them**: Working alongside your staff demonstrates a commitment to being part of the team through actions. It also demonstrates your willingness to dive into a task or challenge.

6. **Be Consistent:** Your leadership is defined and communicated to others through words, actions, and consistency. Inconsistent actions or words send confusing messages to staff.

7. **Trust Your Team:** A trusted team will always work harder and be more productive than a team that is oppressed or in fear of reprisal.

8. **Be Positive and Optimistic:** It can be hard to be positive during challenging times, but you can always be optimistic about a successful future. The leader sets the tone.

Trust and relationships are needed for successful leadership which requires letting go of micromanaging staff in a school. Ultimately there is a sense of liberation when we come to grips with the fact that we cannot do it all and sustain a do it all micromanaging style year after year. Part of leadership should be helping others grow through clear expectations, trust, relationships, and a commitment to empowerment, creating a professional environment where everyone is always better than anyone. Every day is a new day, make a commitment to micromanage less and lead more.

Evan Robb is presently Principal of Johnson-Williams Middle School in Berryville, Virginia. He has over twenty years of experience serving as a building-level principal. Prior to being a school principal, he was an English teacher, department chair, and Assistant Principal. Evan is a recipient of the Horace Mann Educator of the Year Award. In addition, the NCTE Commission on Reading selected him to serve on its national board. As a TEDx Speaker, Evan offers inspirational keynotes, workshops, webinars, and on-going professional learning opportunities on leadership, mindset, culture, impactful change, and how to improve literacy in schools. Evan has shared his ideas with thousands of educators at dozens of workshops across the United States and in other countries.

Stop Drawing Lines-In-The-Sand with Stakeholders
COURTNEY ORZEL, Ed.D.

"At some point you have to make a decision. Boundaries don't keep other people out. They fence you in. Life is messy. That is how we are made. So, you can waste your life drawing lines, or you can live your life crossing them." - Unknown

> "I'm not calling back a single parent about their concern about this topic. I've said all I'm going to say about it."
>
> "I'm no longer going to give an inch more with the teachers after that last staff meeting."
>
> "That's it. I'm not giving one more ounce of effort outside of what's required."
>
> "Ummm, no. We are not doing that, and it's not up for discussion..."

Do any of these sound bites sound familiar? Life is messy. Leaders are tired, and everyone is stressed. All of us. Teachers, administrators, parents, AND students. The job takes a toll on us in any given year, and for all educators. The last year and a half have tested us even more than we could have imagined. Unfortunately, there are times that we respond to daily chaos, tragedy, and trauma by drawing hard lines in the sand.

There are No Absolutes

This is especially true when it comes to leading. In every situation, on any given day, we face complex, challenging, and "you couldn't make this up if you tried" scenarios that test our patience, our memories, and our core leadership values. If leaders are to maximize stakeholder potential, then leaders must no longer draw lines in the sand when working with staff, parents - or honestly, anyone in the school community. No matter how effective and decorated you are as a leader, it won't prevent crazy situations from happening.

Drawing the Line is an Overreaction

Certainly, when we see safety, security, or mental wellness issues arise, we must immediately act to keep our students, staff, parents, and community safe. This chapter is not about ignoring lines in the sand that keep us safe; rather, this concept asks us to think more globally about the day-to-day situations that we face where we "draw the line" against a staff member who irritated us, a parent who took up time that we weren't expecting, or anyone else that disrupted the system to a point that our natural reaction is to "draw a line."

As an example, let's draw the line now by sharing the expectation that cell phones should be stored and in non-use, for teachers in the classroom. We all know that teachers can use cell phones to positively capture a beautiful learning moment and then post it on social media to let parents have a glimpse into the world of the classroom they would never see otherwise. Just because one teacher is using their cell phone to text and make personal calls during class shouldn't mean that everything gets shut down. If we "draw the line in the sand," that moment is lost. Same with students and cell phones- Do students make poor choices at times with cell phones? Absolutely, however, should we "draw the line in the sand" to ban *ALL* phones for *EVERY* student? We have students who can utilize phones and technology in innovative, positive, and transformative ways to create a deeper learning community. Since drawing the line is overreacting, how might the opportunity be leveraged for good? Instead of drawing the line, consider ways to support students in appropriate use that elevates the quality of learning. Instead of forbidding teachers to have access to personal cell phones in class, consider appropriate interactions, apps, and learning experiences that can be captured in real-time. And if there are individuals that compromise the rules, then that is a specific consequence rather than a group punishment that draws a line in the sand. Teach them and learn from them about what we can do to support them?

Instead of creating absolutes and overreacting to those absolutes, consider teaching and learning in the context of, "How can we be better tomorrow than we were today?" "How can we take a situation and think of it differently and explore more options that could create more positivity and engagement for whoever is involved?" Drawing lines doesn't allow for growth based on failure nor innovative solutions.

Empathy Maximizes Stakeholders

Leaders must be able to find a safe space to reflect and ask themselves, "Why did I get into education in the first place?" As leaders, we are pulled in a million different directions. We often start our day before we get to the building, on the phone, reading and responding to emails, most of which include someone that is NOT pleased with something or someone and expects us to take care of it. Before we even begin the day physically, we are mentally and emotionally invested in decisions that impact every student, staff, and parent we serve. This is not easy work, and certainly it is a massive responsibility. If we hear from a parent about a bus issue and draw the line in the sand without really listening, understanding, and showing empathy to a certain situation, we have lost the opportunity to show empathy, understanding and connection.

Focus on What Matters Most
When we think about what matters most to us, we likely think of our family and friends. As leaders, we must remember- how do we want our family and friends to be treated and how do we want them to view us? When we focus on what matters most and find a work/life blend that allows us to better handle stress, situations, and the daily grind of the job…we are better. Is this therapy for you? Is it mindfulness strategies? Whatever it is- we must make it part of our daily routine so that we remain focused on the things that matter most so that we can be our best on the job and make the best decisions. We should never draw a line or decide for our staff, students, or parents that we wouldn't want to be made for our own family. As we move forward with this important work, let's continue to ask ourselves these important questions:

- How is this situation unique?
- How can I show the teacher, parent, or person talking to me that I understand them?
- Am I really present right now or am I already deciding without truly understanding the entire situation?
- What benefit will people in this situation gain by me drawing a line vs. creating a safe space for all of us to learn and grow?
- How do you want to be remembered?

Stay away from drawing lines. No one wins when lines are drawn in the sand as absolutes. No situation is EVER the same. Everything we do is messy. Remember why you got into this important work as a leader of education in the first place. Stay strong and stay humble. Always.

Dr. Courtney Orzel is the Associate Director for Professional Development for the Illinois Association of School Administrators (IASA) and has served as a superintendent, middle school principal, assistant principal, and teacher. She is passionate about women in leadership and moderates the #IASASuperWomen Twitter chat, and she is a co-creator of the Unsupervised Leadership podcast

79

Stop Mocking Parents, Guardians & Families
CARRIE LABARGE

"Opinions don't affect facts. But facts should affect opinions, and do, if you're rational." -Ricky Gervais

Opinions Matter

We all do it. We all have them. We all share them from time to time. What is it? An opinion, maybe two or more. And in my opinion, opinions can be what makes or breaks any relationship. An opinion can take a very benign topic and turn it into an emotional tailspin quickly before someone with a differing opinion really knows what has occurred. Opinions that are shared with another person are words and just like all words, once words are spoken, they cannot be taken back.

Opinions are written on the comment section of surveys, response cards for businesses, and student information cards that are passed to the next year's teacher. Opinions matter, the written ones and verbal ones too! They are especially taken to heart when the verbal opinions come from the school leaders; these are the same people who are tasked with the culture and community of the school. Opinions (that draw the line in the sand as discussed in the previous chapter) can initiate the smallest hairline crack and travel wider and deeper until the opinions penetrate the entire foundation. Those fissures can start at the helm and as they spider out, the culture of opinions can spread to all areas of the school, creating a web of negativity that is often difficult to get back or restore.

Judgments and Opinions are Synonymous

Go ahead, type in the word "opinion", right click (or google), you'll discover that one of the synonym options is judgment. Yes, judgment! Sounds a bit harsher than opinion, but it's an option, nonetheless. This is what we do as humans, we judge, we take the perspective of a situation, we form an opinion (judgment), and all too often, we share it. For the most part, educators and families do their best (their perspective) and both parties pass judgment (have an opinion). Those judgments can be negative or positive. When negative opinions originate from a school leader and are shared with others, it sends a very detrimental connotation to those who hear it. The chances are that judgments will continue being shared with others and grow larger as they go.

Sometimes, opinions come in the form of mocking. Mocking happens for various reasons, it's not right, but we know it happens. Mocking a parent, family, or caretaker only plants seeds of toxicity and division. In difficult situations, emotions run high. Most school leaders mean no ill will by making under the breath comments, rolling eyes, or downright talking poorly about disparity in lifestyles. When someone is called out for being opinionated, it stings. I wonder if it stings as much as the person that discovered they were being mocked or judged by an educational leader. Opinionated people may laugh it off, commenting that their words were a joke, saying that it wasn't the intention. Occasionally the word "sorry" is uttered, or mumbled under one's breath, and the situation is forgotten, and the day continues. Sometimes this is a cyclical occurrence (counted more than a situation at a time) and a cycle that must be broken to maximize the capacity of all stakeholders within the school community.

We Are All on the Same Team
If you are reading this as a leader, most likely you are seeking to align with students, their families, and all stakeholders in the community. Leaders do not take a job of this magnitude with the intent to draw a dividing line between school and home. Every stakeholder has added value to student success; the assumption is that stakeholders unite as a team. Isn't that how all our efforts should align? Families are one of the greatest assets in maximizing student success and academic achievement.

Consider this, families and guardians have their children for sixteen hours a day, we have them for eight (not including weekends). We assume families do their best with their children and families assume we, as educators, do our best. Families send us their precious children. They are doing their very best (regardless of our opinion). Recognize that and lead accordingly. Wouldn't you rather be on the "team," than to have the parent upset that they have been mocked by the very person that should be leading the school? Wouldn't it be more constructive if parents felt comfortable regardless of their abilities or inabilities? Building a team of success that maximizes capacity begins with the superintendent, district leaders, and administration of the school. Being intentional and seeking the strengths of the various stakeholders in your community is the responsibility of ALL LEADERS. Isn't it better to build upon stakeholder strengths, assume positive intent, and work alongside families in such a welcoming way that an allyship of student success is forged?

All Eyes Are on the CEO
It comes with the territory of leadership and whether you like it or not, everyone is watching everything you do. Leaders are held to an even higher standard than everyone else. Assume that they notice your

mood, cadence, response, attitude, facial expression, words, and actions. That's a lot to live up to as the Chief "Education" Officer (CEO) of your district or school.

CEO's are required to take a very diverse group of people and develop them into a cohesive school community all focused on the same mission, vision, values, and goals. The primary goal is to do what's best for students. Clearly, CEO's can take opinions and judgments and set them aside so that parents and families feel included and as highly valued and not mocked. Regardless of the opinion of the district or school CEO, parents need to be spoken about in a positive and meaningful way no matter how ridiculous or unconventional the school leader may think they are. Words have power and the energy that we transmit, typically transpires. At a minimum, keep your opinion to yourself- unless it is positive.

Survival Mode Should be a Judgment Free Zone
I can remember being a fourth-grade teacher and having four children of my own. There were times when, as a parent, I brought my children to their school(s) for a parent night and other times I wouldn't. This was never because I thought education wasn't important, it was always because my tank was empty as an educator-mom. I had enough energy to do homework with my children, make dinner, get them ready for bed, put them in bed, get things ready for the next day, and collapse in bed only to wake up and do it again in the morning.

I had an administrator complain and mock parents about not attending a parent night. She claimed that they didn't care, didn't want to participate, weren't involved in their child's education, and continued to rant other opinions and judgments. I asked her if she felt that way about my husband and I, and she responded, "of course not." I explained our rationale as parents and went on to say that our family came first. We both had good jobs, a roof over our heads, healthy children, money in the bank, etc. and we didn't want to attend parent/family nights, sometimes. Legitimately, that is okay and was a decision we made.

So many of our families are in constant survival simply trying to keep afloat. Maybe it has nothing to do with what we think they do or don't do. It is our perspective. As CEO's, stop mocking and don't allow your faculty and staff to do it either. Greet families with respect and empathy. Be the leader that meets parents and families where they are- with the intention of uncovering strengths that will help maximize the overall capacity of student success.

Carrie LaBarge is an 18-year veteran of education who has taught elementary and adult GED classes. She has worked in only Title I funded schools throughout her career and has served as a Teacher on Administrative Assignment, a Title I Facilitator (liaison) between district and schools . She is now the Early Learning Specialist for the Hernado County School District. She oversees the VPK program for the district and was instrumental in bringing a full day VPK program to Title I Schools. She is a wife and mother of four and has three amazing grandchildren. She is dedicated to education, children, and all those who value education and life . She wishes all to value education and life…enjoy the journey and use both to change the world.

Stop Over-Complimenting Everyone without Specificity
STACEY GREEN

"I can live two months on a good compliment." -Mark Twain

"Great job!"
"You're nice."
"I noticed you."

Compliments make people feel good. Research reveals that the neurotransmitter dopamine is released when a person receives a compliment. The dopamine generated from the compliment may improve the focus and motivation of the receiver. There are also benefits to the one complimenting, as it helps them notice and appreciate the good in their surroundings, creating a more optimistic atmosphere. Appreciation is foundational in building strong relationships as we learned from Melissa Rathmann in Chapter 16. If compliments hold this magnitude of transformative power, then leader's must not only observe the strengths and capacity of stakeholders, but they must also compliment with enough specificity to maximize potential. Compliments assure stakeholders that they are seen, heard, and valued for their individual and unique strengths. In the previous chapter Carrie LaBarge shared this type of connection as the goal with parents, guardians, and families. She also shared that all eyes are on the CEO to lead these interconnections. In this chapter I'd like to take it one step further to demonstrate how complimenting with specificity will leverage and maximize the capacity of community.

Validate Contributions as an Investment
Educators who are investment-based strive to create positive relationships with students, co-workers, families, and communities. In Jimmy Casas' book, Live Your Excellence, he devotes one chapter to the topic of "every contribution, every day". Educators have the power to acknowledge and validate the

contributions of students and staff, no matter how small. If these opportunities are dismissed, the opportunity to strengthen the core of our community and add value to what people bring to the organization are lost also. Casas reminds us trust is cultivated when we invest in others, validating their ideas by words and actions. There are many layers to creating a positive culture and the giving of specific compliments is just one of those layers.

Complimenting is a skill that can be learned. You can easily turn a generic compliment like "good job" into a powerful acknowledgement. As you take steps to improve this skill, you can scaffold your approach by intentionally adding a new component over time. Edmonds suggests these components: be attentive, be specific, and be sincere.

> **1. Be attentive.** First, be attentive to the setting and the situation in which the receiver is making an investment. It's helpful to look for attitudes, abilities, and character traits.
>
> **2. Be specific.** The next step is to make the compliment more precise by dropping generic statements and focusing specifically on what the person did well. Substitute "Good job!" for, "You have a presence for supporting students who are dysregulated by allowing them time to regulate, providing them with space, and offering them their choice of tools. Your ability to stay calm helped everyone involved stay focused on the whole child." It is almost guaranteed that the recipient will replicate the steps they took to earn the compliment. In addition, when you're specific, not only will they hear what you said, but they will also understand that you value them. Consider these examples:
>
>> "You have taken the time to really get to know Joel and he validates this when he enters your classroom and follows your expectations."
>>
>> "Your smile, open body position, and eye contact when interacting with Audrey show her that you are a safe adult."
>>
>> "By pausing, using an appropriate tone and word choice, and then repeating what you heard, assured Mr. Green that you heard his concern. It showed him that you would be committed to delivering his message to the superintendent."
>
> **3. Be sincere.** Sincerity is critical, or the receiver will see right through the giver. A relationship built on trust and investment will assure the receiver that the compliment is based on true merit.

Is it worth the time it takes to formulate an attentive, specific, and sincere compliment? Absolutely.

"You never know if you will simply brighten someone's day or change the trajectory of their life. Either way, it's worth it."-Angela Edmonds

Stacey Green has transformed her school's culture where staff lead with the whole child and whole school in mind, embracing trauma-informed practices, increasing connection with students across experiences, and improving staff's capacity for mutual support, self-care, and vicarious trauma prevention. Stacey was named a National Distinguished Principal for Kansas in 2020.

81

Stop Seeing Students as Numbers
JAMI FOWLER-WHITE

"If you don't educate the whole child, how do you decide which part to leave behind?" -John Michael Lane

Leaders consume a myriad of information each day. The inundation and bombardment of mass information comes at us from every angle: social media, emails, texts, calls, apps, and meetings. Everything we observe and consume through our senses all throughout the day is anecdotal data that can be used to ensure that our students achieve academically and in life.

As a leader of a state, region, or district, focusing on the "students behind the numbers" may pose an even greater challenge because of time and accessibility. Regardless, the real purpose of your work must involve uncovering the needs of the student behind the numbers.

Student Strengths are More than Numbers

We have all felt the pressure of shooting for THE "magic number" of expectation. Our schools are expected to score high enough to show adequate yearly progress, but not too high or it will trigger a "cheating flag." If we are not careful, this pursuit of numbers will cloud judgment and make us forget our sole purpose as educational leaders, which is to educate students. How often have you been in a meeting where you were asked to defend your chronic absenteeism rate because it was above the recommended threshold, told that you did not have enough students score "proficient" on the latest state mandated assessment, or even asked to recite your data on command? I am not saying that as leaders we should not know, understand, or disaggregate our data, but sometimes it is a moot point. Student strengths are qualitative, not quantitative.

In Chapter 73 Brian McCann focused on eliminating extraneous assessments that do not have meaning nor bear an impact on learning. In Chapter 74 Dr. Naomi Ryfun shared the importance of high-quality teaching and meaningful learning rather than obsessing about high-stakes testing. This chapter builds on both premises as we take data and student information one step further. The focus of data analysis must include student strengths, deficits, abilities, talents, involvements, personalities, likes, and dislikes as factors that impact overall student success.

> *Data will talk to you if you're willing to listen to it."* -Jim Bergeson

Factors that Lay the Groundwork to Understanding the Data
Listening to the data talk requires the consideration of multiple perspectives. Any stakeholder who has a vested interest in education–families and educators—should be equipped with relevant data, in a discernible format, in a timely manner, so that the data serves as the driver that advances students strategically on a learning continuum of content and individualized skills. Before diving into summative (or even formative data trend), quality of teaching, interconnections, student motivation, and home life must be considered as factors impacting student achievement scores.

1. Teaching Factor: All students SHOULD receive high-quality Tier 1 whole class instruction. Classroom instruction SHOULD provide individualized, engaging, and equitable experiences that lead to successfully living a good life as educated and productive citizens. Classroom sizes SHOULD be manageable and curriculum resources and supplies accessible. But what happens when a teacher leaves mid-year only to leave the class with a revolving door of substitute teachers the rest of the year? What happens when there are no clear curriculum maps or resources available? Gaps in learning manifest. What happens when those students move on to the next grade level only to experience an ineffective teacher on a performance plan? The gaps in learning widen even more. And what happens when those same students move on to the next grade level and encounter a teacher with poor classroom management? What happens when the gap in learning is so wide that misbehaving seems to be more comfortable to students that are struggling? At this point, the discrepancy between IQ and ability may be so wide that students are identified to participate in special education as a student with exceptionalities. But are they really? The teaching factor is a systemic issue that if not analyzed could be swept under the rug as students move grade level to grade level year after year in a failed system rather than saved. One. Tier. At. A. Time. Students that have had an ineffective teacher two years in a row are not likely to close academic gaps. Avoiding this system failure requires analysis beyond summative numbers.

2. Connection Factor: Students that are involved in clubs and extracurricular activities are more likely to stay actively engaged in the ownership of their learning. The more peer connections, active invested adults, and community engagement, the greater sense of belonging students' experience. It would seem proactive to ensure that ALL students are outfitted with high quality interconnections in school.

3. Motivation Factor: Every student has a distinctive life experience (schema), special gifts (talents), and unique interests that motivate. When encountering low student achievement or academically disengaged students, one of the first questions that should be asked is, "Is it a can't do or a won't do?" Students that can't do the work have learning gaps, cognitive disabilities, medical issues, and possibly visual or hearing impairments. Low achieving students that can demonstrate their learning on an assessment but won't, lack motivation. Getting to the heart of what motivates requires uncovering student schema, talents, and interests. This may be a simple fix by providing opportunities to lead, using high interest text, offering choice, silly contests, awards and recognitions, or better home/school interactions.

4. Family Factor: As many teachers and leaders discovered during the virtual learning pivot from the pandemic, family plays a vital role in student success. For the first time many teachers experienced cognitive shifts because they realized what life was really like for students while at home. At home students may experience a second language, homelessness, bullying, fostering, or crime. Some students are even the caretaker for parents with disabilities, younger siblings, and extended family. Others may be spoiled, entitled, or pressured to be top of their class. High expectations are set by some families while other students are free roaming and experience no structure at home. Some students are in every extracurricular activity feeling burned out and filled with anxiety and others plug into electronics and self sooth through addictions and anxiety until all hours of the night. Understanding what it means to be successful from the perspective of the family is a factor in planning for academic success. Carrie LaBarge shared with us in Chapter 78 that we should not mock parents, guardians, or families. And we shouldn't. Analyzing family factors is a data point that has the potential to leverage success when the information leads to strengthening home and school connections.

A state-assessment is a snapshot of one moment in time for a student. Truthfully, data tied to a teacher's day to day interactions, distributed over time, with evidence of standard proficiency, should matter most. As leaders, do not forget that student success requires taking into consideration contributing factors before analyzing summative assessments. Maximizing academic achievement outcomes requires educators collaborating in pursuit of solutions that impact academic performance. Leaders should encourage the use of all forms of data, not just data that is directly tied to a number.

Create a Robust Plan Utilizing Various Forms of Data
Understanding the qualitative factors above lay the groundwork for deconstructing quantitative data for making future instructional and relational decisions. Data serves to measure progress, proficiencies,

and goals and comes in many forms. There is an overabundance of data that comes in many forms: summative, formative, individualized, adaptive on a continuum, anecdotal, short-term, long-term, historical, qualitative, quantitative, academic, written sample, electronic portfolio, project, demonstration, presentation, medical, socio-economic, mental, perceptual, demographic, social, attendance, behavior, extracurricular participation, and student engagement just to name a few. Creating a robust plan should include the use of all forms of data. A whole child approach for planning high quality teaching and learning cannot stand on quantitative data alone. Before getting started, take a moment to pause and digest the following questions that may guide future analysis of student performance in your state, region, district, school, or classroom.

1. How often do you examine students' quantitative data? (Summative, formative, benchmark, mid-term, end of unit, weekly test, common formative assessment, quizzes)
2. How do you balance the frequency and intensity of assessments with the current reality of student factors and qualitative performance in class?
3. What protocols or systems do you have in place to capture the strengths of every student on a social and emotional level? (E.g., Sports, clubs, talents, passions, family, friends, exceptionalities, motivation)
4. How and when do you discuss outside factors and deficits that may be contributing factors for lagging academic proficiency? (E.g., mental health, traumatic event, foster child, loss of a life, physical health, held back a grade, migrant, refugee, transient, homeless, ELL, victim, poverty, poor Tier 1 instruction, pandemic virtual student with gaps in learning and missing social skills, unmonitored homeschool)

As you work to integrate a whole school approach to data usage, consider leading data analysis with the following suggestions.

Take it slow: To create a data-friendly, student-focused environment, begin by taking it slow. Just because you as the leader understand how to interpret data, be careful not to assume everyone on your staff have been equipped with this same knowledge. It will take time to increase capacity around the plethora of information available. The sheer amount of information can make it overwhelming; many educators wouldn't know where to start. Develop your teachers so they understand the wide array of assessment types and their purpose.

Assemble a team: With so much data available to disaggregate, consider gathering a core team to provide input and help you prioritize where the school-wide focuses should be placed. This type of work is too much for any leadership team to tackle alone.

Organize data into four major categories: After assembling your team, think about beginning with the four major categories of data—academic, demographic, performance, and perception. You may want to organize categories that better meet your needs, the point is to select accurate measures of a school's success and progress. As a team, determine the criteria and specific information to be measured. This will ensure everyone understands the purpose and focus of the team's work. Designate specific steps, processes, or protocols to use when analyzing data (Fitzpatrick, 2004). Resist the urge to only look at the results of one category without considering the strengths, impact, areas of growth, and implications of all four of the major categories.

Craft specific actions aligned to goals: Revisit your mission, vision, values, and goals. Determine your long-term, short-term, and individualized student goals. Researchers have noted when school leaders establish goals for data usage, create the structure and offer teachers the instruments to utilize data, the results can mean significantly increased student learning and achievement outcomes.

Put Data into Action

Utilize all forms of data, dialogue, collaboration, and information to craft specific actions your school will take to increase student outcomes in all areas. These actions should include both quantitative and qualitative measurable results and be revisited in regular intervals using specific organizational systems or school-wide protocols.

> **Create weekly targeted goals in PLC meetings:** Regular intervals could be as simple as a weekly PLC and each teacher selects one student to bring to the team to discuss possible solutions that include both social emotional and instructional approaches.
>
> **Plan for measurable support during the student study team:** Sometimes the team may need to pull in special services like speech, special education, the school psychologist, or even a prior year teacher. Analysis may require more perspectives and minds at the table.
>
> **Facilitate routine student mini conferences:** Sharing academic data, student strengths, and goals with students is sometimes all that it takes. Perception plays a big role in motivation and what better way to act than to ask students what they would like to set as a goal and the contributing factors that may be holding them back from success. Many times, it may be a social dynamic, health impairment, or misunderstanding that is a quick fix.
>
> **Communicate progress to families:** Many schools invite parents in so they can learn to read benchmarking reports and to better understand the student's individual goals to make one year's growth. Provide families with the assessment schedule and how they can support motivation, communication, and academics at home. This may happen during parent conference times at the release of report cards, or it could be a virtual training that a parent can

access at their convenience. Create a relationship so that families feel comfortable enough to call and give a heads-up when there is a change in the family environment, health, social dynamics with peers, medical, or mental health struggles. The perception of the family about your school or district can make or break the academic performance of any student. Reread Carrie LaBarge's Chapter 78 and place families at the center of qualitative data.

Plan for evidence-based interventions and RTI: Most schools at a minimum have adaptive software that provide additional practice for students with gaps in learning. Schools that serve K-12 students likely have an intervention block where students are placed in customized learning sessions for reading and math.

Analyze cumulative standards to adjust teaching during quarterly data days: These are typically days where guest teachers relieve teachers for a full or half day to dedicate fully to the analysis of the most recent benchmark of covered material. During this time teachers can adjust their teaching by spiraling missed concepts, planning for small group instruction, reteaching the whole group, or skip ahead past standards that are already mastered.

Data is a double-edged sword. Don't let the numbers prevent you from using all available information to craft personalized steps for improvement at your school.

Jami Fowler-White is the founder and CEO of Digital PD 4 You, and co-creator of the Ignite Leadership Summit. She has served as an Instructional Coach, a Core Advocate with Achieve the Core, Assistant Principal, and mentor for the National Board of Professional Teaching Standards, and currently a Principal in Memphis-Shelby County (TN). Fowler-White is the author/coauthor of several books including: The Labyrinth of Leadership: Navigating Your Way Through the Maze, Educator Reflection Tips, EduMatch's Snapshot in Education 2020, The Skin You are In: Colorism in the Black Community, 2nd Edition, and Educator Reflection Tips, Volume II: Refining our Practice and blogs at DigitalPD4You.com, provides leadership advice on Insight Advance, and offers mindset strategies on TeachBetter.com.

82

Stop Ignoring the Cultivation of Student Leaders
ISAIAH STERLING

"Student leadership won't work without trust in students. Give them the chance to show how much you can trust them." -Dr. Anael Alston

Take a moment to imagine yourself as a student leader in your school district. You're no longer a superintendent, principal, or teacher who's making a difference in and outside of a classroom. You're now on the sidelines, as a student, trying to make a difference.

You've got this, right?

Imagine, as a student you make every effort to lead change knowing you won't be listened to, and your ideas won't be received much less taken seriously. Yet, you still try. You make an appointment with your principal to share a collection of ideas to positively impact your school. Ideas you've collected from your peers that are well thought out, relevant, and positively impact the learning culture of the school. Your principal listens and acknowledges your ideas and proceeds to pat you on the shoulder while thanking you, looks you in the eye to turn you down, and then sends you back to class. You are beside yourself because you put forth the effort, took a risk, and were willing to put in the work to support the change. But you weren't even taken seriously. Cultivation of student leadership was dodged, avoided, and intercepted in lieu of the status quo. You're told to ask for permission first and to advocate for your needs, so why put forth the effort when you know you'll always be dissuaded with a status quo, no. In an instant, doing what is best for students vanishes into thin air.

A Student Perspective of Hope
In another attempt to dismantle the status quo, a ray of hope shines through when you and a group of student leaders meet with the school principal to discuss ways to boost student engagement and raise morale. Your principal says, "If you guys want to be successful, you can't do whatever you think is best for students because you are the students. That is my job." Silence fills the four walls of the office conference room as your fellow student leaders are dumbfounded. You and your peer student leaders shut down, tuck your tails, remain quiet, and revert to taking your administrators' words seriously as they've crushed all hope of student impact. It was made very clear that engagement and morale will remain a "by teachers for teachers" formality. The cultivation of student leadership was ignored, dismissed, and the instructional authority of the adults was reinforced.

Top-Down Leadership Doesn't Cultivate Student Leaders
Leadership is at the top of a hierarchical organizational structure leading with vision, perspective, purpose, and reality. Hierarchy isn't a bad thing and leaders are trained, educated, and deserve to be respected for their vast experience that they bring to the table. In most school districts, teachers and

administrators work on the front lines of leading students. Policies, curriculum, assessments, and big constructs of education come from the top and are expected to be carried out with fidelity at the school level. Out of fear, or compliance, or habit, teachers and administrators may function in the status quo without ever thinking about what is within their realm of control in cultivating students as leaders within the organizational structure of stakeholders.

School leaders and teachers that view school operationally, shortchange the potential outcomes of a successful academic community. Just as Jami Fowler-White just shared in the previous chapter, students so easily are seen as numbers rather than talented and innovative stakeholders with a perspective that can increase capacity. If leaders aren't intentional about cultivating students as leaders, they aren't maximizing the capacity of their school performance. When student perceptions are ignored, top-down leadership may incite low student morale which leads to low attendance which leads to behavior problems which leads to low academic achievement. Top-down leadership can be a win-win situation when students are valued as a stakeholder of impact.

Place Students at the Forefront of Leadership
School districts that operate under a vision that places student voice at the forefront of leadership, build capacity and maximizes THE most important stakeholder of academic achievement. It is a win for everyone when students are invested in, motivated, encouraged, mentored, and relied upon as part of the solution for high quality teaching and learning. When students as leaders are afforded the opportunity to "be the change they want to be in the world" they become co-laborers in closing achievement gaps, motivating others, behaving, setting goals, and investing in a high-quality life beyond graduation. When students take charge of their education, it creates a united front inside of the classroom and school. Leadership has no boundaries or limits and should be extended to students.

Invite Student Scholars to Lead in the Classroom
All students are scholars. Scholars benefit when they are invited to be a part of the decision-making process in class. As leaders we all know what it feels like to be in charge. We also know how hard it is to work in an environment when we aren't at liberty to add input or leeway in carrying out a required task. When students feel like they are contributing to learning, they feel like they are a student scholar that is part of a learning community. The importance of allowing students to contribute and lead in classroom decisions, is important to meeting the needs of diverse students in a complicated and tech driven generation. As a primary and secondary education student, I had two choices:

1. Stay Silent: Remain silent, obey, and listen to my educators run their classroom the way they wanted causing the least interruption possible. Or,

2. Advocate for something better: Speak up, ask clarifying questions, request to do things a different way, and take ownership for cultivating my own leadership as a scholar seeking to break the status quo mold.

Earlier in my years of education, I chose option number one, like most compliant students do. Speaking up in class, sharing authentic ideals with an educator or recommending something different was interpreted as a behavioral disruption. Later in high school, thankfully, I shifted to option two and brought an army of students with me. To my surprise, I encountered an administrator that recognized my fervor for a high-quality learning experience and listened. She invited a group of us in with the sole purpose of listening. Listening soon turned into action as she invited the counselor and assistant principal to follow-up with our ideas that would lead to high student achievement AND a sense of belonging. Our leadership to light was ignited and our efforts and ideas became the launch pad for maximizing learning, building relationships, and ensuring every student scholar in the school was empowered.

Empower Students Even when they are "Off the Clock"
You may wonder where you should even start in recruiting, cultivating, and building an impactful student leadership environment. A simple invitation is the best place to start. Elicit ideas for leading outside of the classroom and capture your ideas. Ideas may be as small as assigning a student as a leader in class each day to line students up for recess, or as sophisticated as leading a student-based professional development session after school, by students for teachers. Student leaders can connect virtually online after school or meet at a local coffee shop to discuss ways to improve school culture and attendance. Students are social. Students want to be in charge. So why not empower them to be leaders impacting learning on and off the clock of school. Being a leader involves truth, integrity, discretion, creativity, gratitude, motivation, inclusivity, appreciation, confidence, manners, and so many more attributes that future employers desire. Why wouldn't leaders want to empower students to maintain a leadership presence "off the clock" from classroom learning?

A 2017 study by Lead4Change found over 90% of all Americans believe students are more successful in school when they practice leadership outside of the classroom. While in high school the administrators were risk-takers and viewed student scholars and empowered us to lead. One of the ideas that we generated was to record a ground-breaking podcast about student voices that welcomed even more input into learning success. Another idea that they fully supported was contributing as student leaders of professional development. These experiences demonstrated the value of student leadership outside the classroom, and the vulnerability of teachers as learners. Little did I know that our high school student voice podcast would open opportunities for me to meet hundreds of educational leaders, influential authors, and lead to presenting at national education conferences as a student. Leading professional development at my school prepared me for public speaking in higher education, provided me and my peers a greater sense of advocacy for others, and maximized our leadership capacity. These "off the clock" experiences helped us hone skills for professional interactions that prepared us for life beyond graduation.

My peers expressed that they were so excited to be a part of a student voice-based podcast that educators and students could access. The podcast helped student leaders build their professional portfolio. Classmates who assisted or even spoke at professional development sessions had the chance to develop public speaking skills they'll use for a lifetime. I chose to speak up and my high school principal listened. We chose to ask clarifying questions and the school admin team listened. We requested to do things a different way and even more students joined in. We chose to be brave enough to ask and our administrative team was willing to break the status quo mold. To this day I am grateful for the leaders willing to cultivate student scholars as leaders to maximize the capacity of our learning community. I would not be the leader I am today if things had turned out any other way.

Open the Door of Opportunity for All
Embrace the cultivation of student leadership. Open doors harness the power to maximize student growth and hone skills that can impact the future of your school community. Some scholars will wait for you to open a door for them, some are already pounding rapidly with fervor, while others won't even approach the threshold. Student perceptions, voice, and empowerment may be the only thing standing between a student performing proficiently and not.

Educators, remember to place yourselves in the shoes of your students and open the door of opportunity for all student scholars to lead. Student leaders are counting on us. Let's make their time in their K-12 learning community worth their while.

Isaiah Sterling a nationally recognized author, education consultant, journalist, university student and editor. He lives in Tampa, FL and works for Marriott International as a Room Operations Manager. Connect with Isaiah on Twitter @isterlingn or by email at isterlingwx@gmail.com. He is a contributing author in Let Them Speak, Recovery Mode, and the 100 STOP Series.

83

Stop Placing Sole Responsibility of ELL Students on the ELL Teacher
ANDREA BITNER

When a teacher's name is "all called" on the intercom throughout the building asking the teacher to report to the principal's main office, is a moment of trepidation. Imagine the following message booms throughout each classroom, "Ms. Everly, please report to the office...Ms. Everly, please report to the office." Ms. Everly's eyes raise up, her nerves send electrical pulses to every part of her body, and she paces quickly with a racing heart wondering what's next. Her teammates murmur silent thoughts of, "I hope all is okay" and faintly wave as she passes by.

As the only English Language Learner teacher in the building, that experience is the exact opposite for me. When I hear "Mrs. R, please report to the office," I smile. My eyes twinkle. I race down the hall as fast as I can, and wonder what new family, language, culture, experience, strengths, and challenges are standing there, waiting to be shared. This moment is an irreversible introduction to their education, and it is imperative that I make students and families feel safe and welcomed. I'm not the only one there who is able to welcome them...but, we can discuss that later in this piece.

Navigation Station

When a non-English speaking student arrives for the first time to a new school, they deserve "all hands, on deck," in welcoming fashion. Let me repeat that: Your team needs "ALL hands, on deck." Every member of the building will benefit from knowing who the student is, what language(s) they speak, if they were born in the U.S., what communication preferences their parents have, where their formal or informal schooling occurred before, the language level of support he will need to thrive during the entire school day, any traumas incurred, learning disabilities, medical needs, and who the other native speaking contacts are in the district or buildings. Why? Because whether you know it or not, your school just became one of the commanders on their new ship. Do you know how hard it is to navigate eight hours when you are listening to a language you don't understand, at an unprecedented rate, with new accents, local slogans, different teachers that often change every hour, and no parental language support? Mom, dad, or siblings are not there at that moment to help them. That student may even be in foster care, homeless, and/or a refugee tended to by the closest guardian available. Entering school as a non-English speaking native is a life disruption in every sense of the word. While at school, family connections and home comforts are by no means accessible. *YOU* are.

English is one of the most unpredictable, inconsistent, complicated, and fastest speaking languages in the world. When a student is drowning in those panicked moments during the school day, it will require both the life jacket and life preserver to pull them back to shore. A life jacket represents those things that are within your control to plan for before any ELL student ever reaches your front door. A Life preserver represents immediate rescuing from the dangerous waters of unexpected emotions, trauma responses, and frustration. Look at the table below and consider the processes you have in place in your "navigation station."

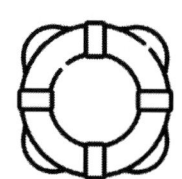

Welcome process for adults & students	De-escalation strategies for students of trauma
Visuals for translation	Therapeutic approach to safe risk-taking
Tour of the school	Comforting objects of familiarity
Labels in English throughout school	Familiar sensory: music, video, food, colors
Name tags for all key adults & students	Translation tools for students to access
Assigned student buddy	Chart with facial mood expressions
Picture of family to add to a binder	Utilize wants & needs list
Picture key of adults & students	Home communication in native language
Picture key of the various spaces in school	Revisit accommodations & supports
Picture key of wants & needs list	School counselor for de-escalation & comfort
Picture key of behavioral expectations	Academic supports
Pictures of comforting things to the student	Review from special education
Designated "safe place" to retreat to	Review from speech practitioner
Visual, daily, color-coded calendar or schedule	
Hearing & vision screening	

Certainly, this is not a complete nor comprehensive list, but it is a great start for you and your school staff to become equipped to maximize your navigation station. The key is that your school is intentional, pre-planned and you have practiced using your life jackets and life preservers. *TEAM UP* and decide what role each of you will play: academically, accommodation-ally, emotionally, socially, and communicatively. Take the time to brainstorm and co-plan the process and resources that you will have available every day of the year. It is our job to ensure that this navigation station is in place. Our kids are counting on *ALL* hands, on deck.

Maya Angelou once said, "When you know better, you do better." We can do better! There are more ELL resources available than any time in teaching history. Reach out to your state, local, or school ELL specialist to learn and gain access to tools, apps, methods, and resources that serve the EL students' and their families. It is our job to seek them out and to commit to using them. Now that you know better, do better.

Some Days Feel Like a Sinking Ship
In a matter of one day, I received a telephone call from the attendance office, an email from the school nurse, a text message from an administrator, and a *TRANSACT* message from a worried parent. Sitting before me were four different time sensitive communication requests. The attendance office asked me to complete an information packet for a new student in Arabic. A text message relayed that there was a fight between one of my students and another young man who spoke Mandarin, and they needed a translation requesting the mom to come in. The nurse was frustrated because she wasn't getting a vaccination request response from a Russian speaking family, and the *TRANSACT* message, in Spanish, said "Mrs. R, please help me! The school called and left a message about my son, and the only words I could understand were "no school" and "Michael." Anyone who has been in education for any amount of time has experienced a compounding, frantic, and emotionally tense day like this one. You can only survive a day like this one as an ELL teacher if you have processes in place, staff trained to support, and a leadership team that makes every effort to prepare for days like this, before they happen. Because they will, and you may need your own life preserver from time to time. And when you do, use "all hands, on deck."

Don't Send Your Message in a Bottle
For fifteen years, I have been one of the most vocal advocates on the planet when it comes to spreading communication strategies with teacher teams to ensure they can successfully access our EL families in

a way that is effective. Every year, we spent time reviewing translation services such as TRANSACT or *INTERPRETALK*, our state department website, the bilingual free text messaging site *TALKING POINTS, GOOGLE VOICE* phone numbers, parent communication preference sheets, translated books, audio options, and more. Teachers and staff are encouraged and equipped to communicate directly with parents or guardians.

Rather than communicating directly with families, sometimes the easiest and fastest way is a quick translation through a bilingual sibling or student's friends to communicate messages to the parent or guardian. Let me caution you, this is a sure-fire way to disempower the leader of the family. Don't shortchange the communication by placing a child as the go-between. This is as effective as sending a message in a bottle out to sea and hoping that it arrives on the precise coordinates at the precise time. It isn't effective. Consider that there may be details that parents or guardians want to share with you without the ears of their children. They are counting on you to provide them with the platform for adult-to-adult communication.

Dock the Boat

The English as a second language ocean is vast, deep, and at times seems never ending. There may be days when you feel that strategies, support, time, and the effort that you place on EL students is at a standstill. Some days it will feel like the ship is in jeopardy of sinking. Sharks will swim and sneak attacks may come in the dead of night when you least expect it. And the sun will rise the next day and the boat will be docked for repairs that will make the next part of the journey even stronger. The steps to success never fall in a straight line while navigating the ELL map. There may also be times you feel unequipped to help them navigate the academic, social, and emotional storm that is waiting for them each day as they arrive on your school door steps.   I'm here on their behalf. Please don't give up. Don't wait for the EL teacher to save you from your uncertainty. Use your resources. Ask lots of questions. Team up. Search for ways to provide academic support. Communicate. Refuse to settle for relying on a child, or your EL teacher, to do it for you. It takes ALL hands, on deck, to dock a boat to regroup to ensure that our treasure (ELL students) make it safely to the shores of success. Maximizing all stakeholders includes building the capacity of the entire ELL school community.

Andrea Bitner is an educator, author, and speaker. She lives in Philadelphia, PA. She has worked with students in grades K-12 throughout her twenty-two years in public education from all around the world.   Her first book, "Take Me Home," was published by Austin Macauley in July of 2021. "Take Me Home" is the true story of 11 of her former EL students who give a first-hand account of what it's really like to become bilingual in America. She is also a co-author of Chip Baker's "The Impact of Influence-Volume 3." She travels the country speaking and teaching educators how to teach and reach EL students, and effectively communicate with EL families! You can find Andrea at www.andreabitnerbooks.com, or on social media @andreabitnerbooks.

84

Stop Fearing or Fighting with the Teachers' Union
DAVID FRANKLIN, Ed.D.

The job of a school administrator is multi-faceted. Part teacher, part counselor, part coach, part lion tamer. The jump from the classroom to the front office is not an easy one to make, like the "sinking ship" day that Andrea Bitner experienced in the previous chapter. As a classroom teacher, I focused my energy on my students and their families just as Andrea Bitner did. I wanted all my stakeholders to have the best possible experience as possible. As a classroom teacher, I had two main stakeholder groups to worry about leading, students and their families.

When I became an administrator, many more layers were added on including community members, school board members, administrative staff, custodians, kitchen staff, security personnel, and district office administrators. However, the biggest and most prevalent group of stakeholders added to my charge were my teachers.

Us to Them
When I made the jump from teacher to administrator, I was given a piece of advice from a colleague. He told me that when you move from the classroom to the front office, you also move from "us" to "them". That day, I spent a lot of time reflecting on that statement and I carried it with me every day from that point forward in my career. This advice held true because I felt the distinction immediately from day one, as my teachers treated me differently than when I was a teacher.

My first interaction with the teacher's union as an administrator happened quickly after I arrived. The union representative from my school came into my office to introduce herself. I knew that she was also sizing me up. I was fresh meat; young and inexperienced, as well as idealistic. I was told that the staff at my school was very involved in the union and that they expected me to follow their contract to the letter. Nothing else would be tolerated.

> At that moment, I saw my opportunity.
> To her surprise, I told her that I agreed with her.

I had heard horror stories of administrators fighting the teacher's union at their sites, feeding into a negative culture fueled by distrust and power posturing. As a new administrator, I wanted to go down a different path. I knew that for my school to support students at the highest level, I needed my teachers to be on my side and they needed me to support them. It was time to stop fearing and fighting with the union and to start working together.

Work Out Misconceptions Using the Collective Bargaining Agreement
My first order of business was to become as familiar as possible with my district's collective bargaining agreement or CBA for short. This way, I would arm myself with the information needed to not get backed into a corner by asking too much of my staff or taking too much of their time. Staying within the parameters of the contract was vital. I also set up a standing monthly meeting with my union rep. Again, she was surprised by my offer. My reasoning behind these monthly meetings was so that we could get on the same page and work out any misunderstandings, proactively, BEFORE they blew up. Expectations on both sides were expressed and agreed upon based on the language in the collective bargaining agreement. I quickly discovered that both the teachers and the previous administration were taking significant liberties with the language in the CBA. While we didn't agree on everything, we both could agree that we would use the contract to determine guidelines and next steps for our school. Once we worked out misconceptions and concerns, we had a strong working relationship. Most importantly, we had built a relationship founded on trust.

Trust Depends on Leaders Doing What's Right, Not Being Right
Over the course of the five years that I served as the principal of this school, I saw many principals in my district come and go. The main reason for them leaving was that they could not create a culture of trust withing their school community. It was more important for them to be right, than to work with their teachers on a solution. Collective bargaining agreements are not perfect documents. In the districts I worked in, there were many aspects in the contract language that I did not agree with. However, this was a contract between the district and the teachers, voted upon and ratified by the

school board. It was to be upheld and followed. Rather than fight and express my opposition to the agreement, I worked with it. Yes, there were concessions that were made to teachers on my part, but gains on my end were made as well. What is most important is that at the end of the day, trust remained at the center of the relationship because I was willing to do what was right.

This trust was tested when I had a significant issue with a teacher at my school. It was the type of issue that, based on the claim, could potentially end the career of the teacher. If the situation was handled poorly, the administrator might be the one left behind. It was also the type of situation where the union could easily rally behind the teacher.

Since I had worked for several years to build up the level of trust at my school, I worked through this issue using the CBA as my guide, ensuring that everything that was done in relation to my investigation of the issue was to the letter of the contract. The trust and respect that I had earned paid off when the facts of the situation came to light. In the end, I spent another two wonderful years at that school, while this teacher quietly resigned in protest without any public fanfare or pomp and circumstance. I took the lessons I learned in working with unions to my next assignment and spent five more successful years cultivating a culture of trust and unity in another school community. My monthly union rep meetings became fun and lighthearted conversations that we looked forward to.

As administrators, we can either choose to fear and fight with teachers' unions to flex our own power, or we can work with them and create a lasting partnership that will benefit all stakeholders, leading to higher levels of student success. Maximizing all stakeholders requires that we do what's right rather than focusing on being right.

Dr. David Franklin is an award-winning school administrator, education professor, curriculum designer, and presenter. He earned a Doctorate in Educational Leadership from California State University, East Bay, and has presented at national and international education conferences. Dr. Franklin is a sought-after presenter in the areas of academic intervention, school leadership, creating a shared vision, creating common assessments, and data analysis.

STOP Making Everything about You

This Type of Nonsense Prevents Dynamic Off-the-Charts Leadership Presence

85

Stop Forgetting Where You Started Your Career
JESSE LUBINSKY

"Leadership is about empathy. It is about having the ability to relate to and connect with people for the purpose of inspiring and empowering their lives." -Oprah Winfrey

Imagine for a moment that you were an executive chef at one of the most acclaimed restaurants in town. Night after night, diners rave about your innovative and modern takes on an extensive array of dishes offered on the menu. You've mastered the art of selecting ingredients, preparing cuisine, and working with your kitchen staff. Now imagine being told that being a great chef means you're qualified to run the whole restaurant. Everything from managing finances and day-to-day operations to handling interpersonal staff conflicts. If it seems like that wouldn't make any sense, you're absolutely correct. It wouldn't. But this is the exact parallel that we see in our schools year after year.

It's become commonplace in education for teachers to be placed on this invisible ladder. If you are a great teacher, you're placed on the fast track to move up the ladder to become a school leader. And yet, being a great teacher is rarely an indication that one will become a great administrator. Sure, having a good work ethic and a solid foundational understanding of good classroom instructional practices are important in both roles but the list of skills required to achieve success on a day-to-day basis in each position are about as different as night and day. And it's for that very reason that so many school leaders who have made the transition from teaching to administration often run into a common stumbling block: Forgetting where they started their career.

The Distance Between Where you are Headed and Where you have Been
One of the moments from earlier in my teaching career that resonated with me as I became a school leader was from my first week teaching in a new school. I had agreed to stay late to provide some technology help to the principal, who was also new to the building. A few days later, there was a letter in my mailbox. It was a thank you note saying how grateful he was for the help I provided. He also made sure to copy the district office on the letter and have it added to my personnel file. And while this letter was only a few sentences long, the gesture has always stuck with me. When I reflect on why

it has, I think it is because it was a sign of respect for the time and work that we all put in as classroom educators. And unfortunately, that respect is often lost on school leaders.

You will never hear a school administrator say they wanted to run a school because they had a passion for excessive paperwork, attending an array of non-stop meetings, handling administrivia, or dealing with frustrated staff members, angry parents, or concerned community members. Almost every single one of them cultivated their love of education in the classroom where they worked tirelessly to inspire students and change their lives for the better. For many, becoming a school leader is a natural next step to expand the scale of their impact. But as anyone who has ever made that transition knows, while the reach of your impact may grow, the work itself becomes all too easy to get lost in as the list of responsibilities and details can grow almost exponentially from one day to the next. And as it grows, so does the distance between where you're headed and where you've been.

A Fool's Errand
As school leaders, we can become so fixated on checking boxes and dealing with issues that we can lose our ability to empathize with our teachers and remember what it felt like to tackle the issues we faced every day in our classrooms. Yes, decisions need to be made, sometimes in the spur of the moment. As Dr. Marcus Belin shared in Chapter 83, those decisions can have consequences and it is important to not only communicate with our teachers but to take a moment to try to place ourselves back into their shoes. It is so easy to roll your eyes or groan when a staff member appears to be complaining. In those moments, it can feel like our agendas and decisions are being questioned. However, what we should do in those moments is to consider how we felt when we were the ones who lacked the power and input to make those decisions. How would we have reacted?

I think we can all accept that trying to turn a school into some form of utopia where leaders and teachers are in full alignment and always in agreement is a fool's errand. But once we put on that leadership hat, it becomes too easy to forget the everyday trials and tribulations of our colleagues still in the classroom. The work of school leaders is not any more important or essential than the work being done by teachers in the classroom. Yes, school leaders have an incredible amount of responsibility for ensuring that our schools run effectively and efficiently. However, as soon as we ignore our teaching roots, dismiss the importance of connecting with our teachers and lose the ability to empathize with them, we have no real chance to be a school leader. And that's the difference between simply administering a school and leading one.

The Value of History

Successful school leaders understand and value history. Not just the history of education in general but of their own personal history and the value that the insights of their own journey can provide them. When we forget to tap into our own experiences as classroom educators, we fall into the trap of failing to think through the impact our decisions would have had on us if we were one of the teachers being affected. And can we really blame teachers for reacting negatively when we ourselves would have reacted the exact same way if we were them?

I think of that note I received often. A simple note being copied to my personnel file felt like gold. Teachers don't require huge gestures or empty platitudes to feel understood and respected. They want to know that the seemingly endless hours of work and dedication are recognized and appreciated. They want to know their voices are acknowledged and heard. Isn't that what you would have wanted when you were in the classroom?

Jesse Lubinsky currently serves as an Education Evangelist for Adobe. He is an Adobe Creative Educator, a CoSN CETL, and an international keynote speaker. He is co-author of "Reality Bytes: Innovative Learning Using Augmented and Virtual Reality" and "The Esports Education Playbook: Empowering Every Learner Through Inclusive Gaming." Jesse is also a co-host of the Partial Credit Podcast and the Ready Learner One Lounge, a virtual reality show focused on innovations in teaching and learning.

86

Stop Assuming Teachers Can Afford It

CATHERINE A. BARRETT

Just as Jesse Lubinsky just shared, leaders should never forget where they started. When leaders are connected to the realities of the day-to-day life of a teacher, they know full well that teachers cannot afford to fund classroom supplies (financially), nor can they afford (mentally) to use their time off for planning or school initiatives. Just because the high-flying overachieving teachers go above and beyond in these ways, most teachers cannot afford it financially or mentally.

Having a visually appealing school environment that is organized and filled with learning resources, books, manipulatives, and prizes doesn't happen without a cost. Setting this level of expectations isn't about you, it is about advocating, sharing, supplying, networking, and giving as much as possible to the teachers to ensure they don't overspend their mental energy and money. Off-the-chart leaders remember the pressures, inadequacies, and financial constraints that it took to provide a flourishing learning environment filled with rich learning experiences.

Summer Planning
During the summer, many teachers relax to decompress and spend time free of obligations. For high flying teachers, within weeks of summer break their minds drift to ideas and planning for the upcoming school year. They think about the content, themes, topics, strategies, and how they will keep it all organized. High achieving teachers typically capitalize on time throughout the summer to dive into a stack of books that they have been eagerly waiting for enough time to read.

Teachers are very social, and the summer break also provides an opportunity for teachers to connect with other teachers both formally in training, and informally at lunch or laying by the pool. When the summer ends many teachers use personal time to plan and make lists of things they need to buy. While these are exceptions to the rule, the majority of teachers value summertime with family in friends and don't want to feel obligated to meet or plan, and on top of it they may be living financially meager as they stretch the budget to make it to that first paycheck of the new school year.

Start to the Year
Every new school year begins with a room assignment. A classroom assigned number as teacher territory. As a classroom teacher, I've been assigned classroom room numbers by administration. One culture norm in our profession is that being assigned a classroom room number may or may not be permanent. In my 20 years in education, I can only count one year in my career where I've remained in the same classroom. When I taught high school, I was even assigned to a closet and informed that I would be traveling and pushing computer laptop carts to the requesting English teacher. Every physical classroom move demands planning for the new space of the environment which also inevitably costs more money that neither the school nor the teacher can afford. Sometimes this means disruption, miscommunication, and chaos can ensue as a result. Look at the following scenario.

An eager first year teacher new to the district arrived early prior to the calendar and contract start date. She decided to visit her assigned room #9000. When she arrived to look around her room, she mentally took inventory of what was available. She noticed furniture stacked, bookshelves, supplies in organizers, and items labeled with another teacher's name. She logged into the district email system and generated an email to the teacher whose name was on the items and boxes.

SUBJECT: *Hi!*

MESSAGE: *It seems some of your items have made their way to my classroom and some are labeled, and others are just randomly placed around my classroom. So, I moved them outside the classroom door and into the hallway. Happy Friday Eve!*

Teachers are notorious for keeping, hoarding, or stealing prized teacher items when they have spotted furniture items, books, supplies and more. In our profession, we gladly accept just about anything we can get our hands on and as if we are treasure finders. Garage sales, Pinterest projects, purchases, and donations fuel the teaching profession. This is sad indeed. In no other profession would a co-worker imagine rationing, borrowing, or scrounging to set up a work environment. In education the answer is simple, they can't afford it monetarily nor should they be required to endure the time and effort to secure and protect belongings. I happened to be the teacher that received the email that my belongings were sorted and some of them placed in the hallway. I was mortified. Clearly, she didn't understand the unspoken rules of teacher property.

As a veteran teacher I wanted to help her understand that we treat one another with dignity. She may not have known that behind the scenes, the assistant principal changed my room assignment two or more times over the summer break. As an idyllic new teacher, she may or may not have realized the effort it took to collect those belongings over the years and that I couldn't afford to replace things. I replied to her email and copied my administrators.

SUBJECT: *Hi!*

MESSAGE: *Welcome to our school. I hope you enjoy teaching in room #9000 as much as I did. I'm sure you are eager to start setting things up as I am too. The principal moved my room multiple times during the summer and the work order hasn't yet been completed to move my belongings. There is a specific district protocol for moving content since the boxes and belongings are required to be in a secure and locked room for safety and security reasons. Please give me a call and I'd love to meet you in person and am happy to meet you up at the school.*

In the email I was welcoming, yet I shared the protocol that hopefully spared any of my belongings from wandering off. The next day I met the new teacher in room #9000 and immediately she was apologetic and on her own she moved the boxes and belongings back inside the room behind lock and key. Had they remained in the hallway it would have been a "picker's" dream of rummaging and I might not have gotten my belongings back. When you are in a profession that can't afford it, "shopping" through surplus items left in a hallway, is FREE for the taking or can even be taken out as trash from the maintenance staff. Leaders, I'm sure you can remember the days of property protection and territorial rationing. Teachers operate in a professional poverty mindset, emotionally and financially, when it comes to finding the resources they need.

Extended Breaks

Fall break, winter break, spring break, and long holiday weekends are another time that teachers use to reflect, grade, collaborate, and plan for the unique needs of their students. Many teachers will redesign lessons for student engagement and motivation based on student feedback. Teachers preview digital lessons that are carried through online platforms, assessing any new features, and learning to use the technology tools effectively. Oftentimes they are closing out a quarter and looking ahead to the next learning segment. During breaks teachers shop and budget for the supplies and resources they will need in the upcoming months. Knowing how tight and restricted school budgets are, teachers spend their own money to ensure classroom success. Out of pride, some districts prohibit crowdsourcing donations or wish lists on websites which leave teachers with no option but to purchase various classroom supplies using personal money or credit cards that they will pay off with another summer job.

End of the Year

As the school year ends, teachers emotionally are spent, and their checkbooks are certainly tapped out. Teaching is a calling and a chosen lifestyle otherwise there wouldn't be so many incredible people still doing it. The reality of life is that teachers still must take the responsibility to manage their personal finances to ensure they live within their salary. To this day I still must balance my finances and decide what I can pay for housing, utilities, meeting my investment goals and having some money left over for savings. Like most teachers, part of this budgeting for expenses involves the amount I will spend to budget for the classroom supplies (which are never enough). My goal is to ensure a well-stocked classroom that is optimal and inviting for learning.

For teachers to stay within a budget, it requires mental discipline and planning. Don't ever forget what it was like to give everything that you had. Look for ways to partner with your local school community, district office, and businesses to help alleviate the mental and financial pressure that teachers undergo.

Catherine Barrett is an Arizona Master Teacher with expertise in K-12 instruction. She is a second career high school reading specialist and classroom technology education educator, all in the state of Arizona. Often referred to as the "bravest teacher" in the state of Arizona by State Senators and Representatives in the House of Representatives as the whistleblower of the REDforED movement.

87

Stop Taking Yourself Too Seriously
BRENT COLEY

Before we jump in, let me start by saying this — being a school leader is a serious job. A very serious job. Please don't let the title of this chapter lead you to think that I believe otherwise. The list of responsibilities placed on school leaders is long and only continues to grow. Ensuring academic success for all learners. Fostering social-emotional wellness in both students and staff. Creating an environment that is safe and inclusive for all involved. Being a good steward of the financial resources allocated to the school. Oh, and then there's bus duty. And IEPs, School Site Council meetings, required staff evaluations, lunch supervision, and email. So much email. In district or county positions, the level of seriousness only increases, as the decisions that need to be made affect a larger number of stakeholders. A serious job indeed.

It's Like Parenting

Now let's compare the role of school leader to that of a parent. A serious job? Absolutely! I'd argue there isn't a more important job than being a parent. As with school leadership, there are so many responsibilities involved in raising children. Working to put a roof overhead and food on the table. Paying bills. Getting the kids to and from school. Preparing meals. Laundry. All important things for sure, but let me ask you a question — what if these things were the only things your children remembered when they looked back on their childhood? What if you worked hard, fed them, provided them with a beautiful home, clean clothes, and transportation around town, but that's all they remembered?

Think back to your childhood. What positive memories of your parent(s) stick out in your mind? Is it that they paid the bills each month? Is it the countless loads of laundry that were run and folded? Is it the nightly ritual of washing dishes after dinner? Or are the memories of mom or dad more personal? My hope is that your head is full of memories that don't solely involve the important-yet-mundane tasks like the ones above, but instead include instances of a more personal nature. Like taking the time to play catch with you in the backyard. Or putting the work aside to play with toys or build Legos with you. Or greeting you with a hug every day when you got home from school. Or just sitting on your bed and listening as you talked to them about what was going on in your life at the time.

What Will They Remember?
Now back to school leadership. Your students aren't going to remember how well you dealt with the school budget, how many committees you were on, nor will they remember all the teacher evaluations you had to do. No matter how serious all those things are, these aren't what they're going to remember. Leadership isn't about you. Yet, they're going to remember you.

They're going to remember what they heard you say and what they saw you do. More specifically, they're going to remember what you said to them, what you did with them, and how it made them feel. So, what's it going to be? Are you going to rush by with a quick reply of, "Sorry, boys and girls. Wish I could chat. Gotta get to a meeting." Or will it be, "Hey, guys! How was your weekend? I'd love to catch up with you later today." Will you be the leader they always saw walking around campus holding a clipboard, on your way to complete the next important task, or the one who made time to stop and talk with them, shoot hoops, or eat a meal in the cafeteria? Will your students even remember seeing you at all?

Here's the thing – If you believe you don't have time to get out of the office and interact with students (because you must devote yourself to the serious work of being a school leader), you're missing the point. Being with students is *THE* truly serious work. Dynamic leaders have fun with students. They know it's okay to be silly at times, that it isn't necessary to ALWAYS act the role of a polished, professional leader (whatever that's supposed to look like). It's okay to unbutton your shirt's top button, to loosen your tie (or even take it off). It's okay to let your hair down (or put it up in a ponytail). It's okay to be real. It's okay to be human. It's more than just okay. It's necessary. Because that's what students will remember. That's the most enduring and important work that we can do as leaders.

The Truly Serious Work
In my 10 years of site leadership as an assistant principal and principal, I've had plenty of opportunities to temporarily place the "serious" parts of the job aside to create memorable experiences for students. I've…

- Sat in a dunk tank at the school carnival.
- Taken a pie to the face after students met a reading goal.

- Been duct taped to a pole when students collected 25,000 Box Tops for Education.
- Kissed a pig after students filled a five-gallon water bottle with spare change for charity.
- Ran a lap around the school quad in high heels when students exceeded their PTA membership drive goal. (Side note: Ladies, on behalf of all men, I'm sorry. You should never have to walk around in those things.)
- Ridden tricycles with kindergarteners and jumped rope with second graders.
- Joined fifth graders in three-point contests at lunch.
- Taken walks with students who were having a rough day and just needed a break.
- Been the hero by helping students get the darn straw into their Capri Sun.

That's *THE* serious work. Those are the things students will go home and mention when asked about their day at school. Devote time each day for *THE* truly serious work. Get out of your office. Put the budget and evaluations aside for a bit. Spend time with students, building relationships that show them you're more than a title -- you're an adult who cares about them enough to spend time with them. Show them it is about THEM, not you.

And smile. Don't forget to smile. Because that's what they're going to remember.

Brent Coley is a former elementary school principal and current district administrator passionate about sharing with and learning from other educators. A firm believer in the power of storytelling, he is also the author of Stories of EduInfluence, The Gift: A Tale of Adventure, Courage and Hope, and host of the Teaching Tales podcast. Learn more at BrentColey.com.

Stop Making Excuses for Your Own Lack of Leadership
ERIC NICHOLS

The district test scores are trending downward. The front of the school needs a facelift and a new coat of paint. The PLCs to be implemented didn't get off the ground in 60% of the school buildings. The high school budget was overspent by 22%. Teachers are leaving school before the contracted end of day and are arriving late. Some school leaders can be heard saying, "This place sucks! Everybody at this place sucks! If they would just do their jobs this place would turn around." This isn't all about you. On the contrary my friend. You, yes YOU, need to STOP making excuses, and LEAD with dynamic off-the-charts leadership presence.

School of Hard Knocks
This just in from "The School of Hard Knocks;" bad things will happen at your school. Your school will have poor performances from staff members occasionally. Parents will be upset now and again, and students will inevitably misbehave. Maybe, just maybe, the school board of directors will make a decision that you disagree with as well. Hey, school leader! Hey, principal! What will you do in these situations? Will you shift the blame to others? Point fingers at those who are not at fault. Bad things will happen within our schools, but as Charles Swindoll says, "I am convinced that life is 10% what happens to me and 90% of how I react to it." What will your reaction be? Successful leaders will not shift the blame. Successful leaders will be seen publicly taking responsibility for *EVERYTHING*!

Quality school leaders, pickup those who stumble. They support and guide failures and mishaps to a better way. Off-the-charts leaders do not point fingers at others who might struggle; the leader points the finger at themselves. The leader takes the blame for missed opportunities. The leader takes responsibility for the bad, the ugly and the gruesome in our schools. As one successful principal noted, "It is my job to take the bad stuff on. It protects my staff, and we regroup as a team and go about getting better." Being a leader is a hard knock kind of life and like Brent Coley just shared in Chapter 87, dynamic leaders most certainly cannot and should not take themselves too seriously. It isn't about you as a leader, it is about remembering where you came from, as Jesse Lubinsky shared. It is about understanding that teachers cannot afford the additional mental pressure that Catherine Barrett shared earlier in this section.

Accept Kudos and Accolades on Behalf of the Team
Just the opposite happens when credit is due to the school leader. Successful school leaders don't accept the kudos and accolades that come their way. Dynamic leaders understand full well that the praise aimed at the leaders is misplaced praise. School leaders should always shift the praise to their staff. Leaders, pass on the credit and as pointed out earlier; take the blame when things go awry. Legendary college basketball coach John Wooden was a master at this and it worked quite well as he won 10 titles in 12 years while embracing this philosophy. As noted in his book John Wooden says, "As my father reminded me more than once, 'Great leaders give credit to others and accept the blame themselves.' If one of my assistant coaches suggested we decide to implement it, I would make sure to praise him for

his foresight in the press conference afterward. But if one made a suggestion that didn't prove to be as successful, I accepted the blame myself rather than pinning it on the assistant. After all, as the head coach, I had decided to go forward with it. I found that this was the most effective way to keep my assistant coaches feeling engaged with the game, willing to make suggestions and ready to contribute to the betterment of the team. It worked with my players, too. I would never publicly criticize a player for poor performance. Even in moments of extreme frustration, I would check myself because it just didn't seem right—because it didn't seem like something my father would have done."

Poor Schools are a Result of Poor Leaders
Quality school leaders can overcome dysfunctional school boardrooms. In fact, effective school leaders can even overcome poor leadership at the district level. Poor schools are not the result of poor board policies, poor district continuous improvement plans or poor district vision statements. School leaders can overcome limited budgets from their Superintendents. School leaders can overcome and rise above poor Superintendents. Effective schools can exist with poor school boards, poor superintendents, but not with poor school leadership.

One such situation involves a rural school district which had continual bickering on the school board, community squabbling on Facebook, multiple Superintendent turnovers and poor school leadership in multiple schools. Two of the district's schools fell into mandated school improvement plans due to poor student test scores and poor student growth. Inserting an effective principal into a school immediately impacted teacher practices, school culture and student growth. Inserting the new principal, led to the school being a top tier school in the state within two years. Another example existed in a booming suburban district where a middle and high school had decades of poor classroom performance. Multiple superintendents had served one- and two-year stints and multiple principals at both the middle and high school had filled the principal's chair. Insert two new energetic, knowledgeable, dynamic, and determined principals and what followed were years of academic success for the suburban middle and secondary students.

What happened in both school districts listed above? A simple recipe of success. New school leadership brought with it dynamic energy, focused culture, new expectations, strategic processes, effective collaboration, inspected accountability, and a new way of doing business. That business was student learning. The school leaders, the principals, realized that great teaching will improve student learning and ultimately the school.

As Dr. Kevin Feldman has been heard saying, "There are only two ways to improve schools, get new students or improve the teachers." The school principal's job as instructional leader is not to bus in new students, but to improve the elements that impact student learning. Principals, your most important job is *NOT* to sit in your office answering emails all day expecting respect just because you are the leader as Dr. Dan Kreiness already pointed out in Chapter 13. Principals, your most important job is not school discipline. Principals, your most important job is not monitoring halls between classes. While these jobs are important to assist with the day-to-day flow of the school, there is nothing more important than improving the teaching practices of the teachers. Nothing is of greater importance to student learning than a quality teacher. High quality teaching practices must grow in each classroom under a principal's leadership. This teacher growth leads to the growth of students and their learning.

Summon Your Inner Harry Truman
When you find yourself in conversations about your school struggling and you begin passing the blame to others, you must summon your inner Harry Truman. Yes, your Harry Truman! Harry Truman's desk had a sign on it that said, "The buck stops here." The buck stops with you as the principal. You are the school leader. You must help improve the teachers. You must bring others up to the level they should be. If your time is occupied with e-mail, paperwork, and phone calls during the school day, well, this may be hard to hear, but...your time is being spent in the wrong area. That's being a paper pusher and you need to reread Christopher Dodge's Chapter 66. You should be spending time in classrooms improving those who directly and deeply impact the students and their academic and future achievement(s). Your time should be spent with the *TEACHER*S!

So What? Now What?
Is your school board a mess? Is your superintendent struggling? Is your teaching staff sub-par? I have a strong message for you, "So what! Now what?" The situation is what it is. What will you do now? It is time for you to look in the mirror. You need to look at your school and how YOU are leading it. Pull up your bootstraps and solve the problem. Start by reflecting on, "What are you doing to make your school better?" Flush it all out on a brainstorm notepad and T chart the problem and next to it the actions you can take to flip it to a dynamic off-the-chart success. That teacher is not using good teaching practices. Your job is to correct that. That custodian is showing up late and leaving early. Your job is to correct that. That paraprofessional is letting students collaborate on a test when it should be individual. Your job is to correct that. That teacher is using effective teaching strategies. Praise and

broadcast that. That bus driver is making student trips safer than ever before. Provide the kudos they deserve. You are the school's leader. My goodness, stop making excuses! Stop blaming your staff. The longer you wait, the longer you hurt kids by allowing poor practices in your school. Don't wait any longer by allowing poor practices to continue, on your watch.

YOU and your school team can overcome poor superintendent leadership. YOU and your team can overcome school board drama. YOU and your team can improve your teaching practices. It is on YOU as the school's leaders. The message is simple, So what! Now what? This is the mindset needed to strategically plan for dynamic culture, dynamic teaching, and a dynamically successful school community. Move forward. Attack the deficiencies and gain momentum with the practices that work. Ditch inefficiency to feature best practices. *YOU* are the driving force behind your school's failure or success. Not the board. Not the kids. Not the teachers. Not the superintendent. *YOU*! Stop making excuses school leader, district leader, instructional coach, or interventionist. This approach applies to every leadership position. Stop making everything about *YOU* and lead your team(s) and department(s) to dynamic off-the-charts academic success.

Eric Nichols serves as the Assistant Superintendent/Principal for the Silvies River/Crane Schools in east rural Oregon. Eric has been advocating for student and teacher voice while serving as a high school teacher and administrator for nearly 21 years.

89

Stop Inadvertently Harming Staff
PAMELA HALL

"With every interaction in a school, we are either building community or destroying it." - James Comer

In various ways, multiple people say great leaders know they're the leader because others willingly follow. Great leaders aren't concerned with titles or directives. And as Eric Nichols just shared, dynamic leaders take full responsibility for failures and strategically coach up, lead up and praise effective interactions along the way. Dynamic leaders intentionally focus on being a servant and helping others rise. They cling to a vision and lead by example. I must assume that you aspire to be an even more effective leader, or you wouldn't have the courage and vulnerability to read this book. Teachers love kids. So why are more than 40% leaving the profession within their first five years? Usually, it's a lack of support and skills. No leader intentionally sets out to harm staff. Leaders must strategically build community and set processes in place to ensure that during the hustle and bustle of the school day, they don't inadvertently harm staff. It can happen as many leaders inadvertently harm staff through their ego, agenda, lack of vision, or lack of skills. Unintentional subtleties can sink a leader and harm staff. How can you avoid such a shipwreck? Be intentional. Plan and gain skills by following the advice of the authors in this book. Give yourself an annual, monthly, and weekly check-up, and consider the following points.

"Managers help people see themselves as they are; leaders help people to see themselves better than they are."
— *Jim Rohn*

Put Your Trust and Faith in People
Researchers weigh in on what I think and know to be true. Micromanaging negatively affects your culture. When you micromanage, you are sending the message, "I don't trust you." If you don't trust your team, they won't trust you. Next, they resent you because they think you think they're so incompetent you must dictate their every move. Micromanagers believe they are in control when what seems counterintuitive to them is true. The more power you inflict, the more work you create for yourself because your team becomes unmotivated by direct demands.

I know an extremely talented, motivated, and high producing teacher who left a school because the leader inflicted micromanagement more and more each year, tightening control like a vice grip. The result of subtle announcements to report to duty stations, staff knows where and when they're supposed to report to duty and scripted pages of how to act created a mass exodus of the most talented, self-motivated, high performing staff members. You see, your best staff doesn't need step-by-step directions, but everyone on your staff needs clear expectations.

Once a substitute administrator came to my school. She stated, "This place runs like a well-oiled machine." "It does," I replied, "It's not perfect, but it runs well because the staff is trusted and supported. Our leader hires the best and trusts us to do the rest." Leaders who feel inferior and lack confidence hire people they feel superior to rather than people with more skill and talent. Inferior leaders micromanage. They must feel in control.

Educational leader and author Todd Whitaker shared in David Schmittou's, The Lasting Learning Podcast, that he asked all teachers to do two things every day: 1. Care 2. Try. He supported his teachers, led by example, and didn't micromanage. knowing full well that this inadvertent practice could harm his staff. The result equaled low staff turnover, high trust, teamwork, and increased student achievement. Micromanaging creates a compliance-based culture. It's a cycle. It harms staff creativity and innovation. It hurts school culture. It harms you, ultimately. Instead, have trust and faith in people.

100 No-Nonsense Things That All School Leaders Should STOP Doing

For more on micromanaging, see Evan Robb's Chapter 77.

Clear Communication is Kind

Educational leader and author Todd Whitaker said, "Good people's lives are driven by guilt. Blanket statements shut down superstars. Best teachers are disenfranchised, and those who the statement was for are either oblivious or unwilling to change." Stop making "all staff" announcements that only pertain to a few. The information makes go-getters question their ability and feel stressed. They feel like they were doing something wrong. In contrast, the ones the announcement was really for continue in oblivion and ignore it. Go directly to the source. Use bold, clear communication instead of passive-aggressive communication.

> *"Leaders don't avoid, repress, or deny conflict, but rather see it as an opportunity."* -Warren Bennis

Embrace conflict with the goal of resolution and restitution. Stop avoiding uncomfortable or courageous conversations. We're all shaped by our experiences. Let everyone share their perspective because it isn't all about you, it's about *THEM*. Bring in all sides of a story. Iron sharpens iron. Build relationships with your team members by communicating that you care. They don't need gifts to know you care. They need you to listen and communicate clearly in a timely fashion. The following scenarios display two very distinctly different ways to communicate corrections or redirection. One way builds a relationship and assumes positive intent. The other is condemning and creating a barrier.

Scenario #1: One year I had an assistant principal who didn't communicate with words. Instead, he used shaming gestures like tapping his watch. One morning, I attended to a parent, which caused me to be a couple of minutes late to my classroom. I was met at my door by my assistant principal, my class, a disapproving look, and his finger tapping his watch. Not once was my past character of being punctual taken into consideration. Not once did he ask why I was running late and how to help. Instead, I was judged and made to feel small and shamed instead of supported. He could have taken my class in and gotten them started by extending positive intent and empathy.

Scenario #2: On the other hand, a different assistant principal used humor for correction. He reached through an open window and picked up a phone from my first graders' dramatic play area, saying, "Mrs. Hall, Mrs. Hall, did you know you left a window open?" Mortified, I could see I left it open because he reached through it. I know leaving a window open is a big deal. Think--security. Because I was corrected in a fun-loving way--I never left the window open again. My opinion of my leader was elevated because he didn't devalue me. I bet I'm not alone on this. Correct with love, care, and maybe a bit of humor. It's far-reaching and received much better than a direct order and disapproving look.

STOP Making Everything About You

I agree with Brené Brown,

> *"Clear is kind. Unclear is unkind. Most of us avoid clarity because we think we're being kind when we're actually being unfair and unkind. Telling half-truths to make people feel better and ourselves more comfortable is unkind. Not giving clear expectations because it feels hard, yet holding people accountable is unkind. Clear is kind."*

Through open and transparent communication, leaders create trust, staff buy-in, and learn staffs' gifts and talents. When you communicate clearly, you cultivate a collaborative environment. Be the leader who builds bridges and relationships.

> *"A leader is not an administrator who loves to run others, but someone who carries water for his people so that they can get on with their jobs."* - Robert Townsend

Too Many Demands Can Be Overwhelmingjac

One of my dear teacher friends was a top performer year after year and season after season. Until one season, she wasn't. For one year, she entered a rough patch. She lost a family member, divorced, and got ill. That's a lot to carry. Instead of her principal supporting her, her principal added to the anxiety by visiting her room more often with critical feedback. Instead of offering counseling or extra help and support, she was under a microscope for performance. We have all been through rough patches in life. You will continue to inadvertently harm your staff unless you consider the following practices.

> **Offer relief to those that you lead.** Layering on more demands will inadvertently harm them until they finally crack. When new directives come from above, consider anything that you can remove from your staff's plate. When more and more gets piled on a plate, but nothing comes off, initiatives slide off and land in a heap on the floor. Choose tasks and responsibilities you add to your staff wisely. Staff can only focus on doing a few things well. Once mastered, then add more.

> **Make time for ongoing self-care.** Allow time for staff to have a few minutes to breathe or take a quick break. One year, our PTA provided a duty-free lunch for teachers once a month. It was a huge help, even if it was only once a month. It raised teacher morale and gave teachers a few minutes alone—self-care in action.

> **Instill a tap-in/tap-out system.** Designate someone to go into a teacher's room when behavior challenges escalate, or they need a break is a colossal help for reducing burnout. A colleague "taps in" while the teacher "taps out" for a few minutes. Again, self-care should be the way we do business during the school day just as Greg Moffitt shared in Chapter 38.

Consult staff and compose a list of top needs. Work to meet their needs the best you can. Implement initiatives specifically to reduce stress and increase self-care. When you take care of your staff, they take better care of students. Ultimately, student achievement goes up.

Delegate and disperse the workload evenly. Stop putting the weight of ineffective folks on the shoulders of go-getters who are already giving and giving.

Show them instead of telling them. You can minimize anxiety by providing teachers with better classroom management skills. Role model, co-plan, and coach them up. As a result, skilled teachers aren't as overwhelmed.

Dynamic leaders encourage growth, teamwork, and always place staff's best interest at the forefront remembering what it was like to be in their shoes as Jesse Lubinsky shared. When you inadvertently hurt staff (because we're all human), your staff will forgive you, apologize and strive to do better. They know your heart, track record, and your vision is worth following. That's how you will know you're one of the greats, (even though it isn't all about you).

Pamela Hall, a multinational award-winning educator, is a speaker and author who's dedicated to helping educators consciously connect with and grow all learners. Pamela's a life-long learner leading and inspiring thousands of students and educators. She's an ordinary cappuccino drinking, chocolate eating mom and wife from Virginia with an extraordinary passion to make a positive difference.

90

Stop Complaining About How Busy You Are
RACHAEL GEORGE, Ed.D.

As an aspiring leader, I distinctly remember hearing my principal reference how busy administrators are and how there is never enough time to complete whatever project we were meeting about. While the response was probably meant to help provide me perspective, all it did was make me think through the long laundry list of things that I was busy with as well, yet I still completed. I was teaching full time, coaching multiple seasons throughout the school year, working two separate side jobs, working on my second master's degree simultaneous to my doctorate along with the responsibilities of home. Little did my principal know, but this comment made me feel beyond frustrated and resentful to the point that I viewed them in an entirely different light. It was at that moment that I promised myself that I would never complain about my business when I became a school or district leader. Like Jesse Lubinsky in Chapter 85 I knew where I came from, how hard it was to pull off, how much it mattered, and I never wanted to fuel frustration and resentment in any future leadership role.

Everyone is Busy
As educators, we are all busy. Changing positions is simply, "different" busy but equally time consuming and stressful because deadlines and people are always involved. As leaders increase in power positionally, the stakes grow higher for the decisions we make, and there are additional plates to spin in the air. Every single person in the school knows that administrators are busy with observations, goal setting, discipline, meeting with families and students, handling the upset parent calls, attending child study teams, and working to plan the upcoming parent night. Life as a leader is busy and the demands are high.

To steal Eric Nichols words from Chapter 88, "So What? Now What?" Leaders are busy, there is no denying it, but it doesn't require exacerbating the fact with negative talk. When we complain about how busy we are in front of teachers, nothing good comes from it. In their eyes, we come across ineffective, ill equipped, and faltering as we make excuses why things weren't done or why we are grumpy. Dynamic off-the-charts leaders demonstrate that they are up to the task and can handle the workload. Instead of complaining how busy you are, take a deep breath and work to be present in each moment.

You Chose this Job
If you find yourself complaining about how busy you are in your head or aloud, stop for a moment and remind yourself that you chose this job. Instead of staying in the classroom, you opted to become an assistant principal, principal, or district leader. You wanted to be a leader and take on the hard work. In fact, we knew it wasn't going to be easy and we still signed the contract. Take a moment and remind yourself why you went into leadership. What's your why? Does your initial why still hold true and align with the work you are doing? And if it doesn't incite passion and a love for leading any longer, then you may want to consider bypassing the following chapters and skipping to Dr. Robert A. Martinez's Chapter 100. If you want to get a handle on leading and reframe and recalibrate, then I urge you to continue reading.

Let's say you think you are too busy and don't like it. Let's play this out further...you chose this job but now you're second guessing if it is a good fit. That's ok, honesty and reflection is great. The beautiful thing about life is that we control our own lives and our own choices. If the decision to go into leadership is no longer the right fit for you, make another choice. Perhaps it is time to head back into the classroom, go into educational consulting, or try another career.

Being a leader is hard, perhaps harder than some of us ever imagined. However, we are still the leaders in our school or district, and we owe it to those that follow our charge to lead dynamically.

Dr. Rachael George is the co-author of the book PrincipalED: Navigating the Leadership Learning Curve and a member of the ASCD Emerging Leaders Class of 2015. She is an award-winning educational leader that has served at the preschool, elementary, secondary, and district office level. She is the co-author of, She Leads: The Women's Guide to a Career in Educational Leadership.

91

Stop Being an Invisible Leader
MATTHEW B. FRIEDMAN, Ph.D.

On a gloomy Monday morning, Paul, the building principal, woke up and drove to work as usual. Very much focused on completing his financial year end budget and scheduling teacher observations, Paul entered his office with one specific goal in mind for the day. He was hoping it would be as easy, trouble-free, and as smooth-sailing as possible. As his administrative assistant read aloud the agenda for the day, he mentally rolled his eyes at the day's schedule. There were too many meetings on the agenda: several with staff, a parent meeting to discuss a situation that occurred on Friday afternoon, a district HR meeting, and a meeting with the school board to discuss the school's handling of Covid-19 in the upcoming months. In mere body language he was already complaining about being busy. Meetings all day? Seriously? Couldn't all this be discussed in an email?

Paul then headed over to his emails and realized that no, in fact none of the meetings on the agenda could be handled in an email because most of the people involved already responded to calendar invitations. He skimmed down the agenda to find a district admin meeting with the HR department, parent X wanted to know more about project Y, and staff member Z wanted to communicate with him regarding a problem he'd been facing with a student. Paul's reaction was that of disengagement. All he wanted was for the agenda to go away. He wanted to tell his assistant only to bother him if it was an emergency so he could prepare for other meetings, and retreat to his office to get his work done. Clearly, he was making everything about *HIM*.

The first meeting on the list was a district all admin meeting, Paul's goal was to keep as quiet as possible, and minimize the chance that agenda items would create more work. During the meeting, Larry, from HR, started the agenda. He explained the problems that many staff had been facing and guided the group through the agenda. In the meantime, Paul was listening but not engaged, as usual. The issues being brought up truly required immediate action and attention, but the process seemed too much trouble. He wanted to wait and see how things unraveled. Paul interjected and shared that no action should be taken. And just like that, Paul solidified his role as an invisible leader.

The next meeting faced parents that felt like nothing was being done to eliminate bullying during recess, and Paul proposed to 'wait things out'. Tired of the nonsense, Paul walked them out and closed his office door in full avoidance of dealing with the situation at hand. Paul had become passive; he wasn't always like that.

When he first took the role, he took initiative as a person always willing to take a risk and invest effort and hope into every situation with the ambition that things would, indeed, get better. Now, Paul had become the type of leader that no longer accepted challenges even if it meant, later, turning into failures. Over the course of his career Paul had increasingly become invisible to his team.

As obtuse as it may sound, the disposition of an apathetic leader is not rare. This downward spiral in leadership is something that happens to countless leaders in education. Slowly, over time, the profession becomes all about *THEM*. As hopeless as Paul seems at this point, in his life as a principal, he is not beyond redemption. Like many leaders across the nation, he can make the choice to lead dynamically. If you have come across colleagues with a disposition like Paul, or if you have found yourself losing steam and just getting by, you may want to consider making changes that will ensure you are visible, proactive, relatable, strategic, and off-the-charts dynamic, again.

Pull Your Head Out of the Sand
Invisible leaders prefer to stay quiet for a variety of reasons. They may not want to offend anyone. Or they do not want to lose face, lose credibility, or jeopardize their relationship with others. In fact, the

latter is potentially one of the biggest mistakes made by leaders – abstaining from voicing concerns and worries, out of fear of not being "liked." In the book, *The Five Temptations of a CEO*, Patrick Lencioni points out the following temptations that leaders can fall prey to as invisible leaders.

1. Choosing status over results.
2. Choosing popularity over accountability.
3. Choosing certainty over clarity.
4. Choosing harmony over conflict.
5. Choosing invulnerability over trust.

As a leader, you may have held back from standing up when you knew that something was wrong. Perhaps you did not want your reputation to be hit, or you wanted to stay credible and respected by your peers. Maybe, like Paul, you are keeping quiet to avoid rocking the boat – you want a smooth sailing journey, or you just have a lot of work to do. This is not just something that makes you invisible as a leader, but it's also something that makes you the 'under-the-radar' leader. Dynamic leaders intentionally stick their necks and take courageous risks to solve problems intentionally, instead of burying their head in the sand (or hiding in your office). Although temporarily it may feel easier to stand on the sidelines while adversity takes place. Pull your head out of the sand, stand tall, and be visible. If you feel yourself in a Paul scenario, then revert to the prior 89 chapters and read them again or skip directly to Chapter 100 and process out of your role as a leader.

Tune In and Face the Music
Your visibility as a leader will greatly be improved if you will be open with staff members and be authentic. Authenticity fosters a community culture that is welcoming, warm, and empathetic. For example, rather than retreating to your office when there are issues being discussed, a visible leader welcomes productive conflicts and arguments from a variety of perspectives, rather than constantly trying to keep conflict at bay. Conflict is not always negative: when it leads to positive changes being instituted, it is conducive to the betterment of the school and its community. In this sense, it is nothing short of positive. By "opening up", I am referring to your ability to be there, to listen, and to be a part of the conversation. Welcome new ideas, thoughts, projects, and perspectives on matters that matter. Don't shoot any stakeholder down trying to avoid shaking the boat, instead present yourself as the leader who always has an ear ready, tuned in, and open to new ideas. Tune in by listening intentionally and proactively face the music (current reality) do deescalate, resolve, or mitigate conflict

Run Your Team, Not Your Emotions

Emotional intelligence (EQ), is the skill whereby you understand, process, and empathize with other individuals' emotions and hence react appropriately. Authors Jean Greaves and Evan Watkins, share in their book, *Team Emotional Intelligence 2.0: The Four Essential Skills of High Performing Teams*, that when emotions run your team, your team will run into trouble. Dynamic leaders focus on the following essential skills:

1. Team Emotion Awareness
2. Team Emotion Management
3. Internal Team Relationships
4. External Team Relationships

Leadership EQ allows you to process your own emotions and to analyze why you act a certain way in certain situations. Visible leaders are adaptable, analytical, self-regulating, deescalating, and empathize to connect to root problems. As the 'leader of the ship', you must learn the ability to navigate your own problems and difficulties, strategically, without letting them affect the way you work, respond to people, or perform your job. A visible leader is available. Dynamic leaders take the time in the moment to set down their pen and paper or stop what they are doing when they hear a teacher crying to spend time connecting to become aware and understand. Meeting a person where they are at emotionally when they are in distress is an entry point to managing the emotions and co-regulating. This is how you create a community culture that is rooted in mutual respect, understanding, collaboration, and viable solutions.

EQ is a necessary leadership skill whether a student comes to school and is visibly upset sitting on the chair in front of you, or a teacher sharing that he or she may need a few days off to tend to their sick parent's needs. A visible leader presents him or herself as someone who will understand, assist with emotional regulation, offer, and consider solutions, and who will seek to fulfill a person's emotional needs.

Take the Spotlight

Being proactive is a way for you to show to those you are leading that you are on top of things, and that you are an initiative-taker instead of only being a reactive person. Whenever adversity comes up – no matter whether it is nonsense or not – if you are seen as the first person who takes the initiative to speak up and outline exactly where the problem lies, you will be viewed as the person who is willing to take the heat of the spotlight. In the context of a school, this can apply to anything from fights on the playground to workplace bullying between two teachers. The key is to take the initiative publicly, diplomatically, and with dignity. Not sticking your neck out whenever something happens where the leader should be present sends a message that you aren't available when necessary, and therefore, will render you invisible. Even if you are available some of the time, the times where you don't take the first step to fix the issues being faced, you'll end up giving someone else the spotlight, which makes it difficult to remain consistent and reliable.

Know When to Stay in Your Lane

What all this tells us is that a certain level of self-awareness is necessary when leading a school. Of course, nobody's perfect. We all have our faults, but we most importantly all have our leadership strengths and deficits. While you want to stick your neck out whenever opportunities arise, you should also know when to stay in your 'lane', as the kids' say, so as not to engage in something that you are not qualified to do. Dynamic off-the-charts leaders know when to delegate what and to whom. Go back and read Svetlana Popovic's Chapter 4 if you need a refresher on delegation. In short, dynamic leaders are self-aware of their skills, strengths, and especially weaknesses. This level of self EQ allows leaders to tune in when there's someone on the team that is more of an expert than them. Effective leaders are willing to stay in their lane specially when someone else could do a better job because their skillset, aptitude, or experience exceeds theirs. Staying in your own lane as a leader can produce two concrete results:

> **1. Provides team members with the independence they need to feel fulfilled at work.** To avoid faculty from feeling like they are only working to make you happy, which shouldn't be the case. They should enjoy their work and have some degree of independence and control over how initiatives are carried out. Your teachers and coordinators will thank you for it – they'll be glad not to be micromanaged.

> **2. Demonstrates that everyone is interdependent.** Staying in your own lane shows to your team that you are not a one man or woman show, and hence that you see yourself as just as 'worthy' or 'capable' as others. When the people you lead feel valued, they will appreciate the egalitarian nature of the work, thereby creating a work culture in which teachers, coordinators, and all other members of staff feel valued. It supports your efforts to create a solid work culture where each member feels like they can rely both on you as a leader and on each other for sources of support.

Know your strengths and capitalize on them. Acknowledge your deficiencies as a leader and know when it's best to give the space for those who are experts in the area to take over and make the best out of a poor situation. Finally, be ready to give the stage to your staff, teachers, and coordinators. A dynamic off-the-charts leader is capable of keeping his or her role as a leader all the while providing space for those who want to showcase their expertise and potential.

Ultimately, becoming a visible leader is possible, even if you are currently struggling to have a strong foothold in your team. Be strong, be bold, and be ready to hold your ground. Don't be worried about risk-taking to the point that you avoid all potential adversity – discomfort will be needed for any kind of growth and advancement. Stick your neck out and become the best person to speak to whenever an issue arises. And just like that, you'll have become a visible leader.

Dr. Matthew B. Friedman is a Superintendent of Schools at Ocean City School District (NJ).

Stop Being an Under-the-Radar Leader
JILL PAVICH & RICK JETTER, Ph.D.

"You can't get anywhere flying under the radar." -Grant Cardone

A Double Perspective
Over the course of the previous 91 chapters, it has been well established that teachers *ARE* leaders. The uniqueness of this chapter is that compared to all the other chapters in this book, this chapter offers a dual perspective. Jill Pavich begins by sharing her perspective as a teacher leader in the classroom while Dr. Rick Jetter piggybacks off her perspective by addressing these same challenges from the perspective of a district leader. No matter your current position or role in education, under-the-radar mindsets prevent dynamic off-the-charts leadership presence. Stop making everything about you.

Be On-Radar in the Classroom
JILL PAVICH

As a leader in the classroom, being 'on-radar' means asking questions, challenging assumptions, and making instructional decisions which involve risk -- all on behalf of the students they serve. Effective, 'on-radar' teachers therefore stick their necks out daily. How possible is it for teachers to have BOTH creative license AND support from school and district leadership as they take these important risks in the classroom?

Giraffes Stick Their Necks Out
Can you visualize a giraffe walking through a zoo attempting to go unseen? It would be so unnatural that onlookers couldn't help but ask what's wrong, thus creating the opposite effect. Under-the-radar leaders can be viewed the same way; it isn't natural for them to crouch so low. And in the end, attempting to pass by unseen ends up causing a much bigger commotion -- for teachers, and more importantly, their learners.

Choosing a low profile prevents other stakeholders from promoting progress and raising achievement. In other words, your decision to shrink makes other campus leaders -- like teachers -- feel small, too. As a leader, not only do you need to stick your neck out, but it is in your charge to support leadership around you to do the same.

> Who leads professional learning communities?
> Who coordinates before and after school programs?
> Who designs common formative assessments?
> Who coordinates your book fairs, curriculum nights, movie nights, and community events?
> Who maintains close communication with families?
> Who coordinates field trips, guest speakers, fundraisers, and spirit weeks?
> Who inspires others to learn and grow in their content, standards, and practices?
> Who maximizes student learning and high student achievement?
> Who comes up with ideas and solutions to challenges and happenstances?

Yet somewhere between top-down mandates and prescribed curriculum, book bans and topic restrictions, the mounting pressures of standardized tests, and overall classroom micromanagement, teachers don't always feel seen as leaders nor trusted like the professionals they are. Sometimes, they can feel powerless in their ability to stick their necks out as high-impact stakeholders. But as Dr. Amanda Shuford Mayeaux points out in Chapter 56, teachers might be the best form of homegrown leadership you could possibly ask for.

The essential question you ultimately need to ask on your campus is therefore two-fold: Are you willing to treat teachers as leaders? And — once you do — are you willing to help them build on their capacity to lead?

If you help teachers tap into their potential for leadership, it creates an automatic ripple-effect in the classroom to match. Teachers are more willing to stick their necks out for students when they see you doing so for them. Your leadership is the catalyst, but the risks your teachers wish to take won't always be comfortable ones. Are you willing to trust them? Are you willing to support them as they lead instruction? This is how you stick your neck out. But there is a choice to be made. It's impossible to lead like a giraffe and stay out-of-sight at the same time.

A Giraffe's Experiment
If there's one thing teaching through a pandemic taught educators everywhere, it's that teaching isn't just a science. It's a science experiment. At the height of remote learning, educational leaders shifted toward power standards, prioritizing what was absolutely essential in terms of cognitive learning goals, while incorporating much more white space for mental, emotional, and personal support.

We recognized more readily that our students' needs stretch well beyond academics. And we knew that if we were going to get through this experience at all, our scholars would need way more help with the non-cognitive parts of their character, from cultivating stronger habits of mind (ex. tolerance, resilience) to building more durable skills that would last long after exams were here and gone (ex. creative problem-solving).

Today, at the crossroads we've arrived at in education, giraffe leaders continue to recognize these critical components in education that the pandemic shed so much light on; and they're still sticking their necks out to nurture them accordingly. Put another way, giraffe leaders pursue soft, social, and emotional skills and habits of mind just as fiercely as they do academic standards because (in the words of expert educator A.J. Juliani), "we're not just preparing our students for something (i.e., a test); we're preparing them for anything (i.e., life)."

The on-radar leader stands tall accordingly and reaches for the highest branches when it comes to curriculum development: weaving collaboration, creativity, empathy, and other critical skills into our otherwise academic-only lesson plans. The key difference is, however -- durable skills like these don't just exist in the giraffe leader's best-laid plans. They're consistently measured, too.

When giraffe leaders stretch beyond exclusively academic data as a measurement for growth, it sends a renewed message to learners about how success can be defined. Isn't that worth sticking your neck out for? Not to mention, it gives teachers license to create the kind of learning experiences that more concretely connect what our students are learning in the classroom with what they'll experience in the real world. This kind of leadership ensures that students aren't just learning about the world, they're learning with it.

If you have been flying under-the-radar as a leader, this is the chapter where we're sticking our neck out for you. Stand up and stretch for the taller tree. Aim for the leaves of high academic achievement -- and beyond.

Jill Pavich, M.Ed. NBCT is an expert educator, published author, and proud business owner. Through her digital courses, workshops, and online community, she helps secondary ELA teachers make writing more relevant, authentic, and empowering for today's learners and tomorrow's leaders. Learn more at www.jillpavich.com.

Stick Your Neck Out and Lead Your Troop
RICK JETTER, Ph.D.

Many principals and district leaders choose to lead like a giraffe in theory, but when earth shattering issues come about, we wonder if they will just work themselves out. We start to make excuses for why we do not step in to address an issue. We think that delay is necessary for seeing where things go or end up on their own before we intervene. But maybe it is too late then. Maybe our under-the-radar mentality made things worse. The nonsense can come from anywhere and it can be about anything. Sometimes, issues are not nonsensical at all. They are real issues that need to be resolved. They are human conflicts that demand human attention. Under-the-radar leadership can become over-the-radar (and even proactive) intentional leadership whether you are dealing with a challenging parent, student, teacher, colleague, supervisor, board member, or community member.

> "Just a few more years until retirement."
> "I've survived for this long."
> "If I put my hand on a hot iron this year, I will surely get burned."
> "I can do this. I can just make it through. No one will even notice."
> "If I just keep my head down and keep this building running, things will be OK."
> "I'm not going to look for (any) trouble this year. This needs to be an easy year."

And there you have it: A "flying under-the-radar" mentality. We've seen it. We've heard about it. Hell, we've even lived it, ourselves. Leaders are tired of nonsense and sometimes when nonsense exists, it is so much easier to stare at the ground or close the office door just as Dr. Matthew B. Friedman just shared in his example in the last chapter. It is so easy to become "invisible," like the principal Paul did, but now, maybe we are finding that some leaders fly under-the-radar on purpose. Either way, when school leaders fly under the radar, they create a ripple effect all the way into the classroom just as Jill Pavich pointed out. And that certainly can't be good for high academic achievement.

Nonsense comes in all shapes and sizes and THIS book recognizes some of the nonsense going on in our schools, along with other truths about nonsense written in Book #1 of the #100StopSeries for Teachers. Nonsense can be relational, positional, stressful, conflicting, passive-aggressive, delusional, and irrational. Nonsense can be emotional, impractical, and sometimes, forever, scarring. Then, we try to dodge the cuts that turn into scars, (because we don't really want to be scarred, after all) but then only find ourselves selling out to passivity.

What is Your Expiration Date?
There is an amazing article by Julia Azari, entitled: It's the Institutions, Stupid: The Real Roots of America's Political Crisis. What Azari's article taught is that, sometimes, we find leaders (or educators) who consciously choose to fly under-the-radar, intentionally. Azari reminded me that many politicians make sure that they always vote their party line platform even if they disagree with the way they actually end up voting on the matter in the end--just so they do not lose potential re-election status or party backing when their term is ready to expire. The problem is that these types of leaders are already expired if they are going to fly under the radar in the first place.

The Neck of a Giraffe
School leaders and educators sometimes sit by the sidelines because it is easier for their career and livelihood to not make the tough decisions. They become paper-pushers, rubber stampers and all of this is typically done for a retirement that awaits them at the finish line of their career or a promotion to a new position that will increase their weekly take home pay. Some just want to get to that beach house that they saved up for by the age of 55. Others want a passive career so they can exit their profession safely with the least amount of resistance possible. This type of thinking is nonsensical.

Yet, workplace bullying, stepping on others to get that promotion, or waging all-out war against our colleagues takes place each day in almost every school on the planet. Think about it for a moment, can you name any setting or environment that is free of adversity? Every educational environment has and always will require leaders to step up, stick their necks out, and do the tough work that demands attention. Our colleagues are counting on us to do something incredibly creative in our jobs, to stick up for those who need our help, and to stick our necks out so others can be defended under our watch. After all, our students ARE counting on us.

> *"Well as giraffes say, you don't get no leaves unless you stick your neck out."* -Sid Waddell

Regardless of your position, whether a teacher or a superintendent, you are a giraffe for a reason and you *ARE* a leader. You are there to stick your neck out. You must. It's part of the job. And you won't get no leaves (high academic achievement) if you don't.

Giraffes Help others Find their Place in this World
Teaching through a pandemic revealed how far behind public education already was in meeting the needs of students. Teachers still forged ahead, some flying under-the-radar while others stuck out their necks and foraged on higher trees discovering a new perspective. Many teachers discovered that students didn't need content knowledge as much as applicable and transferable skills, character traits, and innovative thinking. Many lacked skills outside of academic standards. Grit, tenacity, compassion, problem solving, creativity, and resilience were missing. Many students even apathetically developed a bias toward action, problem-solving, or a knack for resourcefulness. To their defense, these were not attributes they could acquire by locating the main idea or citing 'right there' text evidence. Rather, these are critical components of character that giraffe leaders would need to 'stick their necks out' to nurture and cultivate because no one else was going to officially do it.

Giraffe leaders stand tall and reach for the highest branches weaving collaboration, creativity, and empathy into their lesson plans naturally, all the time. As a state, district, school, or classroom giraffe, how consistently do you measure such leadership capacities? If as a profession we are going to stop flying under-the-radar, then we have got to lead with empathy to ensure that everyone develops habits of mind just as fiercely as we do academic standards. Giraffe leaders commit to deeper learning experiences that more concretely connect what those they lead in the classroom with what they'll experience in the real world. Giraffe leaders deliver on the promise of community transfer.

As you go about your day-to-day duties, use the questions below to help you reflect on whether you're doing so with your head down or your head raised:

Have you kept quiet about something for fear of "offending" someone?

Have you kept quiet about something for fear of jeopardizing your relationship with a supervisor or your job?

Have you failed to stand up for what is right for fear of pressure, because of other's expectations of you, because your reputation must be squeaky clean, or because a new position that you are hoping to be promoted to is just around the corner?

Have you found yourself keeping quiet about something, as to not ruffle any feathers or ripple any waters?

If you have been flying under-the-radar as a leader it isn't too late to stop making everything all about you. You can stand up. Don't worry about what could happen. Be strong. Be intentional. Stick that neck out and lead your tower of giraffes to those leaves of high academic achievement.

Contributing the bare minimum as a leader, is an act of selfish preservation, in any role. If you allow apathy, lack of direction, lack of intention, disempowerment, or any other leadership deficits to creep into your school or teams, you're flying under-the-radar as a leader, and that's weak misdirection. Giraffes stick their necks out to ensure teachers and teams are mentored, respected, and treated as leaders because they want every person on the team to be brave enough to stand tall in order to do what's right.

Being trusted as a giraffe gives teachers a leg up (or neck). Accessing evidence-based practices and high-quality resources give teachers another leg up. Getting to know the strengths and deficits and how to leverage learning is an additional leg up. Unless teachers are embraced as practitioners conducting a science experiment testing what works with their students, they will never make it safely across the Serengeti as a united troop. And any time you feel yourself stuck in the grind that's mucked in bureaucratic red tape, anytime you're feeling the desire to fly powerlessly under that radar, remind yourself why you're here in the first place...

Dr. Rick Jetter is a Co-Founder of Pushing Boundaries Consulting, LLC; author of various books for educators, speaker, trainer, and the Assistant Head of Schools at Western NY Maritime Charter School in Buffalo, NY. Rick is also ranked #6 in the World's Top 30 Global Gurus in Education for 2022.

.

Stop Waiting for an Invitation to Visit Educator Classrooms
JULIE WOODARD

Dynamic off-the-chart leaders are not invisible, nor do they fly under-the-radar as we just read about in the previous two chapters. They are as proactive, involved, informed, visible, and intentional. Like the experienced pitcher on the mound who might enjoy a visit from the pitching coach during a winning game, new and veteran teachers also enjoy a visit from leadership especially when it is not required. Scheduled classroom observations reflect the passive minimum and one point in time. Most teachers collaborate, plan, adapt, research, and network to ensure that the individual needs of their students are met. Teachers work hard and they want authentic feedback, encouragement, and for their strengths to be noticed. Classroom walkthroughs shouldn't be about you, they should be about supporting *THEIR* success.

An Open Door Goes Both Ways
School Leaders set the tone, facilitate the culture, and lead expectations for an open-door policy when it comes to classroom climate. An open door is a welcome sign. As a district administrator or a principal of a school, I'm sure you want to feel welcomed and invited into a classroom experience. If safety regulations allow, encourage teachers to prop open their classroom door as an invitational cue to administrators. Teachers welcome leadership input and participation because it demonstrates presence and the importance of learning in that moment. Dynamic leaders pop in to sit with a student to engage in co-learning as an investor in continuous learning. Teachers crave that adult interaction during their lessons and their day and value collegial communication and participation. Teachers are pleasers like a child looking up to their parents and welcome feedback that is supportive and communicates the value of our instruction. Sometimes simply hanging out in our classroom is all it takes. Teacher mentors and coaches can be that positive bridge when they see something amazing, they can grab their administrator to participate and watch students learn because of effective teaching. An open door goes both ways, administrators set the culture of and open-door policy, and teacher leaders and coaches prop the door open to invite them in. Administrators want to feel welcome and have a place or position in the learning process, too, so let your staff know this.

#Observe Me
This is basically the opposite of Jerry McGuires famous line, "Help me, help you." Rather the opposite is true, "Help you, help me." A few years ago, the "Observe Me" classroom invitation trended on social media among educators. These self-motivated, and dynamic teachers were vulnerable and committed enough to showcase their teaching in real time. They each hung a simple sign outside their classroom door, with the hashtag #observeme. This hashtag served as a sign that the classroom teacher wanted administration (or colleagues) to drop in, watch, and offer some feedback on the specific skill, strategy, or content that they had noted as a focus. For example, a teacher had worked on mastering individualized learning stations deeply rooted in standards. A short explanation was listed under the hashtag explaining to the observer what to look for and provide specific feedback. Observers were invited to leave a smiley face on a note, a suggestion for student classroom management, a pedagogy tip, or a simple word of encouragement. Administrators were invited to provide informal authentic feedback free from the formality and depth of formal observations or review. This trend led to opportunities for relationship building among staff and leadership. It opened doors and forged relationships that led to a culture of, "Help you, help me, and it may end up helping you too." If your school hasn't participated in this movement, type in the #observeme hashtag on social media and introduce #observe me to any staff that may be ready to be a vulnerable leader and ask them if they are willing to give it a try.

Invite Them to Invite You
At the beginning of the school year, or during a reboot in January, share and reshare your expectations of the learning culture. Invite your teachers, coaches, mentors, team leads, and paraprofessionals to invite you in. Express your desire to be visibly involved in classroom learning as a participant in learning. If you are an instructional coach, include your administrators as readers, judges, or participants. An administrator is a great tool for reading a book, kicking off a new lesson or allowing students to ask questions about their experience with an upcoming skill or unit of study. School leaders can be the perfect audience in a class reader's theatre. School leaders are perfect for joining book talks and sharing their personal input. Students, faculty, and the school learning community all benefit when the students see the administrators participating in and valuing classroom learning. Teacher leaders who invite and include administration in their students' learning have modeled to students the importance of community in the learning process. The learning is then focused on the synergy of the community rather than the adult as an untouchable boss who is out of touch.

Your Presence Validates Learning

Forging relationships with administrators can be eye opening for students. In my personal case, my administrators are in and out of my door frequently and not only for observation and conference-required visits. Our students know our leaders as active participants and community builders of culture. Just yesterday, a younger student was shocked to learn that our principal had been a teacher in the past. They connected on a simple matter and bridged a relationship that offered a personal connection of belonging. We all know that building relationships is key to student success; we know that these relationships strengthen student resolve and connect them to personalized and invested learning. District and principal classroom presence is a catalyst to spark individual and community motivation in carrying out the mission, vision, values, goals, and beliefs of the school. Dynamic off-the-chart leaders intentionally carve out protected time to validate the importance of learning.

Showcase Personal Talents, Interests, & Passions

If you follow many dynamic administrators on social media, you will find some that live in their alter ego of Superman or Batman or bring their passions into their school as a history buff, beehive farmer, musician who plays in a weekend garage band, doing a magic trick, or gardening and cooking in a school club. Your perspective may be about playing big league ball and connect to why studying velocity and speed in class matters. Dynamic leaders do not wait to be invited, they are contagiously vocal about their talents, interests, and passions. They just do it because the end goal is to uncover the strengths in others. Showcasing non-academic culture building models healthy well-balanced contentment in life and interconnects leaders as learners of others' talents, interests, and passions. Connecting in this way shines a new light on learning for students. Non-academic connections teach parallel lessons like failure is part of the learning process, or practice is a necessary component to success, everyone has strengths and deficits, or you are never too old to learn.

No Feedback is Negative Feedback

Avoiding classrooms out of trust and respect for efficacious teachers is a myth. No matter how many positive formal evaluations you deliver to district leaders or teachers, that's not enough. Just like high performing gifted students, don't forget about them and leave them alone to self-direct knowing they will pass the state assessment and hoping for one year's growth. We engage, challenge, reinforce, and add a twist to think on. All teachers want feedback informally. No feedback is *ALWAYS* interpreted as negative feedback. Like a pitcher on his way to a no-hitter, he'd love an "atta boy visit" from the pitching coach. He'd love for the game to stop and fans to cheer as the coach approaches the mound.

Why does the coach only come out … when it's too late… to pull him off….?

As teachers we want to make it clear to leaders that you are welcome and wanted. Teachers and students are captivated by your presence and want you to experience their new learning, or smile, laugh, and connect socially with your passion and perspective. All stakeholders want to form relationships that are more than superficial. School communities thrive on moments that connect and celebrate a shared commitment to mission, vision, values, beliefs, and goals.

Julie Woodard just began her 21st year in education as an award-winning elementary Art Teacher who creates custom images and illustrations for authors and speakers.

94

Stop Trying to Be the Smartest Person in the Room
LAURA MCDONELL

A year ago, I did not want to run with people who ran faster than me. It was frustrating to think about the commitment and training involved in maintaining that pace of athleticism. I was afraid I might not have what it takes to run with people who had already achieved what I was aspiring to do. Even now, running with those that are faster, requires me to be vulnerable because their capacity as a runner far surpasses mine. My deficit skills were exposed, and my lack of endurance was amplified.

Last year, I let my own pride get in the way as I chose not to grow as a runner. Rather than challenge myself to step out of my comfort zone and adapt to a faster pace, I chose to train for my race alone. When I ran by myself. I was *THE* top competitor in "my team of one." I could run at whatever pace I desired, no matter my effort or speed, and I always landed first place. At the end of my spring marathon, I realized that being the best in my group and not showing up to run with people who were better than me, did not serve me well. Trying to be the best runner in a "track meet of one" didn't seem to matter. Likewise, trying to be the smartest leader in the room nets the same result.

After learning that my strategy of running by myself did not really work, I knew I had to try a different approach. Being the best runner in my solo group did not help me accomplish my goals. Staying in a "safety zone" by myself was easy, but easy would never make me great. I knew if I wanted different results, I would have to accept the fact that I wouldn't always be the most athletic or the smartest. This analogy to running is very similar to being a leader of students. Sometimes I get nervous before running with a faster or a more accomplished team. When tasked with new challenges I'm unsure of the outcome(s). Choosing to surround myself with colleagues that have different areas of expertise and more miles dedicated to running than me can be intimidating and overwhelming. Just like Dr. Jared Smith shared in Chapter 2, effective leaders admit when they don't have the answers, tap into experts, and ask questions. Goal focused leaders are patient and committed risk-takers *BECAUSE* they don't think, or *TRY TO BE*, the smartest person in the room because it negatively impacts the culture of the people they lead. The same principles to leading students apply to leading teachers and teams of educational leaders at the district, county, state, or national level(s).

Run Alongside, Share the Road, and Offer a New Pace
Dynamic off-the-charts leaders focus on empowering others. In addition to establishing mission, vision, values, and beliefs, your goals and expectations must be communicated routinely and in such a way that your message encourages others to rise to their highest potential as they aim for the finish line of each race.

The group of people I run with today challenge my pace by guiding me to a bigger and more audacious goal. Ultimately, our goal is to empower others to take responsibility and ownership. To produce independent thinkers (students or adults) willing to take risks, we must bring people into new spaces where they have room to stretch their stride and time to practice.

Fortunately, I am with a group of runners who are encouraging and help me ease into a new level by not simply telling me what to do, but by sharing the road. These runners model, articulate, coach, and share with me what it looks like to be successful. Leaders in the classroom, building, or district need to do the same by "running alongside" a person who is less experienced. Rather than tell a group how to handle a challenging situation, leaders can role-play and show what it looks like to thrive in certain conditions. Shared experiences, even if they are experienced through role-play, can create connections. Connection happens when there is vulnerability. Perfection does not allow opportunities for people to form bonds and feel inspired. A focus on creating connections offers opportunities to build new relationships.

Seek Strengths Through Confidence Not Arrogance

There will be situations where a leader is the smartest or most experienced person in the room. There are a few people in my group of runners that stand out. However, when we run together, they don't minimize their accomplishments either. Instead make sure that the conversation is productive and inclusive. Dynamic leaders take every opportunity to ask questions, share experiences, and develop mindsets because each person has something to offer. Sometimes wisdom comes in unlikely places. What if leaders treated everyone as if he or she had something valuable to contribute? Everyone has different experiences. While you may have tremendous experience in a particular position, building or district, there is someone who has far more experience in a different way that is high added value to the team.

As leaders learn more about the expertise, skills, and experiences of the people that they lead, be willing to change your thinking if the initiative or practice no longer serves in the best interest of the organization. Learn everything you can about the people you lead, and their capacity Great leaders empower others to do big things. Dynamic off-the-chart leaders never run alone or make it all about them. Regardless of your position, find people running faster than you and begin training.

Laura McDonell is a high school English teacher in Michigan. She is a mother of three extraordinary kids and a devoted marathon runner. Laura blogs at enjoyingeverymile.com and always encourages students to chase their impossible.

Stop Gloating about Your Accomplishments, Honors, & Credentials
COREY CALDER

"I'm not worried about the awards. The past is the past. I'm living in the moment." -Principal Baruti Kafele

I first need to start out by saying that I have no personal experience with a leadership team who gloats about their personal accomplishments. I have worked alongside five principals and a dozen of assistant principals. These leaders never bragged about their personal past because they were more focused on the moment. They were focused on the students and faculty that were in their building. These are the types of teams that can enhance or change a culture in a school building.

100 No-Nonsense Things That All School Leaders Should STOP Doing

I have heard from countless other educators who have shared how their principal or leadership team bragged about their past accomplishments. Leaders that are all about themselves have awards displayed on the shelf behind them in eye shot and degrees and certifications mounted on the wall. One had been known to say, "I appreciate you all as a team, but I am a doctor. I sit in *THIS* principal's chair. (Pointing at people one by one.) You aren't a principal, you aren't a principal, and you aren't a principal. I make the decisions around here." This is as egotistical, toxic, and insecure as it gets when it comes to leading people. We want to believe that this type of behavior doesn't happen, but it happens all too often. As an administrator it is amazing what I've discovered about leadership in such a short time. One thing is for certain, those that lead with dignity, grace, and presence do not require the showcasing of accomplishments. Like Principal Kafele, I'm not worried about the awards. The past is the past. I choose to live in the moment.

Four Ways to Live in the Moment

1. Create a shared space in your office. Take a moment and reflect on the physical layout of your office and make changes. Consider what is on the walls, bookshelves, and tables. What do students, families, community members, and teachers notice when they walk into this office space? Stakeholders don't care about your diplomas or awards. This is a community space of healing, processing, collaborating, inspiring, planning, and mentoring. Use this space to communicate those messages. Put up artwork that students have created in art class. Have books available to share with teachers and other staff members. Post messages of hope, encouragement, and inspiration. Feature the mission, vision, values, beliefs, and goals in a personalized and inviting way. No matter what you do, create an environment that students, families, and staff want to be a part of when they enter this shared space.

2. Uncover the needs of people and W.I.N. them over. Principal Thompson *(Twitter: VAeducatorDAT)* taught me how to W.I.N. each day. W.I.N. is an acronym for (What I Need). Dynamic off-the-charts leaders set out each day with a mindset to W.I.N. over people. Sometimes all it takes is asking, "What do you need that I can help support?" Sometimes it is sitting beside a teacher making a tough phone call home, a high five, a smile, or a hug. Other times may be opening a milk carton for a student or asking your school volunteers what they are most passionate about. You will find that staff members, students, departments, or families need small things that will make a big difference in supporting student learning. Support stakeholders and teach them how to W.I.N. Each W.I.N. demonstrates meaningful belonging and they play a big role in the school community. If you want to stop making everything about you, then get in it to W.I.N. it.

3. Spread positivity as a beacon of light. Spreading positivity is masterfully contagious. Your previous accomplishments only matter because it helped create the leader you are today. Spreading positivity is what will be remembered. During class exchange, be present. Give students high-fives, fist bumps, or a positive greeting as they transition to class. Be present in your hallway or school. When you pop into a classroom for a walkthrough, leave positive notes. If you see a student working hard, leave them a positive note. If the teacher is being the best they can be for the students, leave them a positive note. Positive praise goes a lot further than previous accolades. Make it a goal that by winter break and by the end of the year to leave a positive sticky note for *EVERY* faculty member. Whether they work in the cafeteria, drive a bus, clean the building, or teach in front of students, *EVERYONE* is important. Make sure they feel that way throughout the year. If you need more ideas, go back to Chapter 16 and reread Melissa Rathmann's chapter on celebrating people or Michelle Osterhoudt's Chapter 46 on understanding the power of empathy. Positivity comes in many forms as words, gestures, silliness, laughter, compliments, sticky notes, emails, and elaborate celebrations. Every form of positivity is a seed planted in the culture and climate leading to success. Principal Sigler taught me to plant seeds of positivity because they are investments into stakeholders that will pay dividends later. Spread positivity in every moment possible.

4. Invest in yourself first. As a leader of people your biggest investment is you. You must take care of yourself. Do you hear me? If you need to better understand this concept, go back and review chapters 38-49 that focuses on getting a handle on anything that is holding you back from a healthy career. I remember the words of wisdom from Ms. Seely, whom I highly respected as a leader, telling me to make sure I was taking care of my at home family. She said that school family was important, but my at home family always needed to be number one. Dr. Ferrell taught me that investing in your own leadership is important because you constantly must learn and grow to be able to serve the students of today. They weren't talking about certificates and accolades; they were talking about the way I prioritized and interacted with people because of my accomplishments.

Your previous accomplishments matter, but what matters most is what's happening in the moment. Living in the moment and leading people to a big W.I.N. doesn't require gloating, accomplishments, honors, or credentials. Living in the moment requires leadership presence.

Corey Calder is a passionate school leader in Richmond, Virginia. He loves supporting the entire school community while connecting with other educators. He believes we all can do anything with a positive relationship with students, faculty, and the outside community. Corey can be reached via Twitter or Instagram (vaeducatorctc).

Stop Power Tripping
MARK FRENCH

Pow·er trip·er *noun*
: a leader with a self-aggrandizing quest for ever-increasing control over others: a person behaving in a way that increases a feeling of power: a person using power to control of other people as pleasure
//*She's been a **power tripper** ever since she was promoted to superintendent.*

Most likely you have known an educational "power tripper" at some point in your life. Many times, this occurs when someone is promoted into a leadership role that they think they deserve, or when they've been in a position so long that they believe themselves to have the most power. Either way, power trippers are a disease that will ultimately kill its educational body if it isn't treated and cured.

One might call leaders on a "power trip" controlling, bossy, self-focused, braggadocious, selfish, boastful, or dictatorial. Power tripping turns off colleagues and those in the trenches carrying out the frontline work. Power tripping educational leaders take credit for others' contributions, ignore members of the team, works as a self-promoter, and make everything about them. Power tripping is a continuation of the previous chapter where Corey Calder shared that "the past is the past" when it comes to accolades and accomplishments. Nobody cares how much a leader knows until they know how much they care (and find it even more repelling when they are on a power trip). A leader on an active rampage flexing their power tripping muscles will add suffrage rather than a healthy culture.

Impacts of Power Tripping
Leadership is developed over time, through practice and hard work. Sometimes being a leader, and owning power, can trip you up. Power tripping is viewed negatively and can cause others to lose respect and appreciation for you as their leader. Some equate power tripping to bullying. When power tripping affects others or is intended to intimidate, demoralize, control, threaten, frighten, or harass, power tripping takes on a form of abuse. This is the harmful consequence of power tripping. When leaders find themselves caught up in this cycle, they must find strategies and solutions to manage, deal with, and eliminate this malpractice.

Power tripping can contribute to a loss of empathy. Sometimes those in power no longer feel compelled to pay attention to the needs of others to ensure their own progression and position. They may develop a lack of both empathy and compassion which transfers to those they supervise and creates an unhealthy work climate and toxic culture. Employees subjected to abuse of power may respond by deliberately reducing their efforts or lowering the quality of their work. Demotivation can be extremely powerful itself. Sometimes the demoralization leads employees to stop caring about their work altogether and seek healthier work environments, better positions, or more fulfilling opportunities.

How to Deal with a Boss on a Power Trip
If you have a boss or supervisor on a power trip, there are things you can do to deal with them and help yourself. It would seem reasonable that you would want to avoid a power tripper but that can be counterintuitive. Instead stay connected to them and work to develop a strong relationship. Engage and let them know you want to present your best work and help them look good. Ask for advice on what you could do to improve your work. Rather than shrink away or isolate yourself from a power tripper, continue to do your best and make sure you are communicating with your boss and work to share any successes together. Be sure to take care of yourself. Even if you are trying to effectively deal with a power tripper, it may not always be successful. Be sure to manage any stress or anxiety their behavior may cause and ultimately you may need to find another place where you are valued and appreciated. Chapters 1-95 prepared you to deal with a power tripping boss. Revisit and sharpen your high EQ strategic leadership skills before making any big moves. If things go further south, you may wish to talk to someone in HR about your experiences and feelings. Be clear, concise, and provide documentation and/or evidence if you decide to have that conversation.

How to Stop Yourself from Power Tripping
It's difficult to know the reasons, intent, and motivation from someone who appears to be on a power trip. Consider the following attributes of a power tripper and what you can do to minimize or resolve this ineffective trait.

You are a Power Tripper if . . .	Do This Instead
Someone has pointed it out to you.	Share this information with a mentor, counselor, or confidant that can support and hold you accountable.
You claim credit for the work of others.	Pass the compliment to those involved.
You micromanage people.	Delegate tasks and projects to others.
You give directives consistently with no rationale or collaboration.	Plan strategically, provide a clear plan for expectations based on
Assume negative intent.	Assume positive intent.
Lack empathy when people fail.	Mentor those that fail and co-plan their success.
You compete at everything to win.	Intentionally step out to observe others win.

Determine Your Intentions

A good leader doesn't need to assert themselves or grandstand as a leader. Create and strengthen your team and promote them. Don't make it about you. Find the gifts that each person brings and showcase those. Include them. You don't have to do everything yourself. You will find that the contributions of others strengthen whatever result you can achieve on your own. Think about what your intentions are for demonstrating power tripping behaviors. Who are you demonstrating these behaviors for? What need do you have for this self-focused or narcissistic behavior? When you examine your need for power tripping, then you can work to change your behavior and stop power tripping. Is what you are doing self-promotion, self-serving, or interpreted as such? Even if you aren't intending to power trip, if others are interpreting your behaviors as such, then you are turning people off.

Power inherently comes with being a leader. Use that power to unite others, create a team, share successes, develop a vision, and bring out the best in everyone. Stop or don't power trip as a leader because ultimately it makes others lose respect and trust for you, causes good people to leave, and damages your organization and reputation.

Mark French is a retired elementary school principal who served students, staff, families, and communities in Texas and Minnesota for 38 years. He is co-author of the book "Principals In Action" and was honored as the 2015 Minnesota National Distinguished Principal.

Stop Thinking You Must Climb a Mythical Superintendency Ladder
RACHEL M. KENT

The field of education is chocked-full of overachievers. Class presidents, valedictorians, college athletes, business owners and those with the penultimate degree-- a doctorate. Yet in education, out of all the positions within the field of public education, there is only one that indicates the ULTIMATE career success--becoming a Superintendent. Many teachers feel compelled to journey from the confines of a sweltering classroom to the comforts of a leather-cushioned air-conditioned office. A myth. The freedom to use the lavatory when you need. Another myth. The power to make decisions that will have a significant impact on the learning of youth. Another myth-- the power is shared and leveraged through collaborative thinking and oftentimes micro-management ensues. Although it may be perceived as idyllic, being responsible for a school building, department, or school district, isn't all that the myths of career success make it out to be.

As you've discovered in the first 96 chapters, being a superintendent (or any school leader) is a big emotional roller coaster with inordinate time restricted demands. Many teachers will ponder, "Should I go into leadership?" That consideration arises for a variety of reasons. Educators may have a desire to make an even greater impact on their school or district, want to advance in their career, draw a greater salary, or genuinely want to use their talents and newfound knowledge utilizing their newest degree. The good news is that all of these are possible without climbing a path to the top position of a superintendency.

All snarking aside, there IS a disproportionately high number of overachievers in the field of education– those full of enthusiasm, and who want to change the world. Unlike other professions, public education lacks a high variety of pathways to advance or change roles at work. For teachers to harness their talents and ability some believe they must progress in title(s) and continue to advance. Not every educator is destined to be a superintendent (or the next step on the ladder). So why do so many teachers accept the myth that they must progress positionally? Leading in your school community and fulfilling your purpose in a career doesn't require a fancy title but rather defining success and leading from within.

Pause for a moment and think about the following questions before you move on to the next section in this chapter. Reflect on your experiences progressing through roles, titles, and contributions during your educational career and how they have contributed to your current perceptions.

>How do you define success?
>What does leadership mean to you?

Success is Winning Every Day
Most dynamic leaders are successful in their role because they demonstrated the skills necessary and developed strong relationships long before they got a new title. It's often said that people are hired for the next role because they already demonstrated proficiency for the job. Plenty of leaders progress through the ranks simply because someone tapped them on the shoulder and asked them to apply. They were already winning every day and that success propelled them on to the next role, authentically.

Natural leaders are team players with high added value that experience winning every day. They are contagiously inspirational and collaborative learning leaders. Do you feel like you are winning every day? Would you consider yourself successful? Do you experience contentment and fulfillment in your current role? Are you doing good, not just doing well? If the answer to these is no, then you may need to spend time in reflection figuring out– why not? What is your definition of success? If you aren't already winning every day, a change in your environment, grade level, or advancing in a role may not ensure immediate success. That too is a myth. Winning leaders take responsibility when things go wrong, they help others move forward, and set the example. These attributes are necessary as a leader in any role from classroom teacher all the way to superintendent. Leading isn't about the position, it is about a multitude of small wins every day that net success in the environments that you can control.

Leading is Everything BUT the Title
At some point in our careers, we imagine the life of an administrator-- air-conditioned office, a lunch break without students, meetings with meaningful agendas, and the power to make decisions that will impact schools for good. Many would love to "be the boss" and have the final say in school district matters. But are these the right reasons to pursue the next title? As we just saw in the previous chapter, Mark French made it very clear that power tripping has no place in any educational leadership role. The superintendency or any administrative role involves many, not so glamorous, "other duties as assigned" and pressures. The pressure behind the expectations is public, of greater consequence, must be answered, and formally accounted in a transcript for the school board and community. A superintendency isn't something that you just apply for, it is one that requires distributive practice, mentoring, high EQ, skill, and knowledge. Leading is a lot of pressure.

As a teacher I had always been told that I would be a good administrator. I experienced encouragement and the proverbial tap on the shoulder. I'd always been ambitious-- working multiple jobs throughout the school year. I'd worked summers in pseudo-administrative roles, experiencing the joy of academic team meetings with real agendas for change. Along the line, I was no longer content with only experiencing the "small wins" inside the classroom. I yearned to accomplish more. Even though I was good at what I did, and was viewed as successful, I was feeling stuck. What I really wanted was an opportunity to make a bigger impact in my school and community– but opportunities for impact weren't available unless I went into administration. I had already been considering the next step in my career path when cancer hit, and my plans were shaken off-track. My life turned upside down and I was left with long strides of time filled with thinking, healing, and aspirations.

During many months of recovery, I reflected, and grew; and decided that I needed a change in my career. I decided to leave teaching in the classroom for a career in administration. I enrolled in a university program to attain a second master's degree. I was set to start classes when an opportunity as an administrator opened. The challenge of launching a local charter school from the ground up seemed like the inspiration and once-in-a-lifetime opportunity that I'd been hoping for. I would get to walk in an administrator's shoes before investing in the cost of a second master's degree. The bonus was a "bigger title" and came with a smaller salary than I would have made had I stayed back in the classroom. I anticipated that the experience was well worth it, I was following my purpose– and the title would help me feel a greater sense of impact in my career. Or would it? Long story short, building-level administration during a world-wide pandemic wasn't for me. I learned early in my administrative experience that I didn't like some of the most important aspects that came with the title.

> I didn't like being "always on call".
> I didn't like having to hold peers accountable.
> I didn't like relying on others' work to be able to complete my job.
> I didn't like the frequent interruptions and lack of control over my day.

As a teacher I didn't have to worry about those things. My classroom was under my control. I was the king of that proverbial castle. I could plan my joy each day 42 minutes at a time. As an administrator the grass was not greener on the other side. In fact the grass was old, stained, brown carpet with a musty odd smell. The "fancy office furniture", really chairs from my college dorm room circa 1999. It may seem odd, but I am thankful and filled with gratitude for that smelly carpet, chaotic, lack of control experience as an administrator. It saved me the thousands of dollars that I was about to invest in my college tuition.

That being said, teachers, principals, and district administrators shouldn't feel an unspoken pressure to pursue a path to superintendency to make an impact or to change things up. All educators deserve built-in opportunities to lead in their schools, utilize their talents, and to help others grow without the need to leave their success zone where they ALREADY experience leadership and wins every day.

Success and Leadership Do Not Require a New Title
Superintendents, district administrators, and building administrators I encourage you to provide opportunities for teachers to lead from within. Many teachers have the same perfectionist type-T personalities seeking to overachieve and maximize their impact. Identify these teachers of excellence and notice their interactions and needs. This doesn't mean giving more work, it means cultivating

leadership skills if teachers are ready, willing, and able to embrace leadership within their school. There is pride in being a teacher and leading from within and everybody doesn't need to advance to the next position. When teachers latch onto these opportunities and succeed, these new wins open the possibility that maybe they will authentically progress in title. Teachers that you see potential in and encourage to advance is a good thing. Mentoring and growing future leaders ensures the succession of high-quality leadership that will last long beyond your retirement. Consider offering small leadership opportunities and mentorship alongside those that are ready. Invite leader-ready teachers to:

- Plan and lead family curriculum nights.
- Attend fellowships and policy advocacy meetings and events.
- Communicate updates on local, state, and federal educational policies or memos.
- Participate in certification programs. (Master Teacher, National Board)
- Build partnerships with local companies, alumni, and nonprofits to support student needs
- Self-drive micro credentialing or certifications. (Digital Promise, Google Classroom)
- Implement problem-based learning. (Buck Institute, Lead4Change Student Leadership Challenge)
- Provide mini-PD for colleagues in a before/after/during school 15-minute soundbite.
- Attend the superintendent forum as a voice representing the teachers at your school.
- Teach community classes. (CTE, Local Colleges, or Online Universities)
- Partner with companies or non-education professionals. (Microsoft, Non-Profits)'
- Pursue Ambassadorships with reputable education agencies (NYSCATE, Donors Choose)
- Lead a social media marketing campaign showcasing themes and good things in your building.
- Facilitate a student-run support center or school-based food pantry (Good Deed Grocery)
- #Observeme (As Julie Woodard shared in Chapter 93)

Education, unlike other fields, is a career of longevity. Teachers join the profession, knowing that the basic elements of their position will remain the same for the next 30-or-so years. Working bell to bell. Training yourself to use the restroom only during breaks between classes. Eating lunch at 10:30 in the morning. Leaders must respect the fact that most educators inside or outside the classroom may reach the point of asking, "What should I become next?" Some feel the pull for a change in scenery, finances, or ambition. Some want to see progress in their career, a title beyond teacher. Some want a greater impact, a greater challenge, and greater responsibility.

Providing a menu of opportunities and encouraging teachers to grow, shows your intentionality as an off-the-charts and dynamic leader. Leading growth has nothing to do with a title, it is about building relationships, capitalizing on purpose, opening doors of possibility, and creating off-the-charts interdependent success. I'm here to tell you that following the path to the Superintendency will not fulfill those goals. Experiencing true happiness because of all the small wins of success in your career, will. And it is possible without a title, without an hour-long lunch break, and without managerial drama, and politics. Dynamic off-the-charts leaders recognize that the success of the organization isn't about them, it is about providing those they lead with what they need, to ensure small wins of success every day.

Rachel M. Kent is a career educator in Western New York in the fields of English, Career and Technical Education and Special Education. Rachel has worked on the NYSED Performance Descriptor Committee for ELA and Common Core/NGLS. Rachel is also a Literacy Design Collaborative module author, National Writing Project and America Achieves Fellow and is a proud supporter of the success of all students. Rachel leads a student-run food pantry at her school, pro bono. Her students won national recognition for student leadership development.

98

Stop Stepping on Others to Get Ahead
CORI ORLANDO

In the previous chapter you just wrestled with what makes a successful leader. Now, close your eyes. Who is the first person that pops into your head as a dynamic off-the-charts leader? In your opinion what made them such a good leader? Their title? Their degree? Their salary? The pace of their career advancement? Surely, it's none of the above. In contrast we can all name leaders (by title) who are not actually leading and instead are power tripping bosses as Mark French shared in Chapter 96. And we know from Rachel M. Kent in the prior chapter that leading isn't a title and success is many small wins. Regardless of position or title, everyone in education is a leader, in their own right, based on their actions and relationships.

True Colors Can't Hide

Over the years, I have gone through many difficult situations that have shown me who people really are at their core. During tough times most people can no longer mask who they really are. I have witnessed "leaders" in a position of power (and title), willing to step on colleagues and even throw their own teachers under the bus to be the hero or to save face. It is still hard for me to accept a boss, colleague, or prospective leader who lacks integrity. I have encountered two types of people.

    1. Bases. Those that continuously create a firm foundation to lift others up.
    2. Climbers. Those that pull others down to step on as they try to climb their way up.

"Bases" and "climbers," both require a tremendous amount of energy. It seems crazy to me that we even need to address "stepping on others to get ahead", in one of the noblest professions on earth. It seems like an oxymoron. Educators are held to one of the highest moral standards as civil servants in a noble profession. Of all the professions in existence educators should have the highest moral compasses. Dynamic off-the-charts leaders recognize bases and climbers from a mile away and have the leadership presence navigate both.

The Bases

Bases are grounded in their "why." They have a solid purpose grounded in impacting students. Everything they do is tethered to high quality teaching and learning to ensure student success. These are the people who suit up, stand up, and show up for kids. Bases are also the ones that collaborate in PLC to ensure their lessons are engaging, align to the standards, and individualized. Bases take the time to get to know the members of their team(s). They seek to know strengths and deficits to balance and leverage their collective talent. They encourage, seek to understand, empathize, listen, and hear. Others rely on their insight and expertise to boost up others, to carry others into the fold. Bases see the best attributes in others that they can't yet see in themselves. They don't consider personal gain or recognition, rather, they synergize the collective and work interdependently to benefit ALL students. These people truly do exist. And even though I am referring to them as bases, this doesn't mean that they are on the bottom leadership wrung. I have been blessed to work with leaders with nearly every title who are bases. I have gained expertise and learned to be an intentionally good human, from bases. If you have invested the time in reading this book, most likely you try your best to be a base for others. Unfortunately, climbers do not seem to like bases. I don't know if it is because it shows the dichotomy, or because it forces them to become even more competitive. Regardless, meet "the climbers".

The Climbers

These are the people that are grounded in themselves. Their "why" is to be at the top. Their goal is to climb the hierarchy until they land in the highest position of power. They proclaim an intent to do right by the students, which they may have originally set out to do, but lost sight somewhere along the way. Like Jesse Lubinsky shared in Chapter 85, they forgot where they started their career. Climbers have distinctive people skills and earn others' trust easily. They have high EQ ability but instead are cunning and intelligent enough to use people's strengths and weaknesses to their own advantage. They will not hesitate to throw someone under the bus for their own gains. They are jealous of other's success and will try to tarnish one's reputation any chance whether founded, or their own manipulated version of truth. To them, making someone else look bad, makes them look better. Climbers are manipulative and many progress far up the chain, leaving smashed and broken bases behind. Where do the students fit into this level of adult malpractice? Let that ruminate.

The Future of Climbers
Unfortunately, I have seen and heard of many climbers making their way all the way to a superintendency. They made it because there was no hesitation stepping on others along the way. I wish I knew why this behavior in education is tolerated because the behaviors are opposite of what is taught in character education. A non-exemplar. A polar opposite. Just because someone has a leadership title, does not mean they are leading with integrity. Climbers that lack a moral compass or authenticity, will eventually get caught. One day they will turn around to find that nobody is following, that scores are in decline, that culture is nonexistent, and stakeholders want answers. When adversity strikes, the base's true colors come out. We witnessed examples of this during the pandemic. When the energy and momentum of the bases was exhausted, metaphorically the base crumbled. If those that climbers depend on to do the work and make them look good are no longer willing to cover for them publicly, who does the climber have left to depend on? Climbers are left standing on their own two watching turned backs walking away. At some point, it will catch up to them and climbers will be left empty handed because nobody will follow.

If You Can Be Anything, Be a Base
So, now what? For me, I hope, hope, hope that I am a base and I'm confident that you feel the same way. If there is one theme that we have learned throughout the entire #100StopSeries is that we must begin each new day with purposefully planned positive intent. A practice that has made a difference for me is tethering back to my very first "why." Seven years ago, I wrote a six-word memoir that defined my "why" as a leader. The following six words still anchor me to my base, "One who inspires and encourages others." When my daily actions and words do not match up to my six-word memoir, I want others to point out that I'm climbing instead of being a base. No leader is perfect and certainly not

every school day is flawless. We all have climbing moments which is why it is so important to know our "why", proclaim our intent, and surround ourselves with others who will lead us back to home base. Integrity is the epicenter of leading people; it is essential to be as consistent as possible regardless of the circumstance. Dynamic leaders mean what they say and say what they mean, consistently.

When You are the New Kid in Town
Currently I'm "the new kid" in my district for the second time in three years, having changed positions and locations. As a new leader coming in, the people have absolutely no reason to believe or trust in me, yet. They don't know me, and they don't know of me, yet. It is my job to try and earn that trust through integrity, authenticity, transparency, engagement, and anything else that shows that I am a base that will always lift them up. This requires me owning the mistakes that I make, (which I do), following through with promises, and communicating professionally. Even though I work at the district office I am my silly, authentic self every time I am with them to put them at ease. Leaders that are new to the district must empower others as professionals to make decisions to best meet the needs of their students. Until trust sets in, you will not be perceived as a non-climber. Leaders must always persevere through personalities, mishaps, awkward encounters, and adversity with integrity. When the climbers in my past tried to rattle me (and I admit, they did) the one thing that grounded me was knowing that I walked through my day with integrity. No one could take that away from me. Remaining steadfast as a foundational base for others to succeed, was within the realm of my control.

My Call to Action Is This: No matter your role. You are a leader. Someone is always watching,

listening, and learning from you. So . . . just keep your integrity intact. When others try to knock you down, let your only reaction be to not immediately react. Keep showing up as your authentic self. Every. Damn. Day. No one can take that away from you. Eventually, everyone's true colors are discovered.

Cori Orlando has been in education since 2001. She has taught grades K-4, been a district ELA TOSA for TK-12, a District Administrator for ELA/SLA/ELD for 29 Elementary Schools and is currently a Lead Instructional Technology Specialist. She presents on all things education in her spare time.

Stop Using Others to Further Your Own Agenda
GREGORY M. GOINS, Ed.D.

"Trust is the highest form of human motivation. It brings out the very best in people." -Stephen R. Covey

Nothing is more difficult than leading change in education, yet many school leaders fall into the trap of moving too quickly in placing their own signature on new organizations. Generally speaking, an impulse to "fix things" often comes from a good place. Those making a transition into new jobs often bring with them proven results from past experience. However, the mad dash to replicate previous success is often met with resistance as each school district has its own climate, culture and steady path to improvement that may not fit with the leader's personal goals and timelines.

Cori Orlando just shared her personal experience of taking time to build trust through integrity in the prior chapter. It takes a while for the people you are leading in a new organization to respect you as a leader and support your agenda. Their biggest fear is that you will add initiatives for the sake of initiatives without ever getting to know the needs of the staff and students. Unfortunately, too many school leaders become impatient and self-serve with a laser focus on racking up an impressive list of accomplishments to move up the organizational chart or into the next big job. In the last chapter we just learned the consequence of stepping on others to get ahead. As this personal agenda is exposed, credibility is immediately lost and replaced by fear, mistrust, and opposition leading to deep problems within the school culture.

Leaders in a position of power with a title on their nameplate who are willing to power trip and step all over others to meet their personal career goals have ulterior motives. Those leaders typically make three mistakes when trying to push others to conform to their own agenda.

Mistake #1 Top-Down Mandates
There's nothing worse than sending out an email or making a big announcement at the next faculty meeting that a decision has been made "in the best interest of the organization." This top-down approach is most always met with resistance, much to the surprise of the superintendent or principal

100 No-Nonsense Things That All School Leaders Should STOP Doing

who assumes that everyone will simply fall in line and conform without question. The top-down mandate is often a rookie mistake that is the first big wake-up call when it comes to developing leadership styles because it is a forced buy-in. Allyson Apsey opened the first section in Chapter 1 cautioning leaders against this very practice. When top-down mandates fail, many leaders shift to a forced buy-in approach that puts pressure on others to toe the line in a "divide and conquer" approach that only creates greater challenges when trying to implement new ideas.

Playing the "blame game" and calling out those that are "part of the problem" are simply dirty tricks designed to shame others into jumping on the bandwagon. This might lead to questions like: "You know this is the right thing to do, right?" or "How can you not go along with my plan when you know how bad our test scores are?" In each case, the leader tries to bully others into compliance which often leads to an even wider gap of disagreement and wreaks havoc on team building. Revisit Chapter 1 to learn additional strategies on avoiding this rookie mistake. If you do not reckon with top-down mandates, ultimately, students will suffer.

Mistake #2 Carrots & Sticks

Once leaders figure out that top-down mandates and forced buy-in are ineffective strategies for change, the mistake they commit is often a "carrots and sticks" approach that rewards those that support new ideas, while punishing those that provide push back. This incentives-based philosophy creates "winners and losers" which generally divides people. "Cutting deals" is almost always the kiss of death for school leaders. In the book, *Drive: The Surprising Truth about What Motivates Us*, author Daniel Pink calls these types of incentives "If-then" rewards as in, "If you do this, then you get that." As an example, the principal may enter negotiations with an individual by saying, "If you will support my ideas at the next faculty meeting, I'll send you to that big, national conference on the beach this summer." Although playing favorites and manipulating others for personal gain seems profoundly unacceptable, it happens. When leaders lean into malpractice it always leads to anger and resentment. Instead, Pink recommends shifting the focus from "carrots and sticks" to intrinsic motivators that include autonomy, mastery, and purpose. Analyze how these three shifts are interconnected throughout the 100 STOP Leaders book and the leadership EQ agility required to make these shifts.

1. Intrinsic motivators that include autonomy. Offer a sense of self-direction with some control over what, when, and how things are done. Revisit Allyson Apsey's proactive approach in Chapter 1 on how to handle when you've already made up your mind. Maggie Cox insists that leaders don't squash staff-generated ideas or interests in Chapter 54.

2. Mastery. Place continuous improvement at the forefront using data and evidence to align to the shared mission, vision, values, and goals. Do not waste time on work that doesn't support the mission and vision. Revisit Sean Gillard's message on this in Chapter 63.

3. Purpose. Clearly define "why" you're doing something in the first place. Maggie Fay shares in Chapter 64 why we should not introduce more initiatives just because we learned something new. In Chapter 51, Aggie Salter reminded us not to carry out initiatives that only we enjoy.

Each shift above serves as a "north star" when leading change in schools. Leading effective change is arduous and strategic work. Creating motivated, masterful and purposeful teams will transpire when the leader has taken the time to establish a collaborative leadership process that values transparency, shares a vision, and empowers those they are entrusted to lead to take ownership of the change process.

Mistake #3 Seeking Consensus Without Ownership

As we have heard from a wide variety of authors in this book, the first step to leading change is sharing your "why." In any organization leaders must facilitate open and honest dialogue to define the problem(s) and root cause(s). This is often the most difficult task as many people shy away from courageous conversations to avoid hurt feelings or creating an environment of finger pointing or blaming others. However, as Jim Collins states in his book, *Good to Great: Why Some Companies Make the Leap... and Others Don't*, "Productive change can only begin when you confront the brutal facts. As such, being fully transparent and putting all your cards on the table in a respectful manner is one of the keys to leading positive change." Ownership is not buying-in to a new initiative but owning past mistakes because of analysis, deep reflection, and collaboration, it's about strategically choosing to make important changes.

Difficult conversations will only be productive if everyone has a voice at the table with a system designed for regular participation and feedback. This can best be described as a "brainstorming" session as teams must work together to reach consensus on the root of the problem before moving to solutions and strategic planning. Keep in mind that sending out surveys to gather feedback via email may be a good place to start, it only scratches the surface. Deep and meaningful collaboration takes place in face-to-face, trusting, vulnerable, risk-taking settings that begin with small group bite size conversations before moving to all-staff large-group discussions. To implement changes effectively leaders must increase in a slow enough progression to build momentum for second order change.

Most importantly, leaders must understand the difference between buy-in and ownership as the two are often used interchangeably to describe internal feelings of support. In reality, "buy-in" is about following someone else's idea and being steered toward support and compliance by those in charge. On the other hand, "ownership" allows everyone to participate in the process with the opportunity to share their "own" ideas and vision for change that ultimately lead to a greater sense of responsibility.

In the end, organizational change is about bringing people together to create a shared vision for the future of your school or district. Once you understand the difference between buy-in and ownership, you will be on your way to leading a team that just might be inspired enough to follow your lead.

Dr. Gregory M. Goins is a veteran school administrator, teacher, and educational consultant with more than 25 years of experience leading transformative change in education. Dr. Goins served 15 years as a school district superintendent in Illinois and is currently the Director of Educational Leadership at Georgetown College in Kentucky. He is also the host of the nationally acclaimed Reimagine Schools Podcast.

100

Stop Leading in Any Role if You Don't Love the Profession
ROBERT A. MARTINEZ, Ed.D.

"I have decided to stick with love. Hate is too great of a burden to bear." -Martin Luther King, Jr.

You Always Have a Choice
If you made it this far in the book you have encountered over 99 choices that leaders make. It is your choice to stay in the profession of education, and I hope that each of you personally choose to become a leader in the field of education because we need good ones. Seriously. You didn't choose to read this book by accident. You weren't selected in a lottery, or by chance to pay tribute like in the Hunger Games. Surely you didn't just happen to stand in the wrong line at educator school and several years later someone just decided to put you in an office to lead. Taking on an educational leadership role was a choice, and I hope one that was made with some forethought, a commitment to serve students, teachers, support teams, parents, etc., and a conscious decision that was made because you love the ideals and people involved in the work of the education profession. All the work!

I'll presume that no one forced you to take the educational job that you are currently in. Nobody forced you to leave the classroom or to stop providing direct service to students. No one forced you to try and make a larger difference in students' lives. No one enticed you to work long days, many evenings, weekends, but rather, there was an internal personal drive that existed to lead schools and districts for the greater good of humanity, for the inherent feeling of making a difference, and God I truly hope that you have loved it all.

I hope you loved the smiles in our students' eyes when they arrived at school. I hope you felt the strong passionate feelings of students learning a wealth of information, ideas, and creating new answers to questions that had never been thought of before. I hope the hair on your arm stands up when you experience accomplishments, awards, and accolades of your students knowing they came to school to learn in an environment you helped create. I hope that you can still smile and giggle a little, when you hear the laughter of a classroom full of students, especially when their teacher shows some vulnerability, acting goofy, sending a funny smile, making a mistake, or radiating sheer joy just because they feel honored to be with students daily.

Know When It's Time to Ride Off into the Sunset
If you don't get goosebumps in these moments, then man, I hope you do make that determination to call it a career, and head off into the sunset, because while you might be coming to work, you are not coming to a place you love for the right reasons. And our collective of students deserve someone who continues to love it all. I sincerely hope that you have not retired in spirit and as a result are manifesting drudgery each day by coming to, staying at, or surviving a position or leadership role that you don't love. If for some reason, the only reason you keep coming to work is a rationale of putting a little more aside for your retirement, then please, take what you have stored away and ride off into the sunset.

I hope you never lose the wonderful memories you have amassed or lose sight of the vision of leading a school or district out of the haze of mediocrity, doubt, despair, frustration, or loss of love for the career you chose. But, if you find yourself, mad, angry, frustrated, perplexed, and wondering why you are there in your office each day, well my friend, if you cannot see and feel the love for the work, then by all means, pack it up and take it home. The profession needs your heart, mind, soul, and actions that continue to carry love in them. Our students, teachers, support members, parents, and stakeholders deserve the best version of you. They deserve the *YOU* they hired. The one who loved all things education. Loved the curriculum, instruction, teaching, planning, designing, collaboration, creativity, and most of all the people. The students, teachers, support staff, colleagues, parents, family members, and even the people who might not always treat us well. Love them too.

Our educational system simply cannot rise to the level we need it to be if educational leaders who don't love the work anymore are still in charge of pieces of the puzzle. If you are still reading and make it through the end of the book feeling inspired, invigorated, challenged, and in the game, then there is hope. I hope you are changed by this book knowing that leaders across this nation rallied together to share with you the value and importance of *YOU* and your role as leader. I hope you are not the only one that finds themselves in rough waters from time to time. I hope that you feel a sense of comradery and newfound colleagues willing to connect and go to bat for you. If you want to simply up your leadership game or overhaul your attitude and leadership practices, we are her for that too. Leaders cannot do it alone and we would be honored for YOU to stay in the profession and thrive in leading.

Stay in Love with Leading
Each of you must find that "thing" that keeps your love alive. Some might call it, your "why" perhaps, but I think it goes a little deeper than that. This "thing" is the reason your love sustains. This "thing" is the basis for your thoughts, actions, daily commitment, and follow through to make other things better. Each of us has at least one. Maybe it's something from your personal story. Perhaps it's a memory of that one time a child under your care truly moved one step closer to their goals. Maybe it's a conglomerate of all the children you taught, or even appreciation from your own heart for your own education. In any case, you must find this seed of love, carry it with you, and never let the bad weather of difficult surroundings loosen it from your grip. Nurture it, take care of it, and let it guide your compass in all you do.

Spread the Love
Like in life, the more love we give, the more love we receive, and that love produces more love that will exist after we depart. Working in the education profession, especially as a leader, connotes the same thoughts for me. I truly believe that the more love you can carry into each of your days for the entire theme of education, the more love will propagate through time. If you feed those in your care, your impact will linger throughout the environment long after you depart, leaving a legacy. All ego aside, dynamic off-the-charts leaders think about their legacies. I simply can't think of a legacy that would be better than to know that the love I have for education, lingers in every environment that I ever worked, even years after I've left. If you still have it in you, or you are considering moving into your first leadership role, do it for you, and more importantly, do it for them, for all of them!

Dr. Robert A. Martinez is currently the Chief Human Resources Officer for the Antioch Unified School District in Antioch, California. Dr. Rob focuses on building the resilience of everyone he works with to support our students. He strives to build leaders across our educational community who can lead into the future... Known as @ResiliencyGuy Dr. Rob often says, "Let the life we help others live be the measure of our success." His new book, "Recipe for Resilience, Nurturing Perseverance in Students and Educators is focused on ways to do just that.

STOP Dismissing Reality

This Type of Nonsense Clings to the Comforts of the Past Rather than Leading Courageously in the Present

Stop Pretending as Though Things Have Gone Back to "Normal"
CHRISTOPHER R. MANNING, D.M.

Many educators and education leaders are still reeling from the very traumatic era that hit schools and colleges across the world. Here in the United States, the COVID pandemic and outbreak of violence within our schools and communities have placed many teachers, students, and families on edge.

Many children spent more than one academic year away from school, away from socializing with their schoolmates, away for the structured/formal learning environment which was a very significant part of their social lives, academic learning, and human development. As a result of this extended separation from a key part of their lives, many children are left changed. Their perspectives of what school is and what school should be, have also changed, and we are only beginning to learn what is on their minds.

Further, many teachers have changed their views of what schools are and what they should be. The absolute worst thing we could do is pretend that everything is "business as usual." I know that many district employees would love that to be the case, for the sake of their own job security. Very large and bureaucratic institutions change their ways about as fast as a cruise ship changes its course—it takes time. For this reason, many people do not wish to entertain the idea of any dramatic changes to how we educate our children.

The October 2022 "The Nation's Report Card," released by the National Assessment of Educational Progress revealed that nationwide test scores were at the lowest level in decades, with historic lows. This dramatic fact requires that we do some thinking. Just how many students are now two to three years behind in content knowledge, thinking skills, social interaction, and human development AND negatively impacted with digital dementia or mental illness because of the isolation induced in 2020. The academic, social, and emotional gaps that already existed were exacerbated by the trauma of society. And even to this day, second graders arrived in face-to-face schooling for the first time in their school experience. The vast needs of students became even bigger than what we could offer with our curricula, assessments, virtual lessons, and grade reports. Students lost loved ones, witnessed violence and division, and experienced bouts of depression and some even PTSD. Just because the 2022-2023 school year opened in-person doesn't mean we picked up where we left off and things are back to business as usual.

Many of us with years of experience and advanced degrees would not want to admit that our practice and education became outdated the moment we, as a nation, removed our students from school for nearly two years (some for two entire academic years). We do not want to admit that teachers are asked to teach under conditions that we ourselves have never experienced. Counselors are maxed out; teachers are overburdened and all the practices that worked before the pandemic don't necessarily work any longer. Adjusting to meet the needs of this new profile of student with far more deficit areas, will require a dynamic shift in our collective mindset.

School culture is created by the interactions of three separate groups: student culture, staff culture, and community culture. All three of these groups have changed tremendously and are still trying to find their bearings in the aftermath of the world shutting down. Millions of people died while packets or computer screens replaced the one constant and sense of belonging in their lives, school. Students took for granted (rightfully so) that they would attend school "normally" from kindergarten on. Parents took for granted that their children would be "off to school" each school day and that they would have that time to work and take care of things on the home front. Educators (of all titles) took for granted that they would "go" to work each day to live out their leadership dreams of changing lives.

This reality was briskly torn from us, and not so gently thrown back at us. Despite the countless hours spent on re-entry planning, the fact remains that many schools are still "re-entering" their buildings, and many students have only physically returned to school, they have not re-entered school emotionally and socially. We have work to do and that starts with leaders not pretending as though we just returned from a long field trip. This was traumatic for all of us, we owe it to ourselves. We owe it to our teachers, and our students to put pretense aside, start listening, and re-create our practice.

Dr. Christopher R. Manning grew up in Claremont, California and Phoenix, Arizona. He is a veteran of the United States Air Force. While in the military he lived and worked in Montana, New Mexico, Washington D.C., South Korea, Germany, Kuwait, and Japan. As an international educator, he lived and worked in Kyrgyzstan and Bangladesh.

102

Stop Trying to Be Somebody that You're Not
SUSAN MACK-OSBORN

Rediscovering who you are as a leader is a process that will take distributed time, multiple experience, and consistent reflection. You will come to the role with ideas, perceptions, and assumptions surrounding what you think the role is and what it should be because of your schema. Invariably there will be a moment(s) when you think to yourself, "This is not what I expected, or I'm not sure how to do this role and do it successfully." During those times of self-doubt, you may find yourself dwelling on your skills, your mindsets, and how you will meet your ultimate goal of high student achievement and success. Discovering who you are as a leader requires that you stop trying to be somebody that you're not.

Determine Who You Are
Working with new administrators and leaders over the past several years, and through my own experiences as a

developing leader, it has become clear that there are stages that most of us go through as we learn a new role and practice it. We arrive to a new position with a variety of skills and beliefs that have been crafted over years in various areas in education and have completed a multitude of prerequisites to land in a 'formal' position of leadership. Once actually in the position, many of us question ourselves with thoughts of, "Now what? Who am I expected to be? And, Who am I as a leader?" It is at this stage that we draw upon our past experiences with leaders, good and bad, and begin to reflect on how we want to lead others. Focusing on the 'how to lead', is the stage where many of us are the most comfortable because we know where to access concrete resources to get us started and answer many of our questions. We know what books to read and who the leading experts are in the field of educational leadership. We have been inundated with information from various leadership training courses and other professional development opportunities. New leaders are well trained, well read and prepared with tools and resources to be successful. They have also had many opportunities to work with and for a multitude of experienced leaders and have a strong sense of what they will and won't do as leaders themselves.

Drop the Persona
After enough time has passed to become familiar with any position of leadership, many begin to question their own expectations. In mentoring new leaders or leaders in a new environment, I have noticed that the conversations inevitably move towards misperceptions of the role and assumptions people have. Their upbringing, past experiences, observations, and previous educational environments all play into their schema. New leaders will often formulate a 'persona' based on their beliefs of what a good leader should be and what is required to do the job successfully. They will emulate others' practices to appear confident and knowledgeable, thinking that this is how they need to 'act' or should 'act' as a leader. This ultimately leads to inner conflict as the person is not being true to themselves as a person, or to their core beliefs as an educational leader. The new leader is trying to be someone they're not and this becomes a roadblock when it comes to making decisions and leading a team. The challenge now is discovering 'who you are as a leader' once you are vulnerable and courageous enough to drop the persona.

Discover Your Authentic Leadership Style
So how do leaders get over this hurdle and find their authentic leadership style? This process takes a great deal of insight, EQ, intuition, and personal reflection to list and flush out all your strengths and beliefs as part of your self-discovery. As a leader gains experience, develops their interpersonal skills and draws upon both internal and external resources, it is imperative that time is set aside to focus on the choices and decisions that you are making.

It took a few years of being an Administrator before I really started to reflect on who I was as a leader and what personal characteristics I drew upon continuously to make decisions. I knew if I wanted to lead authentically, I would need to be intentional in my thought process while making decisions that impacted students, staff, and the community. Early on in my career I spent a great deal of time thinking about what a respected colleague might do or say and base my decisions around those assumptions. I was often hesitant to trust myself in choosing a course of action before I reached out and consulted with a trusted mentor. I tried to emulate their 'style' of leadership and acted the way I thought I was supposed to 'act' as a leader. This of course was all learning and a valuable part of the process but there came a time when I started to question who I was a leader and how I wanted to move forward. I knew that I wanted to be true to my authentic self.

I started asking for feedback from staff and colleagues around my strengths, and where I needed to be more transparent or thoughtful in my leadership style and approach. I spent a lot of time reflecting on how and why I made decisions and what characteristics I drew upon most often when setting direction, accessing resources, building relationships and in all areas of being an effective leader. I began to let go of my preconceived notions around leadership and gained a deeper awareness and acceptance of my own abilities. I worked with increased confidence and trust in myself and discovered who I was as a leader. This was liberating and allowed me to relax contentedly in my role as a leader because I was authentic in all areas of the school and organization.

What driving factors help you to make sound decisions as a leader? Do any of those factors hold you back or impact decisions you might otherwise make? How would you describe your personal style as a leader? Does your personal style seem to be effective? Some leaders have discovered that they lead with their heart first, others utilize their strong abilities of perception, another realized that it was their empathetic nature that drove their decision making, while others, like myself, depend on strategic thinking, data, or evidence when leading in an educational setting. All of these leadership styles are needed to be well-balanced and seasoned as a leader but knowing what drives you deep down will allow you to be true to yourself as you continue your leadership journey.

There is no need to emulate, copy, or try to be someone that you are not. Spend some time alone or with a trusted colleague or mentor and develop a deeper awareness of who you are as a person and what your experiences have taught you. Be confident. Accept yourself for who you are and lead as your exceptional and authentic self.

Susan Mack-Osborn is an Elementary School Principal with the Halton District School Board in Milton, ON, Canada. She has an undergraduate degree from McMaster University in Hamilton, ON, a Bachelor of Education degree from the University of Toronto and a Master of Arts degree from the Ontario Institute for Studies in Education (OISE). She has been a dedicated educator for 30 years, teaching elementary and high school students. Susan has been a school Administrator for over 20 years and has a passion for restructuring organizations, developing teams, and data driven results. She has unwavering support from her parents, is inspired by her daughter Shannon, and shares a joy for life, adventure, and mayhem with her husband and best friend, Vincent.

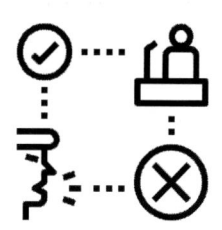

There is No Counter-Argument to Stopping Nonsense
JON CORIPPO

I've had quite an educational journey over the last 24 years: emergency credentialed teacher, two stints at county offices of education, one as an ed tech coordinator doing 3 PDs a week, the other serving concurrently as an Assistant Superintendent/Tech Director/Risk Management. I helped open a high school from scratch. I've taught in four different school districts. For about 6 years, I was a leader of one of the largest non-profit edtech organizations in the US., and in 2019-2020, I fired myself from leadership and went back to teach 6th grade to update my skills and test new ideas. Since summer 2020, I've been consulting full-time, and I've visited over 270 classrooms in three countries, doing demo lessons with pre-k through AP level students.

I've seen a lot of education, worldwide. Here's my first message: the vast majority of kids are fine. They are ready to be led. They are ready to work. School is not ok, but the kids are fine.

Adults Have a Different Timeline than Kids
What's wrong with school then? Schooling is stagnant. It refuses to change. It is proud of the static nature of doing things that it continues to enforce. Worst of all, school continues to be mostly about adults. Board meetings are about adults. Cabinet meetings are about adults. PLCs are about adults. IEPs happen with just adults talking. Everything is about adults.

Here's why going back to the classroom for one last year was so powerful for me: When working alongside other teachers, I realized they really didn't process the tempo we needed - these kids only get *THIS YEAR* one time, we must get high quality engaging instruction right, *THIS YEAR*, not in the spring or over the summer, *NOW*. The urgency is now. Currently, school doesn't seem to be working at such a pace that today matters, because the adults have a different timeline than kids. It's just another year for us. But when you are 10 years old, one year is literally 10% of your entire life. Imagine if you are forty years old currently, that is four years of your life in stagnation, status quo, repetition, standardization, and obedience to a system of conformity.

As you read this book, *100 No-Nonsense Things ALL Leaders Should STOP Doing*, I suggest you glance back at the table of contents and prioritize things we can stop doing to ensure that you stop any malpractice happening on your watch, *THIS* year. Especially the practices, challenges, protocols, systems, and expectations that are about adults. Get passionate and visualize the dynamic success you will experience because you *DID* something about it - and like Rae Dunn says - get a new vantage point. Look through an educational lens that focuses on intentionally leading people in such a way that *THIS* year turns into the most academically, socially, and wildly successful year for *EVERY* kid in *EVERY* class. The good news is that many of the things that you need to put a stop to are laced with adult politics anyway. I don't know who said it first, but it's true:

> *"We are at our best when we are about kids, and we are at our worst when we are about adults."*

There is No Counterargument High Quality Leadership

As leaders, let's analyze both sides of the coin. Consider the possible counter arguments to the argument of eliminating adult-centric practices: Does being student-centered mean we will surrender the class to kids? No. Does this mean school is just fun all day? No. Does this mean an end to order and high expectations for good citizenship in class? No. Ironically, most kids want order, they find stability in predictability. Most kids want real academic challenges, they are curious and like figuring things out. Does this require teachers and admins to become even bigger martyrs with their time and gold? Again, no.

Success is Free

What I'm encouraging you, as the leader of your state, county, region, district, or school is to *DRAMATICALLY* CHANGE your leadership practices to eliminate and cut out anything ineffective or inefficient that doesn't have a laser focus on high quality planning, high quality teaching and learning, or high-quality leadership. This book has provided you with a new network of experts at your service willing to network and share. Hopefully you have discovered that this message isn't about anyone else, it is about how YOU can lead others to success because you were intentional. Streamline. Tighten things up. Investigate. Observe. Listen. Discover what isn't working. A faster operational tempo is free. Better ideas are free. Seeking to understand students and their point of view is free. Being empathetic is free. And many of the things kids would ask for are a flick-of-our-wrist easy, and free. Need some examples?

We did a school survey once and were shocked that 85% of the girls felt "unsafe" in the bathrooms.

We immediately engaged several of the students and found that the way the gap in the door pointed at the mirror allowed other girls to accidentally see into the stalls. Awkward at any age. Our custodian made a few changes and in three weeks we were feeling 98% *SAFE* in the bathrooms. Three weeks. Quick tempo, acting with empathy.

At the HS that we built from scratch, Mike Niehoff and I informed the teachers (all untenured) that we'd be doing an end-of-quarter survey for each class, after each quarter. Several teachers expressed deep concern that kids might say nasty things in the surveys. We simply pointed out that we should all probably be very professional with kids, knowing that the surveys would be coming. How did it go? Teachers were *STUNNED* at all the positive comments. Free. First quarter. Empathy.

We've shared Smart Starts (the idea of truly onboarding kids for the year. It's an amazing collection of Eduprotocols that bind a class together in 3-5 days) far and wide, literally all over. Educators say: I can't wait to do that next year! Wrong. You can Smart Reboot after Thanksgiving or Winter or February break. This year. Now. Free. Build those relationships immediately.

This incredible book is packed with amazing things to *STOP DOING*. I'd implore you to START stopping them as soon as possible. We (collectively) only get *THIS YEAR* once.

Jon Corippo has served as a classroom teacher, high school principal, director and assistant principal while leading educational nonprofits for 25 years. Jon's passion for student learning led to the development of the bestselling book: Eduprotocol Field Guide Series. Jon loves interacting with all types of educators for professional development and is famous for his offer of "free lifetime tech support" both inside and outside of where he resides in California.

References

Adverse Childhood Experiences (ACES). (2022). Nearly 35 million U.S. children have experienced one or more types of childhood trauma. https://acestoohigh.com

Allen, N., Grigsby, B., & Peters, M. L. (2015). Does leadership matter? Examining the relationship among transformational leadership, school climate, and student achievement. *International Journal of Educational Leadership Preparation, 10(2)*, 1–22. http://www.ncpeapublications.org

Azari, J. (2019). It's the institutions, stupid: The real roots of America's political crisis. Foreign Affairs, 98 (4), 52-61.

Birla, N. (2019). Words matters: A time to talk and a time to listen. Thrive Global. https://thriveglobal.in/stories/words-matter-a-time-to-talk-and-a-time-to-listen/

Bravata. C. (2020). Prevalence, predictors, and treatment of impostor syndrome: A systematic review. *Journal of General Internal Medicine, 35(4)*, 1252–1275.

Brower, T. (2021). Empathy is the most important leadership skill according to research. Forbes https://www.forbes.com/sites/tracybrower/2021/09/19/empathy-is-the-most-important-leadership-skill-according-to-research/

Business to You. (2022). Crossing the Chasm in the Technology Adoption Life Cycle. https://www.business-to-you.com/crossing-the-chasm-technology-adoption-life-cycle/

Calvert, D. (2016). 5 tips to become an authentic leader. Kellogg School of Management. https://insight.kellogg.northwestern.edu/article/five-tips-for-authentic-leadership.

Casas, J. (2020). Live your excellence: Bring your best self to school every day. California: Dave Burgess Consulting, Inc..

Child Mind Institute. (2016). Mental Health Report. https://childmind.org/report/2016-childrens-mental-health-report/

Childress, H. (1998). Seventeen reasons why football is better than high school. *Phi Delta Kappan, 79(8)*, 616-619.

Coda, R. & Jetter, R. (2022). *Educational rehab: An unprecedented opportunity to restore K-12 public education.* New York: Pushing Boundaries Consulting, LLC.

Coda, R. & Jetter, R. (2016). *Escaping the school leader's dunk tank: How to prevail when others want to see you drown.* California: Dave Burgess Consulting, Inc..

Conscious Leadership Group. Locating yourself: A key to conscious leadership. https://conscious.is/video/locating-yourself-a-key-to-conscious-leadership

Crowley, M. C. (2011). *Lead from the heart: Transformational leadership for the 21st century.* Indiana: Balboa Press.

Dake, L. (2021). Crisis management: Effective school leadership to avoid early burnout. Maryland: Rowman & Littlefield.

Delahooke, M. (2019). *Beyond behaviors: Using brain science and compassion to understand and solve children's behavioral challenges.* Wisconsin: PESI Publishing.

Donohoo, J. (2018). The power of collective efficacy. *Educational Leadership, 75 (6),* 40-44.

Edmonds, A. (2019). How to Give Sincere, Specific Compliments. Purposeful English. www.purposefulenglish.com/blog/how-to-give-sincere-specific-compliments

Eliophotou-Menon, M. & Ioannouz, A. (2016). The link between transformational leadership and teachers' job satisfaction, commitment, motivation to learn, and trust in the leader. *Academy of Educational Leadership Journal, 20(3),* 12.

Ellis, L. (2005). *The Dash: Making a difference.* Simple Truths Publishing.

Faunalytics. (2012). The Better listener, your husband or the dog? https://faunalytics.org/whos-the-better-listener-your-husband-or-the-dog/

Fitzpatrick, M. (2004). Using data to guide school improvement. *Learning Point Associates, 7,* 1-14. https://files.eric.ed.gov/fulltext/ED518630.pdf

Freire, P. (1972). *Pedagogy of the oppressed.* Pennsylvania: Herder.

Garmston, R.J. & Wellman, B.M. (2016). *The adaptive school: A sourcebook for developing collaborative groups.* Maryland: Rowman & Littlefield.

Gatto, J. (2005). *Dumbing us down: The hidden curriculum of compulsory schooling.* British Columbia: New Society Publishers.

Gray, K. (2019). Dear school administrators: please stop taking away teacher planning periods. https://www.weareteachers.com/i-need-my-planning-periods/

Greaves, J. & Watkins, E. (2022). *Team Emotional Intelligence 2.0: The Four Essential Skills of High Performing Teams.* Talent Smart Press.

Hargreaves, A. & O'Connor, M. (2018). Solidarity with solidity: The case for collaborative professionalism. *Phi Delta Kappan Online.* https://journals.sagepub.com/doi/pdf/10.1177/0031721718797116

Healthy Children.org. (2021). The pandemic's impact on children: COVID vaccinations and mental Health. NIHCM. https://nihcm.org/publications/the-pandemics-impact-on-children-covid-vaccinations-mental-health.

Imposter Syndrome. (2022). Psychology Today. https://monadelahooke.com/

Jetter, R. (2021). *100 no-nonsense things that all teachers should stop doing.* New York: Pushing Boundaries Consulting, LLC.

Lai, M. K., A. Wilson, S. McNaughton, & Hsiao, S. (2014). Improving achievement in secondary schools: Impact of a literacy project on reading comprehension and secondary school qualifications. *Reading Research Quarterly 49 (3)*, 305–334.

Lencioni, P. M. (2008). *The five temptations of a CEO.* New Jersey: Jossey-Bass.

Lencioni, P. M. (2002). *The five dysfunctions of a team.* New Jersey: Jossey-Bass.

Metcalf, M., & Morelli, C. (2015). The art of leading change: Innovative leadership transformation model. *Integral Leadership Review, 15(3)*, 83–92.

Marotta, A. (2020). *The school leader: Surviving and thriving* (2nd ed.). New York: Routledge.

Marzano, R. (2017). *The new art and science of teaching.* Indiana: Solution Tree Press.

Matas, C. (1993). *Daniel's story.* New York: Scholastic Inc.

McNaughton, S., M. Lai, & Hsaio, S. (2012). Testing the effectiveness of an intervention model based on data use: A replication series across clusters of schools. *School Effectiveness and School Improvement 23 (2)*, 203–228.

National Alliance on Mental Illness (2021). Mental health by the numbers. https://www.nami.org/mhstats

National Association of School Psychologists (2021). Comprehensive School-Based Mental and Behavioral Health Services and School Psychologists. https://www.nas Wooden, J. and Yaeger,

D. (2011). A game plan for life: The power of mentoring. ponline.org/resources-and-publications/resources-and-podcasts/mental-and-behavioral-health/additional-resources/comprehensive-school-based-mental-and-behavioral-health-services-and-school-psychologists

National Center for Education Statistics. (2020). Characteristics of public school principals. https://nces.ed.gov/programs/coe/indicator/cls

Open Minds (2020). 2019 U.S. mental health spending topped $225 billion with per capita spending ranging from $37 in Florida to $375 in Maine. https://www.prnewswire.com/news-releases/2019-us-mental-health-spending-topped-225-billion-with-per-capita-spending-ranging-from-37-in-florida-to-375-in-maine--open-minds-releases-new-analysis-301058381.html

Poortman, C. L., & Schildkamp, K. (2016). Solving student achievement focused problems with a data-use intervention for teachers. *Teaching and Teacher Education (60)*, 425–433.

Rogers, E. (2003). *Diffusion of innovations*, 5th edition. New York: Free Press.

Schildkamp, K. (2019). Data-driven decision-making for school improvement: Research insights and gaps. *Educational Research, 61 (3)*, 257-273.

Shanker, S. (2022). The five domains of self-regulation. https://self-reg.ca/

Shappell, J. (2020a). Want to influence others in 2020? Listen to them. Navalant. https://www.navalent.com/resources/blog/want-to-influence-others-in-2020-listen-to-them/

Shappell, J. (2020b). How much does therapy cost? Thervo. https://thervo.com/costs/how-much-does-therapy-cost

Siciliano, M. (2016). It's the quality not the quantity of ties that matters: Social networks and self-efficacy beliefs. *American Educational Research Journal, 53, (2)*, 227-262.

Van Geel, M., T. Keuning, A. J., Visscher, & Fox, J.P. (2016). Assessing the effects of a school-wide data-based decision-making intervention on student achievement growth in primary schools. *American Educational Research Journal 53 (2),* 360–394.

Vygotsky, L. S. (1980). *Mind in society: The development of higher psychological processes.* Massachusetts: Harvard University Press.

Ward, S. (2016). The Analytics Perspective: 5 Ways to Optimize Glance Management Reporting in Your Business. Stoneword. https://www.stoneward.com/blog/2016/04/glance-management-reporting/

Wilcox, K. et al. (2012). Are close friends the enemy? [Unpublished paper]. *Journal of Consumer Research of Columbia Business School,* 12-57.

Willimon, W. (2020). *Leading with the sermon: Preaching as leadership.* Fortress Press.

Wooden, J. and Yaeger, D. (2011). A game plan for life: The power of mentoring. New York: Bloomsbury.

Youngman, E. (2020). *12 characteristics of deliberate homework.* New York: Routledge.

What's Coming Next in the 100 Series?
2023

100 No-Nonsense Things that ALL Parents Should STOP Doing

"Uncontrolled variation is the enemy of quality." -Dr. W. Edwards Deming

This project is designed to equip all stakeholders with a common expectation for quality teacher leadership, community-based school leadership, and parent leadership. Pushing boundaries in education requires a common language, common vision, and controlled variation because everyone brings talents and high added value to the school community.

Bring the 100 STOP series to your school, district, or organization! Let us lead the tough conversation and initiate the heavy lifting. Launch every school year with the powerful content and stories offered in the #100StopSeries to align your staff and proactively equip them to handle adversity.

The Pushing Boundaries Consulting team can deploy one or more of our 100+ presenters to offer no-nonsense guidance on transforming your school culture into a dynamic, synergistic, a five-star community. You can follow the hashtag #100StopSeries on most social media channels to stay up to date on the following books within the **100 STOP Series**. You may also subscribe to our free e-newsletter at www.pushboundconsulting.com and become part of the 100 STOP series "Crumpled-Up-Paper Movement."

Every stakeholder deserves belonging, excellence, and positive outcomes,

. . .**Because our students are counting on Us!**

PUSHING BOUNDARIES
CONSULTING, LLC

PUSHING BOUNDARIES
CONSULTING, LLC

$34.75
ISBN 978-1-7370390-4-4

Made in the USA
Middletown, DE
12 September 2023